VIVA JUÁREZ!

Viva Juárez!

A BIOGRAPHY

BY

Charles Allen Smart

GREENWOOD PRESS, PUBLISHERS
WESTPORT, CONNECTICUT

Library of Congress Cataloging in Publication Data

Smart, Charles Allen, 1904-1967.
    Viva Juárez! : A biography.

    Reprint of the ed. published by Lippincott,
Philadelphia.
    Bibliography: p.
    Includes index.
    1. Juárez, Benito Pablo, Pres. Mexico, 1806-1872.
I. Title.
[F1233.J9535 1975]   972'.07'0924 [B]   74-24538
ISBN 0-8371-6145-2

Originally published in 1963 by J. B. Lippincott Company,
Philadelphia and New York

This edition published by arrangement with
J. B. Lippincott Company, Philadelphia, New York

Reprinted in 1975 by Greenwood Press,
a division of Williamhouse-Regency Inc.

Library of Congress Catalog Card Number 74-24538

ISBN 0-8371-6145-2

Printed in the United States of America

in memory of my father

George Smart (1863–1925)

a tough-minded, serene, and unwearied liberal
who in one way or another enjoyed most people
and most biographies

PREFACE

HAVING lived in Mexico about half of the time during the last ten years, I could hardly have escaped becoming keenly interested in Benito Juárez, who did more for the Mexican people than any other man has ever done, who like Abraham Lincoln had almost no advantages but genetic ones, and who like George Washington raised "a standard to which the wise and the honest can repair." I was fascinated less by the numerous statues of Juárez than by his old black coaches, dramatically but justly exhibited beside the gaudy ones of Maximilian in the Castle of Chapultepec, and by a monument that he himself would have approved: the growing number of schools in which Mexican children, taught by devoted men and women, are preparing themselves to make the Republic of the future. I was also interested in the fact that many of the people in the historic village in which we lived, San Miguel de Allende, did not honor Benito Juárez, and that books attacking him continued to be published in Mexico City, where printing is relatively inexpensive but publishing is relatively unprofitable. Then, as I read about Juárez, I encountered the more difficult and interesting problem of his personality, a problem that the distinguished playwright Franz Werfel gave up and that has seemed to baffle the scholars as well. One of the greatest men in the history of human freedom seemed also to be one of the most self-sufficient, reserved, and hence mysterious.

Having for thirty years earned as much of my living as I could by writing, I inevitably began to think about studying and writing about this man who had somehow moved in on so many of my waking hours. In time I visited every place where Juárez had lived except Chihuahua and El Paso del Norte, now Ciudad Juárez, and at least

9

as usefully (I hoped) I pondered the poor Mexican Indians and the less poor Mexican politicians whom I encountered in one way or another. I found two big, fascinating, and very different books on Juárez, by the Maestro Justo Sierra (1906) and by Mr. Ralph Roeder (1947), but somewhat to my relief, both seemed to be extended political essays rather than biographies, and I seemed to be getting much closer to Juárez himself in the selection of his letters edited by Sr. Jorge L. Tamayo. When even these did not satisfy me, I began to think about going into the whole literature on the subject, and even into the archives. After a while, two things happened: world events suggested to a good many Americans that their interest in Latin America might be too little and too late, and my old friend and first and best editor, Mr. George Stevens, visited Mexico, saw for himself a few absorbing things not unconnected with Juárez, and encouraged me to undertake this biography.

Since this book was written by an American, and primarily for Americans, its limitations of this nature, as distinct from the personal limitations of the writer, should be fairly obvious. I can only hope that my presumption—if it is that—will be balanced by my respect and affection for the Mexican people, and by such little understanding of them as I have been able to acquire. As a quietly patriotic American, I have my prejudices in considering Mexican-American relations, but I have tried not to indulge them or to overcompensate for them. It seems to me that the life of Juárez and the events of his time are full of meanings that are very important and much alive for Americans to-day, in our effort to understand and to help intelligently, in the interest of ourselves and of human freedom, the nations of the world that are struggling out of colonialism and other forms of oppression, and that unfortunately seem to be more sensitive to "intervention" by the Western powers than by the Soviet Union. If the Mexicans seem to have forgotten that the Monroe Doctrine had a part in their liberation in 1867, and that we defended them in two world wars, and if all of them do not seem to recognize that we are defending them now, and that the Alliance for Progress is a tremendous effort by equal partners to advance the democracy for which Juárez gave his whole life; we for our part seem to have forgotten that under President Polk we stole half of Mexico in

1846–48, that President Buchanan and his kind were greedy for more, and that our record since the time of Juárez has not been by any means beyond reproach. In this book I have tried not to labor the meanings that this part of history, between 1806 and 1872, has for us to-day, but I hope that the reader will not misunderstand the points that I have ventured to suggest, and will see more for himself. Scholars, librarians, and many journalists and "common readers" are interested, not without reason, in books that have or profess to have "new material." Originally I hoped, as some fine biographers have done, only to write a biography as reliable, interesting, and artistic as I could make it out of already published material—and that seemed a plan quite ambitious enough for me. Out of dissatisfaction and curiosity, I have gone somewhat further than that, into five archives and into many conversations with well-informed Mexicans. The hitherto unpublished material that I have used or incorporated in this book is chiefly about Juárez' wife and about the naval action at Antón Lizardo in 1860, but there are other new details that scholars can detect for themselves, if they wish to take the trouble.

A definitive biography of Juárez will be written only by a Mexican, only after Mexican scholars have been able to do much more work in collecting the letters, speeches, and personal papers of Juárez and his contemporaries, and only after much more work has been done on the military, political, social, and economic history of the times—work such as Lic. Daniel Cosío Villegas and his colleagues have done on the period after 1867. This work requires institutional support and money, and at this time, with good reason, the Mexican government and universities, and the American government, foundations, and universities are more interested in raising the Mexican standard of living, and then, if any money is left, in investigating the astonishing pre-Columbian civilizations. However, a thorough job of scholarship on Juárez and his times would cost less than one rocket destroyed in flight because a hyphen was not fed into a computer, and it might do as much for peace.

More important, in my view, than my items of unpublished material, is the more extensive use that I have made of Juárez' own letters and notes, hitherto available in Spanish but untranslated into English. Early in my venture I discovered that although these were very objective and reticent, from them there seemed to emerge an impression, a fragrance, of Juárez himself that for me was more interesting and valuable than anything in the long and heated arguments about Juárez' actions, and than any of the stories about him that are passed on and on by his admirers and detractors without any documentation. For that reason this book is the first to publish in English the entire text of Juárez' *Notes for My Children* and numerous passages from his letters and his fragmentary and somewhat cryptic diary. All of the translations are my own. It is a curious fact that although some of the special studies, such as those of Sr. Fernando Iglesias Calderón and Sr. José Fuentes Mares, are properly documented and annotated, this book seems to be—if we ignore the faulty sketch by U. R. Burke (1894)—the first full-length biography of Juárez, in any language, that is annotated. If an undocumented anecdote or detail has seemed to me credible and interesting, I have used it, but an alert reader, by referring to the notes in the back of the book, can check on any detail and on my methods.

In this connection, I might remark that I have a low opinion of biographical fiction and of biographies that slyly introduce thoughts, feelings, and even conversations and events that have been imagined by their authors. The essential value of a biography is in its record, as accurate as an honest and sceptical writer can make it, of what actually happened, and no other value can compensate for the sacrifice of this one. In a few places, in order to make more clear my vision of Juárez, I have suggested what he *might* have thought and felt, but I have done this quite candidly.

Mexican Proper Names

For those not already familiar with this matter, I wish to offer the following attempt at a clarification. Juárez' mother's name before she married was Brígida García and on marrying Marcelino Juárez she became Brígida García de Juárez. When her husband died, she became Brígida García, viuda de Juárez, or widow of Juárez. Our hero's full name was Benito Pablo Juárez y García, or Benito Pablo Juárez García, and as is obvious, he dropped his second given name and his mother's name. Most Mexicans do not drop names, and some, like Jesús González Ortega, are better known by the names of their mothers—in his case, Ortega. The brothers Miguel and Sebastián Lerdo de Tejada had as their surname Lerdo de Tejada, usually shortened to Lerdo, but Antonio López de Santa Anna was known not as López but as Santa Anna. The "de" in a surname, when not indicating "wife of," is sometimes dropped: José María Gutiérrez de Estrada was and is often spoken of as Gutiérrez Estrada.

In Mexican place names, sometimes three are involved in the name of one place: the original Indian name, a Christian saint's name, and the name of a Mexican hero associated with the place. Oaxaca de Juárez has no saint's name and usually the Juárez is dropped, San Miguel de Allende or San Miguel Allende has no Indian name. San Andrés Miahuatlán has no hero's name.

In the use of proper names of persons or places, I have retained the usual Mexican accents, as in Juárez, and the Mexican forms, as in Veracruz instead of Vera Cruz. However, I have thought it better to drop the accent from México, and to refer to Mexico, D.F., or Distrito Federal, equivalent to our District of Columbia, as Mexico City.

On pronunciation, I venture to make only two points: it is *Huar*ess, the *H* having a very slight guttural sound, and *not* Warezz; and Oaxaca is Wa*hah*ca.

I have used the $ sign for both pesos and dollars, since throughout this period the peso almost equaled the dollar in value.

While I am aware that Mexicans are Americans, for convenience I have referred—as many Mexicans do—to citizens of the United States as "Americans," instead of using the awkward "North Americans," which would include Canadians.

Acknowledgments

Besides giving us genetically and by example a taste for people and books, my ancestors and my wife's left us just enough property to permit me to indulge for a while in this arduous and not inexpensive sport of writing biography. These Smarts, Allens, and Duns, these Husseys, Warrens, and Pratts have constituted our chief supporting Foundation, and I regard their help as a fellowship that can be justified, if at all, only by the quality of the product. I think especially of my father; of my grandfather, Charles N. Allen, who fought in Mexico, 1846–48, but learned to love that country; of my father-in-law, the Reverend Alfred R. Hussey; and of the historian Charles Warren. I have also been helped by a grant from the Organization of American States, but no person connected with this organization has had any knowledge of, or any influence upon, my views on past or present relations between American states. Among the living, I am especially indebted to three people, one of whom is probably unaware of the fact. With her unfailing support and constant interruptions, my wife has kept me alive in our own time and place. My editor, Mr. George Stevens, has listened patiently to my little troubles and triumphs, and has criticized with care, candor, and high intelligence. President John F. Kennedy, the father of the Alliance for Progress and the Peace Corps, and a cultivated man, wrote me a letter of encouragement that has made me feel that I might be working for something more than my own pleasure and profit.

All biographers and historians must think as I do that librarians are wonderfully kind and efficient. I wish to thank heartily the following: Dr. Manuel Alcalá Anaya, Director of the Biblioteca Nacional; Dr. María Teresa Chávez, Director of the Biblioteca de Mexico; Mr. Howard F. Cline, Director of the Hispanic Foundation, Library of Congress; Lic. Daniel Cosío Villegas, Curator of the Archivo Romero in the Banco de Mexico; Miss Patricia M. Fox, of the *American Historical Review;* Ing. Juan José González, Curator of the Archivo Municipal of Veracruz; Mr. Vivian S. Heath, of the Admiralty Library, London; Sr. Guillermo Hernández Ávila, of the Cabinete de Manuscritos, Biblioteca Nacional; Mrs. M. W. Hesketh-Williams, who got me materials from the Public Record Office, London; Mr. James M. Heslin, Director of the New-York Historical Society; Mr. Elbert L. Huber, Archivist in Charge, Navy Branch, National Archives, Washington; Sr. Jorge Fernando Iturribarría, Director of the State Library, Oaxaca; Mrs. Concha Romero James, of the Hispanic Foundation, Library of Congress; Sr. José Martínez Hernández, of the Cabinete de Manuscritos, Biblioteca Nacional; Mrs. Mauda Sandvig, Director of the Benjamin Franklin Library,

Mexico City; Mrs. Marie-Louise Sheehan, Director of the Public Library, Chillicothe, Ohio; and Mr. Walter W. Wright, Librarian of Ohio University. In addition, I have received a wide variety of aids and supports from the following: President Emeritus John C. Baker of Ohio University; Mr. Jacques Barzun of Columbia University; Miss Eileen Bowser of the Museum of Modern Art; Professor Salomón Albarrán Bolaños of the public school of Pomoca, Morelía, and his son, Sr. Ubaldo Albarrán Gutiérrez; Mr. Crane Brinton of Harvard University; Mr. James R. Browne of Kenyon College; Mr. William C. Crosby, sailor; Mr. Horace Y. Edwards of the Foreign Service of the United States; Miss Dorothy Farnum, the biographer of Zélide; Mrs. Howard T. Fisher, student of Madame Calderón de la Barca; Mr. Dudley Fitts, poet and scholar; Dr. Charles C. Griffin of the University of Oregon; Sra. María del Carmen Masip y Echazarreta de Hawkins, Director of the Academia Hispano-Americana of San Miguel de Allende, Gto.; Sr. Christian Félix Hernández, Director General de Gobernación, State of Veracruz; Sr. Adolfo Hopp; Dr. Charles N. Hoyt; Colonel John M. Johnson, U.S.A. (Ret.), explorer; Mr. Paul M. Kendall, biographer; Miss Betty Kirk, journalist and student of Mexican history; Captain F. Kent Loomis, U.S.N. (Ret.); Mr. Juan Marichal of Harvard University; Father K. R. McCarty of the Order of St. Francis; Sr. Alberto Misrachi; R. Leoncio Pérez Quiroz, El Párroco de Oaxaca; Mr. Ralph Roeder, who graciously welcomed me into his bailiwick; Mr. Lesley Byrd Simpson, historian of Mexico; Mr. Frederick B. Taylor, artist; Mr. Philip B. Taylor, Jr., of Newcomb College; Sr. José C. Valadés, scholar and diplomat, who warmly welcomed me into his field; Mr. Donald Devenish Walsh of the Modern Language Association; Mr. Lee Weber; Mr. A. Curtis Wilgus, Director of the School of Inter-American Studies, University of Florida; Mr. George H. Willis, Director of the Office of International Finance, United States Treasury Department; Sr. Ramón Xirau; Lic. Leobino Zavala, lawyer, poet, and scholar of San Miguel de Allende, Gto.; and Mr. Leo F. Zee of Hong Kong and Ohio University, who made the maps. To all of these I am deeply grateful.

Permission to publish, or to translate and publish, material hitherto unpublished or copyrighted, has been kindly granted by Lic. Daniel Cosío Villegas, for the Archivo de Matías Romero in the Banco de Mexico; by Dr. Manuel Alcalá Anaya, for the Archivo de Juárez in the Biblioteca Nacional; by Sr. Antonio Pompa y Pompa, for the Archivo Histórico of the I.N.A.H.; and by Mr. Elbert L. Huber, for the National Archives, Washington. Unpublished Crown-copyright material in the Public Record Office, London, has been reproduced by permission of the Controller of H. M. Stationery Office. Identification of these materials is made in the notes.

The frontispiece is a photograph taken in Mexico City in 1867 by a photographer who had recently taken the last photographs of Maximilian. When Juárez was informed of this circumstance, he said: "*Así es el mundo*": Such is life.

In this era of guilt by association, it is necessary to repeat the banal warning that not one of the above persons and institutions is in the slightest degree responsible for any of the statements of fact or any of the opinions in this book. In fact, I could name several of them who will disagree with me sharply.

C. A. S.

*Oak Hill, Dun Road, Chillicothe, Ohio
and Apt. 84, San Miguel de Allende, Gto.*

CONTENTS

PART FOUR

INTERVENTION FROM EUROPE

PART FIVE

THE TINSEL EMPIRE AND ONE MEXICAN

PART SIX

A DEMOCRATIC TRAGEDY

MAPS

There follow four maps—one general and three detailed—of Mexico in the time of Juárez.

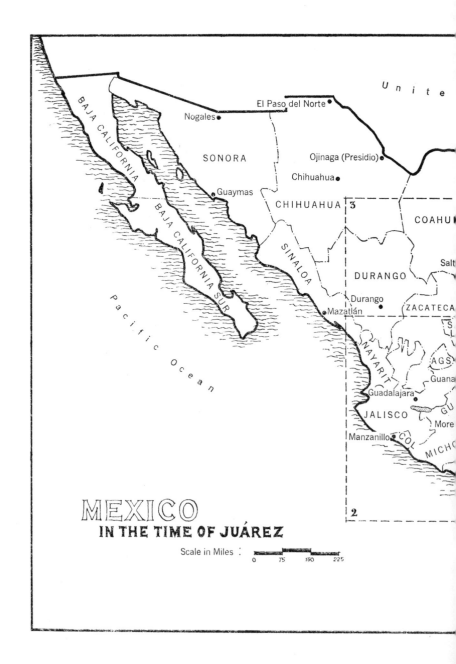

U n i t e

El Paso del Norte •

Nogales •

BAJA CALIFORNIA

SONORA

Ojinaga (Presidio) •

Chihuahua •

BAJA CALIFORNIA SUR

Guaymas •

CHIHUAHUA | 3

COAHU

SINALOA

Salt

DURANGO

Durango •

ZACATECA

Pacific Ocean

Mazatlán •

S
LL

NAYARIT

AGS

Guana

Guadalajara •

JALISCO

GU

More

Manzanillo •

COL

MICHC

MEXICO
IN THE TIME OF JUÁREZ

Scale in Miles :

0   75   150   225

2

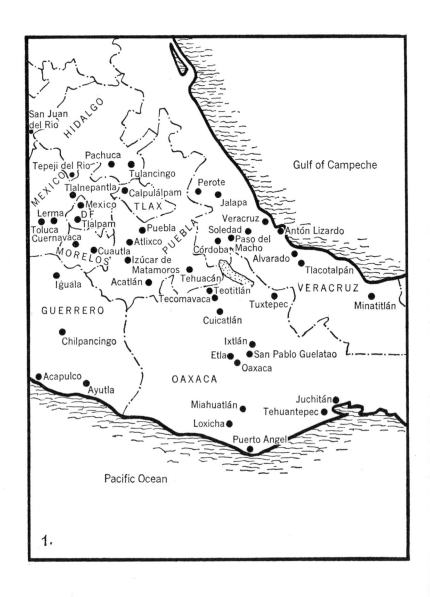

1.

DURANGO

ZACATECAS
Fresnillo ●
Zacatecas ●
●Ciudad
García

SAN LUIS POTOSI

NAYARIT

AGS

San Luis
● Potosí

San Blas
●
● Tepic

Aguascalientes ●

Lagos
de Moreno ●

GUANAJUATO

San Juan
de los Lagos ●

Guana- Dolores Hidalgo
León ● juato ●
San
● Miguel de

'Silao ●
Comon- Allende

Guadalajara
●

Irapuato ●
fort ●

Acatlán ●

Tepatitlán
Salamanca

Celaya ● Querétaro

Salvatierra ● Acámbaro

JALISCO

● Sayula

Morelia ●

Maravatío

● Ciudad
Guzmán

Colima ●
● COLIMA
Manzanillo

MICHOACAN

Pacific Ocean

GUERRERO

2.

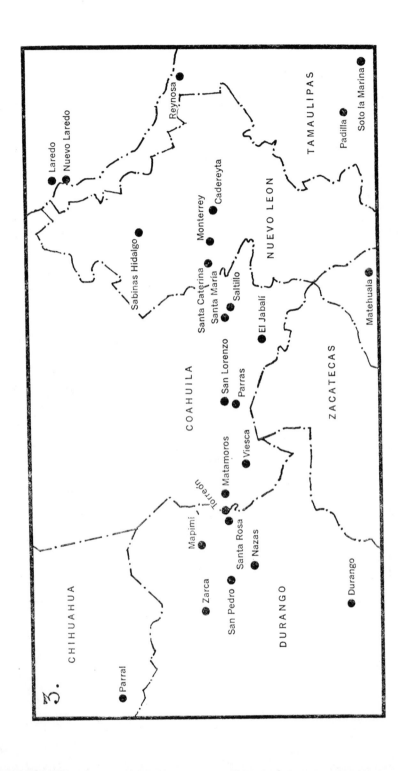

3.

CHIHUAHUA

Parral

DURANGO

Durango

Zarca
San Pedro
Santa Rosa
Mapimí
Nazas
Torreón
Matamoros
Viesca
San Lorenzo
Parras

COAHUILA

Santa Caterina
Santa Maria
Saltillo
El Jabali

Sabinas Hidalgo

Laredo
Nuevo Laredo

Reynosa

Monterrey
Cadereyta

NUEVO LEON

ZACATECAS

Matehuala

TAMAULIPAS

Padilla
Soto la Marina

PART ONE

The Growing Man
and the Awakening People

1

THE BOY FROM THE MOUNTAINS

ON DECEMBER 17, 1818, a ragged Indian boy, alert, unsmiling, twelve years old but small for his age, ran away from his home in the mountains of southern Mexico to the nearest city, to see what he could learn and do. During the next fifty-four years he learned and did enough to be remembered by perhaps most Mexicans as their liberator, law-giver, and savior—a secular saint; and to be remembered by perhaps almost as many Mexicans as an ingrate, a destroyer, a foe of their religion (to them the only one), and a ruthlessly ambitious traitor to his country. To many of the Americans who have looked towards the south he appears vaguely as a dark-skinned, black-coated, flinty democrat of some importance, of the time of our own Civil War, who inexplicably became the executioner of a charming blond young man named Maximilian. All of these opinions and impressions, rising from hero-hunger, fear, resentment, or sentimental ignorance, are superficial and partly or totally incorrect. What this man actually became and did, and why, are matters certainly not beyond all comprehension or reasonable speculation; and an effort to understand Benito Juárez is desirable, because of the importance to-day of Mexico to ourselves.

Juárez' patriotism, like that of most Mexicans, was healthily rooted in a passionate attachment to his own *tierra*, his own part of the country, the state of Oaxaca. This state is located where the cornucopia of Mexico swings eastward, and it includes as its eastern part most of the narrow and fateful Isthmus of Tehuantepec. About the size of Indiana, but much more sensational in landscape, it is bounded on the west by Guerrero, on the north by Puebla and Veracruz, on the east by Chiapas, and on the south by the Pacific

Ocean. The capital city, also called Oaxaca, is only 340 miles by road, via the city of Puebla, from Mexico City, but the trip has always been a rough one. Although the state is mostly mountainous, and has insignificant harbors, there are many fertile if narrow valleys, and the climate, flora, and fauna are as violently varied as the altitudes. The whole rich central valley was once granted by the King of Spain to Cortés himself, with the title of Marqués del Valle de Oaxaca. It is a state that others besides its native sons have learned to love. The people of Oaxaca have always tended to go their own way and to preserve their own stubbornly independent character, religious *or* anticlerical, and in any case somewhat belligerent.

Seeking Juárez' birthplace, you start from the city of Oaxaca eastward, on the road to the great tree at Tule and the famous ruins at Mitla, but you soon turn off into an unpaved road to the north. The rapid, sharply winding climb into the mountains, up from the corn and sugar cane into the pine woods, on a road without any guardrails, can weaken your knees and your stomach. It is also, like almost any trip in Mexico out of the great cities and off the main highways, a move into the past. Except for the infrequent and antiquated bus or truck, there is little on that road or within sight of it that has changed in the last century and a half. Up on those timbered heights there are the wooden and shingled shacks that are so rare elsewhere in Mexico, and from one dark doorway or another a woman or child will stare solemnly as do the small boys herding sheep and cattle, at the passer-by. A man may appear, quickly taking off his hat, with a yoke of oxen drawing a cart with two wheels of solid wood. A buzzard or two soar above the ravines. The city of Oaxaca has a comfortable altitude of 5,085 feet, but within ten miles you have climbed 3,200 feet higher, and at El Cumbre, with tremendous views to the north and south, you are on the continental divide: the river Atoyac, in the city, flows into the Pacific, but the waters of these tumbling mountain streams will find their way down through the hot country of Veracruz, on the northern side, to the Gulf of Mexico. In the vast silence, uplifted in heart by that sea of blue mountains and the thunderheads towering above them, you do not have to remember the exalted, severely beautiful temples crowning Monte Albán, near the city, to know that this is a country fit for gods.

The undulant descent to the north is almost as steep, the air loses its edge, and soon you are back among patches of corn and sugar cane, and among banana and orange trees, while the pines thin out and the wooden houses are replaced by the more familiar adobe ones with roofs of thatch and tile. Across a huge panorama you see a village clinging to the side of a mountain, and after going down to cross the little Rio Grande, above whose banks people live in isolated caves, you climb again to this tree-embowered village of San Pablo Guelatao. It now has about a thousand people, a new school and housing appropriately provided by the government, and in its center is a truly enchanting little lake of clear blue, surrounded by trees, called the Laguna Encantada. Besides the inevitable statue of the most distinguished citizen, in the small public garden, there now rises above the lake a relatively large and rudely modern Palacio Municipal, half of which is devoted to inadequate mementos of Juárez. San Pablo Guelatao has a small chapel, but the parish church of Santo Tomás Ixtlán, a handsome little building, is located in the smaller village of that name a mile or so farther up the mountain. When Juárez was a boy, San Pablo Guelatao had only about a hundred inhabitants and was more primitive, lacking even a school, but it must have been as beautiful as it is to-day.

About 1857, nearly forty years after he ran away from home, Juárez wrote some autobiographical *Notes for My Children*, which begin as follows:

On March 21, 1806, I was born in the village of San Pablo Guelatao, the jurisdiction of Santa Tomás Ixtlán in the state of Oaxaca. I had the misfortune of not knowing my parents, Marcelino Juárez and Brígida García, Indians of the primitive race of the country, because I had hardly reached three years of age when they died, leaving [me] with my sisters María Josefa and Rosa in the care of our paternal grandparents, Pedro Juárez and Justa López, also Indians of the Zapotec nation. My sister María Longinos, a child recently born, for my mother died in giving her birth, remained in the care of my maternal aunt, Cecilia García. Within a few years my grandparents died, my sister María Josefa married Tiburcio López of the village of Santa María Tahuiche; my sister Rosa married José Jiménez of the village of Ixtlán, and I was left under the guardianship of my uncle Bernardino Juárez, because of my other uncles, Bonifacio Juárez had already died. Mariano Juárez lived apart from his family, and Pablo Juárez was still a minor.

The day after he was born, Juárez was carried up the mountain to Santo Tomás Ixtlán for baptism from a font still in use, and this ceremony over "Benito Pablo Juárez" was duly recorded. The house in which he was born has been replaced by a small monument, but on one side of the site stands a rude adobe house, roofed with tile, that is surely much like his birthplace, and is inhabited by a daughter of a great-nephew of Juarez'; a woman of notable dignity and courtesy, she lives there with her aged mother and her baby son, in poverty almost as extreme as Juárez' own when he was an orphan boy. It is easy to imagine Juárez' birth on a reed mat on a dirt floor, and the baptismal ceremony the next day, in that solid, handsome little church, with the relations all standing around the dark, wrinkled, little monkey of a baby, and the priest murmuring above him in the incense.

Although the care taken by Juárez in recording for his children the names of his parents, sisters, and other relations is characteristic of him, there is good authority for believing that among these Indians at the time the family had less cohesion and prestige than the village or whole tribe, led and governed by some aged and highly respected *cacique* or chief. Typical also of the time are Uncle Mariano's separation from his family, and the numerous early deaths. Juárez' father dropped dead while selling fruit in the corridors of the statehouse in Oaxaca. The death rate was of course even higher then than now, and Humboldt, who went through Oaxaca in 1803, reported that the chief causes of death were smallpox, a form of yellow fever to which only Indians were subject, and above all, starvation. Although Juárez almost surely kept in touch with his surviving relations, almost all have disappeared from the documents except his sister María Josefa, who, after her husband took to drink and deserted her, became a domestic in Oaxaca.

The evidence about Juárez' Uncle Bernardino is contradictory. As we shall see, there was mutual affection between the boy and the man who tried to teach him, but later Juárez in carefully correcting a short biography of himself did not alter a passage asserting that his uncle "treated him badly and gave him little care." Probably this uncle was moody, and surely he was hard pressed. There is no evidence that he had a wife or family. Probably he got very drunk on Sundays, and perhaps some stray woman or more respectable female relation appeared from time to time, and before leaving, cleaned up the little bachelor hut beside the enchanted lake. The man and the boy worked very hard to keep themselves alive. One of the boy's chief tasks, in that countryside with only a few stone fences, was herding the sheep, and probably a cow or two and a few pigs, to prevent their being stolen or invading the little patches of corn and beans. Most Mexican Indians are honest, courteous, dignified, incredibly strong and industrious, reserved, and suspicious of strangers and even their friends. Juárez had all these characteristics, to a marked degree, all his life. Spending his early boyhood mostly alone among animals, in that exalting landscape, which may have affected him only unconsciously, and having inherited a tough and curious, if slow-working, intellect, he became intimate very early with the hard facts of life and death, and he learned to face them utterly alone. In those days, he gained the "strength of body, and of spirit in solitude," and the "disdain for perils" of all kinds that he needed and quietly displayed all his life. Surely he learned to fight, with his body and mind, and to go his own way. (At some point in boyhood, he was cut so deeply on the right side of upper lip that the scar remains on his death mask.) In that Indian village, he may well also have acquired "the ancient Mexican idea of voluntary and mutually helpful organization," and perhaps he admired and longed eventually to imitate some tough and venerable *cacique*, who made this idea work, and who knew that people, as well as sheep and sheep dogs, need care and discipline for health, liberty, and growth. In any case, the patriarchal but unsentimental strain in Juárez was always marked. A relation reported later that sometimes this boy would climb a tree and address his sheep in Zapotec, and that "his character was obedient, reserved in his thoughts, and in general, withdrawn. He had friends, but few, and with them was formal and showed good judgment."

"As my parents left me no patrimony and my uncle lived by his own work," the *Notes* continue, as soon as I could think at all, I dedicated myself, insofar as my tender age permitted, to work in the fields. In the few intervals in which we were not working, my uncle taught me to read; he showed me how useful and advantageous it would be for me to know the Spanish language, and since at that time it was extremely difficult for poor people, and especially for Indians, to follow any learned career except the ecclesiastic, he revealed that he wanted me to study for ordination. His desire, and the examples that I had before me of fellow countrymen who knew how to read, write, and speak the Spanish language, and of others in the priesthood, awakened in me a vehement desire to learn, with the result that when my uncle called me, to give me my lesson, I myself took him the whip, so that he could beat me if I did not know it; however, my uncle's work, and my own, in the fields, frustrated my ambition, and I advanced very little in my lessons. Furthermore, in a village as small as mine, which had hardly twenty families, at a time when hardly anyone was concerned with the education of youth, there was no school; and there one hardly ever heard Spanish, because the parents who could pay for the education of their children sent them to the city of Oaxaca for that purpose, and those for whom there was no possibility of paying for board and tuition sent them to work in private homes, on condition that they would be taught to read and write. This was in general the only method of getting an education that there was, not only in my village but also in the whole district of Ixtlán, with the interesting result that at that time most of the servants in the houses of the city were young people, of both sexes, from our district. Thus, from feeling out these facts, rather than from any mature reflection, of which I was incapable, I acquired the conviction that I could learn only by going to the city, and to this end I often urged my uncle to take me to the capital, but either because of his affection for me, or from some other motive, he did not do so, but only gave me hopes that some day he would take me there.

Furthermore, I too was hesitant to separate myself from him, to leave the house that had sheltered me in my orphaned childhood, and to abandon my little friends, with whom I had always had the deepest sympathies, and from whom any separation always wounded me. The conflict that arose within me, between these feelings and my desire to go to another society, new and unknown to me, where I might acquire an education, was cruel indeed. However, my hunger overcame my emotions, and on December 17, 1818, when I was twelve years old, I fled from my house and walked on foot to the city of Oaxaca, where I arrived on the night of the same day.

There are a number of legends about this hegira, the favorite one being that a gypsy on the road to Oaxaca engaged the young shepherd's attention with talk about the big city while another gypsy stole one of his sheep, and that then being afraid to report the loss to his uncle, Juárez fled to Oaxaca himself. Beneath all such stories, what are indubitable are the young boy's affections and loyalties, deeply rooted beneath his reserve, and the courage of that long walk over the mountains and down into the valley of the unknown. There are forty-one long miles between San Pablo Guelatao and Oaxaca, and even if he started and arrived in darkness, and took short cuts, as the country people, who are formidable walkers, always do, that day's journey was a mark of character on the part of a small Indian boy, wearing a ragged straw hat, with worn sandals on calloused feet, and hungry for more learning, more life, than he could find in his native mountain village.

The *Notes* continue:

I lodged in the house of don Antonio Maza, in which my sister María Josefa was serving as cook. During those first days I worked by taking care of the cochineal, earning two *reales* a day for my keep, while I looked for a house in which to work. At that time there lived in the city a pious and very honorable man who worked as a bookbinder. He wore the habit of the Third Order of St. Francis, and although dedicated to devotions and religious practices, was very broad-minded and was a friend of the education of youth. The works of Feijóo and the Epistles of St. Paul were his favorite reading. This man, who received me into his house, offering to send me to school, so that I could learn to read and write, was named don Antonio Salanueva. In this way I found myself settled in Oaxaca on January 7, 1819.

A photograph of Juárez' sister taken in her old age, in her native costume, against a street photographer's backdrop of a stormy seashore, reveals a woman who with any advantages might well have moved out of her background almost as far as did Juárez himself, who remained devoted to her all his life. Don Antonio Maza was a dealer in cochineal, then a chief product of the region, and probably in other agricultural products. His name had originally been Mazza, and he and his wife were either Genoese or Portuguese by birth. Although they were probably members of what was then a very small middle class, and far above young Juárez in status, they must have been more broad-minded than their counterparts then and to-day, for as Juárez grew to manhood he became not their former dependent, their cook's brother, but their close friend. From them, as well as from his patron and his later teachers and colleagues, he must have learned the proper forms for the expression of his innate in-stincts as a gentleman. It was probably his sister or the Mazas who found him a place in the home of don Antonio Salanueva.

The house of this "pious and very honorable man" was a small and ordinary one, of one story, built around a patio. The façade had one big door, and to its left, one big window. This lighted the front room that don Antonio probably used as his bookbinding shop, where customers could come and go without penetrating his living quarters. Although members of the Third Order were lay persons, and could marry, there is no evidence that don Antonio had a wife, but we may assume that he had a *criada*, or maid-of-all-work, and that Juárez was put to work partly as her helper, to wash down the tile floors, run errands, build fires, water the numerous plants, wash dishes, and wait on don Antonio at table. Probably he slept quite happily in some dark little room on a *petate*, or mat of woven reeds. Yet surely all was not housework and school work and no play. Poor Mexican children have almost no toys, and in those days they had no *futbol* or *beisbol*, but they have always had imagination, and one can be sure that—perhaps somewhat quietly—don Antonio's Benito skylarked in the streets and in the public gardens with the other boys of the neighborhood. Also, everything that Juárez wrote about don Antonio, and everything that one can feel in that flowery if dark little house today, suggests gentleness, integrity, and good cheer. This lonely boy and man clearly loved each other, and in the boy don Antonio, like the Maza family, must have felt not only a quiet, rather mysterious charm, but also great latent power that, if it was to disturb the aging man, might yet do great good in the world.

To-day the Third Order of St. Francis is "little more than a parish organization," but in those days it was a more serious affair, and closer to the Second Order of nuns and the First Order of monks. Don Antonio was one of its most devoted members. His house was across the street from the church called "Carmen Alto"; daily, carrying an image of Christ crucified and assisted by his Benito, he made the Way of the Cross; and surely he gave religious instruction to the boy. As Juárez says, he was far from a bigot, and one of his favorite authors, Benito Jeronimo Feijóo y Montenegro (1676–1764), was a Spanish monk who "waged war against the superstition and ignorance of his countrymen," and was the "initiator of educational reform in Spain." Forming a new private library in his last years, after his other books had been lost, Juárez bought the complete works of Feijóo. Of don Antonio's other favorite, the Epistles of St. Paul, perhaps it may be noted that these have always had greater interest for the more liberal Catholics, as well as the Protestants, than for the members of the hierarchy.

Juárez promptly showed an interest in any books he could read, and there is a story that a friendly woman next door gave him a piece of rosin by the light of which—Mexican eyesight being what it was and is—he might read at night. It would seem very likely that don Antonio gave the curious boy at least some lessons in bookbinding, but if he did, I have found no evidence that Juárez ever again touched a bookbinding tool—or any other tool, for that matter, except his formidable pen. Even this early, we find a hint that Juárez' case was one of an extreme concentration of interests and energies. He seems to have been interested in none of the arts except music and the theatre, in which his taste was probably less discerning than it was in human behavior, and judging at some risk from the available documents, he never consciously noticed any of the stunning landscapes among which he passed his wandering life. Like some of his remote ancestors, he was a very great if simple artist, but in his case in a medium much more difficult than obsidian, much more beautiful than gold: the medium of human society.

Although Juárez wrote proudly of the race of his parents, and never forgot his own people, he showed none of the self-conscious and snobbish pride of some Mexican intellectuals of our time in their much less complete Indian ancestry. The ruins at Mitla had been seen by Humboldt in 1803, and had indeed been reported by a Spanish monk as early as 1533, but the superb "acropolis" of Monte Albán has been really known, explored, and unearthed only in the last forty years. Juárez seems to have known and cared nothing about all this. For him it was enough of an honor and a task to be a modern Mexican.

For some time don Antonio's houseboy from the mountains must have walked the streets of Oaxaca in a daze. The city was marked then, as it is to-day, by fortresslike but often beautiful churches and monasteries, then active but used almost as often for military as for religious purposes; by vast, solid, and finely decorated houses surrounding flowering patios; by large, attractive tree-shaded public gardens with fountains; and by the attitude of its inhabitants, poor as well as rich, that life, even when violent, can always be graceful, usually relaxed, and sometimes good. In 1792 the city had an estimated population of 24,400, and the estimated population of the state was 411,000. Although young Juárez knew little Spanish, neither did many others in the streets: an estimated 88 per cent of the people were pure-blooded Mixtecs and Zapotecs. Humboldt also estimated that in 1808 there were about 6,500,000 people in all of Mexico, including two to three million pure-blooded Indians, the same number of *mestizos*, of mixed blood, and the rest Spanish, including those born in Spain and the *criollos*, or creoles, of pure Spanish blood but born in Mexico.

The religious atmosphere that surrounded Juárez was not limited to don Antonio's house and to the Carmen Alto across the street. Two blocks away there was the church of Santo Domingo, which in its relatively restrained opulence and its exquisite fantasy is surely one of the most beautiful churches in the world. Humboldt guessed that the clergy in all of Mexico numbered only some 10,000 persons, plus three to four thousand lay brothers and sisters and servants in the convents; but the proportion of clergy in Oaxaca was probably much higher.

"Oaxaca," says the historian Justo Sierra, "was a city that lived in the shadow of the monastery; there, all were brothers or wished to be, both the unmarried and the married; the soul of Oaxaca lived in ecstasy before the altar of Mary. And Mary was the true conqueror of Mexico, and the race thus saved knelt before her, with lips full of tender and humble confidences, and with eyes full of tears. But beneath this poetry of human sorrow and consolation there was hidden the permanent shadow of superstition, that bound in its cobwebs those spirits that thus could not open their wings; and also the unending and gentle exploitation of that poor person on his knees, whom nobody could rescue from his moral slavery, represented by unending toil, by unending drunkenness, and by the candle perpetually burning on the altar."

For a few years, at least, the young Juárez could not have responded to the clericalism and religiosity of the city in this manner, or in these words of a sensitive and highly intellectual liberal of a later generation. As an Indian, he was at least as profoundly religious as the Spaniards, and he had of course been born and bred a Catholic. How could he have suspected that there was any truth outside that repeatedly proclaimed by the Church, and how could he, like most Mexicans to this day, have found anything in its myths, ceremonies, and fiestas but a magnificent dramatic cycle, repeated yearly, in which he too—even he, a poor little mountain boy hoping to learn Spanish—had a part? To people living in squalor, the Church offered these magnificent second homes, the numerous temples. To people fixed in their places in a feudal society and naturally suspicious and isolated, it offered communion, not only with Mary and all the saints, but also, in a way, with the rich, the powerful, and the strangers kneeling beside them in one kind of equality before God. To people without art except their own crafts and gardens, it offered this superb music and these paintings and sculptures, violently realistic in many cases, but often less vulgar than some are to-day. To people without the science with which to face disease and natural disasters, it offered miraculous intercession that sometimes seemed to be effective. To people without philosophy who, like ourselves, had no answers about "the nature and destiny of man," but who had had no cause to become sceptical about the educated clergy, it offered all the ancient Catholic answers in crude forms that were effective, at least imaginatively.

However, all these offerings had a price: economic, political, legal, and even—as Sierra suggests—moral and spiritual, and down from the mountains there had come this boy, like others already in the city, who had risked everything to learn—that is, truly, to think for himself. The *Notes* continue:

In the primary schools at that time, Spanish grammar was not taught. Reading, writing, and learning by rote the catechism of Father Ripaldo was at that time the whole of primary instruction. Inevitably, my education was slow and in every respect imperfect. I spoke Spanish without rules and with all the errors committed by the uneducated. After some time in the fourth class in writing in the school that I attended—as much because of my work as because of the bad method of instruction—I could still hardly write at all.

Anxious to finish my writing lessons quickly, I asked permission to go to another school, believing that thus I could learn more perfectly and rapidly. I presented myself to don José Domingo Gonzáles, as my new teacher was named, and he promptly asked me in what grade I was writing; I answered him, in the fourth. "Well, then," he said, "write me a page and hand it in to me at the hour when the others hand in theirs." When the usual time arrived, I handed in the page that I had prepared in accordance with the pattern he had given me; but it was not perfect, because I was a student and not a teacher. The teacher was annoyed, and instead of showing me the defects that my page had and showing me how to correct them, he only told me that it would not do, and ordered that I be punished.

This injustice offended me deeply, as did the inequality with which the teaching was done in that school, which was called the Royal School: for while the teacher in a separate department taught with care a certain number of children who were called "decent," the poorer youngsters, such as myself, were relegated to another department, under the direction of another man, called the Assistant, who was as little fit to teach, and of as harsh a character, as the master.

Since I was dissatisfied with this deplorable method of teaching, and since there was in the city no other school to which I could go, I decided to leave the school for good, and to practise by myself the little that I had learned in order to express myself in writing, however bad in form that writing might be—as indeed it is to this day. [It was not calligraphically bad, if less formal than many of that time.]

Meanwhile, every day, I saw going to and coming from the Seminary College in the city [*Seminario Conciliar de la Santa Cruz*] many youths who were studying to embrace careers in the Church, and that reminded me of the advice of my uncle, who wanted me to become a priest. Furthermore, it was at that time the general opinion, not only of the common people, but also of those in the upper classes of society, that the religious, and even those who were only studying to become priests, knew a great deal; and I noticed that they were in fact treated with respect and consideration for the knowledge that was attributed to them. This circumstance, more than the idea of my becoming a clergyman, an idea for which I felt an instinctive repugnance, induced me to ask my godfather—for so I shall call don Antonio Salanueva, because he took me to be confirmed only a few days after receiving me into his house—to allow me to go and study in the seminary, assuring him that I should do all I could to make the fulfillment of my obligations to him, in his service, compatible with my dedication to the studies I wanted to undertake.

Since that good man, as I have already said, was a friend of the education of youth, he not only received this idea gladly, but even urged me to put it into effect, saying that since I had the advantage of knowing Zapotec, my native language, I could be ordained, in accordance with the ecclesiastical laws of America, without having to have the patrimony that others needed to live while obtaining a benefice. With my road smoothed in this manner, I began the study of Latin grammar at the seminary, with the rank of *capense*, on October 18, 1821—of course without knowing Spanish grammar or any other of the elements of a primary education. Unfortunately I was not alone in this deficiency, which marked the other students generally, because of the backwardness of public education at that time.

Thus I began my studies under the direction of teachers who, all being clerical, gave me a literary education that was strictly ecclesiastical. In August of 1823 I completed my study of Latin grammar, having passed the two required examinations with the grades of excellent. In that year the course in arts did not begin, and I had to wait until the following year to begin the study of philosophy in the work of Father Jacquier; but before that I had to overcome another serious difficulty that presented itself, as follows: as soon as I finished my study of Latin grammar, my godfather showed great eagerness that I should go on to the study of moral theology, so that in the following year I could begin to receive holy orders. This suggestion was very painful to me, both because of my repugnance to a religious career and because of the low reputation of the priests who had only studied Latin grammar or moral theology, and who therefore were ridiculed by being called "priests of mass and stew," or "Larragos." They were called the first because, on account of their ignorance, they could only say mass to earn a living, and were not permitted to preach or to exercise any other functions requiring instruction and ability; and they were called "Larragos" because they had studied moral theology only in the works of Father Larraga.

As well as I could, I explained this objection frankly to my godfather, adding that not yet being old enough to be received into the priesthood, I should lose nothing by taking the course in the arts. Luckily, my arguments convinced him, and he allowed me to go my own way.

In the year 1827 I finished the course in arts, having maintained in public two theses that had been assigned to me, and having passed two required examinations with the grades of excellent unanimously given, and with other honors given me by my synodical examiners.

In the same year there began the course in theology, and I went on to study that subject, as an essential part of the career or profession to which my godfather wished to destine me, and perhaps that was the reason why he had not insisted that I be ordained previously.

None of us was ever the child he remembers himself to have been, but in these paragraphs, probably written when Juárez was fifty-one years old, we can begin to trace a few more lineaments of the boy and of the man he was to become.

"This injustice offended me deeply." We may well believe it. Injustice of any kind, to others no less than to himself, offended Benito Juárez all his life. But why so? There had been nothing in his life to lead him to assume that justice was the norm, and that any injustice was a personal offense, an outrage. It may be that resentment at injustice, like jealousy, for example (which Juárez seems never to have felt), comes from something deeper than experience, something in the genes, something that creates also a belief that Juárez had in "a natural faculty of man to establish the just and the reasonable."

Juárez' interest at this time in the "respect and consideration" shown by all classes for the alleged knowledge of the priests, and even of the students in the seminary, might be seized upon by his hostile critics as early evidence of the ruthless personal ambition they attribute to him in his later life; but it seems healthy and natural in a poor boy of his age. More interesting is his scepticism about the soundness and respectability of the knowledge in question. Sr. Valadés points out that Francisco Jacquier's *Curso completo de filosofía*, a favorite text in Spanish seminaries, was cold and tedious, and surely "incomprehensible to someone seeking only the disciplines of personal and communal life." Such studies probably produced a reaction, developing the innate pragmatic and practical tendencies of Juárez' mind. The instructors in the seminary not only played endlessly with abstractions: they were probably also isolated and smug, like the rest of the clergy. They also seem to have been hypocritical, for Sierra says that in Oaxaca at that time, the celibacy of the clergy was almost a myth, and the condition of the Church was comparable to its condition in the Middle Ages, when Hildebrand fulminated his reforms. Facing all this daily, having come from the rough honesty of the Indians in San Pablo Guelatao and from the integrity of the home of don Antonio Salanueva, and having normal, active sexual instincts, Juárez inevitably felt "instinctive repugnance" to the idea of becoming a priest.

Yet this response is not irreligious, an adjective that almost always implies or indicates a certain superficial or trivial quality of mind. On the contrary, Juárez' response to the Church, at this time and later, indicates a deeply religious mind, which took life and virtue, in the old sense of manliness and decency, very seriously indeed, and which was even then, very quietly, beginning to detect an important difference between religion and the merchandise of that Church in that time and place. No thoughtful, honest person, studying the deeds and letters of this man, can disagree with Sr. Valadés that "in Juárez, without any doubt, there lived an exceptional culture of the spirit." As we proceed, the reader may profitably ask himself whether he agrees with Mr. L. B. Simpson the historian that Juárez had the temperament of a Puritan.

But this is to get a little ahead of ourselves, and right now we may observe a trait in this young man that was important to him then and that was to become even more important to himself and to Mexico: his capacity for handling personal relations. The reader will have observed Juárez' respect and affection for his patron and godfather, and also the discernment and tact, helped at critical points by good luck, which, without injuring the old man unnecessarily, enabled Juárez to get his own way.

Even from the remote and somnolent city of Oaxaca, in the years 1806–27, "never send and ask for whom the bell tolls." "At that time," continues Juárez in his *Notes*, "great events had already occurred in the nation," and they touched him, vitally.

2

THE PAINFUL AWAKENING

THE MOST IMPORTANT FACT about the Mexico in which Benito Juárez
lived and worked is that beginning in 1810 it was aroused from a
condition in which it had remained relatively unchanged since early
in the sixteenth century, and was projected violently into the Western world of the nineteenth century.

After many centuries of isolated development under the various
pre-Columbian empires, Mexico was conquered by Spain—or if you
will, collapsed into Spanish domination. It was then held, still largely
isolated, in a more or less enslaved and static condition, for three
centuries, while most of the Western world was experiencing the
Renaissance, the Reformation, the rise of nationalism, the growth of
science, the beginnings of imperialism and of the industrial revolution, the development of democracy, and the various wars that accompanied these upheavals. Then, between 1810 and 1920, while
Western imperialism flowered, intruded upon Mexico, and began to
decay, Mexico had to experience in little more than a century what
the rest of the Western world had undergone in three. In this period, the key figures in Mexico, inspiring, dominating, or merely expressing a multitude of other wills, were Hidalgo—traditionally, but
for whom one alien would prefer to substitute Morelos—Juárez,
Díaz, and the potent but on the whole unworthy leaders of the Revolution of 1910–20.

The conquest of Mexico (1519–30) by Hernán Cortés is of course
one of the most remarkable military exploits of all time, and the
colonization of New Spain, which was effected by 1551 by Zumá-
rraga, Quiroga, Mendoza, and others, and which endured for three
centuries, is a feat equally remarkable. On these achievements, we

find a wide band of explanations and moral judgments of great interest, that can be explored elsewhere. After making such an exploration, we may perhaps decide that while giving Mexico the Spanish language, which is certainly better than a score of Indian languages; a form and degree of Christianity less bloody than the Indian religions; a government more stable and probably no less humane than its predecessors; and many beautiful buildings, the Spaniards, like most imperialists, did everything possible to sweat the subject people for their own gain, to prevent their education and political growth—the early friars being obvious exceptions—and to resist external contacts and internal change. In this view, the astonishing success of the Spaniards was in retrospect, and on the whole, a failure and a crime; and they, even more than the invading Americans and French, were responsible for the anarchy, the loss of territory, and the psychic wounds, still crippling the Mexican people, that followed the achievement of Mexican independence.

In New Spain, the domination by the matriarchal nation was complete. The government was centralized under the Viceroy, who appointed and directed the local authorities, almost all of whom had been born in Spain. Even the creoles were deprived of power, with the result that although they became increasingly restless, they were never able to acquire the experience in politics, law, business, and warfare that characterized the leaders of the American Revolution. Although slavery was illegal in New Spain, the exploitation of the Indians deprives this legal fact of some of its apparent luster. The Spanish sovereigns and the early Dominican and Franciscan friars were much more interested in the Indians, and treated them more humanely, than most of the Viceroys and other political administrators, or than the later clergy. On the great *encomiendas*, plantations and mines owned by the Spaniards, the Indians worked as serfs, and among them smallpox, influenza, yellow fever, and syphilis were rampant. Economically, New Spain was totally subservient to Spain, and was dominated by monopolies. Mining, cattle raising, and only a very few industries, such as textile manufacture, were allowed, plus the overland commerce, by way of Acapulco and Veracruz, between the Philippines and Spain. Almost all manufactured articles were imported from Spain and France. The Church was almost a part of the government, and like it, was dominated by Spaniards. The Catholic religion had merely absorbed and enveloped the cults of the Indians. The Church was enormously rich, in church buildings, in the gold and silver objects within them, and more importantly for the economy, in lands and mortgages. It is generally admitted that the Church owned or controlled at least half the property in Mexico, and that this fact was the second major brake, after the Spanish restrictions, on economic growth and the improvement of the common welfare. There also existed more personal and galling impingements on liberty and equality: tithes were legalized, fees were charged for all religious services, church property was exempt from taxation, and the clergy, like the army officers, had the *fuero*, or privilege of being subject only to their own laws and courts.

Very gradually, during the Silver Age, which Mr. Simpson dates from 1570 to 1821, the severities of life in Mexico diminished, although there were serious but futile riots in Mexico City in 1566, 1624, and 1692. Often the members of the privileged classes had culture of a sort that is evidenced in the paintings of the time, in the university, and in the lives and works of such solitary figures as Sor Juana Inés de la Cruz. The lives of the privileged had grace, and even the Indians managed to enlighten and decorate their short, hard lives, while retaining their incomparable dignity.

The more thoughtful and energetic creoles, the more vital and severely exploited *mestizos* and Indians, and a few priests, such as Hidalgo and Morelos themselves, were growing restless, but the Spanish governors, army officers, and higher clergy were still tough and resourceful, as was proved during the eleven-year war for independence. If history had not been moving outside of Mexico, and if communications had been even poorer than they were, this great colony might have toiled, slept, and smoldered, with little "history," for decades or centuries longer.

But history had indeed not stopped elsewhere. From the sixteenth century, the English, the French, and the Dutch did their own exploring and colonizing of the New World. As pirates and smugglers they terrorized and plundered the Indies and both coasts of New Spain. The successful and more or less democratic colonization of North America, and the American Revolution, provided a startling example of American colonies fighting their way to independence and democratic self-government; and in the following decades the rapid and vigorous expansion of the United States westward produced an increasing threat to the vast, thinly settled, and remotely governed northern provinces of New Spain.

Soon after the American Revolution came the French, quickly followed by the conquests of Napoleon Bonaparte. Meanwhile, the Spanish society and government had steadily decayed. The vigorous, brutal, reforming reign of Charles III (1759–88) and of his Visitor General, José Gálvez, and Viceroy, the Marqués de Croix, with the expansion of the Spanish Empire into California and Louisiana, and the expulsion of the Jesuits, was followed by the feeble reign of Charles IV and Manuel Godoy and (after the effective Conde de Revilla Gigedo) of the worst Viceroys on record. Liberal ideas and ambitions penetrated Mexico, and in 1808 Charles IV and his son Ferdinand VII were imprisoned in France while French armies put Joseph Bonaparte on the throne of Spain. In Mexico, the chaotic and ironic situation developed that the *gachupines* (born in Spain) supported the authority claimed by the liberal *juntas* in Spain, and fought the creoles, who wanted to elect their own Mexican *juntas* while remaining nominally loyal to the imprisoned Spanish king. Liberalism was thus opposed to nationalism. The chief result of all this confusion was the growth of the idea of Mexican independence. In 1810 there began the wars for independence in the rest of Latin America, under Bolívar, San Martín, Sucre, and others, that eventually led to the setting up of nine new republics under creole direction.

In Mexico, in 1810, the scattered rebels and conspirators did not have the support of the creoles, and when on the night of September 15–16 Captain Ignacio Allende of San Miguel and Father Miguel Hidalgo y Costilla of Dolores, warned by the wife of the Corregidor of Querétaro that their conspiracy had been discovered, were forced to go into action and proclaim the independence of Mexico in the famous *Grito*, or cry, of Dolores, they could only appeal to the Indians and *mestizos*, who made up their crudely armed and undisciplined but very brave army of around 50,000 men. Under the banner of the Virgin of Guadalupe, this army swept through central Mex-

ico, savagely stormed the *alhóndiga,* or granary, in Guanajuato on
September 28, and on October 30 defeated the viceregal army in
the "battle of the crosses" in the mountain forests between Mexico
City and Toluca, but did not go on to occupy the city and instead
withdrew to the north. On January 14, 1811, they were defeated near
Guadalajara, and on March 21 the leaders of the rebellion were
captured in the state of Coahuila. In the following months, all were
executed. The last of them, Hidalgo—whom, because he is venerated
in Mexico, an American biographer regrets to have to describe as a
vain and violent, if inspired man—already defrocked and excommunicated, recanted miserably, and was shot on July 31. Less than a
year after he had emitted the *Grito,* his head, and those of Allende,
Aldama, and Jiménez, were hanging in iron cages from the corners
of the granary in Guanajuato. There they remained until 1821.

The next phase of the struggle for independence consisted of guerrilla warfare between the viceregal forces and the somewhat disor-
ganized forces of such rebel leaders as Rayón, Cos, Quintana Roo,
Matamoros, and above all, the priest and statesman José María Morelos, a man of far greater stature than Hidalgo or Allende. Often
mere brigands posed as insurgents, a feature of Mexican warfare
down through the Revolution in our century. In May, 1812, Calleja
besieged Morelos in Cuautla, but Morelos escaped with most of the
inhabitants and later reoccupied the town. He also captured Oaxaca
in November, 1812, and it was not recaptured by the royalists until
March, 1814, so that memories of this period must have been vivid
four years later when the boy Juárez arrived from San Pablo Guelatao. Sierra reports: "You had to hear Juárez say 'el Señor Morelos'
to understand the extraordinary tradition of devotion . . . that the
men of the generation that followed that of the insurgents received
from their fathers." At Chilpancingo in 1813 and at Apatzingán in
1814 Morelos and some delegates sketched a liberal constitution, but
soon after that, Calleja and Augustín de Iturbide, who had fought
at the crosses with the royalists, defeated Morelos and eventually
crushed the rebellion and shot Morelos, in 1815.

In that year, Ferdinand VII was restored in Spain, crushed the
liberals there, and scrapped the Spanish liberal constitution of 1812.
Some of the Spanish liberals went to Mexico to join the insurgents.

However, Apodaca, the Viceroy succeeding Calleja, pacified the country except for two insurgents, Félix Fernández of Veracruz, who called himself Guadalupe Victoria, and Vicente Guerrero, an uneducated man, part Spanish, part Indian, and part Negro. In 1820 the earlier, liberal constitution of 1812 was revived by a rebellion in Spain, was supported by some Mexican conservatives who chose to oppose independence in this way, and was proclaimed by Apodaca. Iturbide had been racketeering, and Apodaca dismissed him, but he curried the favor of the priests, who feared this revived liberalism and forced the Viceroy to give Iturbide the military command against Guerrero. On February 24, 1821, in Iguala, Iturbide proclaimed the Plan of Iguala, with three guarantees: Mexico to have independence under Ferdinand or some other European prince; the Church to retain its privileges; and creoles and *gachupines* to enjoy equal rights. Guerrero agreed naïvely to this plan, and with other insurgents, joined Iturbide. Juan O'Donojú was sent from Spain to replace Viceroy Apodaca, and at Córdoba came to terms with Iturbide. At long last Mexican independence (but little more, except the certainty of further turmoil) had been achieved.

We can now return to Juárez' *Notes* for his impressions of these events recorded for his children thirty-six years later. Since these children surely knew more about these events than we can be expected to do, Juárez was brief:

At that time, great events had already occurred in the nation. The war of independence begun in the village of Dolores on the night of September 15, 1810, by the venerable parish priest don Miguel Hidalgo y Costilla, with a few Indians armed with shotguns, spears, and clubs, and continued in the mountains of the south by the illustrious citizen Vicente Guerrero, came to the end with the conclusive triumph of the army of independence, which, commanded by Generals Iturbide, Guerrero, Bravo, Bustamente, and other leaders, occupied the capital of the ancient viceroyalty on September 27, 1821. [Brevity, yes, but why is the great and revered Morelos not even mentioned?]

Iturbide, betraying the confidence that the chiefs of the army, acting solely as patriots and believing that to him alone was owing the triumph of the national cause, had placed in him, declared himself Emperor of Mexico, thus opposing the will of the republican party and arousing the disgust of the monarchist party, which wished to seat on the throne of Moctezuma a prince of the house of Bourbon, in accordance with the treaties of Córdoba, that Iturbide himself had approved, and that were later nullified by the nation.

Suddenly the silence of these parties, who were meanwhile organizing their projects and combining their factions, and the enthusiasm of the crowd, which rarely examines events to their depths and causes, and always admires and approves anything that seems to it new and extraordinary, gave to the new empire an appearance of general acceptance, while in fact only Iturbide himself supported it. This explains the almost instantaneous uprising that occurred within a few months, forcing him to abdicate and promptly to flee from the country.

Immediately the people were called upon to elect delegates with full powers to establish the nation on the bases of independence, liberty, and republicanism that they had just proclaimed; the elections held, the representatives of the people met in the capital of the republic and opened their debate on the form of government that ought to be adopted. Meanwhile, the unfortunate Iturbide disembarked at Soto la Marina, where he was arrested and beheaded as a disturber of the public order. The congress continued its deliberations. The monarchist-conservative party, which co-operated in the fall of Iturbide more because of hatred for this leader than because of any sympathy with the republican party, was already organizing itself under the name of the Scotch party, and was working in the congress for the centralization of power and for the maintenance of the privileged classes, with all the abuses and biases that had been the support and life of the viceregal system. On the other hand, the republican party wanted the new constitution to embody the federal structure and all the principles of liberty and progress that were making prosperous and happy the neighboring republic of the United States of the North. The debate was carried on with heat and tenacity, not only in the congress but also by the public and in the growing press of the provinces, and in the end the republican federalists emerged victorious, in that centralism was rejected, and a representative, popular, federal republic was adopted; but basically the centralists triumphed, because in the new charter were inlaid religious intolerance, judicial exemption of the privileged classes, the institution of general commanderies, and other contradictory principles that nullified the liberty and the federation that it had been the purpose to establish.

The constitution of 1824 was a compromise between progress and reaction, and far from being the basis of a stable peace and of true liberty for the nation, it was the fertile and enduring seedbed of the incessant convulsions that the Republic has suffered, and that it will still suffer while society does not recover its balance by making effective the equality of rights and duties of all citizens and of all persons who inhabit the national territory, without privileges, without exemptions, without monopolies, and without odious distinctions; or while there remain in force the treaties between Mexico and foreign powers, treaties that will be useless as soon as the supreme law of the Republic is an inviolable and sacred respect for the rights of all men and of all peoples, whoever they may be, provided they respect the rights of Mexico, her authorities, and her laws; or while, finally, there is not in the Republic one single and unique authority, the civil authority as it is established by the national will, without a religion of the state, and wiping out the military and ecclesiastical powers as political entities that force, ambition, and abuse have opposed to the supreme power of society, usurping its rights and prerogatives, and subjecting it to their caprices.

The republican party adopted the name Yorkist party, and from that time onwards there continued a bloody and unremitting struggle between the Scotch party, which defended the past with all its abuses, and the Yorkist party, which sought liberty and progress; but unfortunately, the latter almost always fought at a disadvantage because, enlightenment not having become general in those days, its adherents, with a very few and very honorable exceptions, lacked faith in the triumph of the principles they proclaimed, since they ill understood liberty and progress, and they lightly deserted its ranks, going over to the opposing party, which action confused the efforts of their former fellow partisans, defeating them and delaying the triumph of liberty and progress. This was in general the state of the Republic in the year 1827.

Iturbide was a handsome man, tricky and ambitious, vain and vulgar, and although a patriot of sorts, was altogether too small for the position of leadership in which he found himself; and his establishment of a ramshackle empire, in feeble imitation of Napoleon I, was a crude farce, and a sad one for Mexico.

Besides that of Morelos, another important name was omitted by Juárez from this brief summary: that of Antonio López de Santa Anna, a creole officer from near Jalapa, born in 1795, who had fought in the viceregal army against the insurgents, and who went over to Iturbide just in time; and then, when Iturbide's star began to sink, turned against him and demanded a republic without even knowing what that word meant. Santa Anna's speed in turning his coat was surpassed only by his impudence in ignoring his past, which in turn was exceeded only by the credulity with which, for more than thirty years, the Mexican people and most of their leaders kept overlooking the demonstrated nature of this charlatan and traitor and returning him to supreme power. Gross in feature and vulgar in taste, he could be melancholy and suavely courteous, and with a sinister personal power, he could charm and bemuse men far finer and stronger than himself.

But to Juárez, looking back from a later period, such vivid figures and dramas were evidently less interesting and important than constitutional government and the conditions that he thought it required to be established firmly and to function without "incessant convulsions." The Scotch and Yorkist parties derived their names from parts of the Masonic Order, which had been introduced into Mexico by Joel R. Poinsett, the American Minister to Mexico between 1825 and 1829, and so from its origins there, Freemasonry in Mexico, although more often liberal than conservative politically, cannot apparently be aligned strictly with either side. It has been said that there are many Masons in Mexico who are liberal Catholics. A Masonic lodge was founded in Oaxaca on April 25, 1825, and Juárez, who never actually left the Church, was on January 15, 1847, taken into the order, whose members are proud of him.

Juárez' disappointment in the constitution of 1824 was justified, but Juárez was himself later to realize, first, that some of the reforms he advocated were properly to be effected by legislation or by decree rather than by constitutional law; second, that international law had a long way to go; third, that any constitution and any financial reforms could not be effective without the existence of a viable and somewhat humane Mexican economy, which did not then exist; and fourth, that the imitation of the constitution of the United States, and the federalism persistently advocated by Juárez and the other Mexican liberals at this time, were inappropriate and dangerous in Mexico, whose history, society, culture, traditions, and economic situation were entirely different from those of the United States.

It need hardly be pointed out that federalism in the United States meant a strengthening of the central government, and in Mexico the opposite. In Mexico there were no states, as we understand the term, to be federated, but areas larger or smaller than the states, controlled by military and feudal chieftains who had their own private armies and political machines, and who grudgingly turned over to the federal government its only income except for those customs receipts not mortgaged to foreign powers. The state and national legislatures were often controlled by voluble and violent theorists who represented minorities and pressure groups usually of the left. The judicial branch, based on Roman law, was not sharply distinct from the executive, and was rarely manned by trained lawyers. The executive had by no means achieved separation from and control over the Church and the federal army. In a largely illiterate nation, popular suffrage was not possible, and there was instead an electoral system that left the effective votes in the hands of "electors" who were bureaucrats and political hacks controlled and often ignored by the local and national chieftains, usually military. Furthermore, the Indians on their own ancient communal farms or working on the large private or Church *haciendas*, had no concept of private property and personal initiative. It might be claimed that the Constitution of the United States did as much damage to Mexico as the United States Army. As Mr. Simpson says: "The federal system was probably the worst that could have been devised in the circumstances. . . . The liberals took it for granted that everything in the Spanish system was bad and that the only thing to do was to throw it all out and start over again." It could roughly be said that Juárez and the other federalists could have used a little more "enlightenment" themselves, but this would be grossly unjust, because the Spaniards were not the only tyrants, and the liberals learned the hard way that when the centralist conservatives seized national power, usually under Santa Anna, they were worse than the Spaniards. Also, Juárez himself eventually learned better.

After the collapse of the empire and the adoption of the constitution of 1824, Guadalupe Victoria was elected the first President of Mexico, and Nicolás Bravo Vice-President, but this administration soon proved itself unfit to govern. None of the privileges and monopolies were abolished, taxes were not collected, the government's finances were not reorganized, and a sinister new element was permitted to come into the picture: the invasion by foreign capital, not evil in itself, since it stimulated the embryonic economy, but disastrous because it and foreign governments' loans were secured by liens on the customs receipts. It was in this period also that Mexico began to be cursed by the meddling of such foreign agents as the Englishman H. G. Ward and the American Poinsett, whose intrusive exploits were later to be eclipsed by the agents of the French. It was this period also that saw the appearance of the first great intellectual liberals, José Luis Mora, Valentín Gómez Farías, and—although later a Texan and generally now considered a traitor—Lorenzo de Zavala; as well as of the distinguished intellectual conservative historian and politician Lucas Alamán. To the first three, Juárez, Melchor Ocampo, and the other great liberals now growing up became greatly and consciously indebted. If Mexico had had no experience and traditions of freedom, it quickly produced some intellects that did much to make up for the lack.

This leads us back to Juárez' *Notes*, and to an event in his life, and in the lives of scores of other able young men who were to govern Mexico—an event whose importance cannot be exaggerated. This was the establishment of the Institute of Sciences and Arts in Oaxaca, and of similar secular institutes elsewhere in Mexico. Without this creative and highly fruitful act, by unknown men in the state legislatures, all the heroism and bloodshed that followed the *Grito* of Dolores, and that was unfortunately to continue for many years, might well have proved barren and meaningless.

In the state of Oaxaca, where I was living, there were occurring also, although on a small scale, certain events analogous to those occurring in the nation at large. A constituent Congress was held and it gave a constitution to the state. The liberal and reactionary parties assumed respectively the names of "Vinegar" and "Acid." Both worked actively in the elections of the deputies and senators of the first constitutional legislature. The liberal party triumphed, seating a majority of liberal deputies and senators, with the result that the legislature passed some laws that promoted the liberty and progress of that society, which had hitherto been entirely dominated by ignorance, religious fanaticism, and prejudices.

The measure most important for its salutary results, and one that will always do honor to the members of that legislature, was the establishment of a civil college that was named the Institute of Sciences and Arts. It was independent of the clergy, and it was designed for the instruction of youth in various branches of knowledge that were very hard to acquire in that state. There had been no literary institution other than the seminary, where were taught only Latin grammar, philosophy, elementary physics, and theology; with the result that in order to follow some other career than the ecclesiastic, or to perfect oneself in some art or occupation, it was indispensable for a student to possess sufficient means to go to the national capital or to a foreign country in order to instruct and perfect himself in the science or art to which he wished to dedicate himself. For poor persons like myself, all hope was lost.

At the opening of the Institute in that year [January] 1827, Dr. José Juan Canseco, one of the authors of the law that created the institution, delivered the opening address, indicating the advantages of the instruction of youth and the ease with which, thenceforward, one could embrace the learned profession of his choice. From that day, many students in the seminary went over to the Institute. Whether from their example, or from curiosity, or because of the impression made on me by the address of Dr. Canseco, or from the boredom inflicted on me by the study of theology, with its incomprehensible ideas, or because of my ingrained desire to follow some other career than the ecclesiastic, the fact is that I was not studying with enthusiasm the subject of theology, to which I had changed after finishing the course in philosophy. As soon as I had taken the required examination, I bade farewell to my teacher, Canon don Luis Morales, and in August, 1828, entered the Institute to study law.

It should be noted that the establishment of constitutional government in Oaxaca was, as usual in that ebullient state, accompanied, and followed, by disturbances, and that the creation of the Institute had been preceded by a free course in civics, for the public, that had followed the adoption of the constitution. "The learned profession of his choice" is not quite accurate, because the professions of law and medicine were the only ones open, and then only in a limited way, at that time. Sr. Cosío Villegas points out that the history of the next few decades was considerably influenced by the fact that young men with curiosity and ambition had to become priests or soldiers, lawyers and politicians, or physicians, and that the economy offered no opportunities in industry, commerce, or engineering. Although he handled his own personal economy well enough, Juárez never showed any great interest in money, and did not serve as a soldier longer than necessary. He was to become keenly interested in science, but even as early as this, law and politics seem to have been clearly enough his métiers.

The true awakening had now begun.

3

SEVERAL KINDS OF EDUCATION

THE FIRST DIRECTOR OF THE INSTITUTE, who also taught Spanish grammar, was a well-known liberal and independent Dominican, Fray Francisco Aparicio. It is said that when he took the side of a student who was being harshly examined by a doctrinaire theologian, he said: "St. Thomas Aquinas would surpass me in holiness, but not in knowledge." Other teachers at the Institute were three professors of civil and canon law; two of medicine and surgery; and one each of political economy and government, physics and geography, English and French (taught by an Italian named Bernardo Aloisi), and logic, mathematics, and ethics. There were also a librarian, a secretary, and a porter. The professor of logic, mathematics, and ethics was Miguel Méndez, a young, pure-blooded Indian, an ardent liberal who seems to have had a great influence on Juárez and on other students, and who is reported to have predicted that Juárez, the silent and grave young man, would become a great statesman. Méndez died of typhus in 1830, at the age of twenty-five.

"The Director and professors of the new institution," continues Juárez,

were all of the liberal party, and took sides, naturally, on all the political questions that were being agitated in the state. For this reason, or more likely because the clergy knew that the new nursery of education, where intelligence was not hobbled in the pursuit of truth, would be in the future, as it has been in fact, the ruin of its power based on error and prejudice, the clergy, then using the very powerful influence that it exercised at that time on the civil authority, on families, and on all of society, declared a systematic and cruel war on the new institution.

They called the Institute a house of prostitution, and the professors and students heretics and libertines.

Fathers of families refused to send their sons to such an establishment, and we few students who attended the courses were frowned on and ostracized by the immense majority, ignorant and fanatical, of that unhappy community. Many of my comrades deserted, daunted by the powerful enemy that persecuted us. A very few of us continued to support the institution by our daily attendance at the classes.

There are several facts to be noted about this situation. One is that not only the Director but several of the professors at the Institute were priests, presumably as liberal as Aparicio, or else blandly confident that no conflict would arise between the Institute and the Church. Sierra remarks: "The Institute was not founded on hatred of the clergy, according to a report by the lawyer Dublán, who was one of its directors." He cites the presence of priests on the faculty, and suggests that the conflict was "guarded and suppressed, but always latent in the days when the reaction was strongest." Juárez' memories, written thirty years later, after the conflict between the liberal politicians and the Church had become open war throughout the nation, indicate clearly that here, as later, the conflict was begun and pressed hardest by the reactionary clergy in the very first months of the Institute.

Juárez' memories of dwindling classes and ugly slanders are not apt to have been invented; yet it would be rash to assume that in 1828, when he was twenty-two years old, he was anything but a devout young Catholic who was troubled by this conflict yet hopeful that the liberal priests, such as Aparicio—and such as Hidalgo and Morelos, for that matter—would gain the upper hand within the Church. Juárez seems to have nourished this hope at least until 1857. Despite the attacks of his bitter clerical enemies down to this day, there is plenty of evidence that Juárez himself was never an "ignorant and fanatical" liberal, that he clung to the Church and its nonpolitical doctrines as long as he could, and that in his own isolated and difficult way he remained profoundly religious, and a believer in God, until his death. In all of his decisions and acts to curb the political and economic power of the Church, he was slow, practical, and specific.

In his more purely political thinking, Juárez was plunging ahead. On July 30, 1829, less than a year after beginning his studies, in the course in public law under Vicente Manero Embides, Juárez defended publicly the following three rather vague propositions: constitutional powers should not become mixed in their functions; there should be a force to maintain the independence and balance of these functions; and this force should reside in the tribunal of public opinion. Then on August 12, 1830, he defended publicly the two following propositions: direct elections are the most appropriate in a republican system; and this type of election is all the more necessary insofar as the public is educated.

It is easy now to point out that Mexico had inherited Roman law, under which the functions of the executive and judicial branches are blended; that public opinion, while the ultimate power, can "maintain the independence and balance of these functions," if such is desired, only by accepting the device of judicial review by impartial and trained jurists, who did not exist in Mexico; that the Mexican public was mostly illiterate, and an electoral system, often corrupt, was necessary and could only gradually be replaced; and that in general Juárez' propositions, in that place and time, were more forward-looking and gallant than practical. Yet as quietly startling, here, in its way, as a flash of heat lightning is the emergence, in the incense-laden, bell-tolling air of Oaxaca, of an articulate young liberal. Nor, obviously, was Juárez alone. Besides his teachers, Manero Embides, Méndez, and others, he had classmates such as Manuel Ruiz, Marcos Pérez, and Miguel Castro—names that will recur—and probably not a few quiet or open supporters in the city.

How did this happen? With a new and feeble republic on their hands, and with reaction ready to tighten around their necks, Mexicans had to think about politics and society, but where did they get their ideas? The books owned by the professors or the Institute at this time, or available elsewhere to the students, are not known. The books Juárez collected in his last years, after he had lost those he had collected up to that time, include many volumes of French and Spanish law, a French and an American encyclopedia, Blackstone, Proudhon (of whom he had learned from Ocampo), histories of France and Spain, Bernal Díaz, Lemaire, Quinet, nine volumes of natural history by Buffon and others, church histories and canon law, and among the few works not historical or legal, some by Cervantes, Molière, Pascal, and Fénelon.

But the books of Juárez' youth? Surely our Declaration of Independence, our federal constitution, and possibly *The Federalist*. Where else would Juárez so likely have encountered the non-Mexican, or at least non-Spanish, principles of the separation and balance of the executive, legislative, and judicial powers, and of the federal and state powers; or the even more basic principle, so fragrantly Jeffersonian, that the ultimate power is that of public opinion, to be expressed as directly as possible.

Juárez learned Latin almost before he learned Spanish, and he early acquired French, of which he always had a greater mastery than of English. Some persons have imagined that Juárez might have studied when young such books as the *Pandects* of Justinian, and the works of Tadeo Ortiz (whom Sierra praises as a practical liberal), S. G. Roscio, Benjamin Constant, and Voltaire and Rousseau. About these last two, however great their indirect influence may have been on Juárez, one may be permitted doubts. Although his mind had an ironic turn, Juárez was too religious for Voltaire, and too sensible and classical for Rousseau. He believed in God, and in law and order, but law and order based on the educated will of the people, and maintained for their benefit. This was not inconsistent with his distaste for the volatile enthusiasms of the Mexican crowd—and other crowds are not dissimilar. On September 16, the National Holiday, 1840–to look ahead a few years—the young lawyer delivered a patriotic address to his fellow citizens in Oaxaca, eulogizing Hidalgo, of course, pointing out the evil results of three centuries of colonialism, opposing indifference to civil rights and duties, and urging education and good citizenship. He also urged attention to the example of priests who, like Hidalgo, united Christian morality and civic virtue, and honor to the soldiers who had fought for liberty and independence. This address includes a number of references to Greek and Roman history, from which he chose episodes and figures illustrative of civic virtue or its absence. Juárez was not a showy intellectual, or a broad-minded and passionate one like Ocampo, or an original or subtle thinker, but he digested whatever he did read, integrated it with his own experience, thoughts, and faiths, and fought for his final convictions with a strength of will almost unequaled in history.

Sr. Iturribarría, the expert on Oaxaca, has suggested that at the Institute Juárez got a thorough grounding in the facts of colonial history—in the struggles of the Spanish kings with the Mexican Church—which indicated to him that the powers of the Church came from the state, by whose agency alone those powers could be revised or withdrawn.

But his own background and experience were as important as teachers and books in the formation of Juárez' political views and will. As a Zapotec Indian from the mountains he was the heir of a strong tradition of local autonomy. This fact, plus his knowledge that the Spaniards, foreigners, had governed thoroughly, and entirely for their own gain, from Mexico City, made him even more strongly, if not permanently, a federalist. Yet at great cost, after many years, the Spaniards had been overthrown, and Juárez was now passionately a Mexican and a patriot, as well as a liberal. Nor did Juárez, after his own experiences, have to learn from Jefferson or anyone else the importance of free, secular education for all the people.

By this time, too, Juárez' life in Oaxaca and his political views began to be affected, more frequently, by national events. "In 1829," the *Notes* continue, "there was reported an imminent invasion by the Spaniards of the Isthmus of Tehuantepec, and all of the students in the Institute enlisted in the civic militia; they named me a lieutenant in one of the companies organized for the defense of national independence." Four years later, in another period of service that probably included action, he was made a captain, but he never again served in the army. This military experience may have served both to educate Juárez in the necessity of authority and in the attitudes of those commanding and being commanded that made authority effective, and to give him a permanent distaste for arrogant military men and military privilege.

It was probably in 1829 that Juárez, earning enough money from various odd jobs to support himself otherwise than as a houseboy, and probably not wishing to take further advantage of the kindness

of don Antonio Salanueva, left the home of his godfather and patron; but it is clear that Juárez' gratitude, and their mutual affection,
never grew less. It is not known when don Antonio died.

In December of that year there occurred a curious confrontation
of the two men who can be said to symbolize the worst and the best
in Mexico in their time. Although they probably did not meet again,
their influence on each other's lives, and on Mexican history, had
hardly begun. The administration of Guadalupe Victoria floundered
to an end in 1828, whereupon the Secretary of War, Manuel Gómez
Pedraza, used the army to get himself elected President, defeating
Guerrero. Seeing something in it for himself, as always, Santa Anna
came out for Guerrero. At one point, in that autumn of 1828, pursued to Oaxaca by forces loyal to Pedraza, Santa Anna, in his usual
comic-opera style, had barricaded himself in the convent of Santo
Domingo, and in Mexico City Guerrero was illegally and unwisely
made President. What is now known as "The Age of Santa Anna"
had begun. In July, 1829, hoping to profit from these chaotic conditions by recovering New Spain, the Spanish sent an army from Cuba
to Tampico, which they captured. There, however, they encountered one of the most formidable armies in Mexico, that of the yel-
low-fever mosquitoes. For the victory of the mosquitoes, and of the
Mexican General Mier y Teran, Santa Anna rushed northwards with
forces from Veracruz just in time to take credit.

It was while he was playing with relish the role of "the hero of
Tampico," and already dreaming of greater things to come, that
General Santa Anna sat down to a testimonial dinner, in Oaxaca,
and somehow learned the identity of one of the young men who
waited on his table. Juárez must have known about the episode in
Oaxaca the year before, and about the victory at Tampico, but quite
possibly he knew nothing about Santa Anna's previous tergiversa-
tions. Long afterwards, when they had nearly destroyed each other
several times, Santa Anna wrote: "He could not forgive me because
he had waited on me at table in Oaxaca, in December, 1829, with his
bare feet on the floor and in his linen smock and trousers. . . . It is
amazing that an Indian of such low degree should have become the
figure in Mexico that we all know." Nothing could be more prepos-

terous than to accuse Juárez of snobbish resentment towards a man
he had served at table.

Meanwhile, Juárez was doing very well in his studies, and presumably had earned some shoes. "In 1830," he continues, "I was entrusted, as a substitute, with the chair of physics, with an allotment of thirty pesos to add to the few I had with which to meet my expenses." At a meeting of the Directors of the Institute, Juárez once had to reveal that he actually had no students in physics, because they had not succeeded in passing the required course in logic, and although a technicality permitted him to receive his pay anyway, he refused to take it until he had again acquired some students. However, he asked the authorities to buy a telescope and a barometer. "In 1831, I finished my course in jurisprudence and began to practice in the law office of Lic. don Tiburcio Cañas. In the same year I was named an alderman in the city by popular election, and I presided over the thesis that my student don Francisco Rincón dedicated to the academic body of the seminary."

Here there occurs an omission so important that one suspects it was caused by emotion. In 1830 a rebellion led by the Vice-President himself, Anastasio Bustamente, deposed and treacherously captured Vicente Guerrero, the insurgent hero-President, aboard an Italian ship at Acapulco. They brought him to Oaxaca for a drummed-up trial, convicted him, forced him to kneel to listen to the sentence of the court, took him to Cuilapa, now Guerrero, and there shot him. Bustamente's administration was reactionary, and soon enough Santa Anna sensed in the liberal discontent his own chance.

"In the year 1832," continues Juárez, "there began a revolution against the administration of the President of the Republic, don Anastasio Bustamente, which collapsed at the end of the year, with the Scotch party that supported it." For a while Santa Anna, elected President in 1833, allowed Valentín Gómez Farías, the Vice-President, Lorenzo de Zavala, Governor of the state of Mexico, and José Luis Mora, all ardent and able liberals, to have their way, with the result that for about a year (April, 1833–April, 1834) Mexico enjoyed a brilliant if false dawn of liberal reform, during which Juárez continued to climb the political ladder. However, the reactionaries were aroused, liberal resistance was weakened by a dreadful influx of cholera, and Santa Anna proceeded to establish a thoroughgoing dictatorship. Down with the liberals went the young lawyer in Oaxaca.

At the beginning of 1833, [he continues] I was elected deputy to the state legislature. Because of the Law of Expulsion of Spaniards passed by the federal congress [1829], the Bishop of Oaxaca, don Manuel Isidoro Pérez, although exempted from this hardship, refused to remain in his dioceses, and departed for Spain. Since there was not now one bishop in the Republic, because the few that there had been had also gone abroad, it was not easy to receive holy orders, and they could only be had by going to Havana or New Orleans; for this purpose it was indispensable to have sufficient resources, which I lacked. For me, this circumstance was highly favorable, because my godfather, recognizing the impossibility of my being ordained, permitted me to continue in my career at the bar. By that time I was supporting myself entirely by my own resources.

In the same year I was named Aide to the Commandant, General don Isidro Reyes, who defended the city against the forces of General Canalizo, who had pronounced for the plan of religion and exemptions put forward by Colonel don Ignacio Escalada in Morelia. From that time, the clerical-military party impudently undertook to maintain by force of arms, and by means of rebellions, their exemptions, their abuses, and all their antisocial pretensions. What gave this rebellion of the privileged classes a pretext was the first step that the liberal party took at that time on the road of reform: repealing the unjust laws that imposed civil coercion for the collection of monastic votive offerings and the payment of tithes.

Canalizo besieged the city, and actually took part of it, before he was driven off and had to retire to the coast. It was at this time that Juárez probably took part in the street fighting and saw what was to become too familiar a sight in Mexico: cobblestones drenched with blood.

"In January of 1834 I presented myself for the examination for the practice of law before the State Court of Justice, and I was approved and given the title of advocate. A few days later, the legislature named me acting judge of the court of justice, which office I filled for a short time." Juárez' appointment, so soon after being admitted to the bar, may have been due to his success in passing the test set him by the court: that of reviewing and analyzing, within forty-eight hours, a case on a seizure of lands in 1825. He carried his certificate as an advocate with him until he died, but except when opposing injustice, he was apparently never much interested in the techniques and triumphs of advocates; nor was he by temperament a judge, fascinated by the structure and details of the law. Neither was he temperamentally a legislator, interested in the compromises, maneuvers, and oratorical feats necessary for effectiveness as such. In his brief services as alderman, state legislator, and later a delegate to a national congress, he did not speak one recorded word. He seems to have preferred teaching, for after physics he taught civil and canon law, and as long as he remained in Oaxaca, he continued to promote and support his beloved Institute in every way possible. But above all, of course, as he and his fellow citizens learned rather slowly, he was a born political executive.

Although the insurrection of Escalada, supported by Arista, Durán, and Canalizo, had been suppressed the preceding year, its promoters continued working, and in the end succeeded in destroying the administration of don Valentín Gómez Farías; and to this end there contributed many of the actual partisans of this administration, because, ill understanding the principles of liberty, as, I said above, they proceeded without a compass, and they were easily led into the road towards which they were impelled by their ambitions, their interests, and their rancors. Consequently there fell the public administration of Oaxaca in which I was serving, and I was confined in the city of Tehuacán, for no other reason than that I had served honorably and loyally in the posts with which I had been entrusted.

This confinement was probably to a house in Tehuacán, or to the limits of the city. Juárez seems here rather oddly to have ignored the decisive role of Santa Anna in the events of 1834. In any event, he was soon to encounter an anonymous person whose effect on his life and opinions was comparable to that of Santa Anna.

When the order for my confinement had been revoked, I returned to Oaxaca and dedicated myself to the exercise of my profession. The clergy still found themselves in full possession of their exemptions and prerogatives, and their close alliance with the civil power gave them an influence that was almost omnipotent. The exemption that removed them from the jurisdiction of the common courts served them as a shield against the law of safe-conduct, so that they could indulge with impunity in every excess and every injustice. The taxes that were the rights of the parishes were a dead letter, and the payment of the perquisites was determined in accordance with the greedy wills of the parish priests. There were, however, some honorable and upright priests who limited themselves to charging what was just, and who did not rob the faithful; but these truly evangelical men were very rare, and their example, far from deterring the evil ones from their abuses, resulted in their own censure, on the ground that they were misleading the people and beginning to lose the curacies. Meanwhile, the citizens groaned in their oppression and misery, because the fruit of their work, their time, and their personal services was entirely devoted to the satisfaction of the insatiable greed of their so-called shepherds. Justice, if they took steps to seek it, was usually deaf to them, and commonly they received as their own answer scorn or imprisonment.

I myself have been both a witness and a victim of one of these injustices. The residents of the town of Loxicha appealed to me to take their case and establish their rights before the ecclesiastical court against their parish priest, who demanded of them payments and personal services, without abiding by the established rates. Convinced of the justice of their complaints by the report they made to me and by the documents they showed me, I presented myself before the Steward's Court, as it was called. Doubtless because of my status as a deputy, and because at that time the state was governed by a liberal administration—since this happened early in 1834—my appeal was noticed and the priest was ordered to appear and answer the charges made against him; and he was warned not to return to his parish until the trial that he faced should have been completed.

Unluckily, within a few months that administration fell, as I have already explained, and the priest, who had worked to that end, now more audacious and less prudent with regard to society and to his own honor, returned to exercise his regrettable influence in favor of his corrupt interests. Before the end of the trial that I had instituted, of the priest of Loxicha, the ecclesiastical judge without respecting his own decisions, and without any hearing of the plaintiffs, openly directed that the accused return to his parish. As soon as he arrived at the village of Loxicha, he secured the arrest of all of those who had appeared against him, and with the compliance of the Prefect and the District Judge, put them in jail, where they were held incommunicado. He obtained orders from the authorities in the capital that the citizens of the village who came to the city to see me, or to hunt for another lawyer who would take their case, should be arrested and imprisoned.

At that time, the end of 1834, I was substituting in the chair of canon law in the Institute, and being unable to see with indifference the injustice being committed against my unhappy clients, I sought permission from the Director to absent myself for a few days, and I went to the town of Miahuatlán, where the prisoners were, in order to liberate them. As soon as I arrived at that town, I presented myself to the Judge, don Manuel María Feraud, who received me well and permitted me to talk with the prisoners. Next, I asked him to inform me of the nature of the case against the alleged criminals, and of the motive for their imprisonment. He answered that he could tell me nothing because the case was kept secret. I insisted that he read me the warrant for arrest, which was not secret and which should already have been issued, because the time had elapsed that the law required for its publication. No more did he accede to my request, which obliged me to inform him that on the next day I should present him with a petition that would serve to give me his reply in writing—which in turn would be necessary, in all justice, for the defense, of my clients.

The following day I presented my petition, as I had said I should do; but already the judge had entirely changed: he received me with extreme severity and demanded from me the power of attorney with which I was acting on behalf of the defendants; and I having answered that being a recognized attorney speaking in defense of the impoverished accused, I needed no formal power of attorney, he warned me that I should abstain from speaking, and that I should return in the afternoon to offer my preparatory declaration in the case that he was going to open to judge me as a vagabond.

Since the priest was already in the village and the Prefect was acting under his influence, I feared worse injustices and returned to the city with the resolve of accusing the Judge before the Court of Justice, as may be done; but I was ignored, because in that tribunal also the priest was represented. So the doors of justice remained closed to those unhappy ones who suffered in prison without having committed any offense, and only because they had complained of the oppressions of the parish priest.

Implacable in his revenge, as the adherents of any religion generally are, this one did not satisfy himself with the triumphs he had obtained in the courts, but sought to persecute and humiliate me directly, and to do this, he caused Judge Feruad to write a letter of requisition, to the judge in the capital, that he should secure my arrest and have me sent, under guard, to the village of Miahuatlán, explaining that the only cause of this proceeding was that I was in the village of Loxicha, inciting the citizens against the authorities—and I was at that time in the city, fifty leagues from the village of Loxicha, where I had never been!

The judge in the capital, who was working also with the priest, disregarding the fact that the letter had not been written in accordance with the law, came to my house at midnight and conducted me to the jail without giving me any more reason than that he had received an order to send me as a prisoner to Miahuatlán. Also taken to jail was Lic. don José Inés Sandoval, who also had been asked by the accused to defend them.

So notorious was the falsity of the charge made against me and so clear the injustice to which I was subjected that I believed it to be a certainty that the Superior Court, to which I appealed in complaint of such an infamous outrage, would give immediate orders that I be set at liberty; but I was mistaken, for it was only after nine days that it freed me on bail, and it never took account of my complaints and accusations against the judges who had injured me.

These blows that I suffered, and that almost daily I saw suffered by the unprotected who complained of the arbitrary acts of the privileged classes in close association with the civil authority, showed me most clearly that society would never be happy while those classes existed in alliance with the public powers, and confirmed me in my resolution to work unceasingly to destroy the evil power of the privileged classes. This I did as well as I could, and this the liberal party would do; but unluckily for humanity, the remedy that was then being used did not go to the root of the evil, for although many times a reactionary administration was overthrown and replaced by a liberal one, the change was only one of persons, and there remained active in the laws and constitutions the ecclesiastic and military exemptions, religious intolerance, the state religion, and the continued possession by the clergy of numerous properties that they used wrongly to establish firmly their destructive power. Thus it was that when a liberal administration was established, only a few months later it was overthrown, and its adherents were persecuted.

This passage in Juárez' *Notes* is longer than any devoted to any other episode in his life up to that time, and this emphasis seems just. We may hazard the view that even for a mind as disinterested and stoical as Juárez', it is one thing to observe injustices meted out to others, and to resent them, and quite another thing to spend nine days and nights in a Mexican jail, unjustly, and to ponder the situation at painful leisure there. It seems probable that Juárez was not held in solitary confinement, but was allowed to talk, pace a patio, and sleep with his fellow prisoners, who were also his clients; and also that these men, closer to Loxicha than Juárez was to Oaxaca, were fed by friends who brought them beans and tortillas, and that they shared these with their lawyer and with the unhappy Lic. don José Inés Sandoval, who could be called even more innocent, if apparently less chivalrous! Juárez never failed to feel himself at one with the poor and the victims of injustice, and much more so, apparently, than with the powerful figures, including gentlemen, generals, and bounders, who later surrounded him in high offices, accompanied him on his rigorous travels, and received his orders; but there in the jail at Miahuatlán he was at rock bottom with his own, and he never forgot them or ceased to fight for them. In the endless hours of those nine days and nights there was forged the will that rocked the Church from its gold foundations, destroyed one empire, and helped bring down another.

In his *Notes,* Juárez now skips five years, and then continues almost as meagerly: "From the year 1839 to 1840 I was dedicated exclusively to the practice of my profession. In the year 1841 the Court of Justice named me Judge of the First Prosecution of the civil and economic branch in the capital of the state."

According to Sr. Jorge L. Tamayo, the scholarly editor of Juárez' letters, in these years before his marriage, Juárez fathered two children, named Tereso and Susana. Of Tereso, Sr. Tamayo tells nothing but we *may* catch a fleeting and tantalizing glimpse of him later. Susana, Sr. Tamayo tells us, became an invalid and a narcotics addict who in Juárez' later years was in the care of his old friends Sr. Miguel Castro and his wife, when Castro was Governor of Oaxaca; and he also shows us, in a letter from Juárez to Señora de Castro, that the father showed the most tender concern for this unfortunate daughter. This almost hidden chapter does not seem surprising and may not be of importance; in any case, on the basis of what little we know, it does not call for quick or severe moral judgment. Guessing is inevitable, but we must remember that many young Mexican women, to this day, do not choose to marry the fathers of their children; that marriage is often considered, especially by Indians, less important and natural, while more expensive, than procreation; and that in any event the young woman may have died young. If the situation caused Juárez pain, he concealed it and got on with his work.

We are quite safe in assuming that during all these years, Juárez' friendship with the Maza family continued and deepened, and that this relationship tended to domesticate the young man, and to make his attitude towards marriage and family life more respectful—and more Spanish, if you like. On March 29, 1826, eight days after Juárez' twentieth birthday, when he was still working for don Antonio Salanueva, the Maza family, probably already large, was increased by the birth of a daughter named Margarita. Juárez, as a valued friend of the family, probably cared for and played with the child, like most Mexican older brothers. "On July 31, 1843," Juárez wrote with superlative concision for his children, "I married doña Margarita Maza, daughter of don Antonio Maza and of doña Petra Parada." The bride was then seventeen years old, and the bridegroom thirty-seven. The marriage took place in the church of San Felipe Neri in Oaxaca, and in the record of it doña Margarita is described as the "legitimate daughter" of the Mazas, which seems to dispose of a story—used to explain their allowing her to marry an Indian so far beneath her socially—that she was an adopted daughter.

There exists a remarkable and charming photograph of the young Juárez seated between his bride and his sister, her family's cook. Of her bridegroom, doña Margarita, equally concise but more expressive, is known only to have said: "He is very homely but very good." Almost certainly, she knew all about his illegitimate children, and would have felt astonished and amused by any Anglo-Saxon suggestion of her having to forgive him. Unluckily, we do not know much about this woman, but what little we do know indicates that she was superb. It is equally clear that in a very simple, strong, and deep way, Juárez, as she called him, and his old lady, as he called her, were devoted to each other until death. They had twelve children in all: six daughters (Manuela, Margarita, Felícitas, Soledad, María de Jesús, and María Josefa) and one son (Benito) survived their parents; three daughters (Amada, Francisca, and Guadalupe) died as babies, and two sons (José and Antonio) died during Juárez' lifetime.

Juárez' education already well advanced, was evidently to continue.

4

ANARCHY, INVASION, AND ONE
SILENT POLITICIAN

DURING THE 1830's AND 1840's, while Juárez was learning about politics, the law, justice, the Church, the army, love, and himself, his beloved country was writhing in its inability to go either forward or backward. Orating incompetents, gold-braided hoodlums, and a few able and honest men managed, one group after the other, to seize political and military power. The honest liberals represented "the wave of the future" and could not be denied, but they were rendered ineffective by their inexperience, their unrealistic federalism, and their small numbers, even when they managed to seize the government. The honest conservatives were also a minority, and their centralism was corrupted by the support of irresponsible property owners, the Church, and the regular army. Both groups were inevitably defeated by the ignorance and indifference of the great mass of the people; the stagnation of an economy still undeveloped and shackled by monopolies, which made it impossible for the central government to support itself; the incessant intrusions and demands of foreign diplomats; and the frequent rebellions of the savage Indians, of unabsorbed and belligerent minority groups in such places as Yucatán and Tehuantepec, and of the power-hungry local chieftains. Among these last the most formidable at this time, repeatedly successful in imposing himself as a savior, was Santa Anna. Fortunately, we do not have to follow these convulsions in detail.

It is more agreeable and enlightening to take a look at Mexico at this time, through the eyes of Frances Inglis de Calderón de la Barca (1804–1882), a Scottish lady who, as an impoverished teacher living and working in the United States, became a friend of the American literary lights of the period, and in 1838 married a Spanish gentleman, diplomat, and man of letters named Ángel Calderón de la Barca. He was at that time the head of a special diplomatic mission to Washington, and soon after he was appointed the first Minister of Spain to the Republic of Mexico, where he and his wife lived and did considerable traveling from December, 1839, to January, 1842. In London and New York in 1843 there was published her record of this experience, now a classic, called *Life in Mexico during a Residence of Two Years in That Country.*

Mme. Calderón was an alert, skilled, and for the most part objective reporter, with wide sympathies and a delightful sense of humor, and despite her marked areas of personal reserve, she emerges in this book as a most attractive person. Her husband was an aristocrat, and both were warmly received by the upper classes in Mexico, so that it is not surprising that she favored them—although she took care to remain a detached foreign visitor.

Her book includes firsthand reports of the abortive *pronunciamiento* of Gómez Farías and General Urrea against the moderate but ineffective administration of Bustamente in Mexico City, in July, 1840, during which Santa Anna lurked ominously in the background, and of the more determined and successful rebellion by Santa Anna himself the next year. One interesting aspect of these outbursts of violence, as reported by Mme. Calderón, is the cool and almost cheerful indifference towards them of the mass of people who did not take part. Cannon balls fall into houses and gardens, innocent persons stop stray bullets on the streets, negotiations are held, the leaders issue grandiloquent manifestos, and all the while the life of the city quietly stops, or as quietly goes on—at least as normally as may be. When she first met Santa Anna at his ranch, even this keen woman was impressed by him, but her disillusionment with him steadily grew.

In the middle of the rebellion on September 2, 1841:

Mexico looks as if it had got a general holiday. Shops shut up, and all business is at a stand. The people, with the utmost apathy, are collected in groups, talking quietly; the officers are galloping about; generals, in a somewhat party-colored dress, with large gray hats, striped pantaloons, old coats, and generals' belts, fine horses, and crimson-colored velvet saddles. The shopkeepers in the square have been removing their goods and money. An occasional shot is heard, and sometimes a volley, succeeded by a dead silence. The archbishop shows his reverend face now and then upon the opposite balcony of his palace, looks out a litttle while, and then retires. The chief effect, so far, is universal idleness in man and beast—the soldiers and their quadrupeds excepted. . . .

5th—We went upon the flat roof this afternoon, to have a good view of the city. There were people on almost all the balconies, as on a feteday. A picturesque group of friars of the order of La Merced, in their white robes, had mounted up on the belfry of their church, and were looking out anxiously. The palace roof next our own had soldiers on it. Everything at the moment was still and tranquil; but the conduct of the people is our constant source of surprise. Left entirely uncurbed, no one to direct them, thousands out of employment, many without bread, they meddle with nothing, do not complain, and scarcely seem to feel any interest in the result. How easily might such a people be directed for their own good! It is said that all their *apathetic sympathies* are in favour of Bustamente.

Mme. Calderón's husband, don Ángel, started a literary and scientific organization called the Atenéo, which was very successful, and also a newspaper called *La Hesperia;* both were nonpolitical until the latter became embroiled in the storm aroused by the publication of a pamphlet favoring a monarchy, by don Ángel's friend José M. Gutiérrez de Estrada. Sierra gives Calderón de la Barca, and even that fantastic anachronism, Gutiérrez de Estrada, some credit for a mild cultural flowering at the time.

From Mme. Calderón's reports of their arduous and dangerous travels—in coaches and on horseback, with armed guards, through violently and variously beautiful landscapes; of palaces handsome if barely furnished, tenderly nurtured gardens, convents, and hovels; of balls, masses, plays, fiestas, bullfights, hangings, and enormous dinners; of kindness and brutality, courtesy and vulgarity, humor and superstitious devotion; of fecundity, stamina, and dignity in the midst of outrageous poverty; and of a simmering political atmosphere of scheming and corruption, idealism and heroism—from all this we get an impression of a Mexico that had not changed greatly since 1810, that would not change much more by the time of

Charles Flandrau's impressions in another classic, *Viva Mexico!*, in
1908, and that has remained substantially the same to this day.

But all of these are the impressions, necessarily superficial, of
foreigners. There is another change that is more important, and that
has nothing to do, incidentally, with automobiles, electric signs, soft
drinks, and luxury hotels. This change is symbolized by the contrast
between the chances of the young Juárez, trapped in an inferior
seminary until he was twenty-two years old, and those of thousands
of young Mexican boys and girls to-day who are going to good
schools (they could, like ours, be better) that are free and open
(theoretically, at least) to the pursuit of any kind of truth, scientific,
artistic, political, and even religious, at any cost to any institution,
any vested interest, and any "way of life." For this fundamental
change, Benito Juárez himself must be given much of the credit.

However, in the 1840's, and indeed at almost any time between
1810 and 1940, an institution that was more immediately important
than the school, and that demanded more of Juárez' attention, and
more of the blood and wealth of the Mexican people, was that of
the *pronunciamiento*, or armed rebellion by ambitious chieftains who
"pronounced" against the government in power, and against the
constitution, and who attempted to gain adherents, and to disguise
their personal ambitions for power, by offering a "Plan" for the salvation of the country. No one can study the history of Mexico in this
long and critical period without wondering how these chieftains,
or *caudillos*, managed to get so many men, so quickly, to fight for
them, to supply and pay these forces for such long periods, and
hence to do so much damage.

From the days of the Viceroys there was, of course, a more or
less regular professional army, most of which, until the victory of
the republican and constitutional forces in 1861, and the subsequent
invasion by foreign forces, remained loyal to the various conservative governments. The men who fought for the republican and
constitutional government between 1861 and 1867 claimed with
increasing justice—in regard to the tenure of their commissions,
their pensions, and so on—to be the regular army, and their claims
were justified by their victory in 1867. The rebellion in support of
the Plan of Ayutla in 1854, which succeeded the following year,

and which was backed by Juárez, was literally just one more *pronunciamiento* until it was left, later in 1857, in support of the new constitution, by the *golpe de estado* or *coup d'état* supported by Comonfort. In other words, the forces supporting a *pronunciamiento* might be called, and become later to be considered, the regular army, insofar as they supported the constitution in effect, or were successful, or both.

The chief reason why so many and such successful *pronunciamientos* were possible was that so many brave, able, and ambitious men, living in a society that was still largely feudal, had no property or status whatever, had no other prospect of gaining either, had little regard for their own lives or any others, and were loyal to their feudal chieftains, or to the Church and the old order, or to their hopes for social reform, freedom, and a stable republican government. It is true that as these wars progressed, both the liberal and the reactionary governments, legal or not, and their considerably independent generals, resorted increasingly to drafting or simply shanghaiing men from the cities, towns, and ranches that were under their control, and that this aroused increasing resentment and resistance, but it was possible at all only because of the hopeless resignation of great masses of people. Mexico had a feudal society similar to that of England in the fourteenth and fifteenth centuries, and it was a society in which in exchange for endless, grinding work—punctuated by religious fiestas and softened sometimes by the personal kindness of some of the *patrones*, and by *pulque*, hunting, and gambling—and for unquestioning loyalty, the *patrones* gave a bare subsistence, rough justice, and physical protection. In addition, Mexico was and still is a country in which personal relations are more important than political allegiance. In the light of all this, it cannot seem too surprising that when the owner of a ranch or mine, or the *jefe* of a government office called his men out to fight, they usually went. In the case of many of the liberal politicians and generals, the personal and economic loyalty of their dependents must have been as operative as any hopes of reform, freedom, and peace. If we are tempted to think of all this as being very Mexican, we have only to read about the speed and effectiveness with which the great fifteenth-century English lords of the White Rose or the Red called out thousands of brave and not altogether foolish men to buckle on armor, trudge miles across country, and, in the mud and the fog, beat each other's brains out.

But what about the arms, clothing, and food of these Mexicans in their savage mountains only a century ago? The answer is not clear from the available documents, but it can be surmised. Every *hacienda* had been for centuries a considerable fort in itself, defended by men who had learned how to make shotguns, and how to use them with economy and precision against robbers, wild game, and one another. In the state capitals, as well as in the City, ever since 1810, alert governors had been building arsenals in which were manufactured crude but effective gunpowder, cartridges, rifles, bayonets (triangular in cross section), cannon balls, and pieces of artillery. In the years to come, one side got more of all these from the French, and the other, if unofficially, from friendly Americans; while both sides, when they could, bought arms from Europe, including some that had been used at Waterloo.

For uniforms, the Mexicans had long made textiles, straw hats, and shoes almost everywhere in the country, the generals somehow got themselves rather gaudily if heterogeneously uniformed and bemedaled, and the common soldiers probably wore mostly their own usual white pants and shirts, hand-made by their women, with their armies, units, and noncommissioned ranks indicated (if at all) by colored stripes sewn on the trousers and sleeves. (The historical paintings and the uniforms now in museums suggest a degree of uniformity and even elegance that is a bit implausible.) For food, the ordinary Mexican could work and fight on a few beans and tortillas, plus a piece of goat, sheep, or bony steer shot, cut up, and cooked on the way. Of medical care there was almost none, although Juárez in Oaxaca, and perhaps a few other governors elsewhere, did what they could in this direction. Many of all these things could be brought from home, commandeered, or stolen; there were gifts from private individuals and from the Church; the governors had local taxes of many kinds that were incidentally crippling to agriculture and commerce; and the federal government scrambled along desperately and dangerously on unwilling contributions from the states, such customs duties as had not been mortgaged to England, forced loans, and robberies. In short, then as now mass homicide, like love, found a way.

During all these years of the 1830's and 1840's, and earlier, while Mexicans were sporadically killing one another, an increasingly ominous threat was developing from the north. There, the vast northern provinces of Mexico, partly luxuriant forests and partly sinister deserts, but nearly all fabulously rich, were almost uninhabited except by scattered Indian tribes, and were almost ungoverned. The people of the United States were looking and moving westward with a compulsion unequaled in history. The northern republic also was painfully divided between its forces of growth and reaction, produced its spouters and adventurers, and incidentally, had a melancholy politician watching history from the back country, a man who was to prove equal to his own and his country's destiny. The United States had been luckier and was then stronger than Mexico, human society seems to abhor a power vacuum, and the two young republics drifted into their short but very savage little war. Although it was denounced at the time and later by many Americans, including Lincoln, Grant, and Wilson, it robbed Mexico of half its territory, it left wounds in Mexican minds unhealed to this day, and it should make every thoughtful American sad, and also patient in response to any Mexican suspicion and hostility towards ourselves. The story of that war must be told briefly here, in relation to the emergence in Oaxaca of a governor who thenceforward must always have had the United States of America on some part of his tireless mind.

Since 1814 there had existed an American scheme to establish the border between the United States and New Spain, or Mexico, approximately where it is now; Aaron Burr had, not quite insanely, dreamed of becoming Emperor of Mexico; and many worthies, including even Thomas Jefferson and John Quincy Adams, had openly adopted and elaborated the mystical doctrine that it was the "Manifest Destiny" of the United States, because of presumed economic need and "superiority," to absorb the whole of North America. Insofar as the Monroe Doctrine of 1823 was noticed in Mexico at all—until it was used decisively by the United States to Mexico's advantage much later—it was viewed by Mexicans with suspicion as merely another form of "Manifest Destiny" or imperialism. Even down to this day, it has been viewed in this way and resentfully called *monroismo*.

In 1822 Stephen F. Austin took over a colonizing project of his father, Moses Austin of Connecticut and Missouri, who had died the year before, and with liberal grants from the new Mexican republic, founded a colony of Americans in the part of the Mexican state of Coahuila that is now northern Texas. Thousands of Americans, including Negro slaves, poured into the region, and like other unassimilated minorities before and since, this one began, in part unwillingly, to cause trouble for themselves and for everyone else. Those arch-meddlers, Joel R. Poinsett, for the United States, and H. G. Ward, for Great Britain, of course fished in the troubled waters. Naturally, various Mexican governments took steps to control Texas and defend the national territory. In 1830, further colonization of Texas was prohibited and customs stations were established on the Louisiana frontier. The law against slavery was again proclaimed, and the centralization of the Mexican government obviously meant more trouble for the Texans. Austin failed to influence even the liberal President Gómez Farías, and was imprisoned for a year and a half in Mexico City for urging rebellion in Texas. In 1835 the Mexican General Cos was defeated at San Antonio, and the following year Santa Anna with three or four thousand Mexicans returned to San Antonio, and on March 6, four days after Texas had declared itself an independent nation, butchered about 150 Texans at the Alamo, and many others at Goliad. Soon after, Sam Houston defeated the Mexicans at San Jacinto and captured Santa Anna himself, in his carpet slippers. That statesman traded recognition of Texan independence for his own freedom, but in Mexico he was naturally disavowed and deposed. For nine years Texas was refused admission to the Union—because the North opposed the spread of the slave power—and existed as a republic.

Meanwhile, Mexico approached complete chaos, with rebellions breaking out from the political left and right and the geographical north and south. In the silly "Pastry War" with France in 1838, Santa Anna lost a leg and became again a hero; in 1842 this leg was dug up in Veracruz and solemnly reburied, with immense ceremony, in Mexico City. When he threatened to reconquer Texas, the Texans had to appeal to Great Britain for help, and this step alarmed the American government into taking Texas into the Union, in 1845. The new President of the United States, James K. Polk, in 1846 tried crudely to reach a settlement with President Herrera of Mexico, an honest man who probably could not have survived any settlement, and who in any case was soon displaced. Without consulting Congress, Polk ordered General Zachary Taylor to advance from the Nueces River, the actual southern boundary of Texas, to the Rio Bravo, or Grande, and when the Mexicans naturally put up a fight, he secured a declaration of war. Meanwhile Santa Anna, who had been in exile in Havana, tricked Polk into allowing him to return to Mexico.

In that year, General Taylor, whose officers included Grant, Meade, and Jefferson Davis, took Monterrey, and various roving forces took Santa Fé, and with naval forces, occupied California; Tampico also was seized. The United States had now gained all the territory it wanted, and more, but the Mexican government, having its usual convulsions, refused to concede defeat. In March, 1847, General Winfield Scott landed an army south of Veracruz, by-passing the island fortress of San Juan de Ulúa, and took the city. Meanwhile Santa Anna, again in command, moved an army northward, towards Taylor's forces, as far as San Luis Potosí, and then onward to the north, where he fought Taylor at a place near Saltillo called Buena Vista or La Angostura. In this strange battle, the larger force of Santa Anna came very near to defeating the Americans, but Taylor's personal courage, and an ill-advised decision by Santa Anna to withdraw during the night, saved the American force. Because he had captured a few guns and an American flag, Santa Anna claimed a victory—and as we shall see, was even credited by Juárez with one—but in fact greatly weakened the Mexican army by his long retreat across the desert between Saltillo and San Luis Potosí. In Mexico City the proclerical "Polkos" mutinied and the government was overthrown.

Meanwhile, Scott, with his army of about twelve thousand men, and a staff that included such brilliant officers as Grant (transferred from the north), Lee, Beauregard, and McClellan, was climbing inland from Veracruz, and at the difficult mountain pass of Cerro Gordo, between Veracruz and Jalapa, they met and defeated Santa Anna's force, and then moved onward to Perote and Puebla. Even the anti-American historian Vasconcelos was to admit later that this American force, hampered by disease and lack of supplies, and disapproved of or ignored by most Americans at home, performed feats comparable to those of Cortés and his *conquistadores*. Despite Santa Anna's ineptitude, there followed the bitter and courageous defense of Mexico City at Churubusco, the Pedregal, the Molino del Rey, and Chapultepec, where the famous cadets leaped from the cliffs to their death rather than surrender to the invaders. One outfit of Americans had gone over to the enemy, and some fifty of them were captured, tried, and hanged. Often some American units had to keep watch on others to prevent pillage. Even after the city itself was taken, bloody street fighting continued, and the victorious American officers quarreled with one another and with their superiors in Washington. The Mexicans and the Americans fought this war with great courage and resource for only two years, but it is one of the ugliest wars on record.

Having resigned the Presidency, Santa Anna tried to capture the sick American soldiers who had been left at Puebla, but failed. Then pursued by the Texas Rangers, who still remembered the Alamo, he was denied refuge in the city of Oaxaca—an episode trivial in itself, but of immense consequences. He managed to escape to Veracruz, and thence once more into exile, first in Jamaica and then Venezuela.

At Querétaro, Scott and an American agent named Nicholas B. Trist negotiated a peace with Peña y Peña, the Chief Justice of the Supreme Court now President; this treaty was signed at Guadalupe Hidalgo and given that name. In March, 1848, it was ratified by the United States Senate. By conquest, and for fifteen million dollars and the cancellation of American claims, the United States acquired almost half the territory of Mexico and unbounded natural wealth. Yet by raising again the question of the extension of slave or free territory into the west, this victory hastened our own Civil War.

We can now return to Juárez' memories of those times, beginning with the year after his marriage. Naturally, his interests at this time were less military than civil, and his relative silence about military events must not be taken for insensitivity. Juárez' former chief, don Antonio León, and eight hundred other men from Oaxaca, surely including many personal friends and acquaintances of Juárez, were killed at the Molino del Rey.

"In 1844 the Governor of the state, General don Antonio León," Juárez continues, "named me secretary of the cabinet of the government, and at the same time I was elected a substitute voter in the departmental assembly. A few months later, the magistrates of the Superior Tribunal of the state were reconstituted—and the state was then called a department because the centralized form of government ruled the nation—and I was named Second Prosecutor of the same."

Although León had fought with Morelos, he was by this time a Santa Anna conservative, and Juárez has been much criticized for serving under him at all, and especially for signing a decree for ceremonies in honor of Santa Anna, then President. In view of the total confusion of party lines and loyalties, and of the strangely persistent hope that Santa Anna would save the country, such criticism, even when made by Sierra, and elaborately qualified, seems picayune. As secretary of the cabinet, a post in which he seems to have had considerable power, Juárez began his work as a reforming executive. He effected some reforms in the courts, improved record-keeping, established a sanitary commission, and encouraged the production of iron and silk and the building of a road from Oaxaca to Tehuacán—a project that was to be paid for by tolls and diligence concessions, and that became an obsession of his. Within a few months a student criticized León in public, the Governor ordered him drafted into the army, and Juárez resigned in protest; whereupon the Governor made the former secretary a prosecutor. On Juárez' recommendation, the secretaryship was filled by another liberal, Manuel Ruiz. To find anything in all this with which to reproach Juárez as a renegade seems to require an effort and a motive.

"In the year 1845," Juárez continues,

there were held elections of the deputies to the departmental assembly, and I appeared as one of the many candidates who offered themselves to the public. The electors resolved on me and I was unanimously elected. Early in 1846 the departmental assembly was dissolved as a result of the military sedition led by General Paredes, who, under orders from the President, don José Joaquín de Herrera, to march to the frontier threatened by the American army, pronounced in the hacienda of the Peñasco in the state of San Luis Potosí, and countermarched towards the capital of the Republic, in order to seize the government, which he did, submitting himself completely to the direction of the monarchist-conservative party. The liberal party did not concede defeat. Aided by the Santa Anna party, it worked actively until it succeeded in overturning the reactionary administration of Paredes and in installing General don Mariano Salas provisionally in the Presidency of the Republic.

In Oaxaca the movement against Paredes was supported by General don Juan Bautista Díaz; there was named [August 11] a Legislative Committee and an Executive Power of three persons who were named by a Committee of Notables. The election fell on don Luis Fernández del Campo, don José Simeón Arteaga, and myself, and we began at once to fulfill the duties with which we had been honored. Informed of this arrangement, the general government decided to dissolve [September 10] the Legislative Committee, and to entrust the executive power of the state to don José Simeón Arteaga alone. I had to return to my legal post in the prosecutor's office, but Governor Arteaga dissolved it in order to reorganize it with other personnel, and in consequence he proceeded to its reorganization, naming me President or Regent—as at that time was named the presiding officer—of the Tribunal of Justice of the state.

This very temporary state government was a coalition: Fernández del Campo was selected as an old insurgent, Arteaga as a representative of *santannismo,* and Juárez as the leading liberal.

The general government called on the nation to elect its representatives with full powers to revise the constitution of 1824 [which meanwhile had been illegally set aside], and I was one [of nine] of those named for Oaxaca, and so proceeded to the capital of the Republic, to fulfill my new duties, early in December [the 6th] of the same year of 1846. At this time the Republic was already invaded by forces of the United States of the North; the government lacked funds sufficient to set up a defense, and it was necessary for the congress to afford the means of acquiring them. The deputy for Oaxaca, don Tiburcio Cañas, took the initiative in authorizing the government to mortgage part of the properties administered by the clergy, in order to provide resources for the war. The proposal was admitted and then turned over to a special commission, to which I belonged, with the recommendation that it be given prompt attention. On January 10, 1847, a report was made on this matter, advising the adoption of this method, and it was brought up immediately for discussion. The debate was extremely long and heated, because the moderate party, which had a large majority in the chamber, put up a strong opposition to the project. At two in the morning of the 11th, however, the report was approved in general, but in the discussion of the particulars, the opposition presented a multitude of amendments to each of the articles, with the unpatriotic purpose that even when it was finally approved the act would have so many hobbles that it would not produce the result that the congress proposed. At ten in the morning the discussion came to a close with the passage of the law, but for the reasons stated it did not issue with the desired amplitude.

This seems to have been Juárez' first trip to Mexico City. Pola reports: "In this congress, Juárez was a sphinx, saying only Yes and No, while his colleagues, Francisco Banuet and Tiburcio Cañas, did the talking." This was probably not modesty: Juárez was simply not at home in any legislative assembly.

"From that moment," Juárez continues,

the clergy, the moderates, and the conservatives redoubled their efforts to destroy the law and to eject from the Presidency of the Republic don Valentín Gómez Farías, whom they considered the leader of the liberal party. In a few days they succeeded in realizing their desires by inciting to rebellion a part of the city at the moment when our troops were fighting for the nation's independence on the northern frontier and in the city of Veracruz. This mutiny, which was called that of the Polkos, was viewed with indignation by most of the people; and the rebels, thinking that their plan could not succeed by force of their arms, resorted to subversion, and succeeded in winning over General Santa Anna, who commanded the army that had defeated the enemy at La Angostura, and whom the liberal party had just named President of the Republic over the opposition of the moderate and conservative party; but Santa Anna, inconsistent as always, abandoned his men and rushed to Mexico to give the victory to the rebels. These went to the Villa of Guadalupe to receive their protector, with their chests covered with badges of membership in religious orders and relics of saints, as "defenders of religion and the exemptions." Don Valentín Gómez Farías was removed from the Vice-Presidency of the Republic, and the liberal deputies were attacked and denied the reimbursement that the law allowed them for their subsistence in the capital. We deputies from Oaxaca could not receive any help from our state because there the legislature had been destroyed and replaced by those who supported the rebellion of the Polkos; and as a matter of fact the congress was not holding sessions because it lacked a quorum. I decided to go home and dedicate myself to the practice of my profession.

In August of the same year [1847] I arrived in Oaxaca. Although they were persecuted, the liberals were working actively to re-establish the legal order, and in this effort they were authorized by law, for there existed a decree that, on my motion and that of my associates in the deputation from Oaxaca, was passed and sent by the general congress, condemning the mutiny that had occurred in this state and refusing to recognize the authorities established by the rebels; nor did I hesitate to help in any way that I found possible those who worked for the fulfillment of the law, which has always been my sword and my shield.

This last claim, much quoted, is justified by Juárez' whole life. He was indeed "the man of law," most unusual and necessary in those times, and as such he was to save the Republic. However, it might be noted here that he did not speak of the law as his fortress, or allow it to become a prison. On two occasions, for the good of the Republic as he saw it, he set the law aside or tried to get around it.

On November [actually October] 23d we succeeded very well in a movement against the intruding authorities. The President of the Court of Justice, Lic. don Marcos Pérez, took charge of the government; the legislature met and named me Governor *pro tempore* of the state.

At the age of forty-one this born executive had found his proper job, and in spite of turns of fortune that would have downed anyone else, he did it the rest of his life.

5

THE GOOD GOVERNOR

"On the 29th of the same month, [October] 1847," Juárez continues, "I assumed the power [as Governor] that I exercised provisionally until August 12, 1848, when the powers of the state were reconstituted. I was then re-elected for the second constitutional period, which ended in August, 1852, when I turned the mandate over to the provisional Governor, don Ignacio Mejía."

Except for one short, moving passage, to which we shall return, these few words are all that Juárez chose to say to his children about his first two continuous administrations as Governor of Oaxaca. Yet this first major exercise of power, and Juárez' emergence as a liberal administrator, are of major importance, because if he had not accomplished so much in these years and been recognized later, at a critical turning point in Mexican history, for his achievements at this time, his rise to national stature and power might have been delayed. It could not have been prevented, except by a bullet.

Benito Juárez was now a fully mature man of whom we can form a reliable personal impression. He was little more than five feet tall, with a solid, very strong and healthy body, small hands and feet, a dark Indian complexion, clean-shaven, straight black hair parted at the left side, with a lock that was apt to fall over his forehead, and strong Indian features, the most memorable of which were the penetrating and brooding eyes. He was personally immaculate, and under the most difficult circumstances bathed daily whenever possible. Usually he wore dark clothes—although only on formal occasions the frock coat with which he is too often associated—fine white shirts often made by his wife, black bow neckties, and a heavy watch chain on his waistcoat; and without a straight black cane he evidently felt undressed. He buckled on a revolver only when clearly advisable. He slept little, ate sparingly, and drank only a little wine, but he smoked cigars, whenever he could get them, carrying them in a leather case. He was physically graceful and invariably courteous, and he had "a clear and remarkably pleasant voice."

Prieto, his colleague of many years, reports: "In familiar conversation Juárez was very sweet; he cultivated intimate affections; his pleasure was in serving others, taking care to eliminate discontent, even in the lowest servant; he laughed appropriately; he was careful to pay attention; he encouraged jovial conversation, and after starting it, he fell silent, enjoying the conversation of others and being the first to admire them. I never heard him discredit anyone, and as for modesty, I have never known anyone his superior."

He never talked about his personal affairs or, except when appropriate and necessary, about the political, diplomatic, and military problems that engaged his mind in almost every waking moment. He was profoundly reserved, and the impression is unavoidable that except for his son-in-law, who was in no way his equal, and possibly Melchor Ocampo and a few obscure acquaintances in Oaxaca, he never had or needed a very close friend to whom he could unburden his soul. It could be said that except for these few persons, he never loved anyone except the Mexican people, especially the poor ones, and that he loved these with a passion equal to that which he felt for his own family, while never blinding himself to their limitations and follies.

In his thinking, he was slow, and not very subtle or broad; but from personal experience, direct observation, and reading of history, he derived great practical sagacity and a few basic faiths about people and society. He believed that there was a God concerned about the human race, that the people could discover and express God's will, and that it was their destiny to live in a truly democratic society that would permit the growth of the individual. He considered it the duty of all citizens to serve society when called upon to do so, and to serve it honestly and at any cost to themselves. In all of this he practised precisely what, with economy and force, he preached. His political thinking, based ultimately on his Indian background, was basically paternalistic; it was somewhat remote both from the theorizing of the Age of Enlightenment and from Romantic primitivism; and it was even more remote from any form of personal or class dictatorship.

Juárez' courtesy, reserve, and modesty occasionally deceived some of his associates and some of the diplomats of foreign powers into underestimating him, but sooner or later they all learned that behind his few and simple convictions was an indomitable will. During his life and after it he was often accused of gross personal ambition, but he was moved by something much stronger than that: the will of a craftsman in society who loved and had suffered and had decided to make the city, the state, and the Republic, step by patient step, better than he had discovered them to be. He was also accused of cowardice, but only by fools who had never seen him face death with total and genuine serenity.

But what pleasures did he get out of being alive? Was he, even when alive, a man of bronze, alone on a pedestal? He was indifferent to his surroundings, it seems, both when he worked and slept in some wretched inn and when his wife and daughters made him a stuffily comfortable home of the time. It is reported that he never went to a bullfight, and when it was proposed to have a "human fly" perform on the cathedral, to celebrate his birthday, he stopped it on the ground that no man should risk his life as an entertainment. However, he went to the theatre and to concerts when he could, and was happy when his children progressed in their piano lessons. Like all good Mexican fathers, he enjoyed his children and played with them, and there were times when he was alone with his beloved "old woman," doña Margarita. Above all, he evidently enjoyed his terrifying work, as all the great politicians do; and this pleasure is revealed in his self-confidence, his optimism, and the flashes of irony with which he contemplated men and events. *"No tenga cuidado,"* he would say: don't worry, we are going to win. This Zapotec Indian was something of a Puritan and even more of a Stoic. There are worse things to be, and there are much worse kinds of men to have as governors.

On that day in 1847 Juárez, in accordance with the state constitution, took the following oath of office: "I, Benito Juárez, named Governor of the free state of Oaxaca, swear by God and by the holy gospels that I will defend and preserve the Catholic, Apostolic, and Roman religion, without permitting any other in the state; that I will defend and cause to be defended the federal Constitution and the political Constitution and laws of this state, and that I will exercise faithfully the office with which the same state has entrusted me."

This oath, like all others, Juárez fulfilled. He still hoped, as he had seven years before, that Christian morality would induce the priests to support the liberals in social reform. As Governor, he tried to persuade the clergy to help him to effect his reforms, and for a while, as in the matters of road- and port-building, they actually did so. His ideal of a state was that of a family working together, as a result of loyalty, morality, and reason, and in this work the Church naturally had a part. He supported and demanded the collection of tithes authorized by law and defended the Church's titles to properties. Juárez was still a "good Catholic," if a liberal and questioning one. He was not yet in a position to initiate major reforms in the relation between Church and state, his will to do so had not yet hardened, and the Church had not yet shown clearly its intransigence.

The short inaugural address follows:

Gentlemen deputies and senators:

The oath that I have just taken is the guarantee that I must offer, in accordance with the law, that I will repay with loyalty the confidence you have shown me in naming me Governor of the free and sovereign state of Oaxaca. It is a duty of citizens to give their services, however insignificant those may be, when the country summons them to any public office. However, I have doubted whether I should accept the difficult assignment with which you have honored me, because I see among my compatriots a multitude of distinguished citizens whose experience and talents make them worthy to take the reins of the government. At another time that was not one of transition and testing, like the present, I should have refused the distinguished honor with which I now see myself weighed down, even if that act should have marked me as an egotist. But to-day, when power has neither the appeal nor the fascination that attract the vain in the days of calm and prosperity; to-day, when the fountains of the public treasury are drained and the sources of obedience and morality are exhausted as a result of internal dissensions; to-day, finally, when the unjust invader occupies the capital of the republic and threatens us with the total conquest of our territory, the first magistracy of the state is no more than an outpost of imminent danger and a heavy load that will produce nothing but anxieties, fatigues, and sufferings. With this idea, I have not been able to hesitate, and you see me here, gentlemen, ready to face anything that destiny may bring, with the good faith that I have sworn to you before God and men.

You know, gentlemen, how weak are my powers, how small my knowledge; but I count on your co-operation, I count on the support of the people of Oaxaca, and with such powerful support, I promise myself that we shall go forward, overcoming the obstacles thrust upon us by our unhappy situation.

Fortunately, neither faction, nor favoritism, nor intrigue, but only the free and spontaneous will of those chosen by the people, has put me in this position. There should, then, be no fear that my government will either oppress or favor any class of my fellow citizens. No. The common good, the well-being of all Oaxacans will be the chosen objects of my attention.

We have a fundamental charter in which are stated the rights and duties of the governors and the governed. This charter, then, will be my only guide, and its strict observance and the execution of the laws that come from the legitimate representatives of the people will merit my exclusive dedication. Virtue and merit will be sought out, and honorable and peaceful citizens will always find in my administration the firmest support, the most solid guarantee of their rights. Free, and for me sacred, is the right to think, and my compatriots will not be molested for their opinions revealed in speech or writing. I shall respect them and I shall make them respected. Finally, with forbearance and moderation, I shall see to it that all do their duty; but he who crosses the line drawn by the laws, he who violates the rights of others, he who disturbs the peace of the community, will suffer, I swear to you, gentlemen, every rigor of the law. On this point I shall be inexorable, because only thus can morale be re-established, and only thus can the authorities recover their lost prestige. You see traced here, gentlemen, the line of conduct I propose to follow in my administration.

Gentlemen: we are called upon to witness the anguish of our country in the terrible moments of her agony; she claims our succor; let us draw upon our uttermost strength, and still there is time for us to save her. But if by one of the incomprehensible decrees of Divine Providence, it should be decided that she should vanish from the list of free nations, let us work so that on perishing beneath her ruins, we shall leave to posterity records that will honor our memory.

Politicians have spoken thus in Mexico and elsewhere, and will speak thus again, and we must listen to them sceptically, if also with hope. In this case, the ensuing record validates the humility, integrity, and force of these words. And the danger mentioned was a real one. On this date Trist, whose authority had been withdrawn by Polk, but who dared to go on, and Scott were negotiating with Peña y Peña, and although Trist's instructions were embodied in the treaty that was signed and later ratified, there was indeed some strong American sentiment for the absorption of all of Mexico; so that Juárez' mention of this dread possibility was not mere rhetoric.

It is of this first inauguration that Pola, quoting Felipe García of Guelatao, a first cousin of Juárez', reports that Juárez was

congratulated by a group of his fellow countrymen, pure Indians . . . : "We come to see you, Benito, in the name of your village, to tell you that we are very happy that you are Governor. You know what we need, and you will give it to us, because you are good and will not forget that you are one of us. Since we cannot bring you anything else, receive this that we bring you in the name of all of us." Never did such intense emotion seize the soul of Juárez as on this occasion. What they brought him were hens, cereals, fruits, and vegetables. Juárez limited himself to giving a peso to the leader of the commission, and to saying to them that for this they had made so great a sacrifice. This commission, on the night of this day of congratulation, slept in the corridors of the statehouse, and at dawn returned on foot to Guelatao. To come to the capital of the state, and offer this gift, the village had gathered together, and each of those most able had contributed one *real*. The first help that Juárez gave to his village was to open a school.

Afterwards, on a solemn occasion, August 12, 1849 [his second inauguration], he said the following words, as though remembering that earlier congratulation, to the Oaxacans, on continuing as Governor of the state:

"I am a son of the people, and I shall not forget it; on the contrary, I shall uphold their rights, I shall take care that they become educated, that they lift themselves up, that they make a future for themselves, and that they abandon the life of disorder, vice, and misery to which they have been led by men who only with their words proclaim themselves their friends and liberators, but who by their acts show themselves to be the most cruel tyrants."

It must have been very soon after taking office that Juárez issued an order that was sensible and necessary but for which, nearly six years later, he paid heavily. It has usually been assumed that he did this entirely because he alone suspected Santa Anna and on his own initiative, and that he seemed more rigorous than he was in fact, so that we shall report the episode as he himself narrated it, nineteen years later, in his written corrections of a short biography of himself.

As soon as I took over the government of the state of Oaxaca in 1847, the partisans of the illegal administration that had just been displaced, together with those who desired the return of Sr. Arteaga to the governorship, began to work actively to organize a rebellion that might realize their desires, and they obliged the government, which at that time was busy preparing the defense of the state against the foreign invasion, to take also the necessary steps to preserve the public order. It was under these circumstances that there arrived the news that General Santa Anna, who had already been removed from the command of the army of the Republic, had arrived at the city of Tehuacán, with the intention of proceeding to the capital of the state of Oaxaca. This news alerted the disturbers of the peace in that capital, who redoubled their efforts, writing and sending agents to General Santa Anna, in order to oblige him to hasten his march. The city council sent me a statement, and the legislature an appeal, both to the effect that I should in no way permit the arrival of that General, because his presence in the city under those circumstances would be harmful to the public order. Therefore I ordered the Governor of the Department of Teotitlán del Camino [within the border of the state of Oaxaca nearest to Tehuacán] that in case General Santa Anna should show any interest in the territory of the state, he should be informed that he might cross the state, or remain in any town therein except the capital and its environs. Sr. Santa Anna actually entered the territory of the state and was for some days in Teotitlán, and afterwards withdrew in the direction of Orizaba, without having demanded that any authority be turned over to himself.

Perhaps it might have been better if there had been a showdown at this time, because the old fraud had temporarily lost his nerve, and Juárez was evidently well in control of the state troops and of the situation. Although he was to have other rebellions on his hands, nothing more is reported of the partisans of Arteaga. Even if Juárez had known at this time the later cost of this order to himself, he surely would have given it anyway. He was clearly not motivated, as has been suggested, by personal hatred for Santa Anna, but by his very deep sense of responsibility in public office.

When Governor, Juárez lived, with his rapidly growing family, in a large house downtown, a block and a half from the cathedral and two and a half from the statehouse, which has been rebuilt in the style of the old one. His house is a massive, fortresslike building in the style of the time and earlier, with one great door, an interior court or patio, the living quarters (probably barely furnished, like similar ones described by Mme. Calderón) upstairs, and the servants' quarters and workrooms downstairs. "When the bells of the cathedral sounded nine o'clock, Juárez appeared in his office, so that the astonished people remarked ironically that the Governor seemed to be a common mason."

The new Governor now proceeded to keep his promises and to give the state an administration such as had probably not been given to any state in Mexico and may not have been since. His first concern was naturally that of defense, both against the Americans and against internal uprisings. He asked and obtained authority to reorganize the National Guard, and then did so. He established regional forces of infantry and cavalry, and an arsenal that made cannon; published a manual on guerrilla warfare; placed the state's military forces under the command of Colonel Ignacio Mejía, who had studied under him at the Institute; established a military hospital; and secured pensions for the widows and orphans of slain veterans.

In furthering education he also made great progress, building between two and three hundred schools and eight normal schools, training and employing many Indian teachers, and increasing the registration by several thousand pupils, including many more girls than had gone to school before his time. "Children do not go to school," he said, "only because of the dire poverty of their fathers, which can be lessened by the liberation of trade. The desire to know and to enlighten himself is innate in the heart of man. Free him from the shackles that misery and despotism impose upon him and he will enlighten himself naturally, even if he is not given direct assistance. . . . To form women with all the requirements of their necessary and elevated mission is to form the fertile seed of regeneration, of social betterment. For this reason, their education should never be neglected." Nor did he forget the Institute, which he reorganized and supported, serving as temporary director between May and July, 1848.

He was also a notable builder. He undertook the construction of a road from Oaxaca to Tehuacán and completed 104 kilometers of it; completed work on the façade of the statehouse; extended the road from Miahuatlán towards Huatulco, now Puerto Ángel, on the Pacific; built a bridge over the River Atoyac that for almost a century was the only means of communication between villages in the valley, and financed it with tolls; and took steps to establish a mint, but was stopped in this effort by the federal government, which in consideration of a loan from an English company had agreed not to permit any mint within 150 leagues of Mexico City. He also had maps made of the city and state.

Yet perhaps Juárez' most notable achievement as Governor—an achievement that might be studied by liberals elsewhere—was in doing all this while reducing the state's debt from $124,500 in 1847, representing deficits of eighteen years, to $8,713 on June 14, 1852. He did this by enforcing a tax law of 1843, and indeed by rigorously collecting all taxes that were legal, *and* by spending the money legally, as well as by refinancing the debt he found in 1847. He also collected and paid over to the federal government the taxes legally due it: a duty of state governors that they often evaded. This "fiscal integrity" permitted him to pay the civil servants on time, an unusual action that also permitted him to demand and get more honesty and efficiency in their work. In the same way, and by paying adequate salaries, he improved the ethics of the courts.

But governors cannot devote themselves solely to building of various kinds: they have to face and handle crises and disasters. In August, 1850, there broke out a severe epidemic of cholera, in which 10,698 people out of the state's population of something more than

525,000 died. It was the first epidemic since 1833, and it would have been much worse if Juárez had not appointed an active medical committee and encouraged vaccination. In October, 1850, he had to suppress a reactionary rebellion in Tehuantepec, where there had been before, and were to be later, discords between the people of that region and the state of Oaxaca, of which they were a part, and between the two towns of Tehuantepec and Juchitán. The following September, Juárez went to Tehuantepec and discovered that the troubles had been caused by corrupt local officials. He removed these and granted an amnesty to all but the leaders, who continued the rebellion. One was exiled and another executed.

Probably on numerous occasions, the Governor had to show that he not only could do desk work, but he could face danger personally. On April 1, 1850, a mutiny broke out in the Battalion Guerrero, stationed in Oaxaca, and Juárez himself succeeded in putting it down when he appeared on the scene in the midst of the shooting, armed with nothing but a cane. As a public prosecutor and later, Juárez had had serious difficulties with an Italian offender and slanderer of Juárez himself named Salvador Marcucci. When this man had been in prison again, he was legally released, but on his way home he was attacked and wounded, for some unknown reason, by police officers. The Governor appeared on the scene, effected the arrest of the officers, and dispersed the crowd.

In 1850, probably during the cholera epidemic, the Governor's presence was not enough to ward off death in his own home. In 1829, after an earlier cholera epidemic, a municipal cemetery had been established in Oaxaca, to prevent unhygienic burials in churches and their adjoining lands, but despite the insistence of the civil authorities in 1842, and the collaboration of the Bishop at the time, these regulations about burials and exhortations to obey them were ignored, chiefly because the civil authorities, including the Governor and his family, were exempted.

"In the year 1850," writes Juárez, "my daughter Guadalupe died at the age of two years, and although the law that prohibited the burial of bodies in the churches excepted the family of the Governor of the state, I did not wish to take advantage of this courtesy, and I myself took the body of my daughter to the cemetery of San

Miguel, which is situated outside the walls of the city, in order to give an example of obedience to the law, which conventions nullified, to the prejudice of the public health. Since that time, with this example, and with the energy that I used to prevent burials in the churches, the practice has been definitely established of burying bodies outside the city of Oaxaca."

It is probably the phrase "I myself," and the Indian custom of the father of the dead child himself carrying the small coffin, that have conjured up the image of Juárez' doing so alone, but Sr. Iturribarría reports that when the house was full of persons dressed in black, all expecting the child to be buried in the church of Carmen Alto, the *cortège*, led by Juárez, left the city towards the east, making it clear that the burial would be in the cemetery.

In his addresses to the legislature, Juárez, evidently intent on doing his own job, paid little attention to the ominous drift of events in the nation, but on one occasion, November 19, 1850, when, as he saw it, his state was threatened, he spoke out on the subject in a way that should be remembered. In 1842 Mexico had granted rights to build a railroad across the Isthmus of Tehuantepec to a Mexican, José de Garay, but had canceled them in 1845. Ignoring the cancellation, Garay in 1846 sold his rights to two Englishmen, Manning and Mackintosh. In the peace negotiations of 1848, Trist, on Polk's orders, demanded these rights for the United States, but the Mexicans said that they now belonged to Englishmen, and for some unknown reason the matter was dropped and not included in the treaty. In October, 1848, the Englishmen sold their rights to Hargous Brothers, of New York. Presently Nathan Clifford, the American Minister in Mexico, demanded these rights, as did his successor, John Letcher, in 1850. An agreement was reached between Letcher and Manuel Gómez Pedraza, the Mexican Foreign Minister, which was rejected in Washington as being vague, and was also rejected in Mexico because it gave the United States the right to send troops to guard the construction. Because of the Mexican outcries, including the firm opposition of Juárez, in the November 19 address, the Mexican government canceled all such rights on May 22, 1851. Unfortunately, this did not end the affair.

Meanwhile, the federal Republic was trying unsuccessfully to pull itself together after the war. Presidents Joaquín Herrera and Mariano Arista were honest and able men, but their problems remained well nigh insoluble. The primitive nature of the economy and the theoretical nature of the constitution did not permit sufficient taxation, and the indemnity from the United States of fifteen million dollars, in accordance with the Treaty of Guadalupe, did not solve the problems of the treasury. There were rebellions of savage Indians in Yucatán and in the northern states, besides filibustering expeditions from Texas. The governors of many of the states continued to be independent and recalcitrant, while the liberal governors loyal to the federal regime, such as Melchor Ocampo in Michoacán and Juárez in Oaxaca, alarmed the conservatives and aroused them to cohesion and intransigence. These were led by the distinguished intellectual conservative Lucas Alamán, an anachronistic figure who might have done well as a Viceroy but who now proceeded to turn his country over to a reaction on a much lower level than his own. A local rebellion in Jalisco in 1852 against the liberal Governor, López Portillo, was taken over and supported by conservatives elsewhere, with the result that President Arista was forced out of office, his successor Juan B. Ceballos and other moderate liberals became confused, and the way was opened for Alamán and the army to produce an invitation, in March, 1853, to none other than the fifty-eight-year-old Santa Anna to return to power as President. For a while Alamán, as his chief Minister, was able to restrain Santa Anna, but Alamán died in June of that year, and Santa Anna was then able to rule and ruin at will.

The liberal administration in Oaxaca was now, of course, doomed, and although he had retired from office when his second term expired the previous August, Juárez was a man marked for vengeance. He must have come to recognize the danger to himself, although throughout his life he revealed a blend of optimism, courage, and naïveté that was part of his personal power but also got him into plenty of trouble.

PART TWO

From Exile
to the Presidency

6

ONE WAY TO MAKE A LIBERATOR

"As soon as I ceased being Governor of the state [August, 1852]"
Juárez' *Notes* continue,

I was named [by the Governor who succeeded him briefly, Ignacio Mejía] Director of the Institute of Sciences and Arts, and at the same time Professor of Civil Law. In those days there had already broken out the rebellion called the revolution of Jalisco, against the existent constitutional order and in favor of the reactionary party. Even though I held no office in the state, I was nevertheless persecuted, not only by the rebels who seized the public administration, but also even by those who had been my partisans and whom, under my administration, I had placed in some posts of importance. These were ambitious and vulgar men who made places for themselves among the winners at the cost of the man who during his government only took pains to do his duty without doing them any harm whatever. They had neither firm principles nor any feeling of their own dignity, and so they managed always to be on the side of the winner, even though for him they had to play the part of hatchet men [*verdugos*]. I resigned myself to my fate without a breath of complaint, and without any humiliating action.

Juárez was removed from the directorship, a position that paid only $500 a year, but this removal must have offended and angered him deeply. Probably less important to him were the more personal offenses, of which the following, as related by Sr. Iturribarría, is an example.

In January, 1853, General Ignacio Martínez Pinollos, in the service of the state, was induced to go over to the side of a new rebellion in Tehuantepec and Juchitán, which he was supposed to be suppressing, and to the rebellion in Jalisco, his price being the favors of a woman on the other side whom he desired. Unfortunately we cannot afford the space to narrate this grotesque and sordid farce in detail. Pinollos marched back to Oaxaca and was made Governor. Although he refused, for a while at least, to remove Juárez from the directorship, he and his secretary planned to remove Juárez from the scene more definitively; and for this purpose they enlisted the aid of one Máximo Ortiz, a *compadre* or fellow godparent—a close relationship in Mexico—of Juárez' who had taken part in the 1851 rebellion in Tehuantepec, and whom Juárez had removed from the governorship of that district of the state in favor of Ignacio Mejía. Ortiz came to Oaxaca and rented a house opposite that of Juárez, in order to spy on him. On March 9, 1853, Juárez was seated on the balcony of his house, with his wife, taking his ease, when Ortiz came along the street in disguise and fired on him, but missed. Juárez shut the doors of his balcony, buckled on his revolver, and went down to accost Ortiz, who had taken refuge in his house and told his wife to say that he was not there. Juárez called out in a loud voice, so that Ortiz could hear him: "Tell my *compadre* that if he wants to kill me, to come out, so that he can do it face to face." After waiting a while and listening to the excuses of Ortiz' wife, Juárez withdrew without Ortiz' reappearing. The event caused much talk, and although the liberal party was now weak, Pinollos saw fit to remove Ortiz from the scene by making him Governor of the district of Tehuantepec. However, Pinollos now had the formidable support of Santa Anna, who had meanwhile achieved supreme power.

"On May 25, 1853," Juárez continues,

I arrived at the town of Ixtlán in order to advance a judicial proceeding in the exercise of my profession. On the 27th of the same month, I went to the town of Etla, four leagues from the city, to take the testimony of witnesses in favor of the village of Teococuilco, and when I was engaged in this work, about noon there arrived a picket of armed troops to arrest me, and at two o'clock I was issued a passport with the order that I be confined in the city of Jalapa in the state of Veracruz. On the 28th I departed, escorted by a force of cavalry, and in the company of don Manuel Ruiz and don Francisco Rincón, who were also going to be imprisoned, in other places outside the state. On the 4th of June I arrived at Tehuacán, where the escort withdrew. From that place I issued a statement against the unjust order directed against me.

Sr. Iturribarría offers a slightly different version of these events, to the effect that Juárez was arrested at Etla on the 23d, taken to Oaxaca, fired upon *en route* by a government agent, confined in the convent of Santo Domingo with Sr. José Inés Sandoval (who had shared his imprisonment at Miahuatlán), and on the 29th taken with Sandoval and two other liberals, the lawyers Juan María Maldonado and Félix Romero, to Puebla; and that on passing through Etla, where his wife and children were, Juárez was not allowed to bid them farewell. The charge against Juárez was that he had been inciting the people in the region to a class war.

"On the 25th [of June]," Juárez continues,

I arrived at Jalapa, my [supposedly] final destination. In this city I stayed seventy-five days, but the government of General Santa Anna did not lose sight of me or allow me to live in peace, for a few days after my arrival there, I received [August 2] an order to go to Jonacatepeque in the state of Mexico, the excuse given for this change being that I had gone to Jalapa in disobedience to the order of the government, which had sent me to Jonacatepeque. This was only a pretext for vexing me, because the passport and order issued me in Oaxaca clearly stated that the place of my confinement was to be Jalapa. I stated as much, and received no answer whatever. I was like the lamb in the fable to whom the wolf complained that the lamb was muddying the wolf's water. I was preparing to go to Jonacatepeque when I received another order to go to the castle of Perote. I had not even left Jalapa for this last place when I was told to go to Huamantla in the state of Puebla, for which place I set out on the 12th of September; but I had to go by way of Puebla to secure certain means for living in Huamantla, where I could not easily acquire them.

Having done this, I set my trip for the 19th, but at ten o'clock on the night before, I was arrested by don José Santa Anna, the son of don Antonio, and conducted to the barracks of San José, where I was held incommunicado until the following day, when I was taken out and escorted, still incommunicado, to the castle of San Juan de Ulúa, where I arrived on the 29th. Captain don José Isasi was the commandant of the escort that took me from Puebla to Veracruz. I remained incommunicado in the castle until the 9th of October, when at eleven in the morning, the governor of the castle, don Joaquín Rodal, informed me of the order for my exile in Europe and handed me the necessary passport. By that time I was ill, and I answered the Governor that I should comply with the order he had given me as soon as I was better; but he was inexorable, and told me that he had an order to make me embark in the English packet *Avon,* which was due to leave the port at two o'clock in the afternoon of the same day; and without waiting for any reply, he himself seized my luggage and took me to the ship. Only at that time there came to an end the solitary imprisonment in which I had been held since the night of September 12.

The castle of San Juan de Ulúa, in the harbor of Veracruz, now connected with the city by a causeway, but then a small island, is one of the most sinister places of imprisonment imaginable. Some of the windowless cells and galleries, to the heavy walls of which prisoners were sometimes chained standing up, are partly below sea level at high tide, and water drips from the walls of all of them, as in caves, forming stalactites and stalagmites. It is not known (despite the claims of the guides) exactly in which cell Juárez was imprisoned, but any of them would suffice to break the health and spirit of any man. From time to time the ex-governor, accompanied by guards, may have been allowed to take the air briefly, and to write to his wife.

Meanwhile, doña Margarita was being persecuted by agents of Pinollos, and had to hide for a while at the *hacienda* Cinco Señores of don Miguel Castro, four kilometers east of Oaxaca. After that she established her home with her children, and kept a shop, in Etla. Hearing somehow from her husband, she borrowed $400 from don Bernardo Bergés, owner of the *hacienda* Guadalupe at Etla, and sent her brother, José María Maza, with the money to Juárez in Veracruz. He arrived too late, and agents of Santa Anna took the money from him, but a Spanish businessman, Vicente Neira, and an Italian, Juan Saggianti, managed to get the money back, and accompanied Maza in pursuit of Juárez by sea. In the same ship with these three, according to this version, there were Melchor Ocampo, his convalescent daughter Josefa, and his lawyer, Francisco Benítez, who also were being banished and had briefly been given the hospitality of San Juan de Ulúa.

"On the 9th [or was it the 19th of October, or the 9th of November?]" continues Juárez, laconic again, "I arrived at Havana, where by permission of the Captain General, Cañedo, I remained until the 18th of December, when I embarked for New Orleans, arriving there on the 29th of the same month." He went to New Orleans instead of Europe because it was closer to Mexico, and because there were other Mexican rebels in exile in New Orleans.

We shall go on with the story by Sr. Iturribarría, which has the virtue of a little more detail. In Havana, Juárez and a new friend, José María Mata, met the following ship when it arrived, and Ocampo told Juárez that Maza was aboard her, but was being detained because he lacked the proper visa. With the payment of a fine, he was allowed to disembark. Having heard of more cholera in Oaxaca, Juárez was much worried because Maza had not brought with him a letter from doña Margarita, but to his vast relief, one arrived in the next packet. Presently, Ocampo and Mata urged Juárez and Maza to travel with them in the next ship for New Orleans, since their residence in Cuba was so insecure. Knowing that Ocampo and Mata were going first class, for which Juárez and Maza lacked the money, Juárez and Maza said that they would wait for mail in Havana until the sailing of the next ship for New Orleans. This they did, and made the passage as sailors, or in the third or fourth class.

It is not altogether sure whether this story is true or whether Juárez and Ocampo met for the first time in New Orleans, early in the year 1854, a few days after Juárez' arrival there. The circumstances are much less important than the meeting itself, which was highly important in the life of each man, and in the history of Mexico. Juárez was now nearly forty-eight years old, and Ocampo nearly forty-two. Both had been liberal governors of note, and Ocampo a national figure. In appearance, character, and past, they were totally different, but they shared passions for liberty, equality, and fraternity, and for their country, and each had also a capacity, very rare among the great figures of the time, for viewing men and events with disinterested clarity. Ocampo's character was more complex and in the normal sense, more charming, than Juárez', and his mind was more broad and subtle. He was, however, more opinionated than Juárez, and he lacked Juárez' two great assets: unfailing self-confidence and indomitable will. These were probably the two greatest Mexicans of their time, and it does both much credit that despite frequent and strong differences of opinion on means, if not on ends, they remained close friends for life.

In the year 1812, doña Francisca Xaviera Tapía, a maiden lady thirty-nine years old, was living on and operating her very large *hacienda* of Pateo, in the remote valley of Maravatío, in the extreme northeast corner of the state of Michoacán. This isolated, lush, and very beautiful valley was wholly appropriate for the romantic life of Melchor Ocampo. Ocampo later described doña Francisca as having "marked talent, elevated views, a spirited character, and un-bounded charity." She was living at this time with her younger brother and four orphans whom she had adopted, but on returning from a trip to Mexico City in that year, she brought with her a baby boy, and to this day nobody knows with certainty where she got him or how he acquired the name of Melchor Ocampo.

In any case, from that moment he seems to have had everything that had been denied the ragged orphan shepherd boy in the moun-tains of Oaxaca. If not exactly handsome, Ocampo had a sensitive, mobile, attractive face, quick intelligence, and marked personal charm; and although he was adored by the whole family at Pateo, he was apparently unspoiled. He was sent at twelve to the seminary in Morelia, which, thanks to an enlightened priest named don Ángel Mariano Morales, was far superior to the seminary in Oaxaca. It was incorporated in the University of Mexico, and it offered instruc-tion not only in Latin and theology, but also in law, mathematics, and philosophy. Outside the seminary, Ocampo probably encoun-tered the works of Voltaire and Rousseau, Hugo and Balzac; and also, as a scholarly country gentleman, discovered and fed one of the great passions of his life, natural science. Later he was deeply influenced by the works of Pierre Joseph Proudhon, some of which he translated into Spanish and a collection of which he presented to his friend Juárez. It was evidently the moral and noncollectivist basis of Proudhon's thinking that these two great Mexican reformers found sympathetic.

In 1831, doña Francisca, predeceased by her brother, died and left most of her property, which was very considerable, to Ocampo, with provisions for the care of the other orphans in the family. In that year he began to study law in Mexico City, and two years later began to practise there, but very soon he gave up that profession and returned to Pateo to farm scientifically, to try to keep his accounts, to cultivate species of plants new to the region, to study all kinds of natural science and the Indian languages, and to organize his large library. He was the first to trace the course of the River Lerma, which runs from south of Toluca northwest through the states of Mexico, Michoacán (including the valley of Maravatío), Guanajuato, and Jalisco, into Lake Chapala; and he wrote one of the first treatises on the thousands of species of cactus in Mexico.

Two of the orphans who had been raised with Ocampo, both older than himself, remained at Pateo under his protection, and one of them, Ana María Escobar, became his mistress and bore him three daughters; and she or some other woman bore him a fourth. Perhaps because she was considered his "second mother," Ocampo never married doña Ana María, and the fact that she was the mother of his daughters was rigorously kept a secret, even from them, until the day he died. The whole affair is very odd and unusual in that social context, and it may have caused or been caused by a neurotic strain in Ocampo's mind that manifested itself also in restless melancholy, recurrent withdrawals into solitude, and hypochondria. As Sr. Valadés, Ocampo's sensitive and scholarly biographer, points out, he was as immature and unhealthy in this respect as he was mature and healthy in science and politics.

Driven by remorse over his singular love affair, or by fear that he had given away too much of his property, or by a neurotic escapism, or by all of these, in 1840 Ocampo embarked for Europe. There he wandered about, read history, politics, and philosophy, tried to get work as a literary hack, studied French cooking, and became more Mexican by the minute. On his voyage home he wrote a book on the Mexican idioms of the Spanish language.

In 1842 he was induced to go into politics, and he was elected a deputy to the federal constituent assembly. Already he was an articulate liberal, a federalist, and above all an individualist, advocating education for all and naturally suspecting the army and the Church. There were enough like him to induce Santa Anna to dissolve the assembly, and Ocampo went home—as he always did happily—to farm and botanize professionally, care for his farm hands, observe a comet (March 3, 1843), study the Indian tongues, and father his second daughter. In 1843 he again left home to become a deputy and the director of the national school of agriculture. In the troubles of 1846, Ocampo, then a national figure, took a leading part in opposing Paredes and installing Salas as President. He was then appointed Governor of Michoacán, and after some trouble in removing his predecessor, he took office on September 5, 1846.

As Governor of Michoacán, Ocampo, like Juárez in Oaxaca, was notably successful in reconciling factions within the state and in mobilizing its troops and citizens for the defense of Mexico against the invader from the north. In 1846 he was nearly elected Vice-President. In April, 1847, on the news of Scott's victory at Cerro Gordo, Ocampo resigned—he was always lightning fast on the draw with his resignation—but the legislature rejected his resignation and gave him additional powers. Using these to extract money from the Church for the prosecution of the war—just as the national Congress, including the silent member from Oaxaca, had tried to do—he aroused the bitter enmity of the clergy of Michoacán, and not for the only time. After the fall of Mexico City, he was summoned to Querétaro with the rest of the governors, and there he found himself supported by only four other governors in opposing capitulation. He returned to Morelia and resigned in disgust, turning the office over to his friend Santos Degollado.

After serving again in Congress, where he proposed the decimal system of weights and measures, he dared to serve for two months, in 1850, under Herrera, as Minister of the Treasury, always an impossible job. In this office he was realistic, but also too optimistic, advocating reorganization of the financial structure and freer trade within the Republic, but he was driven out of office by the conservatives in Congress and the weakness of President Herrera.

Returning again like Antæus to his own strengthening earth, Ocampo was distressed to learn that doña Ana María was losing her eyesight, but he proceeded to establish a new, model ranch that he called Pomoca: an anagram on Ocampo. While he was doing this, his liberal friends ran him, in 1851, for President, but in the state legislatures, which then did the voting, he was defeated by Arista.

While Governor, Ocampo had had serious trouble with a priest named Clemente Muguía, who had since been chosen Bishop of Michoacán, and whom Ocampo once described as "an astute rascal who, believing in neither God nor the devil, uses both for his own profit." "To become Bishop in fact, Muguía had to take an oath to obey the constitution, laws, and civil authorities of Mexico, and this at the last moment he arrogantly refused to do. Later both sides weakened a little, and he was allowed to become Bishop, but Ocampo smelled battle and decided that he himself would lead the fight for the civil authority and the poor. There is a story, about which Sr. Valadés has doubts, that—during one of the many absences, presumably, of don Melchor—one Esteban Campos, a loyal employee of don Melchor's at Pateo and Pomoca, lost a child, and lacking money, asked the Señor Cura of Maravatío, one don Augustín Dueñas, for a free burial. The tale goes on that Dueñas refused this, and that when Campos asked what, then, he should do with the body, the priest told him to salt it and eat it. In any case, this Dueñas, supported by the Bishop, engaged in a battle of pamphlets with Ocampo, and in his pamphlets Ocampo, identifying rights with duties, and going beyond the question of tithes and even that of Church and state, into the very structure of society, solidified his position as the leading liberal thinker of Mexico.

However, this controversy also had the unhappy result of inciting numerous lawsuits against Ocampo relative to the vast and vague properties left him by doña Francisca, and some of these lawsuits were brought against him by persons previously friends and good neighbors. To these, Ocampo responded with admirable detachment: he was not in any case greatly interested in property, except for its giving him and others liberty. He once exclaimed: "If only every Mexican could be a proprietor!"

In 1852 Ocampo was again chosen Governor of Michoacán, this time by both direct and indirect elections, and proceeded forthwith to execute further reforms, the most important of which was the elimination of the legal right of the Church to collect tithes. However, it soon became apparent that he did not have the firm support of either Arista or Ceballos, that liberal state and federal administrations were disintegrating all over the Republic, and that even in

Michoacán there were alarming defections in the legislature, the garrison, and the police force. After long hesitation, and in the last moments of power taking steps to secure scientific instruments for his beloved Colegio de San Nicolás Hidalgo, a secular institution comparable to the Institute in Oaxaca, he resigned, on January 25, 1853.

It was reported that a neighbor had hired assassins to kill him, but he paid no attention. While he was planning the publication of a newspaper to expose the administration of Santa Anna and Alamán, he was arrested at his home on April 27, 1853, and carted off to Tulancingo, on the way to exile. While worrying about his daughters and his mortgages and talking politics with his friends, he was, like Juárez, moved from town to town. As already reported, he managed to secure the company of his oldest daughter, Josefa, and of his old friend and lawyer, Francisco Benítez, who soon returned to Morelia to try to salvage some of don Melchor's property after it had been confiscated by Santa Anna's government. Doña Ana María and her other daughters were cared for by friends. Although Ocampo had more money than Juárez, and was being slightly less roughly and decisively exiled, for him also this was no comedy. "To be a complete liberal," he had said, "demands effort, because it requires the spirit to be a complete man."

The constantly changing group of liberal Mexicans exiled in New Orleans and in Brownsville, Texas, included, besides Ocampo and Juárez, some formidable men. Ocampo was at that time the undoubted leader, and the President of the Revolutionary Committee. José María Mata, from Jalapa, was the Secretary, who remained for the most part in New Orleans. He later, after the return to Mexico, married Ocampo's daughter Josefa, and even she said: "Mata is so severe that his rectitude borders on brutality." In 1858 he represented Mexico in Washington, and in 1860 was Minister of the Treasury. Ponciano Arriaga was a well-known liberal from San Luis Potosí, and a man of notable vision and moral integrity. Juan Bautista Ceballos was a weak liberal, but he had nevertheless been interim President of Mexico just before the return of Santa Anna.

In 1854, while in New Orleans, Ocampo, Arriaga, and Ceballos were accused, by the Santa Anna government, of organizing a "traitorous filibustering expedition" against their native land. That all these men were doing anything they could to produce the downfall of Santa Anna is undeniable, but the word "filibuster" seems extreme, and the word "treason" even more so. It seems to depend on who wins, on who is talking, and on when. These three, accompanied by Juárez and Mata, protested to Francisco Arrangoiz, the current Mexican Consul in New Orleans, who had incidentally been Ocampo's disastrous predecessor in the Treasury, but of course nothing came of it.

The then colonel Ignacio Comonfort, whom Santa Anna had removed as Collector of the Port of Acapulco, went to New York, possibly passing through New Orleans, on a very successful trip undertaken for the purpose of purchasing arms for the rebellion that developed in the south. His representative in New Orleans was Manuel or Miguel(?) María Arrioja, "a man of great powers for work." Also present was Manuel Cepeda Peraza, a young army officer from Mérida, Yucatán, who had been cashiered and exiled by Santa Anna for his liberalism, and who from then on fought effectively on the liberal side and died as Governor of Yucatán. To Juárez, more important personally than any of these, including even Ocampo, was a young Cuban writer exiled from that colony of Spain for liberal activity, named Pedro Santacilia. They became close friends in New Orleans, and Santacilia later became Juárez' son-in-law, the guardian of his family, and his constant correspondent.

At this time, however, all these men—like Louis Napoleon a few years earlier—were shabby nobodies, conspirators, and in their case, recent enemies of the United States. Also, most of them, and especially Juárez, had skins almost as brown as those of Negroes, and in New Orleans, of course this fact alone made any of them the gross inferior, in most persons' eyes, of any plug-chewing moron with white skin. There exist a few stories about the life of Juárez in New Orleans that include details which are probably picturesque exaggerations of his hardships, and of those of his fellow exiles, but one or two of these deserve retelling and probably some credit. If the details are inconsistent and not exact, the facts may not have been very different.

At that time there lived in New Orleans, as a printer, Sr. Rafael Cabañas, who later became Professor of English in the Superior School of Commerce and Administration, in Mexico City. He states:

As soon as he disembarked in New Orleans, Sr. Juárez, with Sres. Ocampo, Mata, and Ponciano Arriaga, lodged in the Hotel Cincinnati, where we had various exiles; at about eight of the day they arrived, they formed a committee composed of the above and other exiles, in order to agree on the means of displacing the government of Santa Anna.

After reporting what is certainly in error, that this committee concocted the Plan of Ayutla, sent it to General Juan Álvarez in Acapulco, and named Comonfort as head of the rebellion, Cabañas continues:

On the arrival of summer, the havoc of which was terrible in New Orleans, all the companions in exile went to different places in the United States, and only Sr. Juárez and I remained, but we found it necessary to leave the hotel and move to a house in St. Peter's Street, because of our lack of resources; the terrible disease of yellow fever attacked Sr. Juárez, and his life was saved by chance, although we did not have funds for his proper care. [This occurred in November, 1854.]

When don Benito's health was restored, his daily occupation, from five in the morning until eleven at night, was to go and examine all the facts on the colonial system from which that great republic sprang. We lived a long time together, and this gave me an opportunity to observe his private life, his irreproachable habits, and his dedication to study, which he interrupted only to visit some institutions of instruction and public welfare, and one or another person in the capital.

During the time we lived in New Orleans we suffered some lack of resources, although Sr. Ocampo insisted that we take what he had; but Sr. Juárez, with his characteristic prudence, told him that we needed nothing.

He also refused money from several other Mexicans,

with the result that our misery became so great that at one time we were eating in the lunchroom of the Hotel St. Charles, the meal costing ten cents; and later we met a Negress who boarded us for $8 monthly, each, and we were paying another $8 for the house in which we were living until they sent him from Oaxaca a draft of $600.

One day an official of the Court of Justice came and asked him to go

to that tribunal, so that they might consult him on an interesting case
about a land claim filed in Upper California, and they asked him for his
opinion, which was unanimously approved by the members of the court,
who lavished on him praises that were well deserved.

Which court this was is not known. Probably a translator was
necessary.

Sr. Iturribarría adds that Cabañas printed revolutionary proclamations for the exiles gratis, and shared with them his cigars; then continues:

Their resources vanished, and Juárez and Maza had to accept an even
more precarious life. They rented a garret, in the boarding house of a
French woman who had been a chorus girl, Madame Doubard, that cost
five pesos monthly. Since this swallows' nest was under the roof, the
heat was suffocating. The cot on which Juárez slept had been loaned to
him by a Mexican pharmacist named Cotola. Maza slept on the floor.
Ocampo sought them out and was staggered by such poverty. To be
near them, Ocampo moved to the same boarding house, to a very comfortable floor, and thus their solitude and homesickness were made more
tolerable.

In the same place Juárez and Maza met an old vagabond who agreed
to teach them some sentences in English, which they had tried to use in
the street, in business, without anyone being able to understand them.
The English learned in the Institute in Oaxaca, poorly remembered, was
also insufficient to open up for them any chance of obtaining remunera-
tive work.

Finally Juárez and Maza formed a friendship with a "Doctor" Borrego, a globe-trotter and quack who taught the latter how to roll
cigarettes and cigars in a room in a wretched house in the Street of
Great Men, where a half of this hole, divided by a screen, was the
"consulting room," and the other a "tobacco factory." If anyone appeared, Maza looked out, and if the visitor was an invalid, Borrego took
off his apron, put on his doctor's coat, auscultated, palpated, prescribed,
and . . . charged.

When Maza learned how to roll cigarettes and cigars, he taught the
job to don Benito. At nightfall they went out with their poor merchandise to the saloons in the outer suburbs. Maza would go in to sell them,
and don Benito would stand on the corner with the packages, awaiting
the result. When they had made some sales, they went to drink coffee

with milk and eat black bread at the transient stands in the French Market, and then they would go and sit in Jackson Square until eight o'clock, when they heard the firing of a gun that meant that after that moment no Negro [or presumably, Mexican] could walk or remain in the streets without the written authorization of his owner.

Sometimes, in the mornings, they fished in the Mississippi, and when they had good luck, their catch lightened their misery.

It is also reported, most plausibly, that when Juárez, walking along the river, saw female Negro slaves working in the fields, he was much upset and angered. It is said that walking there with Juárez, and watching the bustle of a thriving commerce, Mata suggested to him that one source of all this activity was a freedom of internal trade that Mexico, shackled by all kinds of internal tariffs, would do well to emulate. Juárez may well have agreed, while wondering to himself when either of them would have any chance to do anything about it. Once Juárez disappeared for an entire day, and that night his friends discovered that he had spent it on the quays, without eating anything, while he waited for a vessel that might bring mail from home.

Early in 1854 the committee of exiles was busy with efforts to publish newspapers. However, Ocampo's money soon ran out, and moving with his daughter to Brownsville, Texas, in hopes of stirring up rebellion in northern Mexico, he also undertook, with a complete lack of success, to buy goods cheap in New Orleans and sell them at a profit in Brownsville. While in Brownsville, this unusual rebel and conspirator made a collection of plants native to southern Texas and northern Tamaulipas. Across the river, Santiago Vidaurri, the *cacique* of Tamaulipas, Nuevo León, and Coahuila, was soon up in arms in Monterrey, but with egotistical ambitions characteristic of the man, he was already talking about setting up an independent republic of the Sierra Madre; while with equal folly, Comonfort was talking about making the state of Guerrero independent in the south. Ocampo appealed to another Mexican exile near Brownsville, José María Carvajal, who proved very temperamental, and in the midst of his political frustrations, Ocampo became involved in a petty quarrel between his daughter Josefa and the daughters of his host in Brownsville, Andrés Treviño. Finally, in June, 1855, towards the end of his exile, Ocampo suffered some kind of a "stroke," but soon recovered. The future of all the exiles was dim indeed. Meanwhile, Santa Anna's rule became increasingly tyrannical, corrupt, and vulgar. State and local governments were almost dissolved, and all offices of importance in the central government were turned over to dishonest favorites of the dictator. The Church was flattered and favored, and the army was increased to 95,000 men, while the state militias were incorporated into it, for better control. All opponents of the regime were exiled or imprisoned, and the press was severely censored. If Santa Anna's dictatorship does not now seem as thorough as those of our own century, it must be considered a good effort for its time. Yet his administration, thanks only to Miguel Lerdo de Tejada, a young liberal, must be credited with one gain: the creation of the Ministry of *Fomento*, or development, which encouraged private industry and commerce and advanced public works. Santa Anna established himself in splendor in a palace in Tacubaya, designed new uniforms and insignia for military and civil officers, and revived the Order of Guadalupe that had been established by the hitherto unlamented Emperor Augustín I. "One of [Santa Anna's] misadventures ended in general amusement; for a woman who had spent a night with the dictator purloined his collection of medals and paraded the streets of Mexico the next morning wearing the cross of the Grand Master of the Order of Guadalupe." There was even talk of making Santa Anna an Emperor, but perhaps because he remembered the end of Iturbide, he shied away from that and contented himself with the title of Most Serene Highness. Santa Anna collected taxes efficiently, but he also spent with abandon, allowed his favorites to get their hands in the till, and borrowed money at home and abroad at absurd rates of interest. Taxation was heavier, and the Church refused His Most Serene Highness a loan. Santa Anna's situation might have become desperate sooner had he not, at the end of 1853, in a treaty ratified in 1854, sold to the United States for ten million dollars a parcel of territory known as the Mesilla or Gadsden Purchase, which eventually became parts of Arizona and New Mexico.

In February, 1854, rebellion broke out in the state of Guerrero, led by General Juan Álvarez, who had supported every liberal rebellion, as far back as Morelos, and who was also to oppose the Intervention and the Empire until his death in 1867, at the age of seventy-seven. Comonfort became his second in command. At Ayutla, on March 1, 1854, Colonel Florencio Villarreal proclaimed a Plan for a new liberal government, and invited Álvarez and others to lead the movement. Villarreal himself, previously insignificant, soon faded from the scene, but rebellions now broke out all over the country, and Santa Anna sent his forces hither and yon, burning villages and shooting any opponents he could catch. After he was defeated twice in Guerrero, the Gadsden Purchase money briefly saved him, but Ocampo's friend Santos Degollado in Michoacán, Santiago Vidaurri in Nuevo León, and Governor Manuel Doblado in Guanajuato were all in revolt. On December 1, 1854, Santa Anna held a plebiscite that was openly devised to prevent any opposition. The portents were clear, and Santa Anna had foreseen and escaped from enough tight spots to recognize this one; but it must be remembered that the exiles in New Orleans and Brownsville heard this news, or, rather, fragments of it, often garbled and mixed with a liberal supply of rumors, only weeks later, and that any premature return to Mexico would have been suicidal.

Despite Juárez' reserve and stoicism, we can watch his passionate concern about all this, and get a few glimpses of his daily life and state of mind from a surviving packet of letters that he wrote from New Orleans to Ocampo in Brownsville. Juárez moved into the rooms that Ocampo and his daughter had occupied, and his letters are full of affectionate and grateful messages to both of them. In one letter he reports sending to Ocampo, by sea, some plants from the housekeeper. In almost every letter he mentions the receipt of mail from Mexico, or his hopes for some, and the problems of the theft of letters and the difficulty of transmitting them to the exiles to whom they were addressed. He mentions that apples (always a great resource of the poor) now cost five and a half or six pesos a keg, but may become cheaper. But these letters are chiefly filled, of course, with reports of the successes and failures of the rebellion. June 19, 1854: Prieto has been confined in a village in Oaxaca, but there is no rebellion yet in that state. July 19, 1854: The heat has been extreme, but it is lessening. During the week ending July 16

there were 129 burials in New Orleans, but in a week in June there
had been 329. There is a revolutionary outbreak in Michoacán,
which Álvarez could help. There is a rumor of Álvarez' death from
an ulcer on his leg, perhaps a rumor put out by the government, but
Álvarez is old. August 2, 1854: The rumors about Álvarez are lies.
The government has had to send forces to Michoacán. There is
trouble in the regular army between Mexico and Spanish officers.
November 30, 1854, presumably soon after Juárez' bout with yellow
fever: After reporting rebellions in the south, Guanajuato, the state
of Mexico, and Jalisco: "There are not enough enlightenment and
patriotism to achieve liberty without committing excesses that will
dishonor it. . . . It can be that these ideas are false and only the
children of the bad humor that now dominates me. I hope they are,
and that events will contradict me."

Juárez' spirits, almost never this low, revived, and on February 28,
1855, aroused by an order by Santa Anna, he sent to Ocampo a
letter addressed to him by the group in New Orleans, urging him
to go to Acapulco, and in a covering letter he says: "Men of capacity and irreproachable reputation must give an example. The presence of yourself and our friend Arriaga in the theatre of revolution
will be enough to raise the spirits of the public. That is why I have
signed this letter that you will receive." On March 14 he wrote
another letter to Ocampo, urging Acapulco as a point of reunion
for all revolutionaries. On March 21, Ocampo and Arriaga replied
from Brownsville that they will go as soon as they can: Ocampo is
sick, numb with cold in a storm from the north. May 16, 1855:
Juárez tells Ocampo he has not gone to the place Ocampo mentions
because he lacks money that he hopes to get from his family. Comonfort asked him to join the forces going to Oaxaca, and he wanted to
do so, but this expedition failed, and Comonfort said that the effort
in the south would be only for its independence. Juárez explains
that he will not spend any money to go anywhere not in Mexican
territory. He will stay in New Orleans until he can go somewhere
in Mexico. May 30 and July 15: He reports victories everywhere,
and effervescence in Mexico. He praises a publication by Arriaga,
"who has intelligence and heart." He reports that some of the exiles
are going to Brownsville to take part in the revolt in the North. On

July 13, 1855, Mata and Ocampo, in Brownsville, acting for the committee, write to Juárez, sending him 250 pesos, and a note on this letter, later, by Juárez, says that the government repaid Mata. On June 19 Juárez sends thanks for this money and says that he hears that passengers are not allowed to disembark at Acapulco, but if he cannot go there, he will go somewhere else.

It is to Acapulco that he sets out, as related in his *Notes:*

I lived in that city [New Orleans] until June 20, 1855, when I left for Acapulco to offer my services in the campaigns that don Juan Alvarez and don Ignacio Comonfort were directing against the tyrannical power of don Antonio López de Santa Anna. I made the journey by way of Havana and the Isthmus of Panama, and I arrived at the port of Acapulco at the end of the month of July. What determined me to do this was the order that Santa Anna gave to the effect that exiles could not return to the Republic without first swearing their submission and obedience to the tyrannical power that he exercised in the country. As soon as this order came to my attention, I spoke to some of my companions in exile, and to those outside the city I wrote a letter—that should be among my papers, in rough draft—suggesting that we should return to our country, not by meeting the humiliating condition imposed on us, but by taking part in the revolution already under way against the tyrant, to establish a government that would make the nation happy in justice, liberty, and equality. I obtained their agreement, and the principal ones were don Guadalupe Montenegro, don José Dolores Zetina, don Manuel Cepeda Peraza, don Esteban Calderón, don Melchor Ocampo, don Ponciano Arriaga, and don José María Mata. All of these departed for the frontier of Tamaulipas and I set out for Acapulco.

Juárez' relief must have been immense. His mind was much more calm, and his character much more solid and stoical, than Ocampo's, but for more than two years he had been cut off from his family, his work, and his country, hounded first as a dangerous political prisoner, and then for the most part pushed around or ignored as an impoverished and undesirable alien. Also, he lacked Ocampo's recourse to botany, or indeed any other nonpolitical interest. Making every allowance for later exaggerations, he must have suffered severely, and now he was going home to fight in any way he could, in Mexico, among Mexicans, for his dream of a better society. Soon, if he lived, he would be with his wife and children.

7

THE NEW LEADERS OF THE NATION

DURING THE NEXT FIVE MONTHS Juárez was only one of the least conspicuous of the five to ten men who were now the new leaders of Mexico, and who were trying to organize a new and a more effective and stable national government, and at the end of this period the new administration shoved him back into the governorship of Oaxaca; but the record of these months is an index of the qualities of the man. With unusual clarity he perceived the characters of men and the meanings of events, he was calm under great pressures, he was ambitious for the nation rather than for himself, and he was quietly but very firmly intent on getting something done. The former prisoner in Miahuatlán and in the dungeons of San Juan de Ulúa, the recently wretched exile in New Orleans, was now ready to remove quickly, whenever they proved useless and hampering, the gloves of persuasion and compromise.

Having crossed the Isthmus of Panama by rail, Juárez embarked in the *Flor de Santiago*, a Chilean vessel bound for San Francisco with stops *en route* at Puntarenas, Costa Rica; Corinto, Nicaragua; Amapala, Honduras; La Unión, El Salvador; San José, Guatemala; and at last, Acapulco. There he sought out don Diego Álvarez, the son of the General, and asked to be conducted to his father, who at that time had his headquarters at Texca. He said simply that he had come to see whether he could be useful in the struggle for liberty. He did not identify himself, and possibly he carried no letters or other papers of identity that might have got him into trouble on the journey or on landing. The younger Álvarez agreed to the request of the aging and nondescript stranger, who was somehow not easily shoved aside. On the way to Texca they passed through a heavy tropical storm, and Juárez' coat was ruined, so that on arrival he was given the usual white cotton trousers and shirt. When he again offered his services, he was asked whether he could write, and when he said he could, he was given some simple letters to write for the signature of General Álvarez. When a letter from Ocampo arrived, addressed "Al Sr. Lic. Don Benito Juárez," don Diego made inquiries among the soldiers until he reached Juárez, who admitted that he had indeed been Governor of Oaxaca. When don Diego, "covered with embarrassment," as he said later, asked him why he had not said so, he replied: "Because, what importance has that?"

Meanwhile, the numerous rebellions had got out of the control of the government, which disintegrated. On August 9, Santa Anna furtively left Mexico City for Veracruz, and on August 12 at Perote he "published a manifesto extolling himself and accusing others," and he also attempted to turn the government over to a triumvirate of his own choosing. On August 17 he embarked for Havana and then Cartagena. He could not, of course, discontinue scheming to get back into power and changing sides whenever that seemed possibly advantageous to himself, and his living presence, however remote, continued to be felt as a promise or a threat, but in any case as a force, in Mexican politics. In Mexico, a political career is apt to be decisively terminated only by death, and this fact must be remembered in relation to the numerous executions.

Juárez returned to Acapulco briefly, and his *Notes* continue:

I found myself at this point when in the month of August there arrived the news that Santa Anna had abandoned the power and left the Republic, and that in the capital the revolutionary Plan of Ayutla, proclaimed five months before, had been approved, and General don Martín Carrera entrusted with the Presidency. The enthusiasm caused by this news gave no place for reflection. The agreement was apparent, but nobody took the trouble to examine its terms, or the antecedents of its authors, in order to know their tendencies and purposes and the consequences of their Plan. There seemed to be nothing more to do than to applaud the event, reproducing the Plan in the press and writing an article to praise it. The editor of the paper that was published there gave me this task.

However, I called it to the attention of Sr. don Diego Álvarez, showing him that although the flight of Santa Anna ought to be celebrated as a fact that was disconcerting the oppressors, while facilitating the triumph of the revolution, by no means should the Plan proclaimed in Mexico be approved, nor the President there named to be recognized. The Plan of Ayutla did not authorize the Junta formed in the capital to name the President of the Republic, and because since the initiators of the movement were the same generals and persons who a few hours before had been assisting Santa Anna in the persecution of the supporters of the Plan of Ayutla, it was obvious that seeing themselves ruined by the flight of their leader, they had decided to enter the revolution in order to adulterate it, to save their jobs, and to obtain immunity for their crimes, taking advantage of the sacrifices of the patriots who had leaped into the struggle to liberate their country from the clerical and military tyranny headed by don Antonio López de Santa Anna. Sr. don Diego Álvarez was entirely in agreement with my opinion, and with his compliance, at the dawn of the following day I went to the printing office to revise the article that they were printing and that praised as legitimate the Plan of the capital.

General don Juan Álvarez, who was in Texca, where he had his headquarters, understood perfectly the tendency of the movement in Mexico: he disapproved of the Plan the moment he saw it, and gave orders to reunite his forces in order to march on the capital and consummate the revolution that he himself had begun.

A few days later there arrived in Texca don Ignacio Campuzano, commissioned by don Martín Carrera to persuade Señor Álvarez of the legitimacy of the Presidency of Carrera, and of the advantages that would accrue to all the leaders of the revolution and their forces in recognizing it. In the meeting that was held to hear the delegate, at which I was present by the kindness of Señor Álvarez, the pretensions of Campuzano were disputed with such reason and energy that he himself was convinced of the impertinence of his mission and did not even return to give an account of the result to the person who had sent him. Thereupon General Álvarez marched with his troops in the direction of Mexico.

At Chilpancingo [where they arrived September 8] there appeared two other commissioners from don Martín Carrera, with the same objective as Campuzano's, and bringing messages from General Carrera. These also were heard in a meeting at which I was present, and since they were patriots of good faith, they also were convinced that the Presidency of Carrera was insupportable because it had been established against the national will and contrary to the explicit nature of the political and social plan of the revolution. On my motion, it was agreed that in a private letter it be suggested to General Carrera that he should not insist on his pretension of keeping the mandate, for the exercise of which he lacked legitimate titles, as his agents would show him. With this letter, these returned, and don Martín Carrera had the good judgment to retire to private life [September 11], leaving in military command of the city one of those generals [Romulo Díaz de la Vega] who had signed the Plan of the capital a few days after the flight of General Santa Anna. The commissioners that don Martín Carrera sent to Chilpancingo were don Isidro Olvera and the father of don Francisco Zarco [an eminent journalist and politician who will presently appear on the scene].

On August 6, Juárez had reported to Ocampo from Acapulco that Santa Anna was surrounded in Mexico, and with the agreement of Álvarez, urged Ocampo, Arriaga, and Mata to join them. On September 10, Juárez reported to Ocampo from Chilpancingo Álvarez' rejection of the claims of Herrera, and urged them to come quickly. He said that in Morelia and Oaxaca there were occurring "farces similar to the one in Mexico. . . . There remain in office egotists who would rejoice if we were shot." On September 17, Ocampo, his daughter, and Mata arrived at Veracruz, and Ocampo soon joined his fellow liberals in the state of Guerrero.

Meanwhile, other complications had developed in the north, and Comonfort was active and effective in handling them. In San Luis Potosí, Antonio Haro y Tamariz, who had openly opposed Santa Anna, issued his own Plan, which oddly included a promise to protect the rights and property of the Church and the army, as well as those of all other classes, while in Guanajuato Manuel Doblado issued still another Plan, and in the capital, Carrera was inviting all the rebels to hold a convention at Dolores Hidalgo on the national holiday, September 16. Comonfort, now a national hero, was welcomed in Guadalajara, rejected Carrera's invitation, and assembling Haro y Tamariz and Doblado in Lagos de Moreno, induced both of them to give up their Plans, accept the Plan of Ayutla, and recognize Álvarez as chief of the revolution. All signed an agreement to this effect on September 16, and Comonfort then joined Álvarez and the others in Guerrero.

"Sr. Álvarez," Juárez continues,

proceeded on his march to Iguala, where he published a manifesto to the nation. [This one, issued September 24, was probably written for him by Juárez, who had rapidly become much more than Álvarez' private secretary.] . . . and [Álvarez] began to put in practice the provisions of the Plan of the revolution; to this end he named a council composed of one representative for each of the states of the Republic. I was named the representative of the state of Oaxaca [and first of three secretaries of the council, whose President was Valentín Gómez Farías]. This council seated itself in Cuernavaca [October 4, 1855] and proceeded at once to elect as President of the Republic the Citizen General Juan Álvarez, who immediately took possession of his post. Next he formed his cabinet, naming as Minister of Interior and Foreign Relations, Citizen Melchor Ocampo; as Minister of War, Citizen Ignacio Comonfort; as Minister of the Treasury, Citizen Guillermo Prieto; and as Minister of Justice and Public Instruction, myself.

Ocampo wrote later that immediately after the *Te Deum* to celebrate the election of Álvarez, the new President, unsure of himself in an exalted political position, asked him to form and lead the cabinet, which he agreed to do, but very hesitantly, because among the leading liberals there was some logrolling for office, as by Generals Vicente Miñon and Florencio Villarreal, neither of whom got one, and because Comonfort took it for granted that he would be named Minister of War. Comonfort also tried to do the selecting himself, and to displace Ocampo. According to Ocampo, Juárez and Prieto were chosen because they were strong liberals, or *puros*, to balance, with himself, the moderate, or *moderado*, Comonfort, who at that time had more prestige than any of them, with the doubtful exception of Álvarez himself; and Ocampo adds that Juárez had to be persuaded to accept any office. Juárez never lacked self-confidence, which he left unexpressed, but he may well have foreseen difficulties in serving with Comonfort. The man who was chosen to inform Álvarez of his election, and congratulate him, was Guillermo Prieto, who had voted for Ocampo for the office, but who had a glib and graceful tongue. When the bluff old insurgent reminded him of his vote, he candidly admitted it.

The name of Guillermo Prieto has appeared but marginally in this story, and this picturesque figure demands a brief digression. He was at this time thirty-seven years old, and if his career had been less substantial than Ocampo's or Juárez', he was at least as well known as either of them. His was an unkempt figure, with very bright eyes behind the small, rimmed glasses of the time, and an unusually ragged beard and moustache. Born in Mexico City, the son of a miller and baker, he was left fatherless at thirteen, and thereafter took care of his mother. Intelligent, cheeky, and romantic, he had a picaresque youth. He got himself a scrappy education, began writing verses when very young, and supported himself by calling them to the attention of priests and politicians and thus getting small jobs in public offices. In 1837, before President Bustamente, he recited a saucy ode on the neglect of culture, and Bustamente thereupon made him his private secretary and the editor of the *Official Daily*. During the Pastry War, he served a brief and comical hitch in the cavalry. Having meanwhile fallen in love with a twelve-year-old girl whom he saw standing on a balcony and talking to her doll, he bided his time until the girl, María Caso, grew a *little* older, and until he himself advanced a *little* in the world. He then borrowed the President's coach, and encountering the girl's father in the Alameda, said to him: "Señor Caso, I wish to marry your daughter as soon as possible. Inform me whether you will continue your opposition or not, so that I can take steps." He was accepted as a *novio*, or fiancé, and married within a year. He became editor of the influential newspaper *El Siglo XIX* in opposition to Santa Anna, and was associated with Ignacio Ramírez in *Don Simplicio* until he was jailed. During the American war, his house was sacked by American soldiers, and he edited a paper in English for the "San Patricios," the battalion made up of those Americans who had gone over to the enemy. Until the triumphant return of Santa Anna, he had served four times as deputy and senator, and for four months in 1852, as Minister of the Treasury under Arista. In this office, like Ocampo, he had attempted radical reforms but accomplished little. During the rest of his life, while not in prison or simply out of favor, he usually had some legislative seat or other public office, and in any situation he continued to deliver himself of quantities of journalism, oratory, and verse (which was much esteemed at the time but that except when satirical, seems poetically unimaginative and dull to-day). During Santa Anna's dictatorship he was banished to the village of Cadereyta in Querétaro, then allowed to return to the City, but promptly arrested again and sent off to Tehuacán—not Oaxaca, as Juárez, in New Orleans, had heard. Álvarez named him to the council from Chiapas, a state in which he seems never to have been. He hero-worshiped one liberal leader after another, including, from time to time, Juárez, who, obviously not a soul mate of a type like this, or of anyone else, seems to have regarded him with mild affection and qualified respect.

On the construction of the new government, Juárez continues:

Immediately there was issued the summons for the election of deputies who would build the nation. Since the theory of the revolution was to construct the country on the solid bases of liberty and equality, and to re-establish the independence of the civil power, it was considered indispensable to exclude the clergy from the national representation, because a sad experience had shown that the clergy, through ignorance or malice, believed themselves to be representatives in the congresses only of their class, and opposed any measures that tended to correct abuses and to favor the rights of ordinary Mexicans. In those circumstances, it was necessary to deprive the clergy of the right to vote, taking this step against principle for the good of society, on condition that as soon as there was a constitution and the reforms had been sanctioned, the clergy would be made equal to other citizens in enjoying the right to vote in popular elections. [Twelve years later Juárez tried to keep this promise.] General Comonfort did not share this opinion because he was much afraid of the privileged and reactionary classes. He expressed extreme disgust because to the council formed in Iguala there had not been named one ecclesiastic, once venturing to say that it would be good if the council were composed half of ecclesiastics and half of the other classes of society. He wished also that there should be left employed in the army the generals and other officers that up to the last hour had served the tyranny that had just fallen. This resulted in a great obstruction of the business of the cabinet at times when it was necessary to work with activity and energy to reorganize the public administration, because there was no agreement on the course that was to be followed.

This disgusted Sr. Ocampo so that he offered his resignation and it was accepted. Sr. Prieto and I also made known our determination to withdraw, but on the insistence of the President, and considering that at that time it was very difficult to form a new cabinet, we decided to continue. What most led me to decide to go on in the Ministry was the hope that I had the power to seize an opportunity to initiate one of the many reforms that society needed to better its condition, thus making use of the sacrifices that the people had made to destroy the tyranny that was oppressing them.

We have already seen evidence of Comonfort's hasty judgment in his scheme to make the state of Guerrero independent, and of his ability in getting arms from New York and in bringing Haro y Tamariz and Doblado—at least provisionally, at a critical time—into the Álvarez fold. His peculiar character, so energetic and able that he could not be pushed aside, yet too unstable to be safe, was now becoming of critical importance. As Sierra points out, Mexico was then in a state of hopeful chaos, and this man, "gross of body, with a swarthy complexion emphasized by a beard that was full and black but thin, with an expression of his eyes that was tender and deep, and with a large forehead that seemed to be full of cares and anxieties," had somehow become in the minds of the people the focal point of their hope. And especially in the minds of the conservatives, extreme and moderate: now that Santa Anna had failed even them, they were eager to support this man who might save them from the doughty old insurgent Álvarez, that radical bastard Ocampo, the extravagant Prieto, and the quiet but sinister Juárez. Unluckily, the attraction was mutual.

Comonfort was an honest man, but not a forthright one, who tried to manipulate others without ever fully understanding them, so that the anxieties revealed in his expression were inevitable and unceasing. He was personally less ambitious than Doblado, for example, but more so than Juárez, perhaps because he lacked Juárez' democratic faith and his vision of a society to be created. He was a man of sincere good will who had naturally fought the tyranny of Santa Anna, but that will was a divided one, attached both to the old and to the new, in a situation in which, increasingly, compromise became impossible and everyone had to choose. He now wanted to reform the Mexican government and society, just as the *puros* did, but slowly, by persuading, harmonizing, and compromising. Unfortunately, however, the conservatives would fight before they would yield an inch, and Comonfort's moderation was caused less by benevolence, patience, and realism than by fear. He was afraid not only of the priests, soldiers, and the rich, but also, and perhaps chiefly, as Juárez noted later, of his own devout and aging mother. Vigorous but half-hearted and stupid, he finally gave the conservatives every advantage they could have hoped for.

In the attempt to displace Ocampo as the chooser and active head of the first cabinet, Comonfort asked Ocampo whether he didn't want to be active in internal affairs, and then went on to ask whether his being head of the cabinet would not prevent such activity on his part. Ignoring his previous record as a liberal, Ocampo replied that yes, for the first time in his life, instead of vaguely wanting to be useful, he wanted to accomplish certain specific reforms, and of course he brushed aside the specious suggestion that as head of the cabinet he would be unable to do so. Besides obstructing the cabinet's business, Comonfort went alone to Mexico City and there issued orders without consulting the President or his colleagues.

On October 21, after only fifteen days in office, Ocampo resigned in disgust. A few days later, he and Prieto induced President Álvarez to invite Santos Degollado into the cabinet, but Degollado replied that he was exhausted, wanted to rejoin his family, and did not have the self-confidence in politics that he had felt in war. This reply was characteristic of this remarkable man, whose career was by no means at an end. As an impoverished student who was handicapped also by near blindness, he had fought his way upwards in liberal politics and war in Michoacán, and become the protégé and friend of Ocampo and his successor as Governor of that state. After imprisonment by Santa Anna, he had led the rebellion in that part of the country. Although he lacked skill as a field commander in action, and was often beaten, he had outstanding ability in recruiting, organizing, and inspiring armies; and although he had great energy and patriotism, and was scrupulously honest, he was mentally unstable, and nobody could ever be quite sure just what Degollado would do next. At this time, as Governor of Jalisco, he was vigorously building schools and taking action against the company of the English and American Consuls, Barron & Forbes, who were making their fortunes by smuggling on the west coast and claiming extra-territorial rights. The American government did not support Forbes, but the English government did support Barron, vigorously.

Comonfort also resigned, but unfortunately he was too important for this gesture to be accepted. These events in Cuernavaca at this time may seem trivial, as the squabbles within one more new gov-·ernment, of sorts, of a Latin-American state in turmoil, but actually they were critical in the lives of all concerned and in the history of Mexico, and indeed of the Western world. Up to that moment, Ocampo was still the unquestioned leader of the *puros,* and if he had had Juárez' patience, self-confidence, and will, he instead of Juárez might well have become a figure in world history. If Juárez had had Comonfort's military and personal prestige at this time, and the *puros* had been stronger and more united, behind him or a younger Álvarez, this minority might have been able to galvanize the Mexican people behind them, and to prevent or shorten the ensuing struggle. If Juárez had been as indecisive as Ocampo or Degollado, his first great work for the nation (the Ley Juárez, to be explained presently) might not have been done, the coming Con-stitution might have been even weaker, Juárez himself might have faded into oblivion, and the deplorable Age of Santa Anna might have dragged on indefinitely. As it was, Juárez remained in action as long as he could, and almost imperceptibly at the time, the new age of law and reform for Mexico had begun.

"In those days," Juárez continues,

I received a communication from the authorities of Oaxaca in which they informed me that don Martín Carrera had named me Governor of the state, and invited me to come and receive the post; but since General Carrera lacked the legal right to make this appointment, I answered that I could not accept it, since it was not made by a competent authority.

The government moved for several days to Tlalpam, and thence to the capital, where it remained definitely established.

Also in those first days of his first Ministry, Juárez wrote identical letters to various governors, seeking their support and active co-operation, as he often did later on critical occasions. While never demeaning himself or whatever high office he held, in order to get the support of the governors, he was always alert to their power. On reading the passage above from Juárez' *Notes*, one wonders whether, upon the establishment of the new government in Mexico City, doña Margarita met him there. Such a happy meeting does not seem implausible.

The *Notes* continue:

Sr. Alvarez was well received by the people and by the notable persons who were affiliated with the progressive party, but the privileged classes, the conservatives, and the circle of the moderates who hated him because, as they said, he did not belong to the upper class of society, and because, as a rigid republican and an honorable man; he had no truck with their vices and abuses, began at once to make war on him, systematically and stubbornly, criticizing even his private and simple customs, in ridiculous and indecent anecdotes that were designed to discredit him. The incident that I shall tell will reveal the nature of the intrigues that were indulged in in those days with the idea of damaging the reputation of Sr. Álvarez.

A dramatic company dedicated a performance to him, in the National Theatre. His enemies resorted to the odd and childish expedient of agreeing to stay away from the performance, and even invited some families of so-called nice people to their houses, to keep them away from the theatre. Since the moderates wished to take possession of the situation and had no other man better fitted by weakness of character to satisfy their hopes than General Comonfort, they surrounded him with flattery of his self-esteem and ambition by making him understand that he was the only one worthy of the supreme power because of the reputation he had acquired in the revolution and because he was well received by the upper classes of society. This unwary man fell into the trap, entering into the petty intrigues that were being hatched against his protector, General Álvarez, whom he did not see fit to accompany to the special performance in the theatre already referred to. I have thought it well to go into these details because they help to explain the short duration of Sr. Álvarez in the Presidency, and the almost inopportune manner of his abdication.

While there were occurring the events that were to precipitate the retirement of Sr. Álvarez and the elevation of Sr. Comonfort to the

Presidency of the Republic, I was occupied with working on the law for the administration of justice. The revolution triumphant, it was necessary to make effective the promises of reforming the laws that hallowed the abuses of the despotic power that had just disappeared. The previous laws on the administration of justice suffered from this defect, that they establish special tribunals for the privileged classes [in this case, the clerical and military], making permanent in society the inequality that violated justice and that kept up a constant agitation of the social body.

Not only in this department, but in all those that formed the public administration, was it necessary to go to work, because the revolution was social. More extensive work was needed, so that the task should be done as well as possible, and for this it was necessary to propose, discuss, and agree upon, in the privacy of the cabinet, a general plan; but this was not possible, because after the withdrawal of Sr. Ocampo, the cabinet was incomplete, and Sr. Comonfort, who was considered its chief, was not in agreement with the tendencies and objectives of the revolution. Moreover, the administration of Sr. Álvarez was tenaciously opposed, with all kinds of obstacles put in the way, in order to discredit it and force its head to abandon the power.

It was, then, very difficult to get anything useful done under such circumstances, and that is the reason why the reforms that I effected in the law of justice were incomplete, limited as I was to the removal of the ecclesiastic exemption in the civil branch and being forced to allow it to remain in the criminal, leaving until later the decision on the best way to handle this matter. To the military was left only their exemption in crimes and misdemeanors that were purely military. I eliminated likewise all the other special courts, allowing to revert to the ordinary courts the jurisdiction in all the cases with which they had been charged.

In order to "set the record straight" and answer later accusations that he had secured approval of the new law by deceiving Comonfort, Juárez later wrote the following account of this important matter:

When Sr. Álvarez arrived in the City of Mexico in 1855, he first gave his attention to the reorganization of the public administration, and for this reason, at the first meeting of the cabinet, he ordered the Ministers to work in their respective fields and to present to him projected laws and regulations that could be expedited with this end in view. From that time I made it clear that in my opinion it was indispensable to introduce into the judicial branch certain reforms, repealing or changing at once the laws that established the special courts, because they were notoriously harmful to society, permitting abuses by those classes in whose behalf they had been established, and also because they were openly inconsistent with the principle of equality that the nation had intended to make effective by means of the revolution that had just been victorious. Sr. Álvarez agreed with this suggestion, and Sr. Comonfort did not oppose it. Accordingly, I drew up the law for the administration of justice that I offered to the President for his consideration. When I spoke to Sr. Comonfort about this matter, he told me that he was so busy in his own ministry that he could not be present at the reading and discussion of the law, but that it could be approved without his presence because he supported it in principle. The President set a day for the discussion of this matter, and when the hour arrived, Sr. Álvarez said that Sr. Comonfort had informed him that he could not be present because he would be out of the city on family business; therefore, because the administration of justice was paralyzed by the lack of legally appointed magistrates and judges, the President decided that the execution of this business should no longer be delayed. When this project had been read, discussed, and approved, Sr. Álvarez ordered that it be printed and published; so that in this matter there had not been any surprise or any stratagem whatever.

"Once my work on the law had been completed," the *Notes* continue,

with the assistance of two young men from Oaxaca, Lic. Manuel Dublán and don Ignacio Mariscal, I presented it to President Juan Álvarez, who gave it his approval and ordered that it be published as the general law for the administration of justice. Having been authorized by me, it was published on November 23, 1855.

Imperfect as the law was, it was received with great enthusiasm by the progressive party; it was the spark that produced the blaze of the Reform that later consumed the worm-eaten edifice of abuses and conventions; it was, in fact, a challenge to a duel, flung at the privileged classes, that General Comonfort and also others, lacking conviction in the principles of the revolution, or for personal reasons hoped to stop in its tracks, compromising it with the demands of the past; but they were obliged to support it in spite of themselves, by the omnipotent arm of public opinion.

Ignacio Mariscal, twenty-six years old at the time, had been exiled only from Oaxaca to Mexico City; later he served Juárez with distinction in Veracruz, Washington, and elsewhere, and still later became his Foreign Secretary. To a lesser extent, Manuel Dublán also rose with the liberal tide. Pola cites evidence that in the writing of this law, Juárez was influenced by the political works of Benjamin Constant. Sierra points out that the Ley Juárez was not a law but a decree, backed only by the power of the revolution, but that it could not be nullified by the states, and that, like later conquests of the Reform, it was amplified but never repealed. The Archbishop proposed submitting the matter to the arbitration of the Pope, but of course the government rejected this proposal. In this instance, at least, Juárez' trust that public opinion would support his own was fully justified. The Ley Juárez, besides doing what it had been intended to do, became a symbol of progress, the very flag of the *puros,* and Comonfort and his supporters did not dare to allow it to lapse.

"However," the *Notes* continue,

the privileged people redoubled their efforts to remove General Álvarez from power, hoping that don Ignacio Comonfort would support them in their schemes. They succeeded in attracting to them don Manuel Doblado, who rebelled in Guanajuato for the ancient plan of Religion and Exemptions. The moderates, instead of uniting with the government to destroy the new leader of the reactionaries, informed Sr. Álvarez that he was the cause of this uprising, because public opinion rejected him as governor, and since the Minister of War, who should have been his principal support, also spoke to him in this manner, he made the patriotic decision [December 11, 1855] to turn the command over to don Ignacio Comonfort as his replacement, notwithstanding that he could count on a strong division [of troops] with which to keep himself in power; but Sr. Álvarez is a sincere and disinterested patriot, and he did not wish that another civil war should break out in his country on his behalf.

Manuel Doblado? Had he not fought against Santa Anna and been induced by Comonfort to support the Plan of Ayutla and Álvarez' rebellion? What was he up to now? Unfortunately, Juárez had to ask himself this last question many times during the years to come.

Manuel Doblado had more intelligence, imagination, and personal power than Comonfort, and far fewer scruples to confuse and handicap him in his drive towards the top. If to the liberal cause he was loyal and useful on occasion, that was because he thought it would triumph in the end, and felt that if he were sufficiently adroit and patient in his scheming, he might somehow displace Comonfort and then Juárez himself.

He had been that sort from the beginning. Born a poor boy in the state of Guanajuato in 1818, he had earned his way in school partly by telling his mates, in exchange for cigarettes that he wanted to sell, enchanting fantasies about his own life; and when a clerical teacher asked him sarcastically for one of these tales, he sought a more respectable status by offering an essay "On the existence of God and His power." As a professor of Latin, then as a lawyer, his rise was rapid, and at the age of twenty-eight he was elected Governor of Guanajuato but was denied the office because he had not reached the legal age for it. Like Ocampo—if in nothing else—he had protested against the surrender to the Americans in 1848, and after that he had actually become Governor, and an active one. In "pronouncing" in 1855, in this shocking manner, for Religion and Exemptions, he was probably merely grasping for the coattails of Comonfort.

His eyes were close together, his nose long, his beard a fringe beneath his chin, his manner impressive. When a young student, Sierra saw him entering the Ministry of Foreign Affairs: "stooped beneath his dark overcoat, very well dressed, his resplendent silk hat lightly shoved back above his spacious forehead, his body heavy and a bit laborious, his complexion white and well shaven except for a small chin-beard, his mouth mobile and rather sensual, his eyes small and dark, and their glance rapid and penetrating; he appeared before us lightly smiling and patient in his perpetual impatience," answering their questions with benevolence and then quickly forgetting the incident. For Juárez, Doblado's fantastic and ephemeral little *pronunciamiento* for reaction on December 6, 1855, seems later to have become an incident to be disregarded, if and when Doblado could be useful to the Republic; but he did not forget it.

During the tumultuous days of November and December, 1855,

the very busy Minister of Justice was sought out by an eighteen-year-old from Oaxaca named Matías Romero who wanted letters of recommendation, hoping to get a job in the Ministry of Foreign Affairs. This very sober young man, also a product of the seminary and Institute, was continuing his study of law in the City while seeking and then getting a job as an apprentice in diplomacy. In a very factual diary that he kept for ten years, Romero records how Juárez helped him, and also a curious and amusing incident: "November 27. At the appointed hour [8 A.M.] I was at the Ministry, and at nine Juárez arrived and took me into his office. He sent for [Miguel María] Arrioja and [Ezequiel] Montes, and he was told that they had not yet arrived. While I was there I offered him a loan of $100, and to serve him in any way I could; both offers he accepted, and then he gave me five letters from various persons for me to answer. . . ." Romero saw Juárez every few days, doing odd secretarial jobs for him while he got a regular job, and on December 22 Juárez repaid the $100. The next day, accompanied by Ignacio Mejía, Manuel Ruiz, Félix Romero, and Manuel Fagoaga, Juárez left on the diligence, or stagecoach, for Puebla and Oaxaca. The editor of Romero's diary, Srta. Emma Cosío Villegas, remarks: "From this height, it may seem incredible that a youth of eighteen years should narrate with such dry sobriety the odd fact that a man almost three times older than himself and already a great republican figure should lack a hundred *pesos* and accept them from a nobody [*desarrapado*, or ragged person, but Romero was not *that* poor] who was asking him for a job without pay. Strictly speaking, Romero does not emphasize the fact that chance made him Juárez' banker: only that Juárez took him seriously enough to give him work." The fact is that Juárez, like other civil servants at the time, often received his pay late, if at all, and unlike others, did not use his office to make up for this on the side. He often had to borrow small sums from friends, and he always repaid them. As previously noted, a peso was then worth almost a dollar.

Juárez' *Notes* continue:

As soon as the administration of Sr. Álvarez had come to an end with the withdrawal of this leader and with the resignation of those of us who were his Ministers, the new President [Comonfort] organized his cabinet, naming as his Ministers, as was natural, persons from the circle of moderates. Regard for truth and fairness makes it necessary to say that in this circle there were not a few men who only out of sympathy for General Comonfort, and because they believed in good faith that this leader was capable of serving his country well, were united with him and were called moderates; but in reality they were decided partisans of the progressive revolution, a fact of which they later gave irrefutable proofs by defending with intelligence and courage the most advanced principles of progress and liberty; just as there were also many who allied themselves with the liberal party as the stanchest defenders of the principles of the revolution, but who later have defected most shamefully, going over to the ranks of the reactionaries and the traitors to our country. The fact is that both types were ill defined and deceived themselves in the choice of sides.

The new administration, in view of the general acceptance accorded the law of November 23, found it necessary to support it and put it into effect. I was invited to continue my services by going to Oaxaca to reestablish the legal order subverted by the authorities and garrison that had served in the administration of General Santa Anna, that in order to corrupt the revolution had supported the Plan of General Carrera, and that finally, had declared themselves against the law for the administration of justice that I had published. As much because of my interest in the execution of this law as because a legitimate authority had called me into its service, I accepted without vacillation the assignment given me, and at the end of December I left Mexico [City] with a small force under my orders.

Although Comonfort may have felt happy enough at this time, when he felt that he did not need Juárez' close support, to remove this marked *puro*, the author of the Ley Juárez, from Mexico City, Juárez was undoubtedly the best man available to be sent to handle a nasty situation in his own state. After the flight of Santa Anna, the liberals whom he had banished from Oaxaca returned, and at this time Máximo Ortiz, who had tried to shoot Juárez, was killed while trying to escape arrest. The liberals installed as Governor and military commander General José María García. This officer had supported the Plan of Ayutla, but he was induced by priests and regular army officers to take up Doblado's cry in Guanajuato for Religion and Exemptions. Colonel Ignacio Mejía led a National Guard unit in opposition, but was tricked out of a victory and had to flee by back roads to Mexico to enlist the aid of the national government and Juárez. The "small force" under Juárez' orders was a unit from Oaxaca that happened to be in Mexico City at the time. Meanwhile, Licenciado and Colonel José María Díaz Ordaz, an aristocratic descendant of the famous *conquistador* Bernal Días del Castillo and of Diego de Ordaz, another *conquistador*, but a strong liberal, with the aid of one Porfirio Díaz and others, was gradually getting the situation in hand, so that a conservative attempt to "intercept the Indian" and his guard came to nothing.

"When I reached the border of the state," Juárez was able to write later, "the rebels gave up their hostile attitude and offered to accept my authority. On January 10, 1856, I arrived at the capital of Oaxaca and took up the post that General don José María García turned over to me without resistance of any kind."

Juárez was now again Governor of his beloved Oaxaca, and could begin to rebuild, but he was also now a marked man, admired and hated throughout the Republic. As he probably knew, his return to the national scene was inevitable.

8

WATCHFUL AND ACTIVE WAITING

WHEN Juárez arrived at Etla, near Oaxaca, the village in which, nearly three years before, he had been seized and carried off to exile, he was met by a large crowd of his supporters and escorted into the city, and when he arrived at the statehouse, he was given a salute by a unit of artillery. What was much more remarkable, the conciliatory Bishop of Oaxaca, don José Augustín Domínguez, as authorized by law and tradition, welcomed the Governor with a service of *Te Deum* in the cathedral. The conservatives must have been annoyed, and the Governor, kneeling with his invariable sincerity, must have had mixed thoughts and emotions, not untinged with his characteristic irony.

The *Notes* continue:

I began my administration by recruiting and organizing the National Guard, and dissolving the permanent force that remained, because this type of force, corrupted by the repeated uprisings in which ambitious and immoral leaders, such as General Santa Anna, had obliged them to take part, gave no guarantee of strict obedience to civil authority and to the law, and their existence was a constant menace to liberty and public order. I proposed to keep the peace of the state with only my authority as Governor, in order to offer obvious proof that the general commanderies were not necessary—the commanderies whose extinction I had sought in the state years before, because experience had shown that they were not only useless but harmful. In effect, a commanding general with exclusive command of the force, and independent of the local authority, was an entity that nullified completely the authority of the state, because the governors themselves could not keep a force sufficient to execute their orders. They were called governors of free, sovereign, and independent states, but they had only the name, being in reality mere wards of the commanding generals. This vicious organization of the public administration was one of the causes of the military mutinies that repeated themselves so frequently during the rule of the Constitution of 1824.

However, since there existed laws that sanctioned this institution, and the government of Sr. Comonfort, despite the power given him by the revolution, did not dare to repeal them, he directed that in the state of Oaxaca they should continue in force, but that I as Governor should also assume the command, which I accepted only so that there should be no other leader to complicate the situation with his demands, for I knew that the civil government of the state could administer and direct this department like the others; but I took care to recommend very particularly from the state to the constitutional convention that they work with special zeal to the end that the new constitution of the Republic should eliminate the general commanderies.

With regard to the military, Juárez did more than this. He enlarged the National Guard as far as the budget would permit, and secured artillery, ammunition, and supplies from President Comonfort. Showing an equally necessary but somewhat more imaginative foresight, he established at the Institute classes in military science, so that promising liberals could become officers in the National Guard, and so that that critical organization's loyalty to the civil government and the liberal cause should be strengthened. It was remarked later that Oaxaca, uniting the toga and the sword, became a nursery of lawyer-generals. Among these there was to be included Porfirio Díaz, a young man who had been briefly a law student under Juárez, and whom, when he gave up the political leadership of the district of Ixtlán to return to the armed forces; Juárez promoted from lieutenant to captain.

Díaz' later life as a dictator, and his portraits as a smug, bemedaled, portly, and cruel old man, are more familiar, to Americans at least, than his violent, romantic, and stanchly liberal youth. "Historians will have to admit," asserts Franz Werfel, "that Juárez was dreamless reason and Díaz the enchanted youth of Mexico." Only until 1867, there is some truth in this vivid contrast conjured up by a playwright, but the present biographer would add hastily that Juárez was driven and sustained, through mental trials as severe as Díaz' military ones, by a dream of the future of the Republic nobler than any of which Díaz was capable; and that in Díaz' character and exploits, even when he was young, and as they are reported in his memoirs, one feels a vein of astute but unimaginative coarseness that dispels much of the enchantment, while not making it less interesting. All the same, he was "a bonny fighter," of enormous value to the Republic, and for about ten years, to Juárez, at a distance, he was "our Porfirio."

Díaz, a *mestizo* partly Mixtec, was born in Oaxaca in 1830, the son of an innkeeper and trader who died when he was three years old. Because the lad engaged in street fighting with gangs, his godfather, Bishop Domínguez, sent him to the seminary, which, like Juárez, he abandoned to study law at the Institute. There, his classmates included Matías Romero and Justo Benítez, and his liberal protector was Lic. Marcos Pérez. Although a good student and briefly librarian, he was more interested in athletics and guns, and he earned his living as an apprentice carpenter and shoemaker. He passed his law examinations and worked for a while in the office of his protector, but he never applied for admission to the bar. During the American war, as a student, he enlisted but never saw active service.

When Santa Anna held his plebiscite, the polls were set up in front of the statehouse, and were watched, among others, by the reactionary Governor, Martínez Piníllos. During the previous months, while Pérez had been imprisoned in the convent of Santo Domingo, which was also a barracks, Díaz had managed to read the official mails, and he and his brother Félix, with fantastic courage, strength, and resource, had scaled the walls of the convent and repeatedly delivered the latest news to the imprisoned liberal leader. When Díaz appeared at the polls, the book for signatures in favor of Santa Anna was open, and that in favor of any other candidates was closed and unsullied. He hesitated but when taunted with cowardice, Díaz opened the second book and wrote down the name of General Juan Álvarez. Promptly hunted down by the police, Díaz hid in the house of a friend until they could get horses and flee to the mountains, where they joined a small revolutionary force. As the leader of a much smaller force, Díaz, remembering a trick he had learned in the military course at the Institute, ambushed a unit of eighty or a hundred reactionary troops in a ravine, released an avalanche on them, and routed them. This was the first of some forty-six actions in which he later remembered that he had taken part. When made a political boss by García, Díaz furtively organized a National Guard unit, and when García turned reactionary, Díaz marched with his men to Oaxaca, took part in its liberation under Díaz Ordaz and returned officially to military service and was made a captain by Juárez.

Soon after his return, Juárez established a weekly liberal newspaper called *El Azote de los Tiranos,* or *The Scourge of Tyrants,* to which all the leading articulate liberals in Oaxaca contributed. Francisco Zarco, the leading journalist of the time, called it "the best newspaper in the Republic."

Juárez' *Notes* continue:

Since at this time, we had not yet received the new constitution, the government of Sr. Comonfort, in accordance with the Plan of Ayutla, exercised its general and all-embracing power, which the people barely tolerated because they hoped that national representation would soon return to them their sovereignty by means of a constitution based on the democratic principles that the last revolution had proclaimed. The spirit of liberty that ruled at that time and that was enlivened by the memory of the recent oppression by the despotism of Santa Anna, made extremely difficult the problem of the government in establishing public order, because it had to use the greatest prudence in its dispositions, to curb the attempts of the discontented without wounding the susceptibilities of the states by measures that would impinge upon or restrict too much their liberties.

However, Sr. Comonfort issued an organic statute [a temporary constitution, May 15, 1856] that centralized the government in such a way that it gave jurisdiction to the general power down to the simple police departments of the municipalities. This caused a general alarm in the states. The authorities in Oaxaca protested aginst this measure, asking that it be in effect suspended. They were not categorical in their protest; in fact, the statute that the government had wished to impose was not enforced in the state, and the government was prudent enough not to insist on compliance.

In wording the protest to Comonfort, Juárez had the advice and support of Manuel Dublán, Manuel Ruiz, Félix Romero (a valiant professor of law and journalist), Marcos Pérez, and Justo Benítez, but "the authorities of Oaxaca" were Juárez himself. In a letter to Matías Romero dated May 29, 1856, Juárez writes: "The Statute has been received here with the deepest disgust because it establishes the government of the republic in a centralized form. God grant that the congress complete the constitution as soon as possible, so that we may hear no more of so many disagreeable problems." If he had read this letter, Comonfort might well have exclaimed: "Disagreeable problems indeed!" He had just been forced to recapture the city of Puebla, which had been seized by armed rebels inspired by the protests of the clergy against liberal measures, including principally the Ley Juárez. After taking the city, he had banished Bishop Pelagio Antonio Labastida y Dávalos, who then proceeded to royalist intrigues in Europe, and he had been relatively merciful towards rebellious officers from the regular army, who were later to cause plenty of trouble. Sierra says that Comonfort punished these with "a kind of military degradation, a humiliation that did not put them out of action but disposed them to implacable vengeance." He also notes that when he and others, much later, begged Juárez for the life of a captured rebel, Juárez consented, but warned Sierra and his companions: "Don't forget that when you absolve one of these men who think that politics consists of disorder and military sedition, you are sentencing many hundreds of innocent people to death." Juárez knew very well that although the love of liberty and the love of power for its own sake are the two chief opposing forces in society, liberty requires order, which can be established and preserved only by governmental power that cannot always be disinterested and just. In his unfailing preoccupation with schools and education, Juárez showed that he knew very well that finally there is no adequate substitute for an enlightened and responsible citizenry.

In January, 1856, immediately after his return, he re-established the Institute, and named Lic. Marcos Pérez director, as well as Regent of the Supreme Court of the state. On swearing in the professors, Juárez said: "The government, which knows the importance of public education, the powerful influence that it exercises on morality and social progress, is resolved to give it all the impulsion that the necessities of the state demand, and to protect its development with tenacity."

And so Juárez, as a self-decentralized governor, as independent and recalcitrant as the governors with whom he had later to deal himself, if vastly more humane, intelligent, and disinterested than most of them, went his own constructive way. "He reorganized the College of Advocates; established a council of health" with powers over medical examinations and pharmacists; founded a hospital; "organized a department of public welfare, with the idea of removing an insulting charity from the hands of the clergy and the rich and giving it a social context"; founded a normal school in Tlacolula; "continued the rebuilding of the statehouse, enriched the museum, abolished passports within the state," and tried to liberalize the administration of village *fiestas.* He also finally succeeded in establishing a mint that was for twenty years a stimulus to local mining.

"In this year," the *Notes* continue,

the Ministry of the Treasury was assumed [May 20, 1856] by Sr. don Miguel Lerdo de Tejada, who presented to Sr. Comonfort the law [June 25, 1856] on the disentailing of the properties administered by the clergy; and although this law left them in the possession of the products of these properties, and only deprived them of the work of administering them, they did not obey the law, they resisted compliance, and they worked to persuade the people that it was heretical and attacked religion; and this quickly dissuaded many liberals from using the rights given them by this law to acquire with one payment the properties that the clergy refused to hold under the conditions that the law required.

Therefore I thought it my duty to comply with the law, not only with measures within my authority, but also with my example, in order to encourage those who because of unfounded scruples hesitated to take advantage of the benefits allowed them by the law. I sought the adjudication of a capital of 3,800 pesos, if I remember rightly, that would cover a house situated in the Calle de Coronel in the city of Oaxaca. A desire to make this reform effective, and not the prospect of speculation, guided me in making this transaction. There were transactions of greater size that I could have made, but this was not my object.

The Ley Lerdo was primarily an economic measure, intended to free the vast lands owned by the Church and so to stimulate the economy. The lands were not confiscated: they were put up for sale to the tenants and others, and the Church could not buy them back again, and could only own church buildings and the money received for the lands. Although ironic about freeing the clergy from work, Juárez' language was accurate. Unfortunately, the law did not result in a more general distribution of the lands. The Church *haciendas*, undivided, and with a heavy tax put on their sale, were bought only by the rich. The law provided that both civil and ecclesiastical corporations could not own lands, so that the *mestizos* were able to break up and buy the *ejidos*, or communal lands, owned by Indian villages for more than three centuries. In short, the new-rich, including many foreigners, merely replaced the Church. Therefore the Indians, already aroused by the clergy, now had more substance for their violent reaction, as the liberals were to learn the hard way.

Always one of the best-informed and most intellectual of the liberals, Miguel Lerdo de Tejada was not one of the most realistic or sagacious among them, and in this important act his limitations were later made apparent. The clergy, too, were not as far-sighted and sagacious as they might have been. It has been pointed out that while retaining their greater interest in their own wealth than in religion or morals, by co-operating with the government in the sale of their not highly productive lands, and investing in and promoting railroads, for example, or other forms of industry, they might have become, for a few decades, at least, even richer, and in doing so they might have saved thousands of human lives.

Miguel Lerdo de Tejada, born in Veracruz in 1812, and his brother Sebastián, born there eleven years later, were half Spanish and half Mexican, and after enjoying a wealthy childhood, were orphaned and impoverished, but fought for education, rose to very high offices, and with Ocampo, Ignacio Ramírez, and Francisco Zarco, were probably the most intellectual of the great liberals of the time; yet after their early years, they seem never to have been very close to one another.

Miguel Lerdo de Tejada was writing forceful political essays, economic studies, and a history of Veracruz in his thirties; and during the American occupation of Mexico City, he served on the Municipal Assembly, from motives strictly patriotic and humane, but was bitterly and unjustly criticized for it later. When Santa Anna came into power, he asked Miguel Lerdo for a paper on the economic situation, and Lerdo delivered a strong one, for which he was made Under-Secretary of Development, but of course he was far too liberal for the dictator, who probably never read his reports, and he soon stepped out. It was natural for Comonfort to make him Minister of the Treasury, and it was natural also that this Lerdo's ideas were too radical for Comonfort, so that he held this office less than a year—although he did serve for a little more than a month, later in 1856, as acting Foreign Secretary. He was an aristocratic-looking figure with a moustache and sideburns, of fastidious morals, and he held numerous opinions, which he vigorously stated. His associates, including Juárez, seem to have been fascinated by his talents, while—perhaps with reason—somewhat distrusting his judgment.

His brother Sebastián had a character both more solid and more mysterious. Sebastián, a profound legal scholar, was definitely a liberal, but more moderate in his views than his brother. From 1852 to 1863, with leaves of absence for political office, he served as the Rector of the College of San Ildefonso, an institution under the control of the Department of Justice, and one of the best in the country. In 1855, as Minister of Justice, Juárez attended a graduation exercise at the College, and presently appointed the Rector one of the two *fiscals* of the Supreme Court, an office strangely combining that of Prosecutor—or as we should say, Solicitor-General—with that of an alternate's seat on the court itself. From June to September, 1857, as a figure previously almost unknown, in contrast to his brother, he served as Comonfort's Foreign Secretary, in which post he made only one thing clear: that he firmly opposed any alienation of national territory to the United States. When the explosion came, he returned to his nonpolitical post as Rector of San Ildefonso. All that was known about him was that his intellectual conceit at least equaled his great abilities.

His scholarly biographer, Dr. Knapp, describes him as:

Poised and gracious, on occasion austere and aloof, the thickset little man of less than average height fitted his somber black suit as well as he fitted the part he played as Rector. He always was impeccably groomed, in the same mournful atttire—black suit, waistcoat, and tie, and a spotless white shirt with high collar. With prominent and penetrating eyes and a fringe of chestnut-colored hair framing an oval face and a spacious bald pate, he might well have passed for a village parson. Although his appearance was easily adapted to caricature, in person he was dignity incarnate. Often, too, there was a cynical twist to his thin mouth which might be transformed into an expression of inflexible determination. When the sketch is completed with his pale complexion, it was certain that his makeup was more Anglo-Saxon than Latin, although he would not have been flattered by the comment.

This academic figure was to go a long way, and when Juárez, sitting on a dais beside him in 1855, decided that he could be useful in government, he did not make a mistake.

All the other events of this time were dwarfed in importance by the framing and adoption of the Constitution of 1857, in accordance with the Plan of Ayutla. The constitutional convention, as we should call it, although it had legislative powers in addition, or the congress, as it was called then, first met on February 14, 1856, and with interruptions, it labored through that year and into the next, until February 5, 1857. Because the reactionaries were not allowed to vote, or refused to do so, and because the approximately ninety-five deputies were elected in a time of turmoil and uncertainty, most of them were liberals, *puros* or *moderados*, and on the whole, the *moderados* were dominant. Forty-six years after the Grito of 1810, and about thirty years after the opening of the secular institutes that trained so many lawyers, the members of this body, whatever may be decided about their product, were clearly remarkable men, superior in political capacity to the gallant insurgents. Their passion and eloquence were more marked than their realism, and they represented a minority and probably knew it, but they had great courage, and they perceived that nearly fifty years of bloodshed for liberty and reform had now to be justified or given up as shamefully wasted.

In the final document, what we should call the Bill of Rights came first, at great length, embodying most of the political principles of the Enlightenment and also the basic concepts of the Ley Juárez and the Ley Lerdo, which by this time none but avowed reactionaries could reject. An article establishing religious tolerance was debated with great heat, then the issue was dropped, but Ponciano Arriaga secured the passage of Article 123, giving the government control of the Church. One original feature established the right of *amparo* or direct appeal to the Supreme Court for the defense of civil rights. A good deal of this part of the Constitution, as of its successor of 1917, now in effect, has been neither enforced effectively nor repealed—and any informed Mexican, checking off the items in our own Bill of Rights, could say the same of it. In 1856 and 1857, in writing their Bill of Rights, the Mexican liberals set up a standard and a symbol. At that time, most of the people did not understand it or even know about it, but as the years passed, more and more of them learned about it, understood it, and found themselves ready to fight for it. The leading conservatives understood it immediately, and with the help of the clergy, were able to persuade a great many Mexicans that it constituted an attack on the Mexican religion and way of life, and therefore had to be destroyed at once.

The structure of government established by the Constitution of 1857 was again, as in 1824, too similar to that of the United States, instead of one adapted to the Mexican "character" and to the Mexican society and economy at the time. It established separate and counterbalancing executive, legislative, and legal branches, but these were not kept sufficiently distinct and separate, the legislature was made more powerful than the executive branch at a time when this was very dangerous, and the powers of the states and the federal government, and the relations between them, were ill defined. It included a system of electoral voting, sometimes replaced or supported by direct elections. Most of the alterations of a constitutional pattern itself unsuitable were not advantageous. Because it was feared that any senate would be reactionary, the congress was made unicameral. Most oddly and dangerously of all, the President of the Supreme Court, as he was called, had to be elected, and was named in effect Vice President.

Juárez went quickly and firmly to work under the new constitution, although he expressed doubts about it that he did not choose to spell out. For this constitution, as at least *a* constitution, and a symbol of democratic law and authority, he soon risked his career and his neck. Yet it must be admitted that he did his greatest work when brutal facts repeatedly forced the setting aside of the constitution for the time being, and the granting of all its powers to the President, who could then govern by decree. During the two periods in which he tried valiantly to work within its letter, he was handicapped by its defects, by the egotism of most Mexican politicians, and by his and others' confusion about "parliamentarianism." Under these conditions, as we shall see, he fumbled.

The Constitution of 1857, however necessary, was a bomb, and the firing mechanism was a provision, equally necessary, that all civil officials take an oath of allegiance to the Constitution. On February 5, 1857, the aged and respected liberal Valentín Gómez Farías took the oath first, on his knees before God and the Congress, and he was then followed by all the members of that body and by Comonfort. The trigger was pulled by the Church when it excommunicated all persons who had taken the oath and would not retract in public. Rebellions broke out again all over the country, including once more in that perennial ulcer of reaction, Puebla.

Among the military leaders of the reaction were Tomás Mejía and Miguel Miramón. "The loyal Mejía was a tawny, unprepossessing Indian, with high cheekbones and an enormous mouth, surmounted by scanty bristles. He was a god among the natives of the . . . Sierra Gorda [near Querétaro], who called him by the endearing name of don Tomasito." He was a brave and able soldier, driven by a passion for the Church and the old order, he had had no education, and he unfortunately represented many thousands of Mexicans like him. Like Miramón, he had fought ably against the Americans. Miramón was a handsome and dashing aristocrat, French in origin, very brave, who had risen rapidly in the regular army, and in 1857 was twenty-five years old and a colonel. Both had already rebelled and been shown an imprudent leniency by Comonfort. The most active priest on the reactionary side, in Mexico, was Francisco J. Miranda, large, handsome, suave, and beardless, a very astute and resourceful man who traveled from city to city, organizing rebellions against the federal government. But even Comonfort was for a while active and somewhat effective in preserving order, and the *puros*, including Juárez, were far from intimidated.

It was provided that constitutional conventions be held in all the states, to frame state constitutions in conformity with the federal one, that state and national elections be held, and that the new federal government, under the new Constitution, be installed on September 16, 1857. The new federal Constitution was proclaimed in Oaxaca on March 23, and the next day—the cathedral chapter, which opposed the Bishop and the Constitution, being absent—a *Te Deum* was sung in the cathedral.

"In 1857," Juárez' *Notes* continue,

the political constitution of the nation was published, and at once I hastened to put it into effect, principally insofar as it concerned the organization of the state. It was my opinion that the states should constitute themselves without loss of time, because I feared that because of certain principles of liberty and progress that had been included in the Constitution, there would soon form and break out a rebellion in the capital of the Republic that would dissolve the supreme powers of the nation; it was better that the states should find themselves already organized to oppose it, to destroy it, and to re-establish the legitimate authorities that the Constitution had established. The majority of the states understood the necessity of their prompt organization, and proceeded to realize it in conformity with the basic charter of the Republic. Oaxaca gave itself its own constitution and put it into effect immediately, and in accordance with it I was elected constitutional Governor by direct election by the people.

The constituent congress of the state of Oaxaca had been called together on June 21, 1857, and in addressing this body, Juárez went so far as to say of the new federal Constitution: "The truth is that even in this constitution there have not been established fully and frankly all the principles that the cause of liberty demands in order that Mexico may enjoy a durable peace." He then went on to say that while the Constitution could be legally amended, the representatives present would have to prepare the minds of the people for changes. In the campaign for the governorship for the period 1856–60, Juárez got 100,336 votes out of 112,541, an astonishing turn-out for such an experiment. A good many of the illiterate Indians may have known whom if not what they were voting for.

Meanwhile, from April 3 to May 7, Juárez had been in Tehuantepec again, settling peaceably one more quarrel between that town and Juchitán, and enforcing the decision of the national constituent assembly to reincorporate the isthmus into the state of Oaxaca, from which it had been separated in 1852 in order to strengthen the centralist regime of Santa Anna.

A fascinating minor event of the time concerned a village priest named Bernardino Carvajal. When José Justo Benítez, the secretary of the state government, became too busy in working on the new state constitution to hold his office, Juárez replaced him with Carvajal. When the bishopric denied him permission to take the oath and the office, he withdrew from the Church.

Towards the end of June, acting under the orders of Lorenzo Garza, the Archbishop of Mexico, a parish priest struck back at the law, and was denounced to Juárez by Nicolás Fernández y Muedra, governor of the department of Villa Alta, whereupon Juárez wrote the following letter to the Bishop of Oaxaca:

Distinguished Sir:

Since the government is certain that the parish priest of Zoochila, don Andrés Jiménez, has denied the sacraments to the deceased Mayor of Tavehua, because he did not wish to give him burial, under the pretext that the said official did not wish to retract the oath of allegiance that he took to the political constitution of the Republic; and in virtue of the instructions that I have from the supreme government of the nation, I have been obliged to order that the said Sr. Jiménez be brought as a prisoner to this city and removed outside the state to the place that the President may determine.

This government cannot view with indifference events that, arousing the consciences of citizens, may cause a disturbance of public order; and determined to have the laws respected, it does not fear to provide whatever the welfare of the people may require; if it views with appreciation and esteem the priest who fulfills religiously his holy mission of producing peace and morality, it does not hesitate an instant to punish the subversive person who by his acts makes clear his hatreds and mischief; for to do anything else would be to abandon society to the destructive attacks of the first person who sought its ruin. Since this motive will cause within a few days the removal of Sr. Jiménez, I request you, distinguished Sir, to send another priest to take charge of that parish.

I assure your Excellency of my esteem and consideration.
God and Liberty. Oaxaca, June 22, 1857.

Benito Juárez

Eight days later, Juárez was sworn in again as Governor, and the *Notes* continue:

It was a custom authorized by law in that state, as in the rest of the Republic, that when the Governor took possession of his office, he and the other authorities should attend a *Te Deum* sung in the cathedral, at the principal door of which the canons would appear to greet him; but this time the clergy were at open war with the civil authority, and very especially with me, because of the law for the administration of justice that I had issued on November 23, 1855, and they considered governors heretics and excommunicated persons.

The canons of Oaxaca took advantage of the incident of my taking office to provoke a scandal. They planned to close the doors of the church so as not to receive me, with the sinister view of compromising me by causing me to use force by opening the doors with armed police and arresting the canons; so that my administration would be inaugurated with an act of violence, or with a rebellion, in case the people, to whom they wished to present themselves as martyrs, took part in their defense.

The repeated reports that I had of this plot that was being hatched, and the fact that the church was closed, against the customs on such occasions, it being even then the hour for the ceremony, assured me of the truth of what was happening. Although I counted on sufficient force to make myself respected if I took steps against the seditious ones, and the law in force on the inauguration of governors authorized me to act in this manner, I decided, however, not to attend the *Te Deum*, not out of fear of the canons, but because of the conviction I had that the governors of civil society should not take part in that or any other ecclesiastical ceremony, except as men able to go to the churches and practise those acts of devotion that their religion may dictate to them. The civil governors ought not to have any religion, because it being their duty to protect impartially the liberty that the governed have to follow and practise the religion that pleases them, they could not fulfill this duty faithfully if they were sectarians of any. This event seemed to me a fitting one for reforming the bad custom that existed of the governors taking part in processions and even in the professions of monks, thus using time that they ought to employ in work useful to society. Furthermore, I thought that not having to exercise any ecclesiastical function, or to govern in the name of the Church, but in that of the people who had elected me, my authority remained integral and perfect with only the oath that I took before the representatives of the state that I should faithfully do my duty. In this way I avoided the scandal that had been planned, and from that time there ceased in effect in Oaxaca the bad custom that the civil authorities should attend ecclesiastical functions.

This passage would seem to establish and date with some certainty the culminating and decisive point in Juárez' probably slow transition from being a "good Catholic," however liberal and reflective, to his being what we can only call an independent and unaffiliated Christian. His later remarks on this subject are consistent with this passage, and there can hardly be any reasonable doubt on the point. There is here a vague suggestion of agnosticism, but Juárez almost as certainly, from his references in his speeches to "divine Providence" and God, references that were clearly not rhetorical, did not go that far. His remaining religious faiths seem to have been vague but strong, and he must have continued to feel affection and respect for the religion of his youth and of the Mexican people, and for priests truly occupied with religion and morality. But now the doors of the Church had been closed to him, in more ways than one, by the Church itself, and his relief on the resolution of this conflict in loyalties may well have been considerable.

The *Notes* continue:

Speaking of customs, there were others that served only to satisfy the vanity and ostentation of the governors, such as those of having armed guards in their houses and of wearing at public functions hats of special design. When I was Governor, I abolished this custom, wearing a common hat and suit of citizens, and living in my house without a guard of soldiers and without show of any kind; for I am persuaded that the respectability of the Governor comes to him from the law and from upright behavior, and not from suits and military pomps appropriate only to kings of the theatre. I am glad that the governors of Oaxaca have followed my example.

On August 13, at Santa María Ixcapa, Oaxaca, forces from that state and from Guerrero put down a minor rebellion incited by priests and led by one Colonel José María Salado, an unreconstructed *santannista*. In this vivid little action, reported later, without boasting, by himself, Captain Porfirio Díaz took charge when some of the states' forces lost their nerve, snatched victory out of near defeat, and received an abdominal wound that became infected and would have cost him his life if Juárez had not sent a Dr. Esteban Calderón to care for him and his wounded comrades.

During this year it gradually became clear that Juárez disapproved of Comonfort's vacillations, yet that he would probably be drawn, in one way or another, into the dangerous confusion within the federal government itself. He kept in touch by means of frequent letters with his young friend Matías Romero in Mexico City, receiving reports on national affairs, offering his comments in reply, and counseling the young man on his studies and career. As early as April 4, he was writing to Romero to discourage any attempts by Romero or other friends to have him nominated for any national office, on the grounds that Comonfort's antagonism would be aroused, to the prejudice of the state of Oaxaca in its relations with the federal government. On June 10 he wrote to Romero that he was less alarmed about foreign affairs than about the too frequent changes in the cabinet, into which had been brought persons who could not inspire the confidence of liberals. On September 8: "There is much talk of a *golpe de estado* [*coup d'état*] and of a change of policy of the cabinet, but I do not believe that Sr. Comonfort would care to precipitate his own ruin by separating himself from the legal order that is going to begin on September 16." On September 17 Romero replied that there were too many rumors to be sure of anything except that Congress was having some difficulty in assembling, because the credentials of many deputies were in dispute; that the cabinet had resigned and some considered this the first step towards a departure from the Constitution, while others disputed this interpretation; and that all that was certain was that Sr. Comonfort did not like the Constitution. To this, Juárez replied on September 22: "Even though the Constitution may not be pleasing to the President, there is no fear that he will destroy it, because since the whole nation likes it, it will always be supported by the national representatives, and I think we shall never go backwards, however much that is desired by the enemies of liberty."

The national elections of that year were extremely confused, with Miguel Lerdo de Tejada as the only candidate opposing Comonfort for the Presidency until he withdrew in June; and then he was elected both to a seat on the Supreme Court and to a seat in Congress, when he chose the former. In spite of his resistance, Juárez was nominated for the Presidency of the Supreme Court. In the troubled period after September 16, when the Constitution came into force but there was no constitutional President or cabinet, "some deputies were maturing a plan to overthrow Comonfort and put Juárez in his place." The Congress was finally convened on October 8, but the votes of the electors did not all come in for over a month.

However, Comonfort proceeded to form a cabinet, and on October 19, Manuel Ruiz, a good *puro*, became Minister of Justice and Ecclesiastical Affairs. Comonfort's actions and motives were never very clear, and now, on October 21, he sent to Juárez, by the hand of Ignacio Mejía, a letter that is obscure as it is interesting and important. Addressing Juárez in the second person singular, which indicated more intimacy then than it does to-day, he asked him to accept the Ministry of *Gobernación*, or Interior, which was responsible, among other things, for the police and the internal order of the Republic. There follows this passage: "You will help me also to calm down certain pretensions of the liberal family that are dangerous in the difficult crisis through which we are passing; and finally, because you are informed on the situation and your knowledge of it would help you to carry on the business if, as President of the Supreme Court, you should have to take upon yourself the supreme command of the nation because the failure of my health or some other grave cause necessitated this step." Comonfort had probably forgotten, or now chose to ignore, just how much of a *puro* Juárez had been during their close association four years before. Comonfort now needed both Juárez' personal strength and his prestige. Juárez, like Comonfort, was not to be sworn into the office to which he had been elected until December 1. There remained forty days until that date, and if they were all still in office and alive at that time,

Juárez' becoming President of the Court might be in effect postponed: that is, he could be sworn in and then given leave of absence, to serve as Minister of the Interior. Comonfort clearly anticipated the possibility, or even likelihood, of his going out of office very soon after being sworn in for four years, although he could not have known exactly the dismal way in which this event would occur, and perhaps he hoped to draw his successor further to the right.

Juárez' formal reply, on October 24, to the Undersecretary of the Interior, to be passed on to the President with thanks, was much more explicit. He accepted the office, he said, because he considered it his duty to do so and because "my convictions put me in a position to co-operate in every way in the development of the glorious revolution of Ayutla." José María Díaz Ordaz was immediately made interim Governor of Oaxaca, and on October 27 Juárez left Oaxaca for Mexico City. He does not seem to have taken his family with him, and that would have been for the very good reason that he foresaw personal danger for every politician and his family in the capital. His parting from doña Margarita and the children would have been even more painful if he had known that he would never see the city or state of Oaxaca again.

Juárez was now fifty-one years old, and he probably traveled in worn clothes, with small luggage, in the stagecoach that crossed some very wild, mountainous country. He arrived in Mexico City on November 2, and the next day took over the Ministry. He was rapidly approaching a major crisis in his own life, as well as in that of the nation.

PART THREE

The War of the Reform

9

THE CRISIS OF THE CONSTITUTION

IT SEEMS REASONABLE to assume that Juárez completed his *Notes for My Children* up to this point not long before leaving Oaxaca, and that after that he was entirely too busy to do more than write the very laconic and fragmentary notes, day by day, that with extensive blanks he continued writing for the next seven years, and that I have called his *Diary*. These later notes were obviously written for his own eyes and use only, and he never filled them in and turned them into a more or less coherent if incomplete narrative like the *Notes*. This is especially unfortunate for historians in relation to the events of the next few weeks, because these events were very complex and important, and because Juárez' part in them raises questions about his motives and character. The other writings by those who took part are self-defensive, obscure, and contradictory, and most of the important events were not of a kind to get into public records. We move now, literally, into the realm of the "smoke-filled rooms," trying to keep our eyes above all on the dark little Indian gentleman from Oaxaca who never said much but whom, because of his relation to the Presidency and his unquestioned strength of character, none of the others could ever long brush aside and forget.

The new cabinet included, besides Manuel Ruiz in Justice and Juárez in the Interior, Juan Antonio de la Fuente in Foreign Affairs (a post he had held previously under Ceballos), José García Conde in War, Bernardo Flores in Development, and Manuel Payno in the Treasury, where he had struggled under Herrera. Fuente was a strong-minded liberal, but like Ruiz, and like Ocampo, Degollado, Mata, both Lerdos, and other liberals who were in Mexico City at this time, he seems to have been left in the dark about these events, and escaped involvement. García and Flores seem to have been insignificant figures, and from Juárez' *Diary* one gets the impression that the Minister of the Interior was at least as active in supplying and directing the forces, chiefly National Guard, that were putting down an outbreak of minor rebellions, as the Minister of War. An odd figure who was far from inactive was one Juan José Baz, who had been appointed Governor of the Federal District by Álvarez in 1855.

Juárez' telegraphic *Diary* indicates that while the central drama was developing and being talked about all over town, he was very busy with his own job. Both Puebla and Oaxaca were threatened by reactionary forces on the march, and loyal forces were deployed to meet them. Political prisoners were tried and exiled. The movements of priests were watched. Editors of subversive newspapers were fined. The fractious municipal government of Mexico City was disciplined. While he was busy with all of these matters, and more, his young friend Matías Romero was politely but persistently importuning him to get him a diplomatic post abroad, preferably in London, and to assist him in securing the publication of his adored brain child, a *Synoptic Table of the Treaties of Mexico with Other Countries*. While Romero was busy pushing these projects, copying out letters to the governors and others for Juárez, studying English and French, reading classical authors, and sitting in on *tertulias* or café conversations, others were busy with less innocent affairs.

Before we consider these in detail, an outline may be useful. On November 16, after the abandonment of the Constitution had been widely discussed for some time, Comonfort, encountering Baz, Payno, and Zuloaga, brought this conspiracy to a head, and committed himself to it. The next day Juárez, unaware of this meeting and commitment, urged Comonfort not to resign. On December 1, Comonfort and Juárez were sworn into their offices under the Constitution. On December 15 the conspiracy was revealed to Congress, and Juárez, questioned by that body, somewhat uncertainly reassured it. On the same day Comonfort revealed his intentions to Juárez but failed to win him over to the *golpe de estado*. Payno, when indicted, stalled. On December 16 Comonfort accepted the Plan of Tacubaya to overthrow the Constitution, and the next day had Juárez arrested and confined. Comonfort still vacillated, while the liberals made overtures to Doblado to lead their cause, but finally organized a coalition of governors behind the Constitution and behind Juárez as legal heir to the Presidency. Meanwhile, the reactionaries, on January 11, displaced Comonfort and made Zuloaga their President. Thereupon, Comonfort released Juárez and himself went into exile. Juárez and the leading liberals then escaped from Mexico City and established the constitutional government in Guanajuato, on January 19, 1858. We can now look more closely at these murky, fascinating, and critical transactions.

As early as October 8, according to his own version of it, Baz, supported by Prieto, had been urging on Comonfort the necessity of replacing the Constitution with a liberal dictatorship, to get more accomplished. Baz then traveled to Veracruz with this inspiration of his, and perhaps misunderstood there, seems actually to have found some temporary support for his inspiration. He says that on his return he found everyone, including the devious Doblado, ready only for change by constitutional methods. We may be sure that Comonfort was also being badgered to overthrow the Constitution by his conservative friends, whose motives, of course, were exactly the opposite. His indecision and his suspicions excited others to action and must incidentally have been very painful to himself.

According to Payno, who seems to have been much more clearheaded than Baz, if rather a weakling, he resigned from the Treasury on November 15 solely because he was having trouble with his eyes, and at this time, to his astonishment, Comonfort broke with him. Baz, a friend of Payno's, was also having difficulties with Comonfort, and Payno hoped to reconcile them. On November 16 Comonfort appeared at Payno's house, found Baz there, suspected them of some intrigue, and took them out to the Archbishop's Palace in Tacubaya, which was then being used as the President's house. There they found General Félix Zuloaga, a reactionary friend of Comonfort's who was in command of two thousand troops stationed near by. Zuloaga and Baz were sent out of the small room, and Comonfort and Payno found themselves alone together and both very nervous and embarrassed, with Comonfort constantly smoking cigarettes and pacing the room.

Comonfort then asked Payno whether he had received the eye medicine from the wife of General Landberg. Bewildered, Payno replied that he had not. Comonfort then asked Payno whether he had not sent Landberg any message through his wife. Payno, still in a daze, replied that he had not. Comonfort then explained that Sra. Landberg's confessor had made her take a letter, written supposedly by Payno, to General Landberg in Toluca, where he was in command of 1,600 men, and that offering help, this letter urged General Landberg to pronounce against the Constitution. General Landberg, furious at his wife, could have killed her, and sent this letter to Comonfort. Was it then a forgery? Payno protested that it was, of course, and there followed a reconciliation. This letter had been the cause of the misunderstanding between Payno and Comonfort. Although he was already ripe, as the next hour was to prove, for rejection of the Constitution, Comonfort had been infuriated, not by rebellion, but by being left out of the plot! In the matter of this letter, and of an even more explosive one to appear presently, Payno was either a consummate liar at the time, and in his narrative of these events, or else almost incredibly naïve and weak for an experienced Minister of the Treasury. This writer takes the latter view.

Baz and Zuloaga were now called in, and for reasons clear to nobody but himself, Comonfort now evidently considered himself in the company of men who were both resolved on the overthrow of the Constitution and strong enough to see it through, so that in their company he could safely commit himself—that is, as far as he could ever commit himself to anything—to one more *pronunciamiento*.

"Where are we going?" he asked these three. "Is this a revolution? What are your plans? On what elements can you count?"

Baz then made an astonishing speech, in which he proclaimed himself a liberal, then insisted that in order to make liberal progress, the Ley Juárez, the Ley Lerdo, the Congress, and the entire Constitution had to be thrown overboard. Payno said that the Constitution was unworkable, that the Treasury was empty, that there was no hope of getting money from the United States for rights on the Isthmus of Tehuantepec, that he disapproved of the Ley Lerdo, and that Comonfort should resign. Even Zuloaga, a mediocre man and soldier, but stronger than these two, chose to hedge. Withdrawing his finger from his mouth, where he had kept it while listening and meditating on the future of Mexico and himself, he said that his soldiers were disgusted by the anti-Church laws, and might easily be seduced by Miramón. Almost certainly by this time, if not long before, this character had plotted a *pronunciamiento* against the Constitution, candidly in favor of the Church. To these three, then, a muddlehead at best, an intellectual weakling at best, and a cheap conspirator in uniform, the popular leader of "the glorious revolution of Ayutla" committed himself, and the four of them began to make plans. Comonfort said they had to have the support of Doblado in Guanajuato, Parrodi in Jalisco, and Veracruz. Baz said he would take care of Veracruz. Zuloaga said he would take care of Huerta in Michoacán. Comonfort said he would explore and follow public opinion. At three in the morning Baz and Comonfort buckled on their revolvers and returned to Mexico, with an escort of dragoons.

Although this unsavory scene in the tragicomedy was the only one of which we have a full report, surely many others of the kind were enacted during the following weeks. Having defeated Tomás Mejía at Querétaro, Doblado appeared in Mexico with augmented prestige and had several interviews with Comonfort, during which, to his credit, he tried to persuade the President to seek constitutional reforms by legal means, but characteristically left the way open for himself to resist or support a *golpe de estado*, depending on which course seemed more promising for his own future.

On November 17, the day after the plotting at Tacubaya, Juárez noted in his *Diary:* "Meeting. Comonfort. The obstacles that he has. The respect for the beliefs of his mother. The relations of friendship with various chiefs of the army. The opposition, for lack of sympathy, of the chiefs, and for this reason he thinks his withdrawal is indispensable. Everything was answered satisfactorily."

Was Comonfort dissembling, in order to sound out Juárez, or had he again lost his nerve and was he thinking seriously of resigning? The latter interpretation seems probable, but by no means certain. On the next day, Romero noted in his diary a rumor that Comonfort would resign. A more interesting and important question is, just how much did Juárez know at this time? Obviously nothing about the plot hatched the night before at Tacubaya, and probably nothing more than that the President was badly rattled. Payno was to report, with no reason for defending them: "The only ones who did not know anything in the first days were D. Manuel Ruiz and D. Benito Juárez." The reflexive verb in Spanish—"*A todo se contestó satisfactoriamente*"—can be annoyingly vague, but it is reasonable to suppose that it was Juárez, the incurable optimist, who attempted to calm and reassure Comonfort, and did so to his own satisfaction, if not to that of anyone else. Perhaps he ignored the dangerous military situation and urged constitutional amendments to strengthen the Presidency, or urged another appeal to Congress for extraordinary powers.

On November 18 the ballots for the Presidency of the Supreme Court were counted, and it was found that neither Juárez nor the other candidate, José María Lacunza, had the majority required by the Constitution. The election then devolved on the Congress itself, which selected Juárez. Although it seems to have been assumed for some time—see, for example, Comonfort's letter to Juárez offering him the Ministry of the Interior—that Juárez would be elected, and although the *puros* had some control of the Congress, this must have been something of a jolt and then a relief to the *puros*, if not to Juárez himself. In any case, it was a narrow squeak for the Republic, because Lacunza, then a *moderado*, kept moving to the Right and eventually became President of the Council under the Empire. Comonfort was elected to the Presidency without incident on November 21. On November 30 Juárez resigned from his Ministry in order to go to the court the next day, when both he and Comonfort were sworn into the offices to which they had been elected. Juárez and Fuente, also elected to the court, were then given leaves of absence to return to their Ministries.

On December 10, Juárez notes that the government was finally given ample powers to restore peace. He also notes cryptically: "a conversation with Doblado and Lerdo," probably Miguel, and one would give a good deal to have a recording of that conversation. They were all rapidly approaching the brink.

On December 12 and 13 there was a religious fiesta. December 14: "Accusation made in the Congress." December 15: "A communication was received from the Congress with a copy of the accusation. Letter from don Manuel Payno and don Félix Zuloaga to [Epitacio] Huerta [Governor and military commander in Michoacán]. Plan: 1. The Constitution ceases and Sr. Comonfort is made dictator. 2. There will be named a Council consisting of a landholding representative from each state. 3. There will be an edict summoning a Congress in which there will be representatives of all classes to amend or make a new constitution. It is said that supporting this plan are: Lamberg in Toluca, Echeagaray in Puebla, Iglesias in Veracruz, Parrodi in Jalisco, Morett in San Luis, and Doblado in Guanajuato. Meeting of Ministers on the decision of the Jury, in which it was revealed that the accusation against the Sres. Payno and Zuloaga had been admitted. Ruiz, García Conde, Flores, Juárez, and Sr. Presidente [were present]. Opinion of Juárez: 'To obey the order and ascertain that the accused hear it and have all legal defenses, and that the judges be impartial. Nothing else can be done, assuming that the measure issues from a corporation acting within its constitutional rights.' It was decided to postpone taking action until the following day."

From subsequent events, it is clear that the governors reported to be supporting the *golpe de estado* did not do so, or were misinformed about it, by Baz and others, or rapidly changed their minds. Baz claimed later that it was he, who had urged a rebellion against the Constitution on the leaders in Veracruz in the first place, who now brought them around to its defense! As for the letter itself, it was written by Zuloaga, with a postscript by Payno, who claimed later that he wrote this postscript because he and not Zuloaga knew Huerta! The letter was turned over to the Congress, with others of the kind, by Eligio Sierra, a deputy from Michoacán. The jury referred to was a grand jury, and the measure it issued was an indictment of Payno. Presumably Zuloaga was to be accused and tried as an officer.

The *Diary* for December 15 continues:

The Congress decided that the Ministers of the Interior and of War should inform it about the state of readiness to keep the public peace, and whether they had taken any steps against General Zuloaga, and if they had enough force to suppress whatever disorders might occur.

The Minister of the Interior [Juárez himself] reported that the armed reaction had not been disposed of, for with new forces it had invaded the state of Oaxaca; that these enemies were advancing towards that capital and had got a second breath; and that the government had taken every measure within its capacity to take control of the situation. That in the capital it could only count on 3,000 men, and could not have more, to make itself respected as it would like, because the resources were exhausted every day, and even the force that existed was composed largely of regulars who could not be counted on with all the confidence that was required. That for this reason it was necessary to proceed with extreme caution and judgment, and to take the time necessary to comply with the judgment of the Grand Jury with respect to the separation of General Zuloaga. The government respected and would execute the decisions of the sovereign Congress, because that was its duty; but that being responsible for the public peace, it would try to comply with those decisions, while never forgetting that responsibility.

The President of the Congress replied that he had heard this report with satisfaction.

The Minister was asked whether he thought prudent the adoption of a bill that was read, to the effect that the Congress should move itself to some other place, should the public order deteriorate in this capital.

The Minister replied that he did not consider the measure opportune under the circumstances, because by suggesting that the Congress was frightened, it would cause alarm, and that instead of causing alarm, we should inspire the public with our energy and our unity.

Assuming, as we can, that Juárez did not yet know definitely how far Comonfort had gone towards himself supporting a *golpe de estado*, what can we make of this report, and of the response it received? Well, it assumes a firm leadership, on the part of the President, and at least some power in the hands of Juárez himself, that even then could be doubted. It reveals an optimism, flavored with legalism, that was not appropriate under the circumstances; yet in view of the facts clearly stated by Juárez, the "satisfaction" of the President of the Congress seems even more inappropriate and dangerous.

After a break, the *Diary* for that same day continues: "On receiving instructions to report to him, I noticed in the chief an extraordinary excitement, because he believed that he was being opposed." By whom, and on what account? By a Congress that had a right to know what the situation was? By a Minister whose loyalty to himself in a *pronunciamiento* he rightly doubted?

At this point, before going on with Juárez' account of this critical interview, let us consider a report of what seems clearly to be the same interview, written later by Payno. "One morning" Comonfort called in Juárez and they spoke to each other in the intimate second person. Comonfort explained his troubles and revealed his decision to change his political position.

" 'I knew something,' answered Juárez calmly, 'but since you had said nothing to me, I did not want to say a word to you.'

" 'Well, then,' said Comonfort, 'now I am telling you. We must change our political position, and I want you to take part and go along with me.'

" 'Truly,' Juárez answered him without losing any calm, and as though they were speaking of the simplest thing in the world, 'truly I wish you good luck and much happiness on the road you are going to take, but I shall not go with you.' "

Now Juárez' own version, in his *Diary:*

"Choose whatever side you like," I said, "for I have already chosen mine. I do not believe that we are involved in this, because up to now all steps have been taken within legal limits. In representative governments, interpellations in the legislative body are frequent and ordinary, because they are of the essence of the institution and do not mean an attack on the person of the chief of state."

That afternoon a communication came from the Jury in which it said that the accused Minister's [Payno's] not having obeyed the summons sent him, it asked the government to take steps to have him appear the following day.

The accused said that he would send in his reply in writing.

Juárez apparently thought that there was still some hope of keeping Comonfort within the limits of the law, and was unaware of the sinister influence and power of General Zuloaga. The next day there is no entry in his *Diary*, but the conspirators were more active than the Minister of the Interior and were interested in legal processes only because of the advantage given them by "the law's delay." While Zuloaga and the others prepared for action, Baz, evidently one of those little persons literally intoxicated by unaccustomed knowledge and power, rushed to the Congress and warned that body, with sad accuracy, that it was holding its last session." That night the Plan of Tacubaya was submitted to the President for his approval. He read it and sank on a sofa, exclaiming: 'I have just exchanged my titles as President for those of a miserable revolutionary; but what is done is done, and there is no remedy. I accept everything, and God will show me the way to take.' "

During that night, Zuloaga's brigade entered the city, posted broadsides of the Plan of Tacubaya, and hoisted flags over the public buildings. When Juárez went to work the next morning, there was a reception committee, armed, waiting for him. His diary entry for December 17 is simply this: "I was arrested in the Palace." Payno was assigned the task of keeping watch on him, ostensibly to prevent any attempt on his life. Fuente, Ruiz, Prieto, and others promptly resigned.

Although we do not know now, and probably never shall know, exactly what was done, said, thought, and felt by every man importantly involved in this deplorable collapse of the new government, the main outlines seem clear enough. While most of the *puros* remained in the dark, the conservative opposition to the Constitution hardened around Zuloaga and the troops under his control, and the conflict within Comonfort reduced him to an impotence that he and others blamed on the defects of the Constitution. And it was not merely ignorance of what was going on that paralyzed the *puros*, because it had been apparent to all for many weeks that Comonfort's indecision could hardly result in anything but a collapse of the government. The liberal governors and Juárez himself must have known that they represented, for the time being, at least, a minority of the people probably even smaller than that of the conservatives; that the government's control of the armed forces, and especially of the regular army, was precarious indeed; and that the response of the local forces and of the people to the Constitution as a symbol and banner could not be predicted with any confidence. Comonfort's indecision spread among the *puros* like an infection, and in some of them it was made more feverish by their personal ambitions and by their fear of the return of Santa Anna. The conservatives were able to take advantage of the situation chiefly because, no matter what they said for effect, like Zuloaga that night of November 16 at Tacubaya, what they wanted was the destruction of the Constitution, and they were ready and eager to fight to achieve that end.

Juárez' own behavior from his arrival in Mexico until his arrest, and his motives therefor, will probably be criticized from various points of view for decades to come. Bulnes of course accuses him of failure to do his duty as Minister of the Interior, and of complicity in the "crime"; and even Mr. Roeder sums up an equally critical interpretation by saying that Juárez' arrest was "an accident that saved his political reputation and transformed him from an apparent accessory to the insurrection into its most conspicuous victim." Sierra says: "It seemed to him [Juárez] that the conspiracy hatched between Payno and Zuloaga would never take possession of Comonfort. This accounts for the reassurances he gave the highly alarmed Congress two days before the *golpe de estado*. In his conversations with the President, who knew that Juárez would never side with him, he was in the line of duty, and had implied his line of conduct." The interpretation and judgment already suggested here is that Juárez did not fail in his duty as a Minister because, as he made clear enough to Congress, he had almost no military power, that he did not know until after his report to Congress on December 15 that Comonfort was definitely committed to the *golpe de estado*, and that his inaction was caused by his helplessness in that time and place, and by his incorrigible optimism. Even had he been more ambitious he could not possibly have hoped blandly to succeed to the Presidency merely by doing nothing and allowing events to take their course, simply because he could not have known that Comonfort, still a liberal after his fashion, would in effect save his life by having him arrested and then by releasing him. The only thing that perhaps he could have done, on December 16 if not before, was to gather together those important liberals who were in Mexico City at the time and prepare to unite them and the liberal governors in a defense, military if need be, of the Constitution; yet until there did actually occur a *golpe de estado*, supported by Comonfort, any such action, he may have thought, would be disloyal to his chief. Until he was arrested, Juárez gives the impression of going about his business in something of a daze, wilfully optimistic about Comonfort, but troubled by doubts. Almost always actively and competently attuned to the facts, however hard, of any situation, he seems this time to have withdrawn into his Indian "labyrinth of solitude."

On December 28, 1857, the reactionary generals and brothers, José María and Marcelino Cobos, having come down over the mountains from Tehuacán, via Teotitlán, took part of the city of Oaxaca. On January 16, 1858, Governor José María Díaz Ordaz, Colonel Ignacio Mejía, Captain Porfirio Díaz, and other officers and lawyers trained in the Institute drove the invaders from the city in a bloody engagement that was only the beginning.

While Juárez was imprisoned in the Palace, the wretched Comonfort found himself alone, helpless, and incapable of arriving at any decision. As soon as the *golpe de estado* became known, the response of Manuel Doblado assumed great importance in the minds of those favoring the *golpe*, and also in the minds of those now opposed to it. Comonfort himself and Payno, among the former, and Prieto and others among the latter, all rushed letters and messengers to Doblado, seeking his support and claiming that if he denied it, or even if he gave it, Santa Anna would return and try to take over. Morett in San Luis and Victoriano Zamora in Zacatecas sought Doblado's opinion before committing themselves. Prieto was especially ardent in his appeals to Doblado to take the leadership of the liberal opposition, and indeed, the Presidency. Doblado hesitated, and wrote of coming to some kind of an arrangement with Comonfort, but a firmer mind—at that important moment, at least—intervened. General Anastasio Parrodi, Governor of Jalisco, wrote to Doblado from Guadalajara on January 6, 1858: "We should not listen to any other proposal than that Sr. Comonfort should turn the Presidency over to Sr. Juárez, and that step alone would serve as a basis for any agreement between the dissidents and the coalition, to restore peace and unite all against the supporters of Santa Anna." General Parrodi had already formed a coalition of states to support the Constitution and to recognize Juárez as the constitutional President as soon as he should appear in any of their states. Supporting Parrodi, now, were Governors José Silverio Nuñez of Colima, Manuel Doblado of Guanajuato, José María Díaz Ordaz of Oaxaca, José María Arteaga of Querétaro, Santos Degollado of Michoacán, Juan Álvarez of Guerrero, and Manuel Gutiérrez Zamora of Veracruz.

The reactionaries, for their part, became equally impatient with Comonfort's vacillation and moderation, and on January 11, 1858, they rebelled again, revised their Plan radically to the Right, and demanded Comonfort's resignation. He refused at first to give in, and promptly set free his legal successor, Juárez. Comonfort was then able to muster a few thousand troops in the City, and there followed a few days of sporadic fighting in the streets and from the roofs and towers of buildings, but Comonfort's troops melted away, and on January 21 he and his family took the inevitable road to Veracruz and exile. On January 24, a group of priests and generals swore in Zuloaga as their President. On February 2 Comonfort issued a statement saying that he had frequently thought of resigning in favor of Juárez. On February 7 he embarked for New York.

On hearing of Juárez' imprisonment, Romero, Juárez' young friend and part-time Secretary, tried repeatedly to obtain permission to see him, but did not succeed until January 10, when Comonfort, in the company of Zuloaga, García Conde, and others, allowed Romero to see Juárez, "that one time only." Romero of course did not hear what Comonfort and Zuloaga, about to dine together had to say to each other at that critical moment, and he did not report in his diary the content of his brief conversation with Juárez. Two days later he heard of Juárez' release, but was unable to find out where he had gone. A few days later he took a brief part in the fighting, from a convent tower, under the orders of a young colonel named Ignacio Zaragoza. When the resistance to Zuloaga collapsed, and he still did not know where Juárez and the liberals had gone, he consoled and diverted himself by reading Racine's *Britannicus*. On January 30, at three in the morning, in the company of "Régules, Zaragoza, Fuentes, a spy, and other persons," he took the stagecoach for the north. Between Querétaro and Celaya they fought off bandits, but arrived at Guanajuato the next day. How they handled the spy is not recorded.

More prominent liberals who were in the City at that time were of course in greater danger. Ignacio Ramírez, *El Nigromante*, or The Magician, a brilliant poet, journalist, and professor of law at the Institute in Toluca who had shaken the constitutional congress by proclaiming his atheism, was seized by Tomás Mejía at Arroyozarco and nearly shot, but escaped "because of the bewilderment of the captors themselves." He was imprisoned, but a year later escaped to Veracruz. Santos Degollado, then a justice of the Supreme Court, escaped on horseback, crouching between bundles, was nearly captured, and brazened his way out of it. Prieto, after various hazards, arrived at Querétaro disguised as a muleteer, and was there greeted by Degollado, who informed him that he had been appointed a Minister "to the amazement and delight of his fellow muleteers." Presumably moved, as in the case of Juárez, by loyalty to the old *puros*, or by a last hope of getting their support, Comonfort had relaxed the watch that had been kept on the movements of Ocampo, who was thus able to escape to the north by way of Salvatierra. Miguel Lerdo de Tejada was for a while given refuge in Mexico by John Forsyth, the American Minister, then made his way north and finally to Veracruz. His brother Sebastián calmly returned to his nonpolitical job as Rector of San Ildefonso. There he was not molested, and later he was freed of any imputation that he might have aided the reaction.

And Juárez himself? "On January 11," he notes in his *Diary*, "I was set free, and on the 12th I left Mexico for the hacienda of Chihuahuacán with don Manuel Ruiz and don Nicolás Suárez Pizarro. On the 13th in the afternoon I left in the direction of the hacienda of San José Acolman. I slept in the fields, and on the 14th I arrived at that hacienda. On the 15th I came to Cuautitlán to wait for the carrier of the mail to go to Querétaro. At two in the morning the carriage arrived, I boarded it, and I arrived at Querétaro the same day." Prieto says that at San Juan del Rio, before arriving at Querétaro, they were nearly captured by Mejía, and "owed their salvation to Juárez' incredible coolness." Viramontes says that "at the moment they left that place [Querétaro] the ringing of the bells of the parish church and the salvos of rockets announced that the authorities of the town had adhered to the Plan of Tacubaya." "On the 17th in the afternoon," Juárez continues, "I left Querétaro, and on the 18th at nine in the morning I arrived at Guanajuato, and on the 19th I declared the government established there."

The lines were now clearly drawn for a struggle that had been almost inevitable since the Ley Juárez of November 23, 1855. The reactionaries had gradually begun their war for privilege, and were now ready to fight it ruthlessly to the finish. The liberals were at last united, and Prieto says they were "happy and ardent, made great by events and believing themselves great." Could their leaders remain united; organize, supply, and control armies; and handle effectively and honorably the watchful foreign powers? Could their officers and men, mostly amateurs in warfare, wear down and defeat their enemies, who were mostly professionals? Beneath these questions there was a greater one: could the great, inert mass of the Mexican people—illiterate, hard-working, silent observers of all these alarums, excursions, and bloody brawls of their old masters and their new leaders—could they be aroused by a dream of a great and democratic Mexico, and of a new life for themselves?

As it turned out, this would depend chiefly on the little Indian lawyer from Oaxaca, then still considerably unknown to the masses, who believed only in God, in the people, in the law as their best sword, and in himself as their servant. Benito Juárez, now fifty-one years old, was the constitutional President of Mexico—if one who lacked a capital, a government, funds, and an organized army; but he was still a tough little Indian who knew what he wanted and who could still sleep in the fields and go on from there, indefinitely.

10

THE FUGITIVE PRESIDENT

In GUANAJUATO, the ancient and picturesque mining town in a deep cleft in the central mountains, where there had been struck the first great blow for Mexican independence, Juárez now organized the constitutional government of the Republic. The whisperings about his Presidency having been brushed aside by Parrodi and the other governors, Doblado contented himself with the command of his own troops. Ocampo was made Minister of War, Foreign Affairs, and the Interior; Ruiz was given Justice, Prieto the Treasury, and Leon Guzmán Development, while Parrodi was made Commander-in-Chief. The Ministers shared one another's labors, which consisted in getting whatever news they could from the rest of Mexico, conferring with one another to arrive at decisions, and writing and sending out innumerable letters and messages with hopes that they would arrive and that the orders would be obeyed. They worked in the statehouse and wherever they managed to get rooms and food, and they were assisted by a number of ardent young liberals such as Romero who, like the President and the Ministers themselves, took their chances on getting enough money to live on, and on escaping sudden death long enough to get something accomplished.

On January 19, 1858, Juárez issued a manifesto to the nation, defending the Constitution and condemning those who had attempted to destroy it. "They have invoked the sacred name of our religion, making it serve as an instrument of their illegitimate ambitions, and [they have sought] to destroy at one blow the liberty that Mexicans have won at the cost of sacrifices of every kind." He promised the Mexican people that from that day onward they would be governed neither by one man alone nor by any faction, but under a Constitution and laws that had been established by the general will; he pointed out that he had come into the Presidency under the Constitution; he said that Congress would be assembled as soon as possible; he promised to punish lawbreakers and to secure respect for the Constitution, the laws, and the elected authorities; and he asked for the co-operation of the Mexican people and the protection of Divine Providence. These last supports the government sorely needed, because it had no others except the characters, brains, and wills of Juárez and his little band, and the far from apparent destiny of Mexico as a nascent modern nation.

Meanwhile Zuloaga, although himself only a mediocre professional soldier, had assets more tangible. His government was quickly recognized by the representatives of foreign powers, who had greater freedom to decide than they have now. These representatives included John Forsyth, the Minister of the United States, who wrote to Secretary Lewis Cass that he would find it neither dignified nor agreeable to become a nomadic diplomat in the train of Juárez. Forsyth had other fish to fry with what he considered the stronger government, and he therefore recognized Zuloaga's government on January 27. Zuloaga quickly restored the privileges of the Church and the army that had been eliminated by the Ley Juárez, and also tried to annul the Ley Lerdo. The latter effort was more difficult, and was actually harmful to his own cause, because under this law many properties had already been transferred to influential people. He also swore allegiance to the Holy See, and thereupon received expressions of satisfaction from Pope Pius IX. His government immediately began to appeal to the Church dignitaries for money, and although these hesitated and qualified, they did turn over large sums to the reactionary government. At this time, the forces of Zuloaga, Osollo, Miramón, and Tomás Mejía were much better armed and supplied than the constitutional forces, and they were higher in morale. They began to move northwards.

Imperiled and anxious as the members of the constitutional government undoubtedly were, we must remember that in those days Guanajuato, some 200 miles northwest of Mexico City, was in travel time for men and weapons farther from it than almost any point on the earth is from any other to-day. In his dry, methodical, and humorless diary, almost without images, Romero recorded that besides working, he, his fellow subordinates, and the friendly Ministers did a good deal of sightseeing of the historic granary and other buildings, a mine, the caves, and neighboring mountains; visited bathhouses and barbers; spent many hours of conversation in cafés; and even had time to listen to guitar music, drink toasts to each other, and see three different plays produced in the local theatre.

However, Guanajuato was becoming dangerous, and after dinner on February 12, Juárez stopped Romero. "He said to me that with the Ministers he was going to leave that very night for Guadalajara, and that Prieto would make the arrangements for the travel of the rest of us; he asked me how I found myself fixed for money, and when I said badly, he gave me $10 for food on the road. I said that I wanted to leave as soon as possible, and we said farewell." Prieto, the poet, was to remember everything more vividly and less accurately: "The departure took place at night, in the vehicles called post chaises that I established, and they went this time with their black curtains drawn and with menservants who carried lighted torches at the sides of the convoy, which looked like a funeral procession, and people watched it passing in silence, as though it were the funeral of liberty." Romero and others left three days later, and with an all-night stop at San Juan de los Lagos, the journey to Guadalajara took two days. In the larger city life continued much as in Guanajuato, but Romero, who was never in very good health, had an attack of dysentery, and greater nuisances still pursued him and the itinerant government of the Republic.

Because it has fertile soil and is known as "the breadbasket of Mexico," and because armies can easily cross it, the high central plain known as the Bajío (or sandbank, of several rivers), northwest of Mexico City, has been the scene of fighting in every Mexican war. On March 9 and 10, at Salamanca, largely because of desertions, Parrodi was disastrously defeated by the reactionary General Osollo, and had to withdraw towards Guadalajara with only 3,000 men. Soon after Parrodi's defeat, Doblado and his forces, at Silao, withdrew from the war.

Of the next event in Guadalajara, which is known to every Mexican schoolboy, we are lucky enough to have reports in Romero's diary, written at the time, and in Prieto's memoirs, written much later.

On March 12, after rising early to go out of town with friends to bathe, Romero returned to town, got a haircut, listened to part of a sermon in the cathedral, and at ten went to work in the Ministry of Foreign Affairs, established in the statehouse with the other Ministries. There he heard of the defeat and offered his services anew to Juárez.

Earlier, Juárez had said to Prieto, of the defeat: "Guillermo, our cock has lost a feather!" Seated beside Ocampo at a conference, Juárez "was dressed in his characteristic black frock coat, alert and courteous as always." General José Silverio Nuñez, the military commandant of Guadalajara, was consulted about the defenses of the city, and then Juárez decided to issue a manifesto to the nation, to reassure the people. Prieto was assigned the task of writing a first draft. At this point, Governor Jesús Camarena of Jalisco appeared with the news that Colonel Antonio Landa of the 5th Regiment had rebelled, and that he and his troops were marching on the statehouse. "Sr. Juárez ordered Sr. Nuñez to go and see what was happening and he returned to us, continuing the discussion that had begun." Hurried on by Ocampo, Prieto took some writing materials and started for the house of a friend to do the task assigned.

Meanwhile, Romero, investigating a commotion in the corridors, found himself facing a group of soldiers who were rushing towards him, armed, and crying, "Long live the army! Long live religion!" Romero and others were seized, and some of these bureaucrats were roughed up by the soldiers. Several groups of them, more than seventy in all, were herded together in one room with Ocampo and Juárez. All could hear gunfire and "furious cries" from a prison near by.

On approaching Landa's headquarters, Nuñez had denounced the rebellion, acclaimed the government, and received a blow on his chest from a bullet that was stopped by his watch, in a waistcoat pocket. Probably escorted by captors, he joined the other prisoners in the statehouse and showed them the pieces of his watch.

The poet and Minister of the Treasury was not getting his manifesto written. On leaving the building, he found himself in the midst of bloody riot. With others, he was seized and thrown into a dark little anteroom. Through a keyhole, he saw in the patio "the most frightful chaos," with prisoners, armed with shackles and daggers, letting themselves down from the windows of the adjoining prison, led by "a priest of ferocious appearance." Some of those with Prieto escaped, but he felt honor-bound to break out, find the leaders of the mutiny in that place, and tell them that he wished to share the fate of Sr. Juárez. When he did this he was knocked down and kicked in the head, and then thrown into the room with Juárez and Ocampo. "Juárez was deeply agitated. Ocampo rebuked me for not having escaped, but was also deeply moved, because he honored me with his tender affection."

Prieto's narrative gives the impression that the crisis came that same day, but Romero's diary shows clearly that it did not. During that afternoon and evening some of the prisoners were released or escaped, and a little food was brought in. As the firing continued, the captives learned that the state forces, under Governor Camarena and Sr. Contreras Medellín, the political prefect, installed in neighboring churches, were fighting the mutineers. At 11:30 that night, one of the mutinous officers asked Juárez to order the surrender of the state forces. "This request he denied in a dignified and decorous manner," saying that as a prisoner he could not issue any commands. They passed a cold and hungry night.

At dawn, the firing was renewed, but during the morning Juárez, his Ministers, and their guards had another idea. Still prisoners under guard, Ocampo and Nuñez delivered a message to Governor Camarena, requesting him to effect an armistice of six days. However, before this could be done, the state forces still unaware of this move attacked the statehouse itself, and this made the mutineers holding the prisoners think they had been betrayed. Furious, they decided to kill their prisoners. A squad appeared and raised their rifles. "Sr. Juárez," as Prieto remembered it, "was in the door of the inner room: at the word 'Aim!' he took hold of the latch of the door, raised his head, and waited." At this moment, Prieto rushed forward, covered Juárez with his body, and cried: "Put up your arms! Put up your arms! Brave men are not assassins!" He poured out a torrent of words, and finally the soldiers withdrew. "Juárez embraced me . . . my comrades surrounded me, calling me their savior and the savior of the Reform . . . my heart broke out in a tempest of tears." Romero's report is drier: ". . . and at that moment Prieto came out of the room to the right and said some things, whereupon the soldiers went out into the corridor."

Aware that the state forces might overcome them, and that Parrodi's army was approaching, the mutineers now lost their nerve. The armistice was effected, Ocampo and Nuñez returned to the statehouse, and negotiations were continued. In the end, the prisoners were escorted to sanctuary in the house of the French Vice-Consul, a Hanoverian named William Augspurg, and the next day were freed. The manifesto to the nation was then finally issued. Juárez' entire narrative of this affair in his *Diary* follows: "On the 13th the guard of the palace mutinied and I was taken prisoner by order of Landa, who led the mutiny. On the 15th I was set free."

Parrodi and his army arrived on the 18th, and although Ocampo had made preparations for all to go to Tepic, Parrodi convinced Juárez that it would be better to go to Colima. After much bustling about by all hands, to share what little money was available and buy horses—Romero got one with saddle and bridle for $18—and equipment, the government left Guadalajara at 3:30 A.M. on the 20th, with an escort of 75 infantrymen and 30 cavalrymen under the command of General Francisco Iniestra, whose cool-headed second in command was one Captain Leandro Valle. This young officer, the son of an insurgent officer of distinction, was also a poet who had recently returned from military and other studies in Paris. Naturally he became friendly with a French liberal and soldier of fortune named Aquiles, or Achille, Collin, and both were happy to discuss political and social theories and the works of Proudhon, in French, in this odd context, with Ocampo. Juárez, Ruiz, and Prieto rode in a calash, and the rest on horseback.

At nine, their breakfast stop was hurried because they received a report that Landa, with a much larger force than their own, was on their trail. They hurried on to the village of Santa Ana Acatlán, under a ridge, arriving there at about 3:00 P.M. The civilians were resting in the small inn of the village when, at 4:30, Landa attacked. Iniestra placed his soldiers in and on the roofs of the inn, the house next to it, and the church opposite, and with the help of the civilians, beat off the attack.

At one point, Collin, on a rooftop, noted the position of an enemy sharpshooter, borrowed a rifle from a soldier, and when the sharpshooter's head became visible for a moment, shot him dead. Then he continued to walk back and forth, smoking. Ocampo, who was standing near by, surprised Collin by congratulating him, whereupon Collin replied: "Señor, a man is always a man. How is it that you, one of the great advocates of justice, a fervent apostle of democracy, can congratulate me for having killed a man?" Ocampo replied: "It is not because you have killed a man: on the contrary, it is because you saved many by making this one victim, in urgent necessity, without hatred and without pride."

However, as the afternoon passed, the situation became less comfortable. Writing eight years later, to correct a story that he had offered to give himself up in order to save the rest, Juárez wrote the following:

With regard to the event at Santa Ana Acatlán, I ought to say that after the fight had broken off, between our little force and that of Lieutenant Colonel Landa, General Iniestra, commanding the escort, told me that if the enemy undertook an assault, our loss would be inevitable, because our ammunition was being consumed, the building in which we were was extremely weak, and the enemy had about 600 men and two pieces of artillery, while we had no more than seventy men. He reported this to me so that I should think of some method of saving myself, and so that I should give him precise orders for the fulfillment of his duty. I told the Ministers what Sr. Iniestra had just told me, and I told them that in my opinion they and the employees who formed our party could leave that place, taking every precaution to be unseen by the enemy, and hide themselves in some of the houses of the town, or else take to the fields in order to escape from the consequences of an assault that the enemy would undoubtedly make later in the afternoon or at dawn of the next day; that I should remain to share the fate of our forces, and that the means of escape that I suggested to them would not be unbecoming, because since they did not exercise any military command at the time, and since they were not required to remain constantly and obligatorily at my side in a situation in which nothing could be done in any branch of the government, they did not have the same strict duty that

I had to remain at their posts under the circumstances. However, they answered me in an energetic and decided manner that they would not accept my suggestion, whatever might be the fortune that came upon us. I thanked them and decided that if during the rest of the afternoon we did not suffer an attack, we should take advantage of the night to break out of the siege: the only plausible method of escape that remained to us. The order was given to Sr. Iniestra, and we renewed our march at eleven that night.

Prieto later wrote a characteristically emotional report of this scene, and in his diary, Romero does not mention it at all. He observed the firing from the door and roof of the inn, counted thirteen killed and five wounded among the enemy and one killed in the escort, noted that they had supper at 7:30, and described their withdrawal in a column of fours and then twos, with the escort ahead and behind. Some said that Landa withdrew before they did, others that he did so afterwards. Once more his uncertainty had been very fortunate. The party marched all night, and Romero, suffering in his stomach and head, was wretched. When they arrived at dawn at a friendly *hacienda*, he fell into the first bed he saw. It was March 21, and Juárez' fifty-second birthday. A crowd of Indians appeared, bearing wreaths of flowers, dancing to the sound of small drums, and crying *"Viva el Presidente! Viva Juárez!"* However, at two in the afternoon, the party saddled their horses and went onwards. They were again greeted with jubilation in the evening, but, noted Romero, "we were feeling the reaction to what had happened the day before."

They crossed a mountain range and then descended into beautiful valleys ever more tropical, but they had to cross steep ravines and accept gladly whatever food and shelter they could find, often sleeping on mats on the ground. At Sayula and Zapotlán (now Guzmán) they were warmly received by politicians and the people, but in the latter town and in Colima, where they arrived March 25, they heard the staggering news that Parrodi had surrendered, with all his forces, at Guadalajara. The entire force of the constitutional government now consisted of 350 soldiers and two pieces of artillery. At Colima, Juárez named Degollado Minister of War and Commander-in-Chief, with wide powers to tax, organize armies, and carry on the war. He may have done so with a sardonic smile, but perhaps not: Sr. Valadés suggests that these men had the ingenuousness of mystics, a formidable power. At Colima, they all wrote letters furiously, Romero tried to get his precious *Table* published and ran errands, such as buying a leather cigar case for Juárez, and they all bathed in the river and even saw a play by the Spaniard Bretón, appropriately called *No ganamos para sustos,* or *We Don't Earn Enough to Be Frightened.*

At Colima, however, Juárez received from Governor Manuel Gutiérrez Zamora an invitation to move the government to Veracruz, and he decided to accept it. That city was full of vigorous liberals like the Governor, it was hard to attack from Mexico City because of the fever-infested lowlands that surrounded it, and last but far from least, as a major seaport, it had customs receipts that were not entirely mortgaged to the British and could help support the liberal government and armies—of the future. There was some question whether it would be wise to allow the ailing Romero to take the risks of the journey with the government, but on Romero's insistence, Juárez allowed him to accompany them. Leaving Degollado, Iniestra, and others in Colima to organize an army as well as they could, Juárez and his party left Colima on April 8 and arrived at Manzanillo the next day.

At that romantic if dirty little seaport, where the mountains come down to the sea, they rested and even frolicked for two days, playing billiards, trying unsuccessfully to inspect the two English men-of-war anchored there, and staring fascinated at the phosphorescent surf and sand. Prieto was ill, and Ocampo and Juárez made a chair of their arms and hands to carry him down to the beach: a triumph for this hero-worshiper that he remembered with pride twenty-one years later. "At that time," he wrote, "Manzanillo was an almost deserted beach, full of fever, and the so-called mercantile center was a tent inhabited by two Germans who interrupted their sleep only to drink tons of beer or to make their excursions to the customs house." Some of them went outside the harbor in a small boat, which made Romero very seasick, but he alone went swimming because, he says, the others were unnecessarily afraid of the sharks.

On April 11 there appeared the large and crowded American

steamer *John L. Stephens*, they all secured passage of sorts, and she got under way the same day, bound for Acapulco and Panama. Romero was horribly seasick on the entire voyage, and was unable, among other things, to attend a banquet given Juárez and his party by passengers who were sympathetic with his ideas. On the 12th they all went ashore briefly at Acapulco, and after a conference, decided to go on to Panama and Veracruz. On the 19th they all disembarked at Panama and made a three-hour crossing of the isthmus by railroad to Colón, where they took passage to New Orleans via Havana in the steamer *Granada*. On the 25th they changed to the *Philadelphia*, for New Orleans, where they arrived on the 28th. Romero was impressed by the city, but shocked by the slave market. On May 1 they embarked in the *Tennessee* for Veracruz, where they arrived on May 4. Juárez noted in his diary that the various passages from Manzanillo had cost a total of $315, that he had received only $400 of his salary in Mexico, and $2,198 since then, and that he, unlike the Ministers and employees, had received no travel allowance.

However, the twenty-one shots from the Castle of San Juan de Ulúa were fired as a salute to the President, and not in an attempt to assassinate him and his cabinet. For a while, at least, they had a capital—or more accurately, a command post.

11

THE BLOWS FOR LIBERTY

A LARGE AND CHEERING CROWD was on hand as the President and his Ministers and other civil servants were escorted to the cathedral to attend a *Te Deum*, which was followed by a reception at the house provided by the state. Juárez was of course given the best room, but he chose another that adjoined the bath. When he asked a servant for hot water, she mistook him for a servant of the President and Ministers and told him tartly to wait on himself. This he did without another word. The next morning at breakfast, when she saw him at the head of the table, she ran off, crossing herself, and Juárez and the Ministers all had a good laugh.

On May 14, Justo Benítez, one of Juárez' young lawyer friends in Oaxaca, wrote to him in Veracruz, congratulating him on his arrival there, and in the most charming manner requesting permission to join Juárez and serve him and the liberal cause in any way he could. At the end of his letter he writes: "The Señora and your children are well and Beno has developed admirably."

The Señora Margarita then did something that has received little attention but that proves her to have been quite as hardy, morally and physically, as her Indian husband. She was then thirty-two years old and had eight children ranging down in age from the fourteen-year-old Manuela to a baby in arms. She took them across the mountains from Oaxaca to Veracruz, to join her husband and their father. Shunning the only actual roads, via Puebla, because that would have made easy the seizure or molestation of herself and her family by the reactionaries, she went by way of Cualimulco, across the mountains. The distance from Oaxaca to Veracruz by air is about 150 miles, and by mountain trails it must approach twice that distance.

On these mountain trails, a heavy truck or a double-traction jeep can get into trouble to-day, and in 1858 no vehicle could travel on them. Almost certainly doña Margarita scraped together the money to buy at least six burros and pairs of baskets to hang over their backs to carry the children and a minimum of luggage, including food, and it seems likely that the nine of them were accompanied by two or three horny-footed burro men with machetes and revolvers, men of proven loyalty and resource. The trip took a month, and they must have slept on mats in the huts of friendly Indians. Perhaps doña Margarita sang to her children and told them stories of their father's boyhood in those mountains, that he had told her alone. Probably the children, mostly girls and we may assume tomboys, found the expedition a wonderful lark, but their mother, alert to hard-looking men, wild animals, and any sickness of the babies from many possible causes, must have had some heart-stopping moments on that trip, before they found the big house in Veracruz, and her "beloved Juárez," and stopped for a little while his anxiety about them.

Veracruz, "the heroic city," was and is a picturesque seaport and small city, then walled, very hot and humid most of the time, but afflicted by cold northern winds in the autumn and winter. The richer people, many of whom are still Spaniards, display themselves in the cafés under the portals, and are gravely watched by solitary ship captains and merchants from all over the world. The band plays in the plaza—which at that time was much quieter, the only vehicles being carts and carriages and the litters or two-wheeled traps of very elegant ladies fanning themselves. It was also darker in the evenings, with only torches, lamps, and candles, and with beggars and thieves waiting in the shadows. The palm trees rattle in the hot breezes, and sailors come ashore looking for liquor, food, and women—all plentiful. Armies, navies, and governments come and go, while angry men argue and fight for liberty and peace, and women, grieving and sceptical, wash and bury the dead. Incense rises continually to "Mary, the conqueror of Mexico," while plenty of young and old men swear they will have none of *that*. And always the repulsive vultures stalk and flap their way about, cleaning up the garbage and the carcasses.

Juárez and his Ministers had three main jobs to do, and each affected the other two. The first was to keep the constitutional armies manned, paid, fed, and supplied with arms and ammunition. Funds were extremely short, and this job often had to be left for the most part to governors and generals who had ambitions and vanities of their own and were only very lightly bound by loyalty, discipline, and political conviction to their civilian superiors. The second was to govern those parts of Mexico over which they had some measure of control, through the governors and the roving armies, in such a way as to take revenues away from the opposing government while giving any Mexicans committed to liberty and the future rather than to privilege and the past a sense that this was their own government, of their own nation, and one worth obeying and fighting for. In this effort their greatest asset was the tenacity, vision, and moral force of Juárez, who was actually to be aided, if at terrible cost to the people and himself, by the foreign intervention. He became a symbol and a catalytic agent, as well as an active force, around which there began very slowly to grow that chiefly psychological and moral fact, a modern democracy. The third was to fight off peaceably and honorably, and even to try to win the sympathy and aid of, the powerful foreign governments to which Mexico was indebted to a paralyzing degree, and which kept sending in warships that were usually threatening and diplomats who were usually intolerably presumptuous. A fourth job, nagging and subtle, at which Juárez was alone a master, was that of keeping these variously able but temperamental men working together as a *government* that functioned and had to be respected.

On the military side, the war was very fluid and confused. In general, the reactionary government held the central states and Mexico City, with forces that were better organized and supplied than those of the constitutional government and that were successful in seizing, for a time, Guadalajara, San Luis Potosí, Tampico, Puebla, and the cities of the Bajío. Among their generals, they had, besides Miguel Miramón and Tomás Mejía, a skillful and ruthless hoodlum named Leonardo Márquez. In pitched battles, these reactionaries usually won, but they did not have enough men to control the whole nation, and when they had to withdraw from any point, the swarm-

ing constitutional armies, made up chiefly of redoubtable guerrilla
fighters, flowed back into the vacated areas. Santos Degollado had
little tactical skill, but he had almost incredible ability in organizing
armies in a hurry. Santiago Vidaurri had an important following in
the northeast, and was usually up to something, but Juárez could
neither be sure that that something was quite loyal to the government nor brush the man off. Old Juan Álvarez still held Guerrero,
but his support of the government was otherwise disappointing. In
Oaxaca, Porfirio Díaz was already making his mark as a daring and
talented soldier, loyal to the government, but that state, and through
it Juárez also, was plagued and weakened by continued internal dissensions among the liberals themselves. In the third year there rose
up on the liberal side three other able soldiers, Ignacio Zaragoza,
Leandro Valle, and Jesús González Ortega. The last-named was
comparable to Doblado (who continued to sit out most of the war)
in that he had ability and prestige—and in his case, good luck—but
also an abounding ego.

Of all the numerous local problems, those in Oaxaca naturally
touched Juárez most closely. After the victory of the liberals over
Cobos in January, 1858, they split into two groups, one of lawyers,
more conservative, called the *Borlados*—satirically, the ones with
doctors' hoods—led by or using Juárez' personal friend Miguel Castro, and the other of *puros*, or *jacobinos*, led by Díaz Ordaz and
Marcos Pérez. At the end of 1858 and beginning of 1859, the reactionary Cobos, who had been defeated in January, 1858, attacked
again from the north. At first, because of bad support and poor
co-ordination of his forces, Díaz Ordaz was defeated, and the *Borlados*, unfortunately with the support of Juárez, who had been ill
informed, deprived him of both his command and the governorship,
to which he had been legally elected on the expiration of Juárez'
term, and made Castro Governor. Juárez sent in two out-of-state but
loyal colonels, and gave the command to the Oaxacan Colonel Ignacio Mejía, who in turn was defeated, so that the reactionaries took
the city of Oaxaca, and the state government had to withdraw to
the mountains. At this time, Díaz Ordaz went to Veracruz to present
his case to Juárez, who reviewed it, recognized the injustice of his
previous position, and restored Díaz Ordaz to power in Oaxaca.

Díaz Ordaz then defeated Cobos at Tlacolula, but was killed just after the end of the action, possibly by the *Borlados* themselves. The internal difficulties, too complex for narration here, continued, and Juárez sent in Manuel Ruiz to try to settle them, but he had no great success; and Oaxaca, as productive of internal dissension and street fighting as of talent and heroism, must have caused the greatest Oaxacan endless and acute anxiety.

However, as time went on, the reactionaries too had plenty of troubles of their own. Zuloaga's restoration of strongly centralized government, complete with spies, his suppression of the press, his attempts to restore lands already sold under the Ley Lerdo, his increasing demands on the clergy, and his confiscatory taxes, all were unpopular, even with the conservatives. In December, 1858, and January, 1859, following a rebellion by the conservative General Echeagaray and brief control by Manuel Robles Pezuela, whose attempts to subvert various liberals were thwarted by Juárez, Miguel Miramón became President of the reactionary government.

In February, 1859, Miramón made the inevitable attack on Veracruz, but his expedition had weakened the conservative forces elsewhere, so that the constitutional armies regained several cities in the north, and Degollado was able to organize and supply a force in Morelia and march towards Mexico City. In March, threatened from the rear and his forces weakened by malaria and yellow fever, Miramón abandoned his siege of Veracruz and beat a retreat to Mexico City. There, Márquez had been pursuing Degollado, and at least partly because Degollado handled his men and supplies badly, Márquez routed him at Tacubaya on April 11, and captured his arms and supplies. When Miramón arrived in the city, he ordered Márquez to shoot commanding and other officers among the prisoners, and Márquez was quite happy to go beyond this and shoot many more, including medical students who had appeared to aid the wounded in both armies. Other civilians, including children, were also murdered. For this act of barbarism, outstanding even in a war that was becoming steadily more savage, the liberals called Márquez "the Tiger of Tacubaya." However, riding with Mejía in a triumphant parade, Márquez wore a sash that had been presented to him by a committee of ladies, and on this sash was the inscription: "To virtue and valor:

the gratitude of the daughters of Mexico." The military victories of the reaction continued through 1859, and these had a marked effect both on Juárez' foreign relations and on his measures of reform. It is not, however, necessary to consider these battles in detail.

With the exception of the final military victory that of course was necessary for any political and social advance, the greatest achievement of Juárez and his government in this war consisted in the decrees of reform issued first at Veracruz, on various dates from July, 1859, to February, 1861. The general program of the Reform, going much farther than these specific decrees, was projected in the manifesto of July 7, 1859.

It had long been apparent to the liberals that although the Ley Juárez and the Ley Lerdo had aroused violent opposition, and when incorporated in the Constitution of 1857 had played no small part in frightening Comonfort, inciting the reactionaries to rebellion, and producing the *golpe de estado*, the Reform had by no means been completed; and that in the middle of a war that was already a brutal war of religion, the Reform could not reasonably be further delayed on the ground that the response of the opposition would again be violent. In Juárez' view, however, he was fighting a war for the Constitution, legality, and order, to be based as soon as possible on the will of the majority of the people and their elected representatives, and *not* a war against the Church, except insofar as the Church used and supported illegal and violent means to defend and regain its wealth, its political power, and its privileges. The Indian Juárez and his friend the intellectual but humane and earthy aristocrat, Ocampo, knew the Mexican people better, and respected more sincerely their religion, and their love of all the old ways, than did the bourgeois lawyer Miguel Lerdo de Tejada, or Manuel Ruiz, or Santos Degollado, and they were both sufficiently empirical and practical, after the partial fiasco of the Ley Lerdo, to have doubts about the wisdom and efficacy of decrees that seemed clearly just and necessary but would probably be misunderstood by the people. Also, Ocampo disliked Lerdo and mistrusted his personal ambition. So these two key figures, Juárez and Ocampo, hesitated, while the others grew impatient. After his defeat at Tacubaya, Degollado rushed to Veracruz to urge more reform laws, and on June 25 and

July 5, only a few days before the publication of the first decrees, Miguel Lerdo, then Minister of the Treasury and of Development, became so annoyed that he tried to resign, but Juárez answered him with his usual calm, refusing to accept his resignation and assuring him that they had already agreed to go ahead. The government sorely needed money, Juárez was still a determined reformer, and he was ready to cripple the opposition in any way that offered itself and that might be accepted in time by most of the people. Above all, Juárez was no Comonfort: he knew what he wanted: a democratic Mexico achieved with as little bloodshed as possible. The nature of his final decision was best summed up when he said: "Better one war than two," meaning one war for the Constitution and another for the Reform. Juárez' action in issuing these decrees was closely parallel, therefore, to that of Lincoln, three years later, in issuing the Emancipation Proclamation.

In these historic and momentous decrees, all Church properties except actual buildings used for religious services and instruction, and their contents, were confiscated and nationalized. This act importantly corrected the defective and destructive Ley Lerdo by going beyond the sale of Church lands, and by distinguishing between these properties and the Indian communal lands. If belatedly, the government took steps after the war to restore some of these to their proper owners. This measure released the economy from strangulation by the Church, and today even Church buildings are legally owned by the federal government. All monasteries were suppressed at once, and nunneries gradually—but this step was primarily economic, a necessary result of the seizure of their property and hence incomes. Nunneries still exist in private, so to speak—the nuns cannot wear their costumes on the streets—and nuns still do much of the teaching and nursing in Mexico, while the Church quietly opposes public education, but their activities as teachers are to a certain extent inspected and controlled by the government.

Cemeteries were nationalized, and more important, births and marriages were made civil events, otherwise legally unrecognized. When Juárez' daughter Francisca was born in Veracruz, soon after the publication of this decree, Juárez registered her birth at once, as an example, and that is the first entry in the first book of the kind in Veracruz, where it is reverently preserved in the city hall. It is probable that Ocampo, who carefully reared four daughters without being married, wrote this decree, and it is certain that he wrote *La Epistola de Melchor Ocampo*, a noble exhortation to brides and bridegrooms, on understanding, tolerance, and loyalty in marriage that, in accordance with the law, is read at civil marriage ceremonies in Mexico and other Latin American countries. Some control of holidays and also of religious *fiestas* was also given to the government, in an attempt to lessen the interruptions of work.

Probably the most important of all these decrees, and the one that alone would have established Juárez' greatness, was the one making Church and state independent and separate and guaranteeing complete religious liberty. This decree was confirmed by law and by the later Constitution of 1917, and it is still fully enforced. The Church still opposes it with quiet tenacity, especially in places on the high central plateau, where Protestant proselytizing by foreigners would be foolish and dangerous.

From this passage in Juárez' letter to Santacilia in New Orleans, dated July 12, 1859, in Veracruz, it seems clear that Juárez knew the importance of his act: "I take pleasure in sending you the decree that I have just issued. As you will see, the most important part of it is the absolute independence of the civil power, and religious liberty. For me, these points are capital ones that should be conquered in this revolution, and if we achieve victory, we shall have the satisfaction of having done something good for my country and for humanity."

Of course the reactionaries, led by Archbishop Garza and Father Miranda, objected violently. The sales of Church lands were slow, and often probably unjust, in that purchasers gained more than the government, but the government did eventually increase its income somewhat in this manner, although just how much money was taken in does not seem now to be known. The notable fact is that during the century that has passed since these decrees, the numerous and violent critics of Juárez, for every possible reason, have hardly even suggested, and not begun to prove, that he or any one of his associates profited personally by these transactions. Every one of them died a relatively poor man. After these decrees, there occurred in the churches a good many lootings and sacrileges, but no army has ever been formed of gentlemen only. The animosity of the devout towards Juárez that resulted from these decrees has persisted strongly down into our own time, and it has probably been the actual motive of many of the numerous accusations that in their official dealings with the United States, Juárez and Ocampo were traitors to their country.

We turn now to these transactions, which are extraordinarily interesting in themselves, and which raise questions that are still very much alive to-day, all over the world.

12

THE CASE OF THE DUBIOUS TREATY

NEXT CAME A DIPLOMATIC DRAMA that to this day has been seized upon with savage delight by the Mexican enemies of the United States and detractors of Juárez (usually the same persons), that has disturbed the admirers of Juárez and Ocampo probably too much, and that has disturbed us Americans far too little, chiefly because most of us have known nothing about it.

In 1856, James Buchanan of Pennsylvania, a Democrat, was elected to the Presidency, and of the fairly numerous holders of that office whom the country could not afford, he remains outstanding. In the House and Senate, as Minister to Russia and Great Britain, and as Polk's Secretary of State during the war with Mexico, he had shown himself both indecisive on the great domestic issue of slavery and an aggressive bungler in foregn affairs; and when he became President, the powers and responsibilities of that office made him even more dangerous. He had long wanted to acquire Cuba, and with regard to Mexico, our stealing half of that country had not satisfied him: he now wanted Lower California, a great part of northwestern Mexico, and exhaustive rights over the Isthmus of Tehuantepec. His Secretary of State was a retired general named Lewis Cass.

Their Minister to Mexico, John Forsyth, like his successors, fancied himself a liberal, but had his orders to extort what he could, and as we have seen, on January 27, 1858, with this end in view, before receiving Ocampo's protests, he rather hastily recognized the government of Zuloaga. Forsyth arrogantly badgered Zuloaga's Foreign Minister, Luis G. Cuevas, and when Zuloaga's government decreed something resembling a forced loan, Forsyth, trying to produce a crisis that would facilitate his attempt at extortion, took the outrageous step of advising American citizens in Mexico who would be affected by the decree to disobey it. Rebuked by Cuevas, Forsyth broke off relations and was recalled. However, he chose to remain in Mexico until October, giving refuge to Miguel Lerdo de Tejada and hiding for the liberals forty-six bars of silver made from the objects that General Epitacio Huerta had stolen from the cathedral of Morelia.

President Buchanan now shifted his felonious attentions to the constitutional government in Veracruz, which had just sent Ocampo's son-in-law, José María Mata, as Minister to Washington. Mata had a talk with one J. M. Cazneau, a friend of the President's, who then wrote to him, Buchanan, the following letter, dated June 5, 1858:

Mr. Mata, whom I named the other day as the Minister of President Juárez, is now here awaiting an interview. He has I believe full powers to raise funds by any means short of alienating territory.

It has been suggested that a free transit at Tehuantepec, with all but free ports at the termini, might be worth a million of dollars to the United States, and that another million expended under the joint supervision of the two republics in improving these free harbors would open that splendid country to the right class of settlers.

If any other nation is willing to pay for similar concessions, there need be no objection, for neither money nor navies can buy the *power of proximity*.

Another million will secure the like advantage of way on the northern frontier, with neutral territory down to 28° N. L., under conditions amounting to sale.

Two millions will give us two free highways to the Pacific and put Juárez in the City of Mexico. Once there, he is pledged to a policy that saves Cuba.

The points I have now stated will be confirmed by Mr. Mata and the Juárez government.

It should be noted that this unsavory letter is full of innuendoes, rather than explicit reports, about the position of Mata and Juárez. It should be read in conjunction with a report made to Juárez by Mata from Washington on July 2, of an interview he had with President Buchanan the day before, and of another interview with

Secretary Cass on the day of his report. This letter shows that Cazneau, and certainly others, had sharpened Buchanan's appetite, but it does not support the implication that Juárez was grovelling and approaching treason in his hunger for American money.

President Buchanan, Mata reports, asked him "a multitude of questions," took notes on the members of the constitutional government, manifested a great interest in Tehuantepec, "showed the greatest sympathy for our cause," urged him to remain in Washington until Forsyth's withdrawal from Mexico had been confirmed, because after that, he, the President, "could do something effective in our behalf," asked for his credentials, said that he would read in English the articles of the Mexican constitution giving Juárez authority as President, and told Mata to call on Secretary Cass.

With this second interview, Mata was disappointed. It was shorter and less intimate, and although the Secretary wished Juárez' government well, he was disposed not to intervene in Mexican questions. When Mata urged that Juárez was President in fact and in law, and that since Forsyth's error in recognizing Zuloaga's government had been acknowledged, it could be repaired at once, the Secretary's reply was very vague.

Mata then discusses the problem more generally. Buchanan wanted a great deal, not only in Tehuantepec, but also railroad rights in the northwest of Mexico. "I told him that I believed you would be willing to sanction any treaty that was based on principles of justice and was to the advantage of both countries. For my part, I consider it to the interest of Mexico to make those treaties, if in them the government of the United States binds itself to recognize and maintain in those transits the sovereignty of Mexico, and only in those treaties do I see a means of suppressing the filibustering spirit so prevalent in the southern states, and precisely in those closest to us. Along with those treaties, another could be arranged in which the American government would guarantee a loan to the Mexican government in which the money could be had at the very low rate of interest of 5% annually; and thus we should ally the two countries and governments physically and morally and bring to an end the rebellions in our unhappy country." He then asks for further instructions, although he does not wish to remain in the United States.

"Perhaps I am deceiving myself," he continues, "but I am convinced that Mexico is necessarily allied with this country, and that in order to preserve our independence and nationality, it is necessary to adopt a policy that is based on fully liberal principles, that will serve the reciprocal interests of both countries, and that will permit the two peoples to come in contact with each other, so that they may know and appreciate each other better, and so that one country will lose its spirit of aggression and the other its mean distrust and absurd resistance. In any case, I think the liberal party should adopt this new policy, which is not only the salvation of the country but is also implicit in the principles we proclaim. . . . Here, the chief desire is to acquire by purchase another part of our territory. This is the motive that trapped Forsyth into recognizing Zuloaga. In view of this tendency, which borders on mania, it has seemed to me necessary to make it clear in all our conferences that although we are disposed to make concessions that are just, and that are advantageous to the development and security of American interests, in no case and for no reason should we consider the alienation of a palm's width of our territory."

Although we do not have Juárez' answer to this letter, it seems clear enough from their later communications and decisions that Juárez and Ocampo supported its views in general, although with good reason Juárez became increasingly distrustful of the United States and wary in his negotiations. Here we see foreshadowed all the later negotiations between the Buchanan administration, voracious and ruthless, and the Juárez administration, hard pressed and therefore too optimistic about American intentions.

In December, 1858, in a message to Congress, Buchanan said he hoped to get more out of the constitutional government in Mexico than he ever could from the reactionaries, and asked Congress for the right to invade—or, as he put it, to establish military posts in Sonora and Chihuahua. These threats, disguised as attempts to pacify Mexico, and to prevent European intervention, were repeated in subsequent messages. On December 27 Buchanan sent a Mr. William M. Churchwell as a special agent to Juárez' government, to ascertain more directly just how much he could get. (There is evidence that at the same time Buchanan considered briefly a parallel but necessarily secret approach to the reactionaries.) Churchwell landed at Veracruz on January 19, made a quick tour of some inland cities, and reported to Secretary Cass that probably everything the Buchanan administration wanted in Mexico could now be acquired. Miramón was then about to make his first attack on Veracruz. On February 22 Churchwell wrote to President Buchanan, from Veracruz, a letter accompanying a memorandum that has disappeared, and in a later summary of this memorandum, given to Churchwell's successor, McLane, it is asserted that Ocampo, in the name of Juárez, has promised the sale of Lower California, and transit rights to that gulf and also across the Isthmus of Tehuantepec. Whether Ocampo ever made exactly such a promise may be doubted, but the covering letter is itself most interesting:

President Juárez is a man of some forty-five years of age, a full blooded Indian, well versed in the laws of his country, a prudent and sound juriconsult, but a distrustful and timid politician, austere and incorruptible, yet of a mild and benignant disposition, in his intercourse modest as a child. He has his voice in the council, and is listened to with respect, but he has no influence over his Ministers and is unconsciously perhaps under their most absolute and unlimited control.

Ocampo is a gentleman of great native intellect, and of considerable parts and learning, inflexible in his resolves, peremptory in his views, rather prompt in discourse and impatient of contradiction; but highminded, honest, and like his Chief, incorruptible.

[Miguel] Lerdo de Tajada [sic] (who is in the Cabinet by the suggestion of your agent) has all the brilliant qualities of the other two, is as pure as they, but possesses more of the practical habit, which constitutes a mind turned towards the actualities of life, rather than towards its dreams.

He is the most popular man among his party, and deservedly considered as the master spirit of the Cabinet. His tendencies are all American; he is the best informed statesman of the political and commercial history and progress of his country.

We should look up to him as the man most reliable in his preferences for us; frank, open, bold, and always ready to approach a question, and to assume a responsibility.

I found them somewhat dispirited on my arrival: they had been made to believe that the U.S. would not take any decided course, but now they seem like new beings, and manifest sincere and earnest friendship.

Churchwell next argues for the inclusion in any treaty of a provision for the extinction of Mexico's crippling debt to Britain from any funds obtained from the United States. Such a provision, he argues, would free Mexico from British meddling and "invite support on the part of England, in favor of any arrangement the U.S. might enter into with Mexico.

"In the present demoralized condition of this country," he continues, "with its eight millions of people degenerate and degenerating, no course can be adopted but one that will give the U.S. an effective but indirect Protectorate, exercising by advice and moral aid, through their officials, our beneficial influence, and thus prepare gradually and well for a result which may well be deemed of doubtful import: but one which sooner or later, will have to be met. If the Constitutional Party are restored to power, we can have much to do with regulating their policy, by careful and prudent council. Their principles are daily becoming more popular, and the recognition of the U.S. it is believed would soon place them again in possession of the Capital."

Churchwell then says that Juárez' government is intent on the separation of Church and state, estimates the Church's wealth at $300,000,000, which will be nationalized; says Mexico's domestic and foreign debt is $120,000,000; dilates on the natural resources of Mexico; and says that at least $100,000,000 has been hidden away. All these figures were wild guesses. "The Programme of the Constitutional Government under Juárez has been submitted to me, in the most confidential manner. It was drawn up by Mr. Lerdo de Tajada [*sic*]. Throughout it is eminently liberal. From it a few extracts for your eye alone have been taken, that you may understand their policy. They show every confidence in us, and seem to regard our Government as their natural friend and ally, in the great cause of constitutional liberty which they are battling for with so much zeal." He encloses a public document by Ocampo, explaining his recent settlement with English and French naval commanders, who had been exigent about their governments' liens on the customs. He reports that Miramón has been allowed to get near Veracruz, so that his retreat may be cut off. "I feel more certain of the success of the Constitutional Government," he concludes, "than when I prepared my report."

Reading this letter, we can only hope, with a shudder, that American diplomats are everywhere to-day more accurate and less arrogant than those sent to Mexico a century ago. Churchwell missed Juárez' age by eight years, but he did not come even that close in judging his character. If he actually attended a cabinet meeting, which seems very doubtful, he must have been misled by the animated chatter of the Ministers while the President calmly listened to them. Distrustful of erratic colleagues, and especially of American agents, Juárez had to be; observant and slow to decide he was, and sometimes misinformed and uncertain, but of timidity there is no trace whatever. To call Lerdo more practical than Juárez and Ocampo seems equally wide of the mark: he obviously charmed the American, partly by being or seeming so impractically pro-American, but while he had been writing essays on the reformation of Mexico, Juárez and Ocampo had been governing states, and this Lerdo was notably a theorist from beginning to end. Churchwell's claim that he got Lerdo his job is preposterous, if only because Lerdo had become Minister of the Treasury on January 3, and is in itself enough to discredit considerably his claim—in the enclosed and vanished memorandum—that Ocampo had promised to sell everything Buchanan wanted.

Churchwell was now replaced by Robert Milligan McLane, a successful lawyer and civil servant, of Maryland, who had supported Polk's war against Mexico, and who was given the higher rank of Envoy Extraordinary and Minister Plenipotentiary. Just what his instructions were is not known, but he was probably told to get everything he could, including the sale of Lower California "promised" in Churchwell's memorandum. Whether to recognize the constitutional government, or indeed the reactionary one, was left up to his own discretion. He arrived at Veracruz on April 1, 1859, and immediately went to work, but since Miramón had just raised his first siege and Degollado was approaching Mexico City, Ocampo

was now evasive. However, on April 7 McLane recognized the constitutional government. Miramón's Foreign Minister immediately
screamed aloud, on the basis of Forsyth's previous approaches to the
reactionaries, that a sale of territory was now projected, and both
Ocampo and McLane attempted rebuttals.

Negotiations continued, and on June 18 Ocampo presented to
McLane an extraordinary proposal, perhaps conceived by Lerdo
and supported to some extent at least by Juárez: that of a defensive
alliance between Mexico and the United States, in relation to other
countries, but also providing that each nation be obliged to help the
other, on request by a legitimate government and the majority of
the nation making the request, to maintain order and security and
"consolidate democratic principles and constitutional liberty," in-
ternally. This proposal found an echo in the final treaty, and will
be considered presently. McLane of course backed away, because
he and his government wanted concrete goods at once, and because
world history had not yet invalidated, for the United States, Washington's warning about "entangling alliances."

Meanwhile, the constitutional government was preoccupied with
the Reform laws, and after they had been published, Lerdo went to
the United States in an attempt to borrow money. He was unsuccessful, partly perhaps because McLane pointed out that a loan
would render unnecessary, for Mexico, the sale of Lower California,
and partly because few Americans thought that the constitutional
government would win.

Ocampo's proposals had aroused opposition among his colleagues,
and this fact, and personal dissensions among them, resulted in his
withdrawal from the Ministry of Foreign Affairs on August 14. He
was replaced by Juan Antonio de la Fuente, who, undoubtedly supported by Juárez, firmly rejected the possibility of the sale of
Lower California, and also refused to allow any unilateral action by
the United States to defend its rights to the transit of the isthmus,
should such rights be granted, and should the United States consider
them endangered. In September, McLane returned to the United
States for a vacation and for consultations.

The constitutional cause now went into a sharp decline. Vidaurri,
in the north, withdrew his forces. The reactionary government,

angling desperately, like their opponents, for outside aid and recognition, negotiated with Spain the Mon–Almonte Treaty of September 26, 1859, which capitulated to every Spanish claim for debts and indemnities and opened the way for Spanish intervention on the reactionary side by way of Cuba. More important, on November 13, at La Estancia de las Vacas, between Querétaro and Celaya, Miramón inflicted a crushing defeat on Degollado, and this was followed by other reactionary victories at Colima and elsewhere. Accompanying these defeats, another ominous element appeared in the situation: before his defeat at La Estancia, Degollado had taken the strange liberty, foreshadowing his future, of offering Miramón command of the liberal army, provided he would accept the Constitution of 1857, which would then be revised by a new constituent congress; but fortunately Miramón had rejected the offer. The liberal and constitutional cause now looked almost hopeless.

In November, McLane returned to Veracruz, and on December 1 Ocampo assumed again the Ministry of Foreign Affairs. On December 14, 1859, McLane and Ocampo signed their much-disputed treaty, which conceded everything wanted by Buchanan, Cass, and McLane except the sale of Lower California.

The United States was given the right of transit of the Isthmus of Tehuantepec in perpetuity. Reciprocal customs regulations were agreed upon. In sudden emergencies, the United States could defend the transit without permission of the Mexican government. Somewhat similar rights were granted the United States in the north, between Nogales and Guaymas, on the Gulf of California, and between Matamoros and Mazatlán, also on the gulf. American citizens in Mexico were given the right to practise their religions freely. The United States was to pay four million dollars for these concessions, but was to keep two millions of these in full settlement of claims of American citizens against the Mexican government. In an attached Convention that is an echo of Ocampo's or Lerdo's proposed treaty of alliance, each nation is obliged to invite the assistance of the other if it cannot alone execute the treaty or maintain order and security.

In Mexico, the treaty was far from having the unanimous support of the liberals, and of course the conservative government, ignoring its own machinations in Europe, protested at once to Washington. In the United States, the response was mixed, but on the whole unfavorable. With good reason, Northerners feared it as a charter for the expansion of slavery to the south. Industrial and commercial interests opposed the implicit liberation of trade and lowering of tariffs, although Mexico at that time certainly offered no commercial threat to anyone. It was recognized that the right to defend the transits unilaterally, and especially the attached Convention, might well force the United States into all kinds of armed intervention and expense in Mexico at a time when the United States itself was perilously divided. There was a certain amount of ugly disdain for the idea of associating ourselves so closely with such inferior people as the Mexicans. The fear of involvement was probably increased by the American naval intervention near Veracruz in March, 1860, to which we shall come presently. On December 10, 1859, having finally had his *Synoptic Table* published in Veracruz, and studied English furiously, Romero sailed from that port to become Secretary of the Mexican Ministry in Washington, under Mata. There, Mata, Romero, and McLane, who had gone to Washington for the purpose, and of course President Buchanan himself, all struggled to get support in the Senate for the treaty, which had been submitted to that body on January 4. In January, Ocampo was again forced to resign, and this time was replaced, oddly enough, considering the attempted transaction with Miramón at La Estancia de las Vacas, by Degollado. In another annual message to Congress, President Buchanan, handicapped the liberal supporters of the treaty in Mexico by again proposing armed intervention. On May 31, the Senate rejected both the treaty and the attached Convention.

In March, McLane had reported that Juárez regretted the delay in the ratification of the treaty, and in May Juárez authorized Mata to extend the time open for ratification another six months. By October, however, a liberal victory seemed possible. The decisiveness of the defeat of any treaty in the United States Senate seems to have been misunderstood in Veracruz, because the issue again arose of extending the time allowed for ratification. Juárez, who has written nothing whatever in his *Diary*, hitherto, about the treaty, records the cabinet meeting on October 5, 1860: "On the appointed day the meeting was opened and Sr. Fuente explained that for various reasons he was of the opinion that the extension of time should not be made. Sres. Ocampo [who had returned to Foreign Affairs four days before], Mata [succeeded at Washington on August 14 by Romero as *chargé d'affaires*], Llave, and Emparán favored the extension, and the President decided that the closing date for the ratification of the treaty would not be postponed." This was the President, outvoted four to two, who made the decision, and who in Churchwell's opinion was dominated by his cabinet.

Defenders of Juárez have made much of the fact that he never actually signed the treaty, and on this occasion sent it to the dusty archives as firmly as the Senate of the United States had already done. He never expressed himself fully on this treaty, but there can be little doubt on two points: first, that he supported and would have signed it at least until Miramón raised his second siege of Veracruz on March 21, 1860, or probably until May; and second, that in view of his later rejection of it, in this meeting, and in view of his extreme caution, forever after, in relation to any support of his government by the United States, he was aware that this treaty, however necessary he and his colleagues considered it at the time, was a very risky one for his country.

Another point that has been extensively debated is whether, as a result of the extraordinary powers granted Comonfort and inherited by Juárez, he actually had any authority to negotiate this treaty at all. This is one for the lawyers: the Buchanan administration, not exactly disinterested, was satisfied, and if Juárez did not have this authority, who did?

Another short American report of this affair, a report that is both saddening and amusing, like Churchwell's, cannot be neglected. Some forty years later, McLane himself wrote the following in his *Reminiscences:*

Mr. Buchanan explained to me that he was not willing to recognize Miramón, but that he did not intend to resent the insult to our Minister [Forsyth] by asking Congress to declare war, and that body would not take that course at that time; he proposed therefore to name another Minister with instructions to go to Mexico in a ship of war, and to recognize Juárez, if the Minister, in his discretion, should think he held sufficient authority in the country to be entitled to recognition, and if not, then to remain on the ship of war until the case could be reported to the President for further instructions. After conference with several Senators, I accepted the mission.

The *Brooklyn*, commanded by Captain Farragut, was assigned to the service of my Legation, and placed subject to my orders.

On arrival, McLane sent Farragut on an inept and fruitless peace mission to the reactionaries besieging Veracruz.

Unfortunately the military and clerical party greatly mistrusted the intention of the Government of the United States, and the people of Mexico were easily excited to believe that we meditated the annexation of their country, with or without their consent. It was well known that Mr. Buchanan himself desired the immediate purchase of Lower California, and the passion of our people for the acquisition of territory was well calculated to inspire their want of confidence in us. I had great difficulty in overcoming the fears and distrust of even the Constitutional Government at Vera Cruz, for Mr. Buchanan urged the purchase of Lower California, and President Juárez, with singular determination, refused to cede a foot of territory, whatever might be the consequences. I was fortunate, however, in gaining his confidence and good-will, and in bringing him to desire the friendship and commerce of the United States, which I thought would result more certainly from intimate commercial relations than from the acquisition of territory, and the mingling of our sturdy population with the Indians and Mexicans who then inhabited Lower California and the northern states of Mexico.

I proposed to open ways of communication between the Gulf of Mexico and the Gulf of California, and between the points of the Pacific and the Gulf of Mexico, establishing bonded warehouses at the termini thereof, with the right to protect these ways of communication and these bonded warehouses, in common with Mexico, at the same time establishing a reciprocity of trade between the two Republics. A treaty of this nature was negotiated and received the sanction of both President Buchanan and President Juárez. It was ratified [*sic*] by the Senate of the United States; however, the Southern advocates of actual annexation of Mexican territory, combining with the ultra-protective and manufacturing advocates from New England, opposed it, and continued its discussion until the extreme difference entertained on the general question of slavery culminated in civil war and secession. Nevertheless, the best

THE CASE OF THE DUBIOUS TREATY 201

men in the Senate were committed to the support of the Treaty. The Senate Committee on Foreign Affairs, who recommended its ratification by that body, was composed of some notable men. Mason, of Virginia; Seward, of New York; Slidell, of Louisiana; Douglas, of Illinois, were on that committee, and voted to report it favorably. Mr. Buchanan greatly regretted the failure of the Senate to ratify this Treaty, which, he believed, would establish commercial intimacy between the two Republics, and prepare the way for the admission of all the Mexican States into our Union. I was requested to visit Washington to make explanations to the Senate Committee of Foreign Affairs, and I never returned to Mexico. My interest in the Mission terminated with the failure of the Senate to ratify this Treaty, and the imminence of the Civil War made me unwilling to leave my country and family at that time.

Actually, McLane returned to Mexico late in March, 1860, and remained there until November. In 1885 he became President Cleveland's Ambassador to France, where he died in 1898.

Obviously the President gave McLane more instructions than those he chose to remember here. Captain Farragut was of course David Glasgow Farragut, who had served under Porter in the Gulf in the twenties, who spoke Spanish, and who was soon to become the conqueror of New Orleans and Mobile Bay. The difficulty that McLane records here, in overcoming the fears and mistrust even of the constitutional government, is echoed in a letter that he wrote to Secretary Cass on the day of the signing of the treaty. In this letter he reported that Juárez' cabinet objected to the Convention, and was brought around only by his pointing out that the American government would take action in defense of its rights and its citizens, without asking the consent of any government whatever. Defenders of Juárez have claimed that this threat, implying that the Convention could be a face-saving device, exonerates Juárez and Ocampo, and Sr. Fuentes Mares disputes this claim on the grounds that Ocampo had suggested the Convention, or its prototype, in the first place, and that McLane was boastfully lying. But perhaps the most interesting and depressing feature of this memoir is its bland assumption of the superiority of Americans to Mexicans; and perhaps its most startling detail is the American President's fantasy, in the year 1860, about the incorporation of the Mexican Republic into the United States. Presumably this whole strange Union would be ruled by Southern planters and slave owners, from their verandahs, each with a mint julep in one hand and a shotgun in the other. Since this treaty was never ratified by either government, why have thousands of pages been written and printed about it? For two reasons: because many Mexicans, including some respectable scholars as well as the rationalizing devout and the mental patients, think that it throws grave doubts on the patriotism and loyalty, or at least the wisdom, of Juárez and Ocampo; and because it raises a question more vital even to-day than it was a century ago, and that question is: when, if ever, can political loyalties to the Left or Right be allowed honorably to displace nationalistic and patriotic ones? These are rather dreadful questions, in any biography of Juárez, and we had better glance briefly at some of the intellectually more respectable opinions about Juárez and Ocampo and this treaty.

Sr. José Fuentes Mares (1960) considers Miguel Lerdo de Tejada the most inventive and most disloyal figure on the constitutional side at this time, with Ocampo and Juárez close behind him. He calls them fanatics rather than governors, and heirs of *poinsettismo* and of Lorenzo de Zavala, the early *puro* who became Vice-President of Texas. In American history, this would be like calling Franklin D. Roosevelt the heir of Aaron Burr—which, of course, has in effect been done. As far as they go, Sr. Fuentes Mares' facts seem trustworthy, but his judgments from them are biased, probably by his candid hatred for the United States. "In improbable conditions," he says, referring to the rejection of this treaty by the United States Senate, "Juárez escaped going down to posterity as the most sinister figure in the history of Mexico."

Justo Sierra's judgment of this affair (1905) is much more extended and complex. After pointing out at length the threats to Juárez' government from the United States and Spain, the military disasters, the bankruptcy, and all the rest of the pressures, he calls the treaty "the constitution of an interminable servitude." "And those men of celebrated patriotism," he concludes, "after a year of the deepest conflict in their consciences, and in the midst of a gigantic moral and political struggle, convinced that thus they were saving what could be saved of their country, in order to remake its destiny, calmly accepted entire responsibility for their act; for them, the McLane Treaty was a flaming coal in their hands, and in signing it, one of them signed his own death warrant. . . . [Of the treaty] there remains only a shadow, but this shadow clouds the figures of the leaders of the Reform. They accepted that sacrifice, believing it to be their grim and inevitable duty. Thus we explain the McLane–Ocampo Treaty. . . . Men like Juárez, Ocampo, and Lerdo were not and could not be traitors."

The most interesting defense of the treaty has come (1954) from Sr. José C. Valadés, the scholarly biographer of Ocampo, who has himself served Mexico as a diplomat:

There is, unquestionably, a sense of anguish in Ocampo's project, but there is also a patriotic and democratic conviction that is very great. As a superior man, Ocampo does not see a menace in the United States. He knows, as one who has the habit of taking all problems to the laboratory of judgment, that when nations seek to use force, it is not conventional agreements that prevent foreign intrusion, and that the only thing that will eliminate impulsive action and lessen the aggressive passions of opponents is unity and understanding in principle. Mexico and the United States, thought Ocampo, could make an offensive and defensive alliance not only for military advantages, but rather "to begin to form, in particular, the public law of America," to realize and further "the rooting and development of democratic principles," and to "oppose the conservation of the remains of feudal abuses."

In other words, Ocampo was anticipating the Organization of American States.

The pressures of many kinds were great. On the long, miserable record, and in view of Buchanan's more or less open imperialism, the dangers to Mexico from the United States, in this treaty, were obviously very great. However, as no one perhaps has pointed out in this connection, Juárez, Ocampo, and Mata had all lived alertly in the United States, and may well have recognized that the risks of this treaty actually were not as great as they have since been pictured by the critics of these men and of the United States. Manifest Destiny and Buchanan were ugly enough, but the American people, as frequently underestimated and maligned as the Mexican people and Juárez, were rapidly outgrowing them and sloughing them off.

In Illinois, as a little earlier in Oaxaca, there had appeared a formidable democrat, long hostile to imperialistic nonsense, and the strength of a better United States was rising with and behind him. To say that the United States Senate, in rejecting this treaty, saved the reputations of Ocampo and Juárez is to assume, in obvious error, that Buchanan, McLane, and their like still represented and governed the American people. Even if the treaty had been ratified, the Southern expansionists would soon have been kept busy at home. In rejecting the treaty, what the Senate did was to cancel this test of the disinterestedness of the American people and of the judgment of Ocampo and Juárez. It said in effect: "No: this could be a scheme to promote slavery, not democracy, and we are having too many troubles with oppression and disunity of our own to be bothered with yours."

It was not a bad answer, at that time, under those circumstances, despite the nasty overtones in the press about the degeneracy of Mexicans; and Juárez could not have been wholly disappointed by the cancellation of the test. Before that answer came, something else had happened: Juárez had encountered the American people, not through arrogant diplomats, or through a properly hard-headed Senate, but through United States naval officers and their men.

13

THE AFFAIR AT ANTÓN LIZARDO

WHEN MIRAMÓN was first besieging Veracruz, in February, 1859, Juárez received from Commander Thomas Turner, USN, commanding the U.S.S. *Saratoga*, anchored off Veracruz, a courteous and respectful letter offering Juárez "the hospitalities of the ship under my command, whenever in the judgment of your Excellency, it may be deemed a measure of safety to retire from Vera Cruz, in the event of its investment by a hostile army." Juárez thanked him warmly, while declining his invitation because "my duty demands that I remain among my compatriots in order to direct such actions as the circumstances may demand."

Not all of the relations of the constitutional government with foreign naval officers in ships anchored off Veracruz were so friendly. Early that year, because of irregularities in the payment of debts, a forced loan in Tampico, and acts of violence against their citizens, Spanish, English, and French naval forces threatened the city, and Ocampo, then Foreign Minister, had to buy them off by the old method of guaranteeing them percentages of the customs receipts.

A year later, the dubious treaty had been signed but not yet ratified. Captain William Cornwallis Aldham, RN, commanding H.M.S. *Valorous* in those waters, and also setting himself up as a diplomat, reported on March 2, 1860, to Lord John Russell, Palmerston's Foreign Secretary, that as a part of his diplomatic maneuvers, he had told Miramón that the treaty would be ratified by the United States without doubt, which act "would be in fact a declaration of war against him," and that meanwhile the American naval forces also present would prevent Miramón's getting any supplies by sea. As we know, Captain Aldham's opinion on the future of the treaty was erroneous, and there is no evidence that its having been signed, and its being then considered by the Senate, had any direct or even indirect effect on United States naval operations in those waters. Juárez and his colleagues might well have been hopeful in this respect, but could have had no assurance of American help.

Meanwhile, in the interior of Mexico, "the beautiful reaction," as Miramón called it—while he was called its Paladin, its "Young Maccabee"—had swept everything before it, and on the constitutional side there remained only scattered fragments of armies and the citadel of Veracruz, which by all accounts, including Captain Aldham's, was a military stronghold. Despite its victories, the reaction was nearly bankrupt. The fact that when one constitutional army was destroyed, another took its place, indicated the enduring and increasing popular support of his enemies, and Miramón knew that unless he besieged Veracruz again, and took it this time, he would lose the war. On February 8 Miramón left Mexico City for Veracruz with about 3,000 men and a large supply of artillery and ammunition, and on the road he received about 2,000 additional troops. On the way, he was seriously harassed by guerrillas, and the liberal forces, retreating into Veracruz, left the earth scorched and empty behind them. Miramón arrived at Medellín, near Veracruz, and set up his headquarters there on February 29. He knew that he had to take the city within a few weeks, before the mosquitoes and fevers could weaken his army, and he could not have been exactly cheerful, but this time he thought he held a high trump card.

This was to consist of his receiving simultaneous naval support and additional ammunition from vessels fitted out by the Spaniards in Havana and commanded by an extremely reactionary soldier from Yucatán named Tomás Marín. Early in January one John Black, former American consul, wrote from Mexico City to McLane in Veracruz, reporting the purchase of two vessels by Marín and the proposed attack on Veracruz. After the event, George W. Mathew, the British Minister in Mexico City, reported to Lord John Russell: "It had been for some time a matter of notoriety here that vessels purchased by the Government were fitting out at Havana under the command of a Mexican officer, and the Government papers in Mexico had announced their early arrival and their avowed design to blockade Vera Cruz and force all commerce to Alvarado, of which General Miramón intended to take previous possession." McLane of course informed Juárez, and then wrote to Secretary Cass suggesting that since President Polk had ordered American naval forces to defend the coast of Texas before that country had actually become a state of the Union, it would now be well if American naval forces were ordered to act as though the treaty had actually been ratified, and to defend the port against attack from the sea. He also went so far as to say that he would ask the American naval authorities to help Juárez defend Veracruz against Miramón's attack. Commander Turner and his senior officer present, Captain Joseph R. Jarvis, in the U.S.S. *Savannah*, could of course act under no other orders than those from the Navy Department, and their last order, dated July 27, 1858, had been simply to "protect the persons and property of citizens of the United States."

Juárez and his colleagues were not inactive in the face of this threat. They discovered a treacherous conspiracy that General Robles had somehow managed to organize within the city, and imprisoned those involved in it. They chartered and armed two small American merchant steamers, the *Indianola* and the *Wave*. On February 24, Juárez issued a proclamation declaring Marín and his forces to be pirates, chiefly on the ground that they were operating illegally, without the right to raise the Mexican flag, or, since the vessels had been purchased from the Spanish in Cuba, any other flag. The legality of this proclamation has been disputed, on the ground that pirates are robbers at sea, enemies of the human race, and it has been defended on the ground that piracy consists, as Juárez claimed, in operating without the support of any legal government. This problem we shall leave with the admiralty lawyers.

As Foreign Minister, Ocampo had been replaced, as already noted, by Degollado, and when McLane went to the United States to explain the treaty, the American Legation in Veracruz was left in charge of Charles LeDoux Elgee. In sending a copy of Juárez' proclamation to Elgee, Degollado asked him to pass it on to the American naval officers, so that they might take action against the pirates and help defend the city, including the American Legation, against any attack by them.

On February 26, Juárez' government withdrew all of its forces from Alvarado, the somewhat isolated small seaport some thirty miles to the south of Veracruz that could easily be cut off by an attack from the sea. It also expedited the arming of the *Indianola* and the *Wave*.

On February 27, a conference was held between Degollado, Elgee, and Captain Jarvis. Resisting all of Degollado's arguments, Captain Jarvis stated that unless he received concrete instructions to do otherwise, or unless Marín tried to blockade the port, and thus prevented the free movement of American shipping, he would preserve strict neutrality.

On February 29, when Miramón arrived at Medellín, there began the prolonged and complex efforts of Captain Aldham, acting for the British government, to effect an armistice, efforts that are relevant here only because they opened up a grave difference of views within Juárez' cabinet about the nature and future of the war and thus subjected Juárez himself to another terrible strain just at the time when he was trying to direct the defense of the city by land and by sea, and to carry on the very critical and delicate relations with the American naval and diplomatic officers present.

On March 3, Commander Turner visited Miramón at Medellín to arrange for the protection of the lives and property of American citizens, should Miramón take the city. Miramón, "grave and reserved but respectful and courteous," gave Turner every possible assurance on this point; and General Robles showed him the "utmost cordiality." There was evidently, and naturally, no discussion of the armistice negotiations, and if they had any views on the matter, Jarvis and Turner seem to have considered the fall of the city quite possible, and to have had no idea of taking part in its defense.

Meanwhile, Marín in the *General Miramón*, which he had rechristened in Havana, supported by Captain Arias in the *Marqués de la Habana*, was foolishly approaching Veracruz, when he perhaps could have reached his destination down the coast without calling the attention to himself that proved his undoing. Later, four members of the hired crew of the *General Miramón*, Arturo Connly, Jean Durand, Robert Dantz, and Leon Aubri, named here to indicate vaguely the nationalities involved, signed a report of the trip that shows clearly the shoddy nature of their commanders and of the whole expedition. These four, and probably most of the others, did not sign on to do any fighting, and were unhappily surprised to discover arms and ammunition on board, and to be forced to wear naval "sailors' effects." The *Marqués* had some mechanical troubles, and they made contact with two vessels that undoubtedly reported their approach to Veracruz.

We turn now to the action report made by Commander Turner to Captain Jarvis on March 8. This report was later supplemented by the reports of his junior officers and of the four men named above, and also contradicted by the "protests" filed by Marín and Arias, but the latter documents also contradict each other, and are full of obvious inventions. Any detached and detailed examination of the evidence will support Commander Turner's report.

On the morning of the 6th inst. two large steamers appeared off the harbor of Vera Cruz, without any flag being hoisted, altho' a gun was fired from the Castle, and the Mexican flag run up at the same time to induce them to do so. They were evidently confederates, as they were hove to for some time, communicating with each other.

After several hours, and after communicating with the Spanish vessels of war at Sacrificios, which sent out a boat to them, they stood down the coast in the direction of Antón Lizardo.

You directed me immediately to place my ship in tow of two small American steamers here, the *Wave* and *Indianola*, which were placed at your disposal, to follow them, and to ascertain their character, where they were from, of what nation, where they fitted out, and what was their object upon this coast, and to report to you the result of these enquiries with all practicable dispatch. [It should be noted that these are not orders to attack.]

In obedience to these orders I left here about sunset, in tow of these vessels on board of each of which I placed a detachment of about thirty-five men and marines, in case they might go into shoal water, where my ship with her large draft could not follow and communicate with them. . . .

I proceeded down the coast, making direct for Antón Lizardo, fifteen miles distant, where I expected to find them. About midnight two large vessels were reported at anchor at Antón Lizardo; I stood directly for them; I had directed my pilot to anchor me immediately between the two vessels. [Marín had "hit the sack" and now appeared on his deck without shoes.]

At the moment when I had nearly reached this point, and the tow was cast off, both the little steamers being ahead of me, they hailed and reported that the larger steamer of the two [*Miramón*] was underway and endeavoring to escape through the Southern passage. I hailed and ordered them to pursue him, and to get on board of him if possible, as I was ordered to communicate with the Senior Officer, who I supposed was on board this vessel; at the same moment I fired a shot ahead of him to bring him to.

As soon as they got close to him, which was but a few moments, to my extreme astonishment, he opened a heavy fire of great guns and musquetry upon them; and it was reported to me at the same time the other steamer [*Marqués*] was slipping her cable. I immediately gave him a broadside as I had not the remotest doubt of his being in complicity with and under the orders of the officer of the other steamer, and I was afraid he would go to his assistance, in which case I should have been obliged to recall my vessels, or to have witnessed their capture or destruction, and as he had had the audacity to fire into me, without any provocation whatever, I was determined to seize him if I could. He ran up the Spanish flag as soon as I fired.

In the meantime the larger steamer [*Miramón*] was hotly engaged with the forces on board my two little steamers in a running fight. Finding that he could not get out of the Southern passage, he immediately changed his course, put his head to the northward, and passed inside of me to gain the Northern passage, and to keep out of the way of my guns, followed by my vessels, warmly engaged with him all the time. He was evidently too fast for and was gaining upon them, as he shot ahead of them. I got a gun to bear upon him, and shot away his smoke-stack. I found now that it was impossible to fire without danger to my vessels, as they were all together. The chase was continued in the midst of a hot fire on either side. I could not but admire at this moment the daring gallantry of these fine fellows contending with so superior a force. They closed in upon and grappled with him in spite of his efforts to shake them off. Finding it impossible to escape, I suppose he ran his vessel on shore; at all events, pressed closely by them she grounded, which I was not aware of at the time.

They were then distant about a mile from my ship, and my anxiety was intense for their safety. I could afford them no possible aid, my three largest cutters were inboard, and before I could have manned my boats and got to them, the affair would have been ended. I was not however kept long in suspense, for almost immediately I heard three cheers, and was informed that they were boarding her over the bows, which could be distinctly seen by our glasses.

I now return to the steamer anchored close to me. Whilst the engagement continued between the other vessels, and at the moment that they were passing this ship, the First Lieutenant who was on the poop called to me to say that this steamer was firing musquetry. I directed again a division of guns to be given him, which was done. I then hailed and ordered him on board; as he did not come at once, I sent Lieut. Chapman on board to say if he did not come instantly on board I would send a guard to bring him. He came on board and informed me in answer to my enquiries that his ship was the *Marquis of Havana*, that he had been employed by Captain Marín, who commanded the other ship, to transport stores and munitions of war, and that he was Spanish.

In the meantime I had sent an officer to bring Captain Marín on board. As soon as he reached my cabin, I asked him how he had dared to fire upon my vessels. He replied unhesitatingly, and in the presence of a witness, "That when he observed my vessels steaming into the harbor, he had informed his crew that he was sure they were American vessels of war, and positively forbidden them to fire, but that it was a mixed crew of various nations, having been but recently taken on board, and not being yet properly disciplined, he found it impossible to control them." I observed to him that it was a great outrage for which he would have to answer, which he pretended most deeply to regret—all of which I knew to be untrue because during the action he was distinctly heard calling upon his men to board with him. You will perceive how all this conflicts with the accompanying depositions of four of his crew, who claimed that the officers did all the firing. . . .

It now becomes my painful duty, to speak of a circumstance which has caused me the deepest concern and regret. About two hours after the engagement a boat came alongside from the *Indianola* with a person very badly wounded, dressed in citizen. Upon inquiry I was informed it was "General Llave" of the Mexican Army. I immediately had him taken to my cabin. It seems by his own account as he related it to me, that as I was about leaving Vera Cruz, he was sent off to the *Indianola* by this government to obtain some information as to my movements, and that in the hurry and confusion of getting underway and towing out, his boat left him. The officers commanding those vessels . . . did not know that he was on board until he saw him wounded. Immediately on my arrival here I sent him in a cot to the Castle, where he now is.

General Ignacio de la Llave was none other than Juárez' Minister of War. His wound was in the head, but he survived to fight again, only to be killed three years later by a treacherous escort. If he sneaked into this action, he was not the last minister of state to attempt something of the kind. Sir Winston Churchill attempted it on June 6, 1944.

The engagement lasted between one-half and three-quarters of an hour. Turner reported, in his forces, "one man mortally wounded who is still alive, one seriously, and several slightly. . . . Twelve [Mexicans] were brought on board my ship severely wounded, three of which have died. I have sent all the others to the hospital on shore."

In his letter to the Hon. Isaac Toucey, Secretary of the Navy, dated March 11, forwarding Commander Turner's action report and supplementary documents, Captain Jarvis comments on the action: "I do not see how it was possible for Commander Turner to do otherwise than he did, and I think that he and the other officers deserve great credit for their promptness in defending their Flag." He says that he will send the two steamers to New Orleans as soon as possible, under the command of Commander Jenkins of the *Preble*. "This place is at the present time closely besieged. On the night of the 6th instant, they attempted to carry it by storm, but were beaten off, and from present appearances, I think the same result will occur should they again attempt it. From all I can learn, they have as many troops in the city as the besieging party's."

The senior Spanish and French naval officers protested to Jarvis, the former on the grounds that the captured vessels were Spanish, and the latter on the grounds that they were neutral, both premises being obviously false. Captain Aldham, perhaps only because he was so busy at the time as a diplomat, did not protest. Of course Miramón's Foreign Secretary protested. In New Orleans, the United States District Court, acting as an admiralty court under Judge McCabed, decided on June 28 that Marín, his men and ships were not pirates, and ordered their release. In 1870 the United States Supreme Court confirmed this decision.

On March 21, the United States Senate, thoroughly hostile at this time to President Buchanan, passed a resolution requesting him to inform it concerning the orders issued to the American naval authorities in Veracruz, and the authority for the seizure. When the resolution was sent to the Secretary of the Navy, he replied to the President by sending him the order of July 27, 1858, for the protection of American lives, property, and commerce, under which Turner had acted. The actions of both Captain Jarvis and Commander Turner were approved. Both fought with distinction in the Union Navy; Jarvis died as a retired Commodore in 1869 and Turner as a retired Rear Admiral in 1883.

So much for the facts of this affair. Around them there have grown up many flowers of legend. Choking these out, there has also grown up around this incident a thorny thicket of attack, defense, and recrimination. The burden of the attack is that this incident was merely the last phase of Buchanan's and McLane's diabolical scheme to get control of Mexico; that Juárez and his Ministers were their conscious, willing, and traitorous tools; and that Jarvis and Turner were viciously illegal meddlers who did in fact bring victory to Juárez' side. As Sr. Fuentes Mares chooses to put it: "Turner—although [sic] a Protestant—took the part in the history of Mexico of a kind of Guardian Angel of the Reform."

In our view, Buchanan, McLane and the McLane–Ocampo Treaty had little or nothing to do with the affair, and although Jarvis and Turner were given rather wide room for choice and action among these legal rocks and shoals, they might well, in those days long before radio, have had as much latitude whoever was President. In chartering the *Indianola* and the *Wave*, issuing the proclamation of piracy, and urging the American officers to take action under it— since the constitutional government could not in this case act for itself—Juárez and his Ministers acted patriotically, decisively, and with a degree of legality unusual in civil or any other wars. Finally, Jarvis and Turner and the other American officers and men obeyed their orders responsibly, were indeed surprised by the violent reaction they met, were still not quite unhappy to get into a brisk fight with the enemies of their friends, and to win it, and decided only then that their captives—what else could be done with them?—might be pirates after all. They were, in short, good and perfectly normal American sailors, and a credit to their service and their country.

But was this little incident actually decisive in the war? This is a difficult question, probably unanswerable, and it will be considered very briefly and more chronologically in the course of the next chapter.

14

EXHAUSTION AND ENDURANCE

In 1860, the question was: who will endure?
The whole nation had suffered, and was still suffering, terribly.
Our immeasurably more destructive weapons, our genocides, and
our more refined tortures of fifty and a hundred years later must
not cause us to minimize or to romanticize the destruction and suffering in these Mexican wars of so far away and so long ago. Men
leaped or were dragged away from their families and their work in
the shops, the mines, and the ranches and led into combat with little
or no training, with inferior leadership, food, supplies, and guns,
and with almost no care provided for the wounded. The women,
children, and old men were not only left to do the work, and to
suffer bombardment in the cities, as in all wars; they were also subjected to endless demands and robberies by the passing armies, and
if the head of a household was known as a reactionary or liberal,
opposing forces were just as likely as not to drag him from his home
and shoot him, and then burn and pillage his home, leaving his family
to starve. Taking advantage of the general chaos, bands of hoodlums
robbed and shot travelers and plundered *haciendas*. Internal commerce had almost come to a halt, and food, clothing, and all other
goods were running short. These wars were comparable to the
religious wars in Europe in the seventeenth century, pictured in the
engravings of Callot; to the horrors of the French invasion of Spain
in 1808, pictured by Goya; and to the meaningless brutalities of the
Mexican Revolution that began in 1910, pictured by Orozco. Our
own contemporary Civil War was not pretty, but these wars in
Mexico were worse.
Juárez and his colleagues in Veracruz must not be thought of as

sitting comfortably around their desks and café tables, holding conferences and writing letters while remaining oblivious of all this. Most of them were separated from their families, and if Juárez was not separated from his, he must from time to time have seen the bleeding bodies of women and children in wrecked houses or stretched on the cobblestones. These also were his family: "I am a son of the people, and I shall not forget it."

Could he hold on, and finish the job, so that these pitiful deaths would at least have bought for others a little more liberty and law? The news from the interior, in those months of spring and early summer, was usually bad. The government received unceasing and just demands, and there was only a trickle of money coming in with which to answer them, because the revenues from the sale of Church property were disappointing, and tariff receipts had naturally shrunk. There would be no more aid now from the United States, and if that was a relief from one political anxiety, it did nothing to relieve deeper financial ones. Probably the most severe strain on Juárez himself, aside from the visible death and destruction in a war in which *he* had decided it was necessary to fight back, came from the increasing evidence that two of his Ministers, Miguel Lerdo and Santos Degollado, who had endured much, whom he saw daily, and on whose experience and will he had to count, were losing their nerve. This dreadful evidence appeared when the mighty government of Great Britain, which ruled most of the world, decided to step in and try to stop this nasty little war that interfered with their income and that evidently seemed to them basically absurd.

Britain, which like all the other governments except the United States had not yet recognized the constitutional government of Mexico, was represented in Mexico City by George W. Mathew, an intelligent but somewhat lordly man who got reports, judged them, summarized them, and passed them on to London. In Veracruz, Her Britannic Majesty was represented by Captain Aldham, senior officer present, in H.M.S. *Valorous*, a brave and intelligent but somewhat officious sailor of fifty who reported to and received orders from both Mathew and London. In London there were Lord John Russell, an ardent and remote Protestant, and above him at the time, Lord Palmerston, one of the most astute schemers and meddlers in

Europe. What these men wanted was first of all peace, and then their money, and they showed no comprehension of or interest in the basic struggle between liberals and reactionaries, except for Russell's intrusive and persistent demand for religious toleration as a part of any settlement. For three months these Englishmen were all very patient and tenacious. They harped to each side about its weaknesses and hopelessness, and minimized the importance of both the Constitution and the reactionaries' implacable opposition to it. Finally they became impatient and had to fall back on the old threat to "protect British interests."

For his part, Miramón was having troubles of his own at least as great as those of Juárez. His government, too, was nearly bankrupt, and the illegality of his office as President, with Zuloaga still circulating in the background, was an unexpected embarrassment, his Foreign Minister, Octaviano Muñoz Ledo, was stupid, the reactionaries in Mexico were more articulate than powerful (a fact noted by Mathew), the capture of the two ships was a blow, and above all, the fever season was coming on rapidly and he had not yet taken Veracruz. In all these transactions he was very proud, very courteous, unyielding in defense of religious privilege and in rejection of the popular will, and quietly but clearly almost desperate. He would dicker if he might get his way, but he would not yield a palm's breadth, and was prepared to go down fighting.

Juárez knew or guessed Miramón's troubles, and was prepared and determined to fight for the Constitution and the Reform to the end. Towards Captain Aldham and his gloomy predictions and importunate demands, he was, through interpreters, courteous, patient, quietly suggestive of his superior rank and of the limitations of the Captain's function, and icily ironic. This Captain in the Royal Navy had encountered such an attitude in the Lords of the Admiralty and of the Foreign Office, but when met in a Zapotec Indian ruling one little pestilential city on the coast of Mexico, it must have shaken and galled him a little. Most of the Ministers backed Juárez, but the moral and possibly mortal disease of depression, uncertainty, and even hysteria, appeared in two of the accepted leaders, Santos Degollado, the upright and excitable soldier on leave as Foreign Minister, and Miguel Lerdo de Tejada, the ambitious and brilliant intellectual who had insisted on taking every risk for the Reform, who now insisted on the extreme hazard of suspending payments on the foreign debts in the midst of a civil war, and who nevertheless now came out for abandoning the Constitution, which was the symbol and bulwark of the entire cause. In the end, Miramón gave up the siege, Lerdo resigned, Degollado went back to the army (but without ceasing to make his neurotic mischief), Aldham went back to his ship, and Juárez, the Constitution, and the Mexican people endured.

But there were plenty of bad moments on the way. Russell's opening proposal was for an armistice of from six months to a year, to permit the calling of a new constituent assembly; and Degollado told Aldham, with gross inaccuracy, that this was just what Juárez wanted, and just what Miramón had rejected before the battle at La Estancia. Degollado was corrected, and Aldham rushed off to Miramón and talked him into making vague proposals, but these were addressed to Aldham, and Juárez refused to answer them, saying that when Miramón, the rebel, made more explicit proposals, to the government itself, they would be considered. Then, as he had done with Miramón, Aldham tried to discourage Juárez, saying that Alvarado had been taken and the Americans would remain strictly neutral. "He was told," Juárez noted in his diary, "that the government was well aware of all that, and thus ended the visit of Sr. Aldham."

This interview occurred on the day before the action at Antón Lizardo, which Juárez noted very briefly, adding in parentheses that he had sent his family to the Castle—where, incidentally, there was one decent if grim house for the commander, besides the appalling dungeons. It is possible but doubtful that everyone in Veracruz heard the gunfire on the night of March 6. On March 11, and from time to time thereafter, Juárez joined his family in the Castle, but the Ministers remained in the city.

The seizure of the vessels did not hearten Lerdo and Degollado, because it was at the cabinet meeting on March 13, Llave alone being absent because of his wounds when a stowaway, that they argued for accepting Russell's proposal of a long armistice and a new constituent assembly. Juárez pointed out that any such move would surely result in the eventual triumph of the reactionaries. He was strongly backed by Manuel Ruiz and others, including Llave by proxy, and it was decided that no sacrifice of legality would be made. In the negotiations on March 14, Juárez was represented by Degollado and José Empáran, and Miramón by Manuel Robles Pezuela and Isidro Díaz; and of course they came to nothing. The next day, the fighting, including further bombardment of the city by Miramón, was renewed, and during the following week thirty-eight women, children and old men were killed. "Captain Aldham," as Mathew reported to London, "justly indignant at so disgraceful and useless a mode of warfare, felt it his duty to address him [Miramón] a protest against such barbarity." Captain Aldham was obviously a fighting man of the old school, long since outdated by the successors of Miramón in the theory of total warfare and possibly total extinction. Miramón, however, was a primitive in the newer mode, and Commander Turner, representing the brutal and hypocritical "colossus of the North," had deprived him of the tools for further butchery on this trivial scale. The cargo of the two captured ships had consisted of "1,000 fourteen-inch bombs, 2 brass mortars, 4,000 stand of arms for infantry, and upwards of 60,000 rations," but this must be only a guess, because before she was boarded, the crew of the *Miramón* had thrown a good deal of her cargo overboard.

On March 21 Miramón raised the siege and withdrew towards Mexico, harassed by guerrillas and desertions. Mathew reported that Miramón attributed his failure to the seizure of the two vessels, but in Mathew's opinion, this excuse was "without sufficient warranty, for the place was well defended, and I suspect greatly that the United States vessels in the Vera Cruz harbour would, if needful, have taken part with the besieged." Whether Jarvis would have landed marines and sailors in the city itself, to fight beside the constitutional forces, may be debated, as may be the success that Miramón might or might not have had with the additional supplies. A reasonable guess might be that Turner saved a few score lives of civilians, but not the constitutional cause, which was saved instead by Juárez' handling of his cabinet and the Mexican men's handling of their rifles and machetes.

Captain Aldham wrote to Juárez rejoicing in Miramón's failure, and was praised by Degollado for his behavior, but continued impatiently to press for an armistice and further negotiations. Towards the end of March Degollado was sent back to the army and replaced by Empáran, whose diplomatic messages give an impression of much greater coolness and firmness. On March 27 Empáran had to correct an impression unfortunately given by Degollado to Aldham and Mathew on March 16 that Juárez and his government were ready to accept Russell's proposals, whereupon Mathew accused the constitutional government of misrepresentation and incompetence. Mathew insisted the British government did not wish to dictate the form of any Mexican government, and Empáran had repeatedly to point out that the Reform had already proclaimed religious freedom, that Miramón would not accept it or do anything to prevent a new constituent assembly from destroying the Constitution, and that even if the constitutional government were willing, as it definitely was not, to accede to the British proposals entirely, it would be overthrown by the governors of the interior, just as they had banded together against Comonfort and in favor of Juárez. The British became increasingly irritated and frustrated by both of the belligerent parties, as they by the British.

On April 20, in the cabinet, Lerdo again argued his defeatist position—abandonment of the Constitution—even more strongly, and again Juárez rejected it. Miramón had not proposed anything, Juárez repeated, and "for this reason the constitutional government had finished, for its part, and was in no way compromised, either with Miramón or with the English government." The next day, in the name of the Emperor of the French, the French Consul offered to mediate, proposing again an armistice and a general assembly, whose rights were unspecified. Juárez knew that Mexican reactionaries were concocting a monarchist plot in Europe, although Napoleon III had not yet committed himself, and he also knew that all French agents had been thorns in the flesh of any Mexican government. His polite declination of the French proposal with thanks, was English in its restraint and understatement. On April 23 Lerdo and even Llave came up with another dangerous proposal, that of consulting the governors and through them, public opinion, on the question of abandoning "legality," that is, the Constitution. With the support of Ruiz and Partearroyo, Juárez succeeded in rejecting this proposal as impracticable. Meanwhile, Muñoz Ledo, Miramón's Foreign Minister, had made the fantastic charge that Juárez' government was being disloyal to the Plan of Iguala of 1821, as though nothing had happened since that date.

While these fruitless negotiations were dragging on and petering out in some acrimony, Lerdo was insisting to Juárez that the only way in which bankruptcy could be prevented was by suspending payments on the foreign debts, and although Juárez agreed with this proposal on May 29, the next day he changed his mind, Lerdo resigned in disgust, and his resignation was accepted. Juárez left no record of his thoughts at this time on this proposal, which became so vital a year later. But it seems reasonable to assume that he decided that however necessary this step, almost certain to arouse wrath in Europe, might be later, it could not be taken with the nation still involved in civil war. Meanwhile, there were other lesser but still acute irritations.

In May and June there occurred an interesting exchange of letters between Juárez and one Joaquín F. Pacheco, Minister of the Queen of Spain to the Republic of Mexico, that is, the government of Miramón. From a vessel at Veracruz, addressing Juárez without his title, Pacheco asked him for permission to go ashore and proceed to Mexico City with an escort. Juárez politely granted permission and even supplied the escort. A few weeks later, from the City, Pacheco addressed an offensive letter to Juárez about attacks on Spaniards by constitutional troops, and about attacks on Spain in a constitutional newspaper. He used such phrases as this: "As long as I am here, and as long as the government of the Queen has a ship that can cross the ocean and fire projectiles, you had better understand that this is not a matter that will be endured." Juárez replied that the offending troops had already been ordered punished, and that this order would be repeated. "You may rest assured," he concluded, "that I offer to do this because duty and conscience oblige me to do so, and not the menacing words and offensive and abusive expressions that you permit yourself to use in your letter, and that I refrain from using in reply because my doing so would reduce me to a level to which the dignity and decorum of the office I hold will not allow me to descend."

On August 14, Mata sailed from New York for Veracruz, and Romero, who in the intervals between his arduous letter-writing and studying had made numerous American friends and acquaintances, and done some sightseeing that included Niagara Falls, was left in Washington as chargé d'affaires.

On his retreat to Mexico City, Miramón may have known that his cause was lost; still, during the rest of the year, he, Mejía, Márquez, and other reactionary generals put up stout opposition and won several battles, but on the whole were forced steadily back towards Mexico City by the constitutional forces under Degollado, González Ortega, Zaragoza, Doblado (now back in action, after his extended rest, at a time when there seemed to be a definite prospect of victory), and others. Jesús González Ortega, a florid and erratic personality, won a major victory at Silao on August 10. The constitutional commanders and their troops had gained experience, and the withdrawal of Miramón from Veracruz must have been heartening to them and discouraging to the reactionaries, but in reading the military history of those months, and in considering also the later records of the commanders, it is hard to avoid the hypothesis that the result was caused less by superior military leadership than by a rising will to win, and a new sense of unity, on the part of the Mexican people, expressed through their fighting men. Other elements in a military situation being more or less equal, it is the fighting spirit of the men in action, and the tenacity of those behind them, that are decisive.

If morale was now higher among the unknown liberals, and in the mind and heart of Juárez, mere money—which, except in a police state, can also be decisive—was almost nonexistent, and one of the technical and moral mysteries of these wars is the absence of fiat money. Apparently unwilling or unable to use printing presses, the leaders on both sides began to look around for something else, and to consider more carefully the mule trains or convoys of silver passing steadily from the mining regions of the central and northern mountains to the seaports on the Gulf of Mexico. The foreign owners of these convoys paid taxes on them, and if the convoys were touched, the foreign governments could become even more intrusive than they already were. Furthermore, the liberal generals

who controlled the terrain through which the convoys passed had
shown strict moral scruples with regard to robbery that are now
almost as astonishing as the rashness with which the owners sent
these convoys through a countryside ravaged and impoverished by
a civil war approaching a crisis.

However, time was running out, and in the autumn of 1860 a
convoy worth $1,127,000, made up of consignments from Zacatecas,
San Luis, and Guanajuato, owned mostly by Englishmen, and bound
for Tampico, came under the protection of General Ignacio Echeagaray, a subordinate of Doblado. Under orders from Doblado,
Echeagaray seized the convoy at Laguna Seca, near San Luis Potosí,
on September 9. Doblado then informed Degollado of what he had
done.

As we have already had occasion to notice, Doblado's moral scruples were not conspicuous, and he was now able to argue reasonably
that without the seizure the constitutional cause and perhaps even
the country's independence would have been lost. Sierra adds that
the probability, at this point, with the additional resources, of a
victory by the constitutional side, which still could repay such
"forced loans" from the nationalized wealth, differentiated this act
from similar ones by the reactionaries. Such a robbing is hardly
shocking, but Santos Degollado was an early Christian in temperament, not physically strong, emotionally unfit for military command
in an especially brutal war, near exhaustion and mental collapse. It
was the culmination of a predictable psychological and moral tragedy. Having accepted or demanded personal responsibility for the
seizure of the convoy, he now suffered tortures. He wrote: "Who
deceives his own conscience? Who has not thought, in his conferences with God and with posterity, of the meaning of such a deed?
I had given everything to my country, and I had kept a spotless
name to leave to my children. Necessity came, however, knocking
at my door and begging me, in the name of my cause, to turn my
reputation over to mockery and obloquy, and I, after a horrible
agony, murdered my name, cut myself off from any future, and
declared myself a criminal." This was evidently written later. To
Ocampo, Degollado wrote from Lagos de Moreno on September 16:
"If you do not condemn me in your heart, and sympathize with me

in misfortune, I hope that your brotherly love will represent me, in order to excuse me, before the President, whose friendship I hope to save, even though as head of the nation he has to punish me."

He now made things worse by paying back 400,000 pesos, chiefly to the English, while the generals under him naturally protested that necessity had justified the deed, all of the money was required, and it could be paid back after the victory of the constitutional cause. Degollado wrote later to Juárez that he had made this repayment to prevent certain attack on the gulf ports by the foreign powers concerned—but even in those days, considering what had happened at Antón Lizardo, such an outcome was most unlikely, at least until after consultation with London, Paris, and Madrid. Juárez must have been disturbed by Degollado's mental condition when he heard of it, but perhaps he did not hear of it until it had manifested itself much more dangerously.

Meanwhile, England, France, Spain, and Prussia, probably at the suggestion of Almonte, had come to some kind of an agreement to offer to settle Mexican affairs by having a Mexican congress make a settlement subject to their approval. The United States refused to have any part of this scheme, and of course Juárez rejected it, while disclaiming any personal ambition.

Degollado tried to drag his leader, cause, and country, to which, as he had truly said, he had given everything, down with him. He had already been in touch with and probably influenced by the formidable Mr. Mathew, and he now offered to this interested diplomat a "Plan of Pacification." "He proposed that a congress should within three months decree a constitution, on the basis of the reform laws; that the diplomatic corps, together with delegates of the two rival parties should name a President, who was to be neither Miramón nor Juárez." From Lagos on September 23 he sent this plan to Juárez, in the form of a copy of a letter he had already sent to Mathew. In a covering letter, he says that if Juárez approves, the triumph of the liberal cause is certain; and if not, will he please accept his resignation already offered in Veracruz. "Sr. González Ortega agrees with the bases expressed here, and Sr. Doblado will do whatever the government decides."

In a reply from Veracruz dated October 4, Juárez courteously but vehemently rejects the whole plan, citing eloquent statements made by Degollado himself, when Foreign Secretary, to Captain Aldham, in defense of the Constitution and of Juárez as its embodiment. Juárez says that the plan was the same as that proposed to him by Mathew on September 18, and rejected by him on September 22. He will not try to dissuade Degollado, "and I shall only permit myself to answer that in no manner do I approve of your project of pacification, and that in the fulfillment of my duty I shall employ every legal means within my power to defeat it." As for the resignation, Juárez demands a new one that will explain the new causes for it.

In a letter to Juárez written at Tepatitlán (between Lagos and Guadalajara) on October 16 before he had received Juárez' letter of October 4, Degollado passes on copies of letters between González Ortega and Doblado on one side and Mathew on the other, but says he does not forward the generals' letters to himself because, in rejecting his peace project, their language is too disrespectful. He says that he is sorry to report that Doblado and González Ortega had given his project their full support, but had since rejected it with as much heat as bad faith. He says that he will explain his motives to the nation later. It is in this letter that he offers his explanation of his return of 400,000 of the stolen pesos. In a postscript he adds that he is being calumniated by General Huerta in Morelia, and in a later letter to Ocampo he expresses a fear that Doblado or Huerta may attack his family or himself. In reading Degollado's letters at this time, it is impossible to avoid a strong suspicion that he was suffering from paranoia, yet through it all he retains his faith in Ocampo and Juárez. Only they "have been motivated by a sense of justice, unlike Llave and the others. I feel myself relieved of my moral evils, and have only one desire: to see as soon as possible the virtuous and distinguished Sr. Juárez in the Palace in Mexico."

Juárez relieved Degollado of his command and ordered his trial by court-martial. Through the Minister of the Interior, Juárez also sent a circular to all of the liberal governors, repudiating Degollado and his project; but in a personal letter to the Governor of Chiapas he added that he would never forget Degollado's previous services to the Republic. As soon as Juárez' position became known, Degollado and his project received no further support, and somewhat unfairly, his trial was indefinitely postponed. The collapse of Degollado is one of the most poignant episodes in the entire war.

It seems all the more so because Doblado and especially González Ortega were almost equally guilty. They were not exhausted and neurotic, they may on their whole records be more reasonably suspected of personal ambition, and they got away with it. It seems likely that they did at first respond to Degollado's project as he reported them to have done, and then lost their nerve. With regard to González Ortega—or Ortega, as he is more frequently called—the evidence is too clear. He was at this time besieging Guadalajara, and at the beginning of the siege, without any authority whatever, he tried to reach a settlement with his opponent, General Castillo, by offering to abandon Juárez. Luckily Castillo rejected this offer as insufficient, and when Juárez received documentary proof of this transaction from Degollado, he calmly noted on the margin: "Degollado and Ortega exhort the President to forsake his post." As early as February 17, 1860, Ortega had self-righteously reported to Juárez his rejection of a proposal by unnamed persons in Monterey for the secession and coalition of northern states.

On November 4, from Jalapa, even Miguel Lerdo de Tejada—at least loyally keeping him informed and seeking his authority—wrote to Juárez to inform him that, he, Lerdo, had been approached for peace talks by "persons of high character in the capital." Juárez replied that such persons, including Miramón, who could not now hope to get the terms he desired, could openly approach Juárez himself, who would then consult the cabinet and other persons such as Lerdo.

This whole crisis of unauthorized attempts to make peace was clearly as dangerous as any Juárez had surmounted, and it must have been more harrowing to him than Miramón's bombs had been, in Veracruz. It is easy for us to say now that he might have been less harsh towards Degollado and given Doblado and Ortega, or at least the latter, equal treatment, but although the constitutional forces were now finally winning, the victory had not yet been secured, and to cashier all three might well have resulted in losing everything to an open and successful *pronunciamiento* supported by Mathew and the other diplomats and seized upon by Miramón. As possible replacements of all three, Zaragoza and Valle had shown their military skill and their loyalty but were not yet comparably influential. In any case, the imminent result was to justify Juárez' tolerance of Ortega. In this situation, and in later ones, the personal response of his colleagues to Juárez himself must be considered. The fact that the evidence is tenuous indeed in itself indicates that both as a man and as the legal President increasingly known, trusted, and even venerated by the soldiers and people, Juárez commanded his colleagues' respect and even fear. They had been confronted in January, 1858, by his legal title, as President, which they needed, but by December, 1860, his acumen, tenacity, decisiveness, and luck, known more and more beyond the cabinet room and beyond the sea, had made him a force and a symbol that they were apt to forget while off campaigning, or while talking or writing very privately among themselves, but one that sooner or later they had to face. When they did face him personally, or one of his letters, they invariably had second thoughts on the matter in question, and the quietly, courteously expressed will of Sr. Juárez prevailed. Miguel Lerdo, Doblado, Ortega, and plenty of others were personally ambitious for the Presidency, while he was clearly not so—a fact that baffled and must have irritated men who remembered that he had acquired his office almost by chance, and who shared but dimly, if at all, his compelling vision of a democratic and orderly Mexico. Many of them were soldiers who, however ineptly, had commanded men in action, while almost all that he had done in that way was to face assassination with serenity. Many of them were still governors—or rather, feudal barons —with political and economic power over huge areas and thousands of people, while Juárez (again like Ocampo) had previously been successful only as a democratic if paternalistic civil servant in a state now torn by dissension among the liberals themselves, a state now completely out of his control and only recently salvaged, for the time being, for the Republic, by a soldier named Porfirio Díaz. Finally, many of these men, always excepting the brothers Lerdo, were by temperament truly romantic, embracing each other easily (invisible knives in their hands), while Juárez, except in relation to his family, Santacilia, and Ocampo, was genial but immensely reserved; he was also obviously sincere, and startlingly willing to make use, up to the last, impossible point, of men who had failed or who had betrayed him personally but who might still, conceivably, serve the Republic. Integrity, disinterested concentration on one job, stamina, and above all, extreme self-sufficiency, seasoned only by graciousness and a certain disillusioned and ironic humor—these are not common human traits, shared and hence easily understood and loved by the rest of us. To Juárez' colleagues he must have been what he has been to many persons since his time: a mysterious power rather than a man, with a charm, if any, that was most elusive. To them he must also have been a very present help in trouble or a profoundly baffling and irritating burden, or even both at once. It is no wonder that they argued and plotted behind his back.

Whatever they made of him then, whatever others make of him now, there can be no reasonable question that this crisis, among the leaders, as in others before and later, it was Juárez, and Juárez alone, without egotism or rancor, using every human resource available to him, and implacable of will, who saved the situation, the liberal cause, and the nation.

At the siege of Guadalajara, Ortega became seriously ill, and the command was temporarily taken over by a relatively new and obscure figure, General Ignacio Zaragoza from the north, who managed to conquer the city in time to defeat an attempt by Márquez to relieve it. Constitutional forces now began to close in on Miramón in Mexico City, from all sides. His financial position was also desperate, and on November 16, he authorized the robbery of $700,000 belonging to British bondholders, from the British Legation. Miramón was never lacking in courage or resource, and in a quick foray from the City on December 8, he reached Toluca and captured almost all the constitutional forces assembled there, including Generals Degollado (without command) and Felipe Berriozábal and a large supply of arms and ammunition. (On December 22, from prison in Mexico City, Degollado wrote a pathetic and moving letter to Ocampo in Veracruz: he is very nervous about the imminent battle for the city, but of course wants the liberals to win it, even if it costs him his life; for if he escaped, where could he go and what could he do?) Ortega, with a growing army, now approached from the north, while desertions from Miramón's forces increased. Hoping to prevent the union of all the constitutional forces, Miramón went out to the northeast with about 8,000 men, and at Calpulálpam, on December 22, he met a force about twice that large, under Ortega, and was decisively defeated.

Returning to the City, Miramón surrendered it to his prisoners, Degollado and Berriozábal, then divided the remainder of his loot, $140,000, with Zuloaga and other reactionaries, and after narrowly escaping capture at Jalapa, managed to reach the coast and be taken aboard a French naval vessel, *Le Mercure*, which took him to France. This method of escape aroused the ire of the British, including Captain Aldham, who now regarded Miramón as a simple thief, and of Juárez, who later ordered the confiscation of Miramón's property. Marquéz, Zuloaga, and other reactionary chieftains took to the mountains as leaders of very dangerous and destructive bands now lacking any government or military status.

In Veracruz on the night of December 23, Juárez, his family, and Gutiérrez Zamora were in a box at the theatre, listening to Bellini's opera *I Puritani*. In the middle of the performance there arrived a formidable horseman who had left Calpulálpam only the day before. Having ordered the curtain lowered and the music stopped, Juárez rose and quietly read the news of the victory and the end—as was supposed—of the war. Ignoring the Mexican national anthem, first sung six years before, the opera singers, with unconscious irony, broke into the *Marseillaise*, and bedlam broke loose in Veracruz.

On January 1, 1861, General González Ortega led his 20,000 troops into Mexico City, where they received a tremendous welcome. They did not pillage the city, as the trembling reactionaries had feared. Ortega was a dashing and glamorous figure with a pale face, brilliant eyes, and wide, sharply waxed moustaches. Riding at the head of his troops, in the pealing of the bells, the shouts of the crowd, and the rain of flowers, he caught sight of his former commanding officer, Degollado, on a balcony of the Hotel Iturbide, and made him come down into the street, where he gallantly embraced him and made him share in the triumph. It was their finest hour, and Degollado had few left. It might have been better for Mexico if we could say the same of Ortega.

The means of travel in those days gave Presidents some mental if not physical rest. Juárez, his family, and his Ministers took ten days to move from Veracruz, which he never saw again, to Mexico City, and although the war was at least nominally ended, Juárez needed all the change and rest he could get.

15

TURMOIL, BANKRUPTCY, AND MURDER

VICTORS IN WAR have rarely if ever been able to relax, but the constitutional government of Mexico now moved into an extremely tense and difficult period of "peace." Nominally, the War of the Reform came to an end with the year 1860, but during the bitter year 1861 reactionary forces, without any legal status, continued to strike painful blows, and at the end of that year other reactionaries accepted the support of a foreign invasion that therefore only partly united the nation in a continued struggle for independence and self-determination as well as for reform. The bloody birth of this nation was prolonged for ten years, 1857–67, often called "the great national decade."

On January 11, 1861, after an overnight delay at Guadalupe, Juárez entered the capital and received a tumultuous welcome. He knew that action had to begin at once, and he called a cabinet meeting for that very night. A manifesto was issued to the nation, praising the heroes of the war and emphasizing legality and the continued Reform. Even the day before, Ocampo had urged upon Juárez the resignation of the whole Ministry, in order to give the President new freedom of action, and he had rejected the idea, because of his loyalty to his colleagues; but now he agreed to the first changes, giving Ortega the Ministry of War and Francisco Zarco Foreign Affairs. By January 21, Prieto had returned to the Treasury and Ignacio Ramírez had become Minister of Justice, Public Instruction and Development. During the following months the extreme difficulties of the government with finance, foreign affairs, and internal disorders, the irresponsible pressures and demands of the radicals and the press, the ambitions and fears of the leading liberals, a general impression that the Constitution required or permitted a degree of parliamentary government, and even a new and temporary indecisiveness on the part of Juárez himself, all resulted in frequent cabinet changes of which we shall note only the most important.

The immediate problem on January 11, one that harassed the government for months, was how to handle the reactionaries. Some of their leaders were now in the government's power, and the radicals were screaming for vengeance, but as Prieto pointed out later, in connection with the Treasury, some of the reactionaries holding public office were the only competent bureaucrats available. It was decided that night to try the leading reactionaries according to the law on conspiracy, to expel Pacheco of Spain, the Ministers of Guatemala and Ecuador, and the Papal Legate, to banish the leading bishops, and to give amnesty to the rest. In at least one case, Juárez had to give in to public opinion, or at least to its most vociferous expressions. Isidro Díaz, a close associate of Miramón's, had been caught on the way to the coast. He was ordered tried for conspiracy, and as a soldier, which meant immediate execution upon conviction; but a few days later, Miramón's wife, whom he had left in the care of the chivalrous General Leandro Valle, appeared with "don Benito Gómez Farías, who explained that Isidro Díaz had recommended that neither he, [Gómez Farías] nor Sr. Degollado be shot when they were prisoners in Toluca," just before the reactionary defeat. Juárez reported this to the cabinet, and it was unanimously agreed that Díaz should only be banished for five years. The next day, however, there was an outcry over this decision in the powerful political clubs, the University, and the press, and also from Captain Aldham in Veracruz, because of Díaz' alleged part in the burglary of the British Legation. Juárez and the cabinet backed down, ordering Díaz' transfer to the City for trial as a conspirator. He was finally acquitted, but Juárez admitted that this outcry had influenced his appointment of a more radical Ministry, including Ramírez.

Ocampo had gone happily home to Pomoca, to his now motherless daughters, to his precious plants, and to his translation of Proudhon. Miguel Lerdo de Tejada had become President of the Supreme Court, and like Ortega, an active candidate for the Presidency. As early as November 6, 1860, and then again on January 11, 1861, Juárez issued the decrees for the elections of the deputies and of the President, but it would take several months to hold these elections, first of the electors and then of the officials themselves, and to have Congress meet, count the votes and declare the results. Unfortunately for the Republic, Governor Manuel Gutiérrez Zamora of Veracruz, who had been a bulwark of strength during the war, died on March 21, and Miguel Lerdo de Tejada, who, despite his defeatism and his impractical radicalism, had been one of the vital intellects on the liberal side, also died on March 22, in the midst of the elections. Ortega was a popular hero, ambitious and erratic, rather than a statesman. Prieto, Ramírez, Zarco, and their successors in the cabinet, such as Mata, Zaragoza, and Zamacona, were forceful and talented men, as well as remarkably honest ones, but unfortunately it takes more than a powerful President, a handful of such men, and a brief interlude of "peace" of sorts, to make a strong democracy. The still primitive economy was now in ruins, the foreign powers were still voracious, most of the governors and other politicians were irresponsible egotists, and the masses were still uneducated, exhausted, and indifferent.

Another serious problem was that of financing and strengthening the federal government. The value of the Church properties had been overestimated. During the most desperate days at Veracruz, the government had had to sell many of them at a fraction of their value. Many others had been seized by governors and generals, and not always or even often for their own gain, but to pay their troops and get on with the war. In their own ways, the reactionaries had despoiled the Church also, and by trying to undo the effects of the Reform Laws in places under their control, they had compromised legal titles to former Church properties irretrievably. As a result of this chaos, the human vultures, neither liberal nor reactionary, schemed successfully for themselves only, became rich, and exploited the peasants more grievously than the Church itself had ever done. The war had damaged the economy so seriously that there was not much production, income, or commerce, internal or external, to be taxed. The system of having the states collect most of the taxes and then turn over stated parts of the receipts to the federal government was as ineffective as ever. At least half of the federal income—some $13,000,000 in all—should have come from the shrinking customs receipts, but most of these were mortgaged to the three European powers, 100 per cent on the Pacific Coast and 85 per cent on the Atlantic. The monthly deficit was about $400,000. Lacking solvent banks and an investing public, the government was forced, like some desperate householder, to borrow repeatedly from *agiotistas*, or usurers. Juárez' *Diary* of this year records repeated steps taken to raise a few thousand pesos to pay the police or some unit of the army in order to preserve order within the City, or to repel reactionaries and bandits within a few miles of it.

Prieto, assisted by his able Under Secretary, José María Iglesias, found few records or personnel, so that the figures above, and all others, must remain doubtful. He worked from seven in the morning until midnight, but was sharply attacked in the press and even personally, in the streets. He suggested obtaining somehow a release from the liens held by foreign nations on the customs receipts, reducing the army, and taking a firmer hand with the states in the matter of taxes—all steps as sensible superficially as they were dangerous. Juárez made every possible reduction in administrative expenses, such as reducing the number of Ministers and their salaries, and cutting his own salary from $36,000 to $30,000. On April 22 Prieto gave up and was replaced by J. M. Mata, who lasted only a few weeks.

While the government tottered on the verge of bankruptcy and collapse, the raids of the reactionaries increased, and the army could hardly keep them out of Mexico City, the governments of Great Britain, Spain, and France turned their screws a little deeper into the Republic.

The British, already getting most of the Mexican customs receipts, were now demanding, besides the money stolen at Laguna Seca, which was being repaid, that stolen from the British Legation by Miramón. Zarco had to accept this responsibility also, and then a nasty incident exacerbated these relations. An attack by reactionaries on a stagecoach resulted in the serious wounding of Captain Aldham and the death of a young French lady. Sir Charles Lennox Wyke, the new British Ambassador, replacing Mathew, on landing at Veracruz in May, "haughtily demanded a salute of fourteen guns, instead of the eleven that had been given him there." He was received by Juárez on May 25.

Before and after the expulsion of the insolent Spanish Minister Pacheco, the relations between Mexico and Spain were inevitably hostile. The oppressions of the colonial period, the brutalities of the War for Independence, and the arrogance of the Spaniards still living in Mexico, almost all reactionaries at heart if not openly, could not yet be forgotten, and Spain, as a reactionary Catholic power, having troubles with the liberals in her Cuban colony, was naturally hostile to the Mexican reformers. Spaniards in Cuba had supplied Marín's two vessels, and now Spain was trying to force upon Juárez' government the illegal and humiliating financial claims of the Mon–Almonte Treaty, signed by Miramón, that had preceded and encouraged that attempted intervention in his favor. It was known to Juárez and his government that Mexican monarchists had, if unsuccessfully, approached don Juan of Bourbon, the Spanish Infante, with the idea of his claiming or accepting the throne of Mexico. An attempt at a second Spanish conquest of Mexico, and a tripartite intervention, although already rumored, were not considered likely. Spaniards were hated but not greatly feared.

The real danger, from France, was not at this time clearly perceived by the Mexicans, chiefly because Mexican liberalism, from its beginnings, had fed on French political thought and revolutionary action, and the second culture of such educated and cosmopolitan Mexicans as Ocampo and Valle was French. Juárez himself, it will be remembered, had a better command of French than of English, and a friendly Frenchman, Armando Montluc, was acting as Mexican Consul General in France. What had been forgotten or minimized were the facts that for ten years Napoleon III had ruled in France, that his liberalism was superficial and opportunistic, that he had a scheming, rabidly Catholic, Spanish wife, and that longing above all to equal his uncle, and dissatisfied with the results of his military adventures in the Crimea and Italy, he was already dreaming of a satellite Empire of Mexico that would prevent further Protestant intrusion from the north and would add to his own power and prestige in the world.

In 1859, for a quick loan of $750,000, Miramón had turned over to a Swiss banker named Jecker Mexican bonds to the amount of $15,000,000, and the Duc de Morny, money-mad half-brother to the Emperor, now owned many of these bonds or backed the attempt to have them recognized for a commission. The Conte Dubois de Saligny, the arrogant and intrusive new French Minister, received formally on March 16, now demanded payment on all of these bonds. One of his arguments was that Juárez and Zarco had accepted the responsibility of the Mexican nation for Miramón's burglary of the British Legation—ignoring, of course, the difference between recognizing a very doubtful debt of $700,000 to the British and allowing the Duc de Morny to burgle the Mexican nation to the tune of $14,250,000.

Now the admirable and beloved Sisters of Charity, "Daughters of St. Vincent de Paul," still had at that time an establishment in Mexico City, and hearing that they were hiding Church property, General Valle sent one Colonel González to investigate. The Colonel found some hidden money, suspected there was more, and was somewhat rude to the Mother Superior; whereupon that lady appealed for help to Saligny, as the representative of a Catholic power. Saligny then protested abusively, claiming that all over the world these Sisters were under the protection of Napoleon III. There were other offensive performances by this nobleman, and in response, Zarco and his successors could only evade and procrastinate.

On January 19, 1861, in Springfield, Illinois, whither he had traveled for the purpose, Romero had an interview with the President-Elect, Abraham Lincoln, which he recorded in his diary as follows:

I told him the object of my journey and read to him the note from the Foreign Minister in which I had received my instructions; then I explained to him that the only cause of the revolutions in Mexico had been the clergy and the army, which, in order to retain their privileges and influence that they had enjoyed during the colonial regime, had rebelled against all of the constitutions; but now that they had been completely conquered, there were solid hopes that Mexico would enjoy peace and prosperity. He said to me in reply that during his administration he would do everything in his power to favor the interests of Mexico, that it would be justly treated in every event that occurred, and that it would be considered a friendly and sister nation. He added that he did not believe that anything could occur that would make him change his mind. He asked me for the copy in English that I had read to him of the note of the Foreign Minister and said that he would repeat in writing what he had just said to me. Then I said that Mexico had rejoiced in the victory of the Republican Party, because it hoped that the policy of this party would be more loyal and friendly, and not like that of the Democratic Party, which had amounted to nothing but an attempt to steal Mexican territory for the extension of slavery. He asked me about the condition of the peons in Mexico, because he had heard it said that they lived in veritable slavery, and he was much pleased when I told him that the abuses existed in only a few places and violated the law. He asked me the population of Mexico City, and he was agreeably surprised when he learned it, for he had thought it very small. We spoke of the nomination of Mr. Seward as Secretary of State, and of other matters. He expressed himself very strongly against slavery. . . . In the interview with Mr. Lincoln I left him various papers that I had prepared and taken, on Mexico, so that he could study them, because he did not seem to be well informed on events in Mexico.

As always in his diary, to our loss, Romero gives no visual or intuitive impression of the person interviewed, or of the setting, which in this case was the modest Lincoln house.

During the remaining four years of his life, despite his inevitable support of Seward's cautious policy, which in that tremendous crisis had to be as wary as Juárez' own, and which often exasperated Romero, Lincoln kept his promise. During his administration and President Johnson's, despite the vagaries and errors of hotheads on both sides of the border, the records of Lincoln, Johnson, and Juárez, in the relations between the two countries, need no apologies whatever by anyone, and in all reasonable minds they have wiped out forever the records of such figures as Polk, Buchanan, and Santa Anna. However, on April 12, 1861, General P. G. T. Beauregard of South Carolina opened fire on Fort Sumter, and it became clear in Mexico and Europe that Captain Jarvis and Commander Turner and their comrades would now find grimmer duties in the north, and that except for odd lots of arms and ammunition not at the moment needed at home, the United States could give the Mexican government little but moral support, which was not however negligible. One dangerous element in the whole picture was the relative ignorance of Napoleon III of the strength of the North, and he was by no means the only person in power in Europe who expected an early dissolution of the American Union.

The new American Minister sent to Mexico by Lincoln and Seward was Thomas Corwin of Ohio, a much more distinguished man than his predecessors, who had served in Congress, as Governor, as Senator, and as Secretary of the Treasury, but whose great advantage in Mexico in 1861 was the fact that as Senator he had valiantly imperiled his career by leading the opposition to the war of 1846–48. He was received by Juárez on May 21 with a greeting clearly much warmer than such diplomatic formalities usually are. If Corwin's mission was disappointing in its concrete results, that was only because under the circumstances in the United States, Europe, and Mexico, no man in his position could have accomplished much.

The Confederacy sent to Veracruz a man named Pickett, whom the government ignored, and another named Quintero to Vidaurri to protest against a reported imminent attack from northern Mexico against Texas. With unaccustomed correctness, Vidaurri pointed out that he could not conduct diplomatic relations, and then denied that any such attacks were planned. This was only the beginning of a prolonged threat, of no mean proportions, both to the United States and to Juárez' government: that of a possible union of France, the Confederacy, and reactionary elements in Mexico.

Because of the disorganization of the Mexican states, the elections to the Congress and of the President proceeded slowly, but the unicameral Congress was able to convene on May 9. Yielding up the extraordinary powers he had inherited from Comonfort, Juárez declared: "Before this assembly and before all of my fellow citizens, I accept the responsibility for all of the measures decreed by my administration that were not in the strict bounds of the Constitution when, rejected and tenaciously opposed, it had ceased to exist, and was, instead of the rules of [political] combat, the objective of the Republic." Among many other matters, he reported the beginning of the construction of a railroad to Veracruz and the renewal of the schools; he also explained that the expulsion of the Papal Legate did nothing to hinder Mexican Catholics in their spiritual relations with the Papacy.

Promptly Juárez encountered another prolonged cabinet crisis, reported in some detail in his diary, that was caused partly by the extreme difficulty of the times and of the tasks that Juárez had to offer his Ministers, partly by the rebelliousness of the politicians now in Congress who had for the most part been voiceless and powerless during the preceding three years, and partly by Juárez' own attempt to get along better with Congress by establishing a quasi-parliamentary form of government, within the Constitution, a form in which the members of the cabinet should also be deputies seated in Congress and responsible in part to it as well as to the President. This vague concept, separating the cabinet somewhat from the President, had already received some acceptance, because the Foreign Ministers had acted as chiefs of the cabinets under Álvarez, Comonfort, and Juárez, and resignations, for example, had been offered not to the Presidents but to the Foreign Ministers; and Ministers had appeared in Congress to answer questions. This project was also consonant with the Roman legal system used in Mexico, and with the Mexican practice, under French influence, that is so baffling and alarming to Americans, of allowing executive, legislative, judicial, and even military offices and functions to overlap each other. Juárez himself, it will be remembered, had in 1857 served as Minister of the Interior while on leave from the Presidency of the Supreme Court; and Ortega, who had no legal training or status, was at various times Governor of Zacatecas, President of the Supreme Court, Minister of War, member of Congress, and a General in the field; sometimes, in fact, he was several of these things, and even a voluntary exile or deserter, at the same time. This parliamentary project, at this time, must be counted among Juárez' few mistakes, and it is probably fortunate that Congress rejected it, if only in order to maintain its own nuisance value uncompromised.

Towards the end of May the rebellion of Congress became very serious when it almost set up a Committee of Public Safety, talked of overthrowing Juárez, and dragging up the McLane–Ocampo Treaty, accused Juárez and Ocampo of treason for negotiating it. Juárez, after a defense by Zarco, received a vote of confidence, and

Ocampo, then a deputy, was ordered to come to Mexico and explain the negotiations. This was on May 29, and before he heard from Congress, Ocampo met another appointment.

On May 4, from Pomoca, Ocampo had written to his old friend and colleague Juárez: "I was planning not to go [to Congress] until I had brought in my little harvest of wheat and had finished planting my corn. Now I am only waiting to send to that city the remainder of my old crop [of corn], which will be from what is still standing there. I have my credentials. I am grateful for the kindness with which you urge me to go. I do not think that in the first days the Congress will do any mischief; and I shall be glad to help them avoid going astray in their misguided zeal. Greetings to the Señora and the girls."

On May 14 he wrote—perhaps half ironically, although he was then financially hard pressed—that he had been officially rebuked for not appearing in Congress, that he was nearing the end of his career, and that he had to be sure of his subsistence, while the payment of travel expenses by Congress seemed to him very uncertain. "Therefore I shall not go until the defense of Sr. Degollado requires it." Then he sends thanks to the Señora for a jar of conserves she had sent him by the diligence, and says he will send her a letter in care of the carter whom he has finally secured for his wheat, and who will leave Pomoca within a week.

On May 21: "The carter who was to have taken my wheat came yesterday, but in the end he did not take it, although we had already come to terms; but he did take three small boxes for you and my *comadrita* [fellow godparent or dear old friend, the Señora Margarita]. One is a wine of this region. They make it fourteen leagues [forty-two miles] from this your house, on a mountain called The Saint Andrew, harvesting the wild grapes from an area with a radius of as much as thirty-six miles. It is an industry that is growing rapidly, and that I believe will come to have a certain importance, for in the third year, which was last year, they made more than three hundred barrels. I do not send it to you to drink as it is, because it retains a wild flavor, but so that you may observe an oddity on tasting it with tea. It has seemed to me and to many of us that when one puts from an eighth to a sixth of a cup of this wine, poured out at the time of drinking it, into a cup of good tea, it gives it the scent and taste of strawberries. When the occasion presents itself, I hope that you will allow our friends the Sres. Mejía, Ruiz, Goytia, and Zambrano to try this also. The other boxes contain various preserves, of which I have already recommended to the Señora the *chirimoyate*. They will no longer say that guava jelly is the only industry of Michoacán. In the last few days, erysipelas of the face has returned to plague me, but I am now recovering."

Peaceful and inwardly rich as don Melchor Ocampo's life was, there in that remote, enchanted valley with his remaining daughters, a new mistress, his farming and gardening, and his intellectual pursuits, he must have remembered that two years before, the forces of Márquez had penetrated his Eden and tried to catch and hang his servant, Esteban Campos; and he must have known that Márquez' surviving bandits were roaming and pillaging near by, in eastern Michoacán. On May 30, the day after he was called a traitor in Congress, warned more precisely that hoodlums were near and probably hunting him, Ocampo, against the protests of his younger daughters and his latter-day mistress, Campos' daughter, sent them off to a fiesta at Maravatío. At noon there was a beating on his door, and Lindoro Cajiga, Márquez' gunman, with others, forced his way into the house and, refusing the refreshment Ocampo offered them, took him prisoner.

He was given a pair of chaps, ordered to mount a horse, and taken through Maravatío, where Cajiga kept him from meeting his daughters, to various villages to the east, and finally, on the morning of June 3, to Tepeji del Río, about forty miles north of Mexico City. A few yards from the simple inn room in which Ocampo was imprisoned, Márquez and Zuloaga, who still had the effrontery to call himself President of Mexico, decided, without seeing him, upon Ocampo's death. There was some confusion about Ocampo and another prisoner who was let go, but there is no doubt about the guilt of both Márquez and Zuloaga. Later, in the classic style of teamed murderers, each tried to blame the other. The actual gunmen were Cajiga and a General Taboada.

At ten in the morning Ocampo was told he would be killed, and was given pen and ink with which he wrote his will, acknowledging his four natural daughters, adopting Clara Campos as a daughter, naming his executors, and concluding: "I say farewell to all my good friends and to all who have helped me in little or in much, and I die believing that in the service of my country I have done what I believed in good faith to be good." At two in the afternoon he was mounted on a horse between files of armed and mounted men. Before leaving the town, he was approached by a priest, and he said: "Father, I am well with God, and He is well with me." When the party reached the near-by *hacienda* of Caltenango, he was given permission to make an addition to his will, which he wrote under the portico of the *hacienda*. In this addition, he said that the will of doña Ana María Escobar, the mother of his children, not here named as such, was "in my notebook in English between the fire screen of the sala and the window of my bedroom." In this addition, he also left his books, which numbered about ten thousand, after his executors and a named friend should have chosen those they wished, to his beloved Colegio de San Nicolás in Morelia.

The dreadful company again proceeded, and not far from the *hacienda*, Ocampo was ordered to dismount, was there shot in the head and chest, and dropped dead in the dust of the road. Securing a cord under the arms, the assassins hoisted the body into a pepper tree and fled. "Hours later, kind hands recovered and washed the body, which was covered with mud made by dust and blood."

On the day before, Sunday, June 2, the fiesta of Corpus Christi, in the midst of a severe financial crisis involving the borrowing of a million pesos to pay back the last of the money stolen at Laguna Seca, Juárez noted: "It was learned that the forces of Márquez had arrested Sr. Deputy Don Melchor Ocampo, and also don Francisco Schiafino." While struggling on June 3 with financial problems, and with the arrest of Zuloaga's mother on a charge of aiding reactionaries—proofs disappeared and she was released—Juárez must have felt and perhaps shared with his wife the most dreadful forebodings about his old friend, and the next three days must have been among the worst in his life. When the blow fell, however, it and the violent public response aroused Juárez to his old vigor and decisiveness. In his entry for June 4, he wrote:

At seven in the morning Sr. Pietro told me that according to what he had been told by one of the menservants who were in the enemy camp, Zuloaga and Márquez had ordered Sr. Ocampo shot. Within half an hour he returned with a letter from Márquez himself, directed to a Sr. Carrillo, in which this fatal news was confirmed. Considering the violent sensation that this lamentable misfortune was going to produce among the people, and fearing that an attack would be made on the persons of the political prisoners, I gave orders that the guards at the prisons be doubled, and charged the Governor of the District [Berriozábal], the Military Commander, don Leandro Valle, and the Minister of War [Ignacio Zaragoza] to show the greatest vigilance.

In a little while the news spread through the city, and persons of all classes were presented to us, begging that the political prisoners be executed at once, and even declaring that if the government did not do this, they and the people would do this duty of justice. I did everything within my means to dissuade these people from committing the least offense, since I as the legitimate governor of the society should do everything possible to have the offenders punished in accordance with the laws, but I should never permit the use of de facto methods against the criminals who were under the protection of the laws and the authorities. [I told them] that they should note that those who sacrificed my loyal friend Sr. Ocampo were assassins, and that I was the governor of an enlightened society. Sres. don Leandro Valle and don Aureliano Rivera witnessed this scene.

Young General Valle did more than witness this scene. In another one, apparently at the gates of a prison, he, like Juárez, did more than defend the Republic: in standing up to the mobs, they were *making* a Republic. "He was extremely popular," says Sierra;

his rôle during the war of three years, always fighting, squandering his labor, his intelligence, and his life in Jalisco and then in the Bajío, where he had been one of the principal organizers of the victory; his chivalrous conduct with Miramón, his schoolmate, who on fleeing had entrusted to him his family; his radical anticlericalism; his temperament—articulate, jovial, candid, and witty; even his figure—the very short hair, the complexion white and almost beardless except for a pointed little beard on his chin only; the body medium in size, tough, light, and supple; the frank and sparkling expression; and even the small black hat always worn on the back of his head, leaving his high forehead exposed—all this had fixed him deeply in the affection of his party and in the admiring regard of the people. When these, like beasts set free, sought to seize the political prisoners, they found themselves facing Valle; almost alone, opening his arms as though better to protect the prisoners, he promised justice but repudiated the crime; and he imposed his will on their frenzy, so that groups of those madmen abandoned for the moment their thirst for a lynching and cried: "Death to the *mochos* [shorn persons, the current slang for reactionaries], but long live *el pelón* [Baldy] Valle!"

Juárez' entry for June 4 continues:

The excitement increased with the reunion of Congress. This body took various steps, among them that of giving the government power to get resources by whatever manner seemed fit. Sr. Degollado presented himself to Congress, asking permission to take part in the campaign. To this Congress assented, with the proviso that afterwards his trial should take place. Plans were then made in the cabinet for punitive expeditions of cavalry, commanded by Ortega, Degollado, and others, under the direction of Zaragoza.

At half past three in the afternoon, I was told that the diplomatic corps wished to speak with me. I went out with Sr. [León] Guzmán [the Foreign Minister]. Sr. Pastor, Minister of Ecuador, said that the diplomatic corps begged the government to suspend the execution of the political prisoners, because they had learned that it had been decided that they be executed that same afternoon; and that for the sake of the honor of the government they made this entreaty, because they did not want it to debase itself to the level of Zuloaga and Márquez, who were bandits.

They were answered with appropriate energy to the effect that the Mexican government, understanding its duty and its dignity, had never thought or allowed others to think of proceeding in a barbarous manner against persons who were under the shelter and protection of the authorities and the laws; that I regretted very much that they had formed so base an idea of the government of the Republic, judging it capable of an action so villainous and degrading, that they should accept as true a rumor spread by the common people, and that I wished them to disabuse themselves of an idea so offensive to the first authority of the state. The Ministers begged to be excused, saying that they had not believed such a rumor, and that they had taken this step only in order to do their humane duty, and without any intention of intruding upon the politics of the country.

The order for the protection of the prisoners was repeated, and Juárez made arrangements for Ocampo's funeral, while asking Congress "to grant some help to the family of Sr. Ocampo." General Valle caught one Pantaleon Moret, a reactionary, and with the permission of the cabinet, and in accordance with the law of conspirators, had him executed. Ocampo's nonreligious funeral was held on the afternoon of June 6, and Sierra suggests that this ceremony, and many others like it at the time, affected these Catholic people with a deep *malaise*, while at the same time planting in their minds a seed of religious liberty, and of their entire future.

In the midst of these painful excitements, the presidential campaign was finally somehow completed with the election of Juárez. It was objected that he had not received an absolute majority of the possible electors, but this legal quibble was put aside by the Congress when on June 11 it declared him elected by the close vote of 61 to 55. Among the electoral votes, Juárez had received 5,289, Lerdo (because the voting had proceeded before the receipt of the news of his death) 1,989, and Ortega 1,846. Corwin, no political neophyte, had reported to Seward that Ortega would probably replace Juárez. On June 27, perhaps illegally, Congress declared Ortega elected President of the Supreme Court. In his inaugural address on June 15, Juárez again disclaimed personal ambition and promised to uphold the law and pacify the country.

In these days the government continued to struggle with all kinds of administrative, judicial, and financial problems, but the chief concern of Juárez and his Ministers was of course the destruction of the reactionary guerrillas, which meant enlisting, organizing, equipping, and paying forces, chiefly of cavalry, and of getting them into the field under accepted patterns of command and tactical plans. Ortega kept insisting that he never had good enough horses or sufficient equipment to go out and fight, and although he clearly exasperated Juárez with his demands, the disastrous events of the next few days tend to give some credit to his caution, and to suggest that Juárez, his changing Ministers, and their more impetuous soldiers might have dealt with the situation more slowly and with greater care.

On June 15, the day when Juárez took the oath, Degollado, with a small force, was marching from Toluca and Lerma towards Mexico City, through those very high, pine-covered mountain passes, when his force fell into an ambush and he was killed. Thus came to an end the indomitable will, supersensitive conscience, tumultuous emotions, and finally muddled intellect of a gallant, nearly blind officer and gentleman named Santos Degollado.

While with an agony certainly felt and concealed, Juárez was trying to make sense out of the contradictory reports of this event, his leading Ministers resigned, and he had to begin again, with infinite patience and forbearance, to form a new collection of more or less able egotists into a cabinet that might have some support in Congress and that might be able somehow to get on with the nation's overwhelming work. To one hesitant gentleman he suggested that there was such a thing as patriotism, and he might have said the same, "with appropriate energy," to Manuel Doblado, to whom, by special courier on June 17 he sent a letter offering him Foreign Affairs, the Interior, or the Treasury, and from whom, on June 22, he received the answer "that he could not accept the Ministry because, the situation being so difficult, he would not last more than a few days, at the end of which he would depart as discredited as had all the others."

Luckily there were some more modest and patriotic men left in Mexico who were prepared to risk and lose more than their political reputations. On June 22 General Valle left for Toluca and the enemy with only eight hundred men, hoping to join the forces of Colonel O'Horán and General Arteaga. Before he could do so, at a place in the mountain heights near which Degollado had so recently been killed, he encountered some 3,000 reactionaries under Márquez, somewhat rashly gave battle, and was captured. Told that Márquez had ordered him shot after half an hour, he said that he would have given Márquez three minutes. When ordered to turn his back on the firing squad, he protested that he was no traitor, and was told that he was—to his religion. His body, like Ocampo's was strung up in a tree, and when a mission was sent to get it, the killers demanded and received $500 for their merchandise. Aquilas Collin was probably killed in the same action.

As Juárez must have known, endless hardships lay ahead for Mexico, and for his family and himself, but he may also have felt at this point, when Valle's mutilated body was brought into the City on June 28, that there was now no other direction in which they could move but upward.

PART FOUR

Intervention from Europe

16

THE JACKALS AND THE WOLVES

WHILE the military struggle continued, against the reactionary jackals who roamed about in the center of the Republic and came often to the outskirts of the capital itself, Juárez finally managed to recruit and have approved by Congress still another cabinet. It con-* sisted of Manuel M. Zamacona, Minister of Foreign Affairs—a man of talent, culture, and self-confidence, but dwarfed, as anyone else would have been, by the facts of the situation; Ignacio Zaragoza, of War—another superior character, who had to handle the incorrigible egotism and the popularity of Ortega as Commander-in-Chief; José Higinio Nuñez, of the Treasury; Blas Balcárcel, of Development; and Joaquín Ruiz, of Justice.

A minor but delicate problem presented itself to the cabinet on July 15, when Juárez notes: "The official newspaper of Nuevo León was read, in which it appears that don Santiago Vidaurri gave permission to don Ignacio Comonfort to live in that state. It was agreed to tell Sr. Vidaurri, by special courier, to arrest Comonfort and to send him, with appropriate security, to this capital, so that he may be judged in accordance with the laws." Vidaurri ignored the order, but by January 13, 1862, Juárez had softened somewhat; Comonfort then took advantage of an amnesty; and by September 2, 1862, he had been restored to grace and even given command of a division in the north. As usual, Juárez quite impersonally upheld the law unless and until the exigencies of the situation forced him to change or ignore the law for the benefit of the Republic alone.

The financial problem had now become so extreme that unless radical action was taken at once, the armed forces would desert or rebel and the government would collapse. A temporary suspension of payments on the foreign debts had been considered and rejected at Veracruz, and the idea had again been considered in Mexico on May 28, also without action. It was now clear that something had to be done, at any risk. On July 13, as soon as the new cabinet had been formed, and three days before he took his oath as Minister of the Treasury, Nuñez broached the plan anew, and this time the entire cabinet approved it, although Zamacona was very hesitant. Secretly the proposal was taken to Congress, which debated it and then approved it, by a vote of 112 to 4, on July 17.

At first the English and French Ministers, Wyke and Saligny, could not believe that this had happened, but by July 23 Saligny was asking for special treatment for his government, by the 24th he and Wyke were issuing threats to sever relations, and on the 26th relations were severed, pending approval by the English and French governments. On this date the government argued that since the conditions that had caused this action still existed, it could not be revoked.

On July 27 Juárez wrote a long letter to Sr. Juan Antonio de la Fuente in Paris, who was representing Mexico in all of Europe. He reviews the dreadful events of the year and the causes of the suspension, and states the government's hopes of pacifying the country, rescuing the economy, and eventually resuming payments "with due scrupulosity." In reply to the complaints that the suspension was passed without warning, Juárez says that none of the foreign governments would have agreed to it anyway, that they would only have delayed their replies, and that the matter was too urgent for any delay; also, that Saligny had already rejected a suggestion of settling the French debts by means of titles to and notes on Church properties. He also asserts that under the circumstances, public discussion would have been even more destructive. He complains of the tone of the responses of the Ministers, especially Saligny, and he hopes that the Emperor Napoleon and Queen Victoria, once informed of the facts, will respond otherwise. He encloses $5,000 to pay for a trip to London, and if advisable, to buy the support of French and English journalists, adding that more will be available if required. "I have firm hopes," he concludes, "that the respite afforded us by this law will produce the complete pacification of the country and the restoration of our Treasury and credit, saving us quickly from anarchy and the complete dissolution of our society. It is with this conviction that we have adopted this method, and we are resolved to put it into effect, facing with a firm spirit the risks and dangers that may follow, and that in any case will be less disastrous than the imminent suicide that was threatening us."

Fuente passed this explanation along to Thouvenel, the French Foreign Minister, along with a complaint about Saligny's protection of rebels against the Mexican government, but his message was rejected. The Spanish government also supported Saligny and his protests. The English, characteristically, remained open to negotiation, while considering the use of force.

At this time the Confederacy became a nuisance. Its agent, Pickett, threatened the seizure of Monterrey; talked, as a bribe, of returning California and New Mexico; and even made advances to reactionaries and Spaniards—all in an effort to break down friendly relations between Mexico and the Union, or to break down Mexico itself, if the Confederacy might profit thereby.

These intrigues, and repeated threats of filibustering expeditions from the Confederacy into Mexico, merely strengthened Lincoln's and Seward's sympathies with Juárez' liberal and constitutional government, now faced with the likelihood of a European intervention that would, while bleeding Mexico, brush aside the Monroe Doctrine and surely cause the United States trouble during and after our own frightful war. More than once, Seward made it very clear that he wanted no part of Mexico and no more enemies, but would make almost any kind of a deal with Juárez that would keep the Confederacy and Europe at home and unallied.

Seward, Corwin, and Romero now tried to begin negotiation of a treaty whereby the United States would make a loan to Mexico that would pay interest at 3 per cent for five years, from July 17, 1861, on Mexico's foreign debts, then estimated at $65,000,000, this loan to be secured by a mortgage on the public lands and mineral rights of Lower California, Chihuahua, Sonora, and Sinaloa. Before actually negotiating, Seward tried to get the approval of the idea in general by the Senate, and to get the British and French governments to postpone intervention meanwhile, but failed in both efforts. Furthermore, Juárez rejected the project. This episode has been pictured as one more nefarious scheme, in the style of Buchanan, to seize Mexico, and as a horrible temptation to Juárez, whereas it was nothing of the kind. It was important to the United States to keep the European powers out of Mexico, if possible, and to help the Mexican government to be strong and independent, while the American taxpayers, in the midst of a war that had begun badly, and not yet introduced to Lend Lease and foreign aid, had to be offered some kind of security. Once again the United States Senate thought it was going too far, into too many imponderables; and for his part, Juárez, who did not even mention it in his diary or letters, and who had his hands very full at home, probably doubted that the mortgage could be paid off in time to prevent some kind of a foreclosure, after the end of the American Civil War. At great risk, he had just told Britain, France, and Spain that they could not get blood out of a turnip, and if he had to fight them off, when would he have money to pay off the United States? Seward was no Buchanan, and Juárez was no Micawber.

While the skies darkened, amidst an ominous calm, over the seas to the east, Juárez and his Ministers continued to have plenty of trouble within Mexico. On August 13, Ortega managed to defeat Márquez at Jalatlaco, near Lerma, an action in which Colonel Porfirio Díaz again made his mark, and after which Ortega made him a General, giving him his own insignia—a promotion confirmed by Juárez. This victory provided a respite from the jackals, but Márquez and Mejía still had forces in the field, and Ortega kept demanding more money and supplies for his forces before he could or would continue the campaign. On September 3 there was a stormy session between Ortega, Juárez, and the cabinet, at the end of which, notes Juárez, "I showed Sr. Ortega that what was necessary was to work, and to work energetically, without the need of a large army, and without the trains and expenses of opulent nations." Ortega remained recalcitrant, resigned as Commander-in-Chief on September 10, and was replaced two days later by none other than Manuel Doblado. On October 2, however, Ortega returned as second in command. When his military duties allowed, he returned to his duties on the Supreme Court. Finally, in October, near Pachuca, Generals Tapía,

Díaz, and others decisively defeated Márquez and Zuloaga. These two managed to escape, and like Tomás Mejía, later joined the invaders of their country, but at least Lindoro Cajiga, the assassin of Ocampo, was caught and executed. The War of the Reform was at last ended.

The financial and political problems continued to be appalling. There was a delay in reorganizing the custom houses on an independent, Mexican basis, the military expenses had continued, and Nuñez had to go on borrowing at outrageous rates, and making forced loans, a brutal necessity that alienated even the more liberal members of the property-owning class from the government. Nor, at this anxious time, did the Jacobin and juvenile Congress deny itself the luxury of harassing the President. On September 3, the day when Ortega was being his most difficult, a committee from Congress suggested to Juárez the resignation of the cabinet, to appease its opponents in Congress, and this time, at least, Juárez sent them packing. Four days later, however, fifty-one deputies took the extraordinary step of signing a petition asking Juárez to resign, and of course if he had done so, Ortega would have replaced him. At once, however, fifty-two members signed a vote of confidence in Juárez. We have seen that on September 10 Ortega resigned as Commander-in-Chief, was replaced by Doblado, and became his second in command. It has been thought, not unreasonably, that Ortega, and probably the devious Doblado also, had something to do with this illegal and most dangerous attempt at impeachment. In general, it was supported by newcomers hungry for power, and frustrated by men who, as soldiers or civilians, had fought behind Juárez in the war. The critics blamed the crisis on Juárez alone, although it is clear enough now, as it was to some persons at the time, that the crisis was the inevitable result of Mexico's not yet having achieved a modern, taxable economy or a united and vigorous democracy rooted in the minds and hearts of the people and of their politicians; while the great powers of the world had not yet learned the hard way that imperialism has a delayed but bitter price, and that young but true democracies can and must be helped only to help themselves. Two curious facts about this affair are that Sebastián Lerdo de Tejada, now a rising power in Congress, remained aloof from it, and that Juárez did not mention it in his diary until three weeks later. In his address to Congress on its reunion, September 16, he referred to it only in the most veiled and gentle terms: one of Juárez' great talents was that of not holding a grudge, and of refusing to stir up unnecessary difficulties. In this address he also expressed a hope of achieving a reasonable settlement with the European powers.

On October 9 and 10 Juárez fought off another attack on his administration by the Congress, and in doing so, called attention to the habit of the opposition of encouraging noisy vagabonds to enter the galleries and interrupt the sessions of Congress, thus discrediting democratic institutions, not only the administration. On October 24, he demonstrated his confidence by buying a house. On October 25 and 26 he managed to settle a constitutional problem that had caused some of his troubles with Congress, including the noisy claques in the galleries—namely, that of the suspension of the guarantees of civil rights, in order to secure the prompt punishment of rebels and bandits. He found a settlement that was both constitutional and effective.

All this time, nothing had been heard from Europe, and it may have been almost a relief to Juárez to learn that in London, on October 31, Britain, France, and Spain had agreed to act together in an armed intervention. In this Convention it was stated, thanks chiefly to Britain, whose government still had some scruples, and wanted only to get the money due its bondholders, that: "The high contracting parties bind themselves not to seek for themselves, in the employment of coercive measures foreseen by the present convention, any acquisition of territory, or any peculiar advantage, and not to exercise in the subsequent affairs of Mexico any influence of a character to impair the right of the Mexican nation to choose and freely to constitute the form of its own government." Great Britain seems to have signed this document in good faith, and aside from being intent on getting the money by any means, to have wanted only to have a hand in any such operation by the other powers, and to keep an eye on them. Spain had a decadent government still smarting over lost empire, and its subsequent withdrawal does much to redeem its part in this affair. Napoleon III, on the other hand, had already been dealing with Mexican monarchists and with Maximilian, and France's adherence to this statement was soon proved to have been completely mendacious and cynical. There were three wolves in the beginning, but without Juárez' knowing it at this time, and (one hopes) without Palmerston's being fully aware of the exact nature of an operation that might not have been risked without his initial support, the wolf that was intent on the jugular vein of Mexico was the elected Emperor of the French.

Included in the Convention was an invitation to the United States, which also had claims against Mexico, to join the three powers in the intervention. It should be remembered that the Union was already having trouble with Great Britain over the blockade of Southern ports that prevented the shipment of cotton to British mills, and over the seizure, on November 8, by Captain Wilkes, USN, of the Confederate commissioners, Mason and Slidell, from the British mail steamer *Trent*. It must also be remembered that Napoleon III was sympathetic with the Confederacy. In the midst of the Civil War, involvement in hostilities with Britain and France would have been disastrous to the Union. On December 4, 1861, Seward replied to the three powers, on behalf of President Lincoln, that he conceded their right to make war against Mexico; that he was glad that the three powers did not intend to dictate the nature of the Mexican government; and that the United States, he said, would not join in the intervention because it shunned alliances, and because "Mexico being a neighbor of the United States on this continent, and possessing a system of government similar to our own in many of its important features, the United States habitually cherish a decided good-will toward the republic, and a lively interest in its security, prosperity, and welfare."

For some time, Juárez and his Ministers believed that the interests of Britain and France were "purely pecuniary." On November 5 he noted in his *Diary* that the cabinet agreed that "as soon as possible agreements should be reached with the American and English Ministers," and that "the necessity of a tax be recommended to Congress, so that if and when the law of July 17 should be repealed, the Treasury should not be left without resources." However, all the governors were alerted and steps were considered and taken for the defense of the country. In November, Juárez wrote in almost identical terms to Vidaurri in Monterrey and to Arteaga in Querétaro, reporting the Convention and his hopes of a peaceful settlement with Britain and France, and adding: "It is a serious evil, certainly, to have to fight a war with a foreign power, but the degree of this evil diminishes when it is Spain that attacks us, because she supports an unjust cause, and because the struggle she provokes will serve to unite firmly the liberal party, and to eradicate once and for all the abuses of the colonial system, guaranteeing forever the independence, liberty, and reform of our country." It also became apparent to Juárez, later, that those who aided the intervention could not claim to be merely devout, conservative patriots. They would be traitors, and Juárez issued one decree to that effect on January 17, 1862, and a stronger one on January 25, 1862. The latter decree had not been forgotten five years later.

Meanwhile, in November, Zamacona was negotiating with Wyke a new treaty that in effect restored the *status quo ante* with Great Britain, while even giving the British some additional advantages. Juárez was hesitant about this treaty, but allowed it to be signed on November 21. Within a few days, thanks chiefly to Sebastián Lerdo de Tejada, then chairman of the congressional committee on foreign affairs, who claimed with good reason that the treaty went much too far, the Congress rejected it, and instead, merely renewed the previous arrangements in effect before July 17. As a result, Zamacona resigned and Wyke left Mexico City for London, only to discover, when he reached Veracruz, that he had been appointed diplomatic representative of Britain in the intervention. As usual in those days, Britain had got practically what it wanted, and now had no excuse at all for taking part in the intervention. This was one case in which more rapid communications between the capitals might have prevented serious trouble. More dangerously, Juárez remained in the dark about the actual situation with respect to France.

Zamacona's resignation precipitated another cabinet crisis in which Juárez vainly offered Foreign Affairs to several persons, including Lerdo, before he turned to Doblado, who accepted only on condition that he, Doblado, appoint the other Ministers and direct them. This, in effect, made him a Prime Minister and Juárez a mere ceremonial Head of State. Juárez exclaimed to him that under the Constitution, the President chose the Ministers and assumed executive responsibility, but the two men reached some kind of an agreement that is not made clear in Juárez' *Diary*, and proceeded to organize a cabinet and to get themselves granted additional powers to meet the crisis. Doblado did not think his new powers sufficient and tried to resign, but Juárez persuaded him to remain. In the midst of this cabinet crisis, the news came that the Spanish forces had arrived off Veracruz.

Of the last meeting of Congress (in the Palace on December 15), in which the President had been granted additional powers, the curious and condescending English traveler Lempriere reports: "At about three, the President, Juárez, entered amid an astounding din of cannon and trumpets. He is a dark, small man, quiet and self-possessed. He is affectionately termed in Mexico 'the little Indian.' Juárez is a very respectable, well-meaning man, and of fair talents. . . . On taking his seat he bowed gracefully on all sides, and immediately made the following address in a clear and remarkably pleasant voice." In this address, Juárez described the circumstances as the most difficult in which Mexico had found itself since it gained its independence, thanked the Congress for the increased powers, which meant also vastly increased responsibilities, and expressed a hope that the foreign powers would be reasonable enough to see that the financial difficulties were the result of an internal revolution that would in the end benefit them also. In his manifesto to the nation issued three days later, Juárez reported the occupation of Veracruz by the Spanish, reviewed Mexican relations with Spain, and called for firm resistance, as well as for justice and security for unarmed Spaniards within Mexico.

At about the same time, Lempriere had another lucky and interesting encounter, in Guadalupe: "As we sat in the waiting room in the station, the President's family arrived and took seats. There was no fuss or attention paid them, except that they were unpleasantly stared at. The mother is a nice-looking, lady-like dame of forty, graceful and dignified. Her three daughters, from twenty to thirteen, were rather tall, rather stout, and fairly good-looking." Doña Margarita was then thirty-four years old, and her oldest daughter, Manuela, about seventeen.

On December 29, Juárez wrote to Vidaurri in Monterrey that the Spaniard Gasset had landed in Veracruz with 6,000 men, and had so far remained inactive there; that Gasset had not yet shown the courtesy of issuing an ultimatum or an explanation; that since the lack of any Mexican navy made the city indefensible from against an attack from the sea, General Llave, under orders, had withdrawn his men and equipment to Cerro Gordo and Chiquihuite; that the enemy had no fresh food, while the Mexican army was very enthusiastic and eager to attack the enemy when they came out of Veracruz; and that Juárez still hoped for a reasonable settlement.

On January 6 and 7, 1862, the British landed 700 marines and the French 2,500 soldiers. The allied commissioners were Sir Charles Wyke and Commodore Hugh Dunlop for the British, Conte Dubois de Saligny and Admiral E. Jurien de la Gravière for the French, and General Juam Prim, Conde de Reus, for the Spanish. Prim had been very successful in Spain's wars in Morocco, and at this time briefly esteemed by Napoleon III, was in the beginning the leading interventionist. This was lucky for Mexico, because he was married to a niece of Sr. Echeverría, at that time Juárez' Minister of the Treasury. Accordingly, his sympathies were clearly with the Mexicans, and he had the audacity to express and act upon his views. He has been called vain, ignorant, and reckless, and he may have been, but in this instance, at least, he proved himself a statesman. He knew what the French really wanted, and with the support of Wyke, he stood up to them when immediately the three powers began having disagreements about their claims. After various manifestos and fruitless attempts at negotiation, the allies requested permission to move their troops to more healthy locations inland. Juárez replied that this could not be permitted until some kind of agreement had been reached, and offered to send commissioners to meet those of the allies in Orizaba.

When the allies agreed, Juárez named Doblado as his commissioner. "The instructions given to Sr. Doblado are that if the Allies do not recognize the constitutional government, and do not offer to respect the independence and sovereignty of the nation, with all its consequences, it will not be possible to give permission to the troops of the Allies to take up quarters in Jalapa and Tehuacán." The meeting took place at La Soledad, near Veracruz, and the agreement signed there by Doblado and the Allied commissioners on February 19, and by Juárez on February 23, included assent by the Allies to Juárez' stipulations, permission for the Allies to move their troops up out of the tropical swamps to Córdoba, Orizaba, and Tehuacán, provision for a further conference at Orizaba, and provision for withdrawal of the Allied troops toward the coast as far as "Paso Ancho on the Córdoba road and Paso de Ovejas on the Jalapa route if the negotiations broke down." By circular, Juárez informed the governors of this agreement. He also kept his powder dry by making further preparations for armed defense.

"The Preliminaries of La Soledad," as this agreement is called, may sound quixotic in giving invaders permission to save their troops from yellow fever, instead of letting them rot on the coast or putting up a fight at Cerro Gordo or some such strategic place on the road inland, but actually, in its results, which presumably Juárez anticipated and hoped for, at least in part, it was a diplomatic triumph. Before dealing again with the Mexican government, which they had recognized and vowed to respect as sovereign, the Allies had to reveal their purposes more candidly to each other, the French plans forced the English and the Spanish to withdraw—obviously a tremendous gain for the Mexicans—and when the French did unmask themselves to the Mexicans and the world, their perfidy was more clearly defined. Acting under Juárez' instructions, Doblado had performed the only unquestionable and major service to his country in his dubious career.

The British marines remained in Veracruz, the Spanish troops moved up to Córdoba and Orizaba, and the French occupied Tehuacán. In the following weeks, the Mexican government, while still harassed by reactionaries and by cabinet changes, negotiated with the British about the return of the control of the Veracruz customs to Mexico, and more sharply with Admiral de la Gravière about what was to be done with Almonte and other reactionaries who were returning from Europe to take advantage of their country's distress, and were consorting with the French. (Miramón, returning, had been arrested by the British, over the protests of the French, and packed off to Havana as a burglar.) It also negotiated with General Prim, Mexico's new friend, privately, about the movements and demands of the French and English, and with Ambassador Corwin about a loan from the United States. Like other Presidents elsewhere, Juárez could be more decisive and effective in handling the world at his nation's throat than in handling his own Congress.

In a letter dated merely "March," Juárez wrote to Vidaurri:

> On foreign affairs, there is nothing new to report to you, even though there are rumors that the French are on the point of opening hostilities and retiring to their former positions, but this does not seem to me plausible, because even if General Lorencez, who has come with the latest expeditionary force, should bring from his government orders to that effect, he faces the obstacle that the Commissioners of the Allied Powers are solemnly committed, by virtue of the "Preliminaries" agreed to on the 19th of last month, to enter into conferences, and with these in view, to wait until April 15. I do not know up to what point these rumors may be true; but I believe that the representatives of the Allied Powers cannot wish to cover themselves with infamy by trampling in such a shocking manner on their promises.

The allied commissioners met at Orizaba on April 9, and on that occasion Saligny, knowing what the Emperor really wanted, exasperated by the scruples and criticisms of Prim and Wyke, and moved by his own arrogance and impatience, reasserted his fantastic financial claims, and made it clear that he was going to violate both the Convention of October 31, 1861, and the Preliminaries of La Soledad. On April 11 Juárez noted: "Received a communication from the Allies reporting that the Convention of London had been dissolved, that the English and Spanish will re-embark, and that the French will go to Paso del Macho to operate with the liberty of action they desire. It was decided to give a manifesto to the nation, informing it of this event, and summoning it to the defense." In this manifesto, published the next day, and in his address to Congress on its opening session, April 15, Juárez reviewed these events with clarity and with dry vigor, summoned the nation to the defense of its independence. On April 11 the cabinet also decided that "the

English and Spanish commissioners be told that the government is disposed to make a settlement," that Fuente in Paris be informed and recalled, and that this decision be reported to the other Ministers of foreign powers in Mexico. On the same day came a report of a victory by Márquez and Zuloaga, still raiding in the state of Puebla. On April 14 there was an extensive redisposition of armed forces and commands, in an effort both to stamp out the reactionaries and to get ready for the French.

Meanwhile, although the dreadful battle of Shiloh took place on April 6 and 7, in the midst of these events, the United States did not remain indifferent to them. Corwin in Mexico and Romero in Washington repeatedly warned Seward of the monarchical designs of the French, and Seward repeatedly stated President Lincoln's opposition to any attempt to impose a monarchy on any American republic. He also protested directly to Thouvenel and his successor, Drouyn de Lhuys, both of whom brazenly denied any such intention as long as they could. Although Juárez became very impatient with Corwin, and Romero with Seward, on April 15 Corwin signed a treaty with the Mexican government providing for an immediate, "well secured" loan of $2,000,000 to Mexico by the United States, but President Lincoln refused even to submit this treaty to an already hostile Senate, on the grounds that it would not even be considered, "at the time when the French forces occupied a portion of the territory of Mexico." Union sentiment remained strongly in favor of Juárez and the Mexican Republic, but the dangers of massive aid at that time were obvious, and inevitably, Lincoln and Seward were bitterly criticized, both for going as far as they did, and for not going further. The fate of this treaty was foreshadowed in an amusing way in Mexico. Mr. Edward Lee Plumb, the American attaché, in the company of Lempriere, was taking down to Veracruz "the American despatches and the new treaty going to Washington to be signed." Say instead to be filed. These documents were all in saddlebags on a mule that walked into a stream to drink and was only with great trouble recaptured.

On April 23 and 24, Juárez instructed Doblado, who was still in Orizaba, and who had received proposals from Wyke, to renegotiate the Wyke–Zamacona treaty, with changes that would permit the government to pay off the French and the Spanish as well as its own expenses. It would eliminate British inspectors in the customs houses. However, Doblado could not persuade Wyke and Dunlop to accept these changes, and the new treaty, signed by Juárez on April 29, was even more severe on the Mexicans than the earlier treaty had been. Prim did not remain to negotiate a settlement for his country, although one was made later, and the British and Spanish forces all departed. In all of these decisions and actions, both Wyke and Prim, who earlier had been criticized in Spain, were finally supported by their governments.

Juárez, in his manifesto of April 12, and Doblado in a letter to Montluc in that month, both expressed hope that Napoleon III, who had been misinformed, would see the error of his ways, but both gestures were ignored. The French kept pouring in reinforcements, and on April 16 they issued a proclamation at Córdoba, calling themselves liberals and pacifiers, yet insolently asserting that the French flag had come to stay and could be attacked only at great peril. The next day the reactionary Almonte issued a supporting appeal to the Mexican people to adhere to a government suited to "our nature, our needs, and our religious beliefs," and on April 19, at Córdoba, he had himself declared President. General Manuel Robles Pezuela, the reactionary general, violated an oath by going over to the French, but was caught and shot. The French forces began to withdraw, but never went as far as they had agreed to go, and on a pretext returned to Orizaba. There was a skirmish involving forces of General Porfirio Díaz, and on April 27 a French force of 6,000 started towards Puebla. The next day, at Acultzingo, they attacked a smaller Mexican force, which after five hours of fighting withdrew in good order.

Juárez and the Mexican people now faced again their old enemies of the reaction, and a new one, the formidable French army, acting as an instrument of imperial dreams. "We must now prove to France and to the entire world," wrote Juárez, "that we are worthy to be free," and: "The moment has come to act with the speed of lightning. Redouble your efforts and exhort the people to the defense."

Why, then, were the bodies of thousands of good Mexicans and good Frenchmen to drop dead in those jungles and deserts and ancient streets, and rot, and be torn apart by vultures? Because the Mexican Republic was so young, because England and Spain showed no humility and little patience or good sense, because the Americans were busy killing each other, and above all, because the French people, the poor Mexicans who were ready to die, as they thought, for religion, and a silly Hapsburg princeling all trusted their destinies to the dreaming nephew of the Corsican, whom he had been unable to rival in Europe.

17

PROFESSIONALS USUALLY WIN

BUT NOT ALWAYS. The Mexicans, commanded by General Ignacio Zaragoza, and under him by Generals Ignacio Mejía, as Quartermaster General, Miguel Negrete, Antonio Álvarez, Francisco Lamadrid, Felipe Berriozábal, and Porfirio Díaz, with Lieutenant Colonel Félix Díaz in command of the Oaxaca Lancers, retreated to Puebla. This city was always strongly reactionary in its sympathies, but it was protected on the north and east by some low hills, two of which, Loreto and Guadalupe, were fortified. On the night of May 3, Zaragoza pointed out to his officers that the French were running out of supplies and would have to take the city. Although his forces were inferior in number—about 4,850 to more than 6,000 Frenchmen—and much more inferior in artillery and other equipment—he felt it was high time for a nation of eight or ten million to put up a fight and give the government a chance to organize the defense of the country. "As was natural," wrote Díaz later, "we all agreed . . . as was shown by what we accomplished two days later." The neglected fortifications were hastily strengthened, and Zaragoza placed his forces: 1,200 men under Negrete in the two forts to the northeast of the city; 3,100 under Berriozábal, Díaz, and Lamadrid across the road from the east, whence the French would have to advance; and a small force of artillery within the city itself under General Santiago Tapía.

The Mexicans were astonished when at dawn on May 5 General Charles Ferdinand Latrille de Lorencez, advancing as expected from the east, split his forces and sent the larger part sweeping across the rugged countryside to bombard and then attack the two forts. The superior firepower of the French, and the protection afforded by hillocks on their line of attack, permitted them to come very close to the forts, but Zaragoza rapidly reinforced these with Berriozábal's troops and others from the plain, and hid his cavalry and infantry in ditches and behind rows of *maguey* on the flanks of the forts, so that when the French became visible, the Mexicans swept down on them from three angles, and forced them back. The French attacked very bravely three times, and once nearly took Fort Guadalupe when some Mexican recruits momentarily lost their nerve and hid in the church within the fort until their officer, Colonel Arratia, killed three of them with his sword and pointed out that the enemy was already fleeing. With this encouragement, Díaz reported, they returned to their trenches and fought so effectively that they turned the tide of the battle. Meanwhile, the other French force was heavily attacking the remaining forces under Díaz, who managed to drive them back with only two mortars. When the two French forces joined each other in retreat, Zaragoza found himself still outnumbered, and thought it unwise to pursue them. At this point Díaz, fearing that unless he kept up his "sham attack" on the French, with his small force, they would reorganize and come back for more, disobeyed Zaragoza's orders and continued his harassing action until night fell. When he was able to explain this disobedience to his commander, Zaragoza approved of it.

The French retreated to Orizaba to await reinforcements from France. They had lost about five hundred men killed and wounded, and the Mexicans about half that number, while almost no prisoners were taken by either side. On Juárez' unusual orders, the French wounded left on the field were cared for and then returned to the French command in Orizaba. Perhaps Juárez was not yet fully aware that the French attack on the republic was no mere gesture. In his report to the Minister of War, Miguel Blanco, Zaragoza modestly explained that if the brigades of O'Horán and Carvajal had not been off fighting the reactionaries at Atlixco and Izúcar, his Army of the East "might have defeated the enemy completely in a victory that would have immortalized its name." In his more personal report to Juárez, he noted a few defections, asked Juárez to give no more amnesties, and suggested that medals were cheaper than promotions.

Juárez, having received on May 3 an appeal from Zaragoza for two thousand additional men the next day, sent off a force under General Antillón, but clearly it arrived too late to make the victory more decisive. On May 5, Juárez noted simply: "Received by telegraph a report that the French have been defeated," but in later letters and speeches he expressed his deep enthusiasm and gratitude. The rejoicing in the capital and all over the nation, when the news came, was very great. The Mexican army, so long despised, had defeated a part of what was then considered the most powerful and famous army in the world. This pride is still felt in Mexico, and any American who, considering the small size of the forces engaged, in comparison with those in the battles of our own Civil War, and the indecisiveness of the victory, finds himself surprised, should also consider the little noticed but probably very important effect of this battle on our own nation's history. If the French had taken Puebla at this time, they would also, in the light of later events, have taken Mexico City. Napoleon's plans certainly would have been much more quickly and completely realized, and France would probably have openly recognized and supported the Confederacy, and England might well have done the same. In short, the battle of *Cinco de Mayo* was an important victory not only for the Republic of Mexico, but also for the United States.

When the news of Puebla reached Paris, there was an outcry against the war by liberals in the legislature, but additional funds were finally voted, and four months later, thirty thousand more French soldiers were sent to Mexico under a new General, Élie Frédéric Forey. This change of command was not surprising, after Lorencez' unsuccessful attack on the forts. Zaragoza had reported to his Minister of War: "The French army fought with much gallantry: its Commander-in-Chief behaved stupidly in its attack."

At this time there began a long series of efforts to get arms and ammunition from the United States. On May 28, 1862, Colonel Juan Bustamente of San Luis Potosí, a deputy in the Mexican Congress, arrived in Washington. He and Romero were shunted from office to office and worked hard all summer, seeing President Lincoln and all the busy cabinet officers before they managed to buy from a Mr. James Whiting and others a supply of ammunition. They then tried to get permission to ship what they had bought. This permission was finally denied. During the years that followed, numerous shipments were made without permission from both the east and the west coasts of the United States, and across the border. However, as we shall see, too many Mexicans acted in the United States without authority from their government. There was much red tape, there were many delays and losses en route, and by April 13, 1866, Juárez was expressing himself as being heartily sick of the whole effort.

On June 11, Juárez wrote to Montluc with his usual optimism: "Next week our army will begin its operations against Orizaba. The triumph of our arms is not to be doubted. The entire nation is full of enthusiasm. The constitutional government is each day more strong and respected. The French intervention, with the alliance of Almonte and Márquez, is in my opinion lost."

Yet now, as throughout the war, if Juárez was supported by most of the Mexican people—and if the ordinary soldiers fought bravely, and with occasional success, against very heavy odds, Juárez' energies were repeatedly sapped, and the cause threatened, by the vagaries, personal ambitions, and vanities of some of his most important colleagues, political and military.

On June 10, for example, in the midst of operations against Orizaba, Ortega wrote a letter to Saligny to inform him that the republican government was widely supported in Mexico, and that no monarchy would be tolerated; and to suggest that since the French expedition was costly and futile, an armistice and settlement seemed to him reasonable and creditable to both sides. Ortega sent a copy of this remarkable letter to Juárez, with a covering letter of his own to explain this step and to explain that he had taken it with the approval of his superior officer, General Zaragoza—although in the letter to Saligny, all such support is disclaimed. On June 13, Juárez replied to Ortega, recognizing his good intentions, but reminding him of the mendacity of the French, and telling him firmly to limit himself to military operations and to leave diplomacy entirely in the hands of the government. On June 14, some of Ortega's forces were defeated, and on June 17 he wrote to Juárez, accepting the mild rebuke and the orders he had received, enclosing a copy of Saligny's reply that rejected the proposal. He stated that since the matter had been kept confidential, no harm had been done, and promised that his forces would regain their lost ground.

For another example, on July 25 Juárez appealed to Vidaurri in in Monterrey to send supplies and cash for the army, so that it might be more effective before the French received reinforcements, and as usual, he got no response. Vidaurri was too busy taxing goods coming into Matamoros from Texas. On a later occasion, Juárez wrote to Santacilia; "I agree with you that it is necessary to win over Vidaurri or to eliminate him. I am for the first alternative. Only if that does not suffice to use him for the good of the nation we must resort to the second. Work, then, for the first."

Private life never waits for a lapse in even the most serious public affairs. In July, Juárez and his wife lost their infant daughter Amada, and by the next mail from Oaxaca, on July 25, Justo Benítez had to inform them of the death of doña Margarita's father, don Antonio Maza. Perhaps Juárez felt even more deeply than the death of the child that of the man who had taken the ragged boy from the mountains into his home and family.

On August 13, Doblado persuaded Juárez to accept his resignation as Minister of Foreign Affairs, on the ground that there had been an outcry against him "in distant states," and that if he did not withdraw, he might unwillingly provoke an armed outbreak against the whole cabinet and government. Insofar as it existed, and Zarco denied it, this opposition to Doblado came about because he had tried to win over the hated conservatives, Márquez and J. M. Cobos. He was given an army command and replaced at the Foreign Ministry by the able Fuente, while Nuñez returned to the Treasury.

On August 28 Juárez wrote to Montluc in Paris to thank him for his services in trying to present Mexico's case to the French government, but also stating frankly that he considered this effort futile. A month later he wrote to Montluc in good cheer that Puebla was perfectly fortified, and Mexico City would be soon, while the morale of the army and the people was excellent.

Throughout the latter part of this year, 1862, and early into the next, in response to reactionary political activity by the clergy, and to the urging of the radicals, the government continued the reform of the Church, reducing the number of convents, taking over hospitals, making it a crime to preach against the government or the laws, and forbidding the wearing of religious costumes or the holding of religious ceremonies outside the churches. It must also be recorded that acts of violence were being committed by republicans against the clergy and the churches.

In the autumn, Romero in Washington, already discouraged by the collapse of his and Bustamente's efforts to have arms shipped to Mexico, was completely downcast by the revelation in pro-Juárez Northern newspapers that mules and many other utilities of war were being successfully shipped from the United States to Forey's forces in Veracruz and the interior. When Romero protested, Seward replied that the United States had not recognized a state of war in Mexico. (Seward might have said, like Mayor La Guardia of New York, long afterwards: "When I make a mistake, it's a beaut.") On November 20, Lincoln issued an order stopping all arms shipments, but it was frequently ignored. Romero was a tremendous worker, and his health, never very good, became steadily worse. He tried to resign, in order to return to Mexico and join the army, but his resignation was not accepted.

Most unfortunately for the Republic, General Zaragoza died of typhoid fever at Puebla on September 8, at the age of thirty-three. He was replaced by Ortega, and the two other important commands were given to Doblado and Comonfort. On Comonfort's restoration, old Juan Álvarez wrote to Juárez on December 8, courteously but firmly objecting, and refusing to serve under Comonfort. These appointments were easier to criticize than to improve upon. If more a hero than a soldier, Ortega had at least learned his lesson, for the time being, about meddling in diplomacy. When he received from General Forey a letter containing offensive remarks about Juárez, he sent the letter to Juárez and then, as instructed by Juárez, returned it to Forey with the comment that it did not affect Juárez personally, but was an attack on the dignity and sovereignty of the nation.

In his address to the Congress on its opening session on October 20, Juárez said in part: "We should have only reasons for congratulating ourselves when we remember the glory of May 5, were it not for the death of the vigorous and virtuous commander who raised so high the name of his country. But the sorrow that filled every mind on the news of this grim loss did not lessen the hope nor weaken the renewed determination of the nation. . . . The morale of all our troops could not be better: the revolution of four years, and the encounters with the foreign enemy have given courage to the whole army . . . and discipline has been improved accordingly; the patience under suffering of our soldiers is, as always, incomparable, and it binds the troops and their officers together in deep, reciprocal confidence." If Mexico was weakened by poverty and disorder, France was threatened by troubles in Europe, and Mexico had already done wonders. "To proclaim, as our enemies do, that they are not making war on the country, but on its present government, is to repeat the foolish declaration of whoever undertakes an aggressive war. Besides, it is clear enough that anyone insults the people when he attacks the power that they have chosen and wish to support. . . . I am profoundly convinced that we shall maintain our independence with all its rights, and that we shall win for [the Republic] the respect of all governments and the sympathy of all men who love liberty."

Forey had arrived in Veracruz on September 21, but he did not reach Orizaba until October 24, and he did not get along any better with the Mexican reactionaries, such as Almonte, whom he removed from the "Presidency" he had claimed, than he had with the anopheles mosquitoes on the coast. Also, he enjoyed life in Orizaba, and his delays permitted Ortega to proceed with the fortification of Puebla. Meanwhile, Juárez, as usual, was scraping about for money and supplies, and trying to get along with Congress, to suppress banditry, to keep the governors lined up behind the national government, and even vainly to win over such determined foes as the Indian General Tomás Mejía, who was established at this time in the eastern mountains of the state of San Luis Potosí. Early in February, Juárez went to Puebla to inspect the fortifications and review and decorate the troops. Comonfort was moving his force to the north of Puebla, as a threat to any besiegers. Meanwhile, French naval forces had bombarded Acapulco, and other French forces had been ejected from Tampico, while the Mexicans had recovered

Jalapa; but clearly the decisive action of this phase of the war was again going to take place at Puebla.

There is a curious incident of this time. A seer wrote to Juárez to communicate his predictions about how the French planned to take the city and then cut off the retreat of the Mexican army. Juárez thanked him for this letter and asked for more, but did not acknowledge the four letters that followed from the same person. He did not ignore them, however. In one letter the seer reported that a Mexican bugler had been bought by the enemy and at a critical moment would blow the call to disperse. Without explaining why, Juárez ordered Ortega to take precautions against such an event. Ortega did so, and who knows that this was not a valuable item of "intelligence"?

On March 16, 1863, the French appeared again before the city, and within five days they had completed its encirclement and were beginning to bombard it with eight mortars and fifty heavy pieces of artillery. In his command, Ortega had about 22,000 men, including many of the best officers in the army, while the French force consisted of 26,300 men, including 2,000 Mexican reactionaries.

The bombardment began on Juárez' birthday and although totally preoccupied with the imminent battle at Puebla, he tried to prevent any form of celebration, a memorable one took place spontaneously. He received a large group of poor families, and at a dinner, Sr. Jesús Terán, Minister of Justice and of Development, offered a toast so graceful and apt as to deserve recording here: "Among the great men of the earth, I know only one who has achieved the glory of reforming his country and of assuring its independence by triumphing over the strongest nations. That man, whose merit is heightened by his modesty, occupies a distinguished place on the earth, and without any doubt the first place in the hearts of his fellow citizens. We toast that patriot, the Citizen Benito Juárez, and may his days be as long and as happy as those that he has given to the Mexicans." It is only to be hoped that Juárez got some added strength from such praise: he needed it. It was at this time that Victor Hugo, then in exile, did something to redeem his country, and perhaps cheer Juárez, by declaring with passion and courage that the Empire, not

France, was fighting Mexico, and that he himself was on Mexico's side.

Before the French had solidified their encirclement of Puebla, General Díaz proposed to General Ortega a plan for attacking isolated units of the enemy, and so beating them off, but his plan was rejected. When the French attacked the fortifications, and then the various outlying blocks of the city, the Mexican resistance was vigorous and effective. When the French guns destroyed parts of the walls, and the infantry rushed in, they were repeatedly forced out again, and the walls and barricades were rebuilt, while the firing was continued from the housetops, and both sides burrowed under the walls. The streets and the tiled patios, so recently filled with sunlight, flowers, and children, were now filled with dust, smoke, rubble, and shattered human bodies.

When the defenders began to eat the city's dogs and cats, and even the leaves of orange trees, Forey, who had once seriously considered abandoning the siege to push on to Mexico City itself, had a conference with Lieutenant Colonel Togno, an aide of Ortega's, and offered to promote Ortega for the Presidency of Mexico, if he would surrender. On hearing this, Ortega, now a soldier and a patriot, firmly spurned the offer to treat on any such terms.

Meanwhile, Comonfort was assembling forces on the road between Puebla and Mexico, and Juárez, in the City, was organizing a force to repel Tomás Mejía and Butrón, who were attacking it from Toluca on the western side. They came as close as the historic Mountain of the Crosses before being repulsed.

On May 8, while trying to get a train of supplies into Puebla, Comonfort was inexcusably surprised and defeated by Márquez and by General Achille François Bazaine, the French second-in-command. Comonfort lost a thousand men killed and wounded, another thousand taken prisoner, and a large quantity of valuable supplies. This defeat at San Lorenzo seems to have been caused by ineffective liaison between Ortega and Comonfort, as well as by the latter's poor judgment. Ortega and his men in Puebla heard the firing for a day and a half before they learned the news that spelled also their own defeat.

By May 17, having exhausted their supply of ammunition and

consumed anything that might be called food, Ortega and his army had to destroy their own weapons and surrender. This disaster did not lessen the courage and skill with which they had fought, for two months, against overwhelming odds. Because he feared their potential as guerrillas, when they all refused to lay down their arms permanently, Forey ordered the general officers to be sent to Veracruz under guard and thence to France. However, in Puebla or on the trip to Veracruz, most of these soldiers escaped to fight again.

General Díaz escaped in Veracruz on May 21 by changing his uniform for a plaid cape and calmly walking out among the relatives and friends of the prisoners who had been allowed to say farewell to them. In order to add plausibility to this act, he was about to exchange a few words with the Captain of the Guard, one Captain Galland, when he recognized this officer as a former prisoner and even friend of his own. When Díaz had saluted him and disappeared in the street, Captain Galland had an idea and rushed upstairs to look for Díaz, too late. The Mexican generals who were sent to France, with General Epitacio Huerta as their senior, suffered various hardships before they managed, in one way or another, to return to Mexico. Among these was General Ignacio Mejía of Oaxaca, who was sent to Toulon and Evreux. When Napoleon finally—and naïvely—allowed them to go to any country they chose, except Mexico, Mejía went by way of London, New York, Kansas City, Santa Fé, and El Paso, to Chihuahua.

However gallantly, the amateurs and improvisors, including Juárez, had suffered a crushing defeat. At first, Juárez decided to fight for Mexico City, but when it was discovered that only about 14,000 men were then and there available for the defense, with almost no resources, the President and Congress agreed that this force should be saved for later enlargement and equipment, and that the government should withdraw to San Luis Potosí and carry on the war from there. Juárez was given every power except that of dealing with the enemy in any way that might admit foreign interference in Mexican affairs, and this power was to hold good until thirty days after the unknown date when Congress could be reassembled.

Berriozábal had escaped with Díaz, after capture at Puebla and according to the latter, Juárez now offered to make one the Minister of War and the other Commander-in-Chief, as they should settle it between them. Díaz said that he preferred the command in the field, but that in view of his youth and the seniority of many other able officers he thought it would be unwise for him to accept it; and the next day, having slept on the problem, Juárez agreed with him. Berriozábal became Minister of War, and Juan José de la Garza, who had beaten the French at Tampico, Commander-in-Chief. These two offices were now for some time to change hands very frequently.

In addressing the closing session of Congress on the afternoon of May 31, 1863, Juárez thanked the deputies for their grant of power, referred to the fall of Puebla as "a glorious disaster," and said: "Adversity, Citizen-Deputies, dismays only contemptible peoples; our people are ennobled by great deeds, and the country has far from lost the enormous material and moral obstacles that it will place in the way of its unjust invaders." Four days before, he had written: "Great has been the reverse that we have suffered, but greater are our constancy and resolution, and we shall fight on with greater ardor, and with the certainty that victory will be ours, no matter what may be the elements on which the enemy can count, because the nation still has life, and strong sons to defend her."

Congress adjourned at three that afternoon. Warnings had come of the approach of the French, and it was decided that the government and the forces within the city would leave that evening. At sundown, as usual, the flag was lowered from above the National Palace, while the troops presented arms and the national anthem was played. When the flag was handed to Juárez, as he stood on the balcony with the cabinet, he raised it to his lips and then cried out: "*Viva México!*" The crowd thundered back: "*Viva México!*" while parents held up their small children to see and remember the temporary farewell of the Republic, once more embodied in the dark little Indian in a black suit. That evening, accompanied by a few officials who were left to their own resources, but carefully removing what little money was at hand, and the national archives, Juárez left the City for the north.

Meanwhile, the various brigades and divisions that had not been captured at Puebla were reorganized by the generals who had escaped and placed in various positions around the capital to cover the government's withdrawal and to harass the advancing French. New arms and materials of war were at last coming in from the United States through Acapulco.

On June 10, Forey, Almonte, and Saligny rode into Mexico City at the head of the French army. In a message to the French Minister of War Forey reported that the entire populace gave the invaders an ecstatic welcome, but a French captain wrote home that the Mexicans in the City appeared only out of curiosity and tossed flowers that had been paid for by the French.

18

THE CONFIDENCE GAME

It is a curious and depressing fact that most of the Americans who have heard of Benito Juárez remember him only from a film or from a fictionalized biography of Maximilian and Charlotte as the implacable Indian who is interesting only as the destroyer of that poor, dear, romantic pair. This immature romanticism distorts Mexican history and the life of Juárez, falsifying their meanings and lessening their grandeur. Actually, Maximilian and Charlotte were the victims of a grandiose confidence game, and although they were youthful and idealistic dreamers, they were also ignorant, grossly presumptuous, and moved by an ambition hardly distinguishable from simple greed. Napoleon III and his formidable Eugénie were also dreamers not without their shreds of honor, and if Napoleon did a few good things and operated on a grand scale, in this case his hunger for hard cash and his betrayal of his dupes when the going became rough are only too clear. Altogether, these four, and other characters who came out of the ancient woodwork of Mexico and Europe to promote and get what they could out of this enterprise, are somewhat dignified, and they are lifted out of the annals of crime into history, only by the forces and men that they challenged and that ruined them. The first and foremost of these forces was the hunger of an indomitable core of the Mexican people for independence and liberty, and this force of the young Republic in agony was focused and embodied in one man, Benito Juárez. The other forces were of course the distaste of the battle-weary but still armed American people for the sinister tinsel empire on their southern border and the embryonic German Empire embodied in Bismarck. Inevitably Maximilian, the confidence man himself, and finally, many years later, the very tough Eugénie, and poor Charlotte, went down into the shadows and dust, into the trash can of history.

Among Mexican reactionaries and foreign cynics, the notion of a Mexican monarchy had already had a long history. As early as 1783 the Conde de Aranda had proposed having three Spanish Infantes rule Mexico, Peru, and the Costa Firme. Then there was Aaron Burr's not wholly mad and silly dream, 1805–7. The reader may also remember that at the very moment, in 1821, at Córdoba, when the last Viceroy, don Juan O'Donojú, of the County Andalusia O'Donojús, came to terms with Iturbide and conceded independence to Mexico, it was agreed by them—this was the salvage sought by O'Donojú—that Mexico would be an empire ruled by a Bourbon prince. In that same year, during the ensuing shuffle, before Spain repudiated the agreement, and before Iturbide had himself absurdly crowned as Augustín I, Emperor of Mexico, a delegation of Mexican royalists went to Europe and offered the crown to the Archduke Charles Louis of Austria, the winner at Aspern and the loser at Wagram, who politely declined this honor.

In this unauthorized delegation there was a twenty-one-year-old "Young Conservative" named José María Gutiérrez de Estrada, who thus began young a career, certainly long and gruesomely successful, as a professional Mexican royalist. In 1840, during the brief liberal period, he had returned to Mexico long enough to publish a monarchist pamphlet, only to have it suppressed and find himself exiled. He married a rich Austrian countess and lived usually in Rome, in luxury, writing long, grandiloquent letters to every European politician of note, on the virtue of royal blood, on the commercial advantages that would accrue to European powers if there existed a Mexican monarchy, and on the always imminent danger, then, of having Mexico seized by the United States. In 1854, Santa Anna, desperate, commissioned Gutiérrez de Estrada to find a European prince who would take on the job—with Santa Anna himself, of course, as the power behind the throne. Sierra professes a qualified admiration for Gutiérrez de Estrada, calling him the only pure and disinterested one of the conspirators.

Gutiérrez de Estrada's assistant was one José Manuel Hidalgo y

Esnaurrizar, a butterfly who was neatly pinned down by Sierra as follows: "His evolution had been that of most of the Mexican bourgeoisie of good family in similar circumstances: a man of more urbanity than culture, not educated but well bred, superficially informed on the European literary and political movements, of a mediocre intelligence excessively inferior to his pretensions, Hidalgo Esnaurrizar, like all those of his class, had a patriotism that was composed of these two elements: abhorrence for the Yankees and love of our Spanish past. We can unite these elements into one only: absolute devotion to the religion of the fathers: *ubi crux ibi patria:* such could have been his device." With other elegant young men, he fought well, it is assumed, against the Americans in 1846–48. He served as a second secretary in the Mexican legations in London, Washington, and Madrid, and secured the blessing of Pope Pius IX when that pontiff was in exile at Gaeta. "He thus felt himself to be an armed knight of the ancient ideas, and as a new crusader he penetrated salons and boudoirs with the airs of a conqueror of hearts both for his cause and his bed; thus the holy and the sensual were confused in a delicious blend."

A more sinister and important figure in this cast is that of Juan Nepomuceno Almonte, supposed to have been the illegitimate son of the great Morelos himself, and so named because when a battle was imminent, Morelos would order the boy taken for safety *al monte,* to the hills or woods. Educated in the United States, he began his political life as an ardent liberal and was one of those who roundly condemned Gutiérrez de Estrada's 1840 pamphlet advocating monarchy. He was long closely associated with a similar figure, Santa Anna, and was captured with him at San Jacinto. He rose to very high posts, including the Ministry of War, and was at various times Minister to Washington and Paris. He fell out with Santa Anna, and in 1856 Comonfort sent him to London, where, having drifted far to the right politically—or rather, having decided to forgo all other principles for that of self-advancement—he now hitched his malodorous wagon to the artificial star of Mexican monarchism. When Juárez promptly dismissed him, he thus acquired a new resentment. His return to Mexico on the coattails of the French army, to claim the Presidency, has already been noted.

In this conspiracy, the Church was represented chiefly by two very different priests. Archbishop Pelagio Antonio de Labastida y Davalos of Puebla, but originally of Zamora and Morelia in Michoacán, was a learned, cultivated man, of high character, who tried to keep his oath to the government but was deeply opposed to all the acts of the Reform affecting the Church. Because of the armed resistance to the Reform at Puebla, he was banished in 1856 by Comonfort, and he settled down in Rome, where he represented later reactionary governments at the Holy See. In his own way, he was a Mexican patriot, he distrusted Napoleon III, he called Maximilian and Charlotte "the doves of Miramar," and he was sceptical about the whole imperial project, supporting it in the end only as a means of defeating the Reform and restoring the power of the Church.

Father Francisco Javier Miranda, in contrast, was a scheming politician and operator—in fact, Minister of Justice in the illegal cabinet of Zuloaga—who merely happened to be a priest. Usually he was traveling somewhere in Mexico, and later in Europe, and usually wherever he had been soon became the scene of trouble for Juárez' government. He was a politician, says Sierra, "who believed in the virtues of holy water a little tinted with red. . . . He was implacable; he was a cold and imperturbable fanatic."

As early as 1858, Hidalgo, who had become acquainted with the Countess Montijo and her daughter Eugénie, was invited by Eugénie and Napoleon to Compiègne, and there Hidalgo broached the idea of a Mexican Empire, an idea Napoleon had already discussed with a not unsympathetic Palmerston. Sierra records: "As soon as the possibility of a French intervention appeared, according to Saligny and the agents of M. de Morny, Hidalgo maneuvered with such zeal that Eugénie, who, they said, had the blood of Moctezuma in her veins, could not in the middle of 1861 cherish any idea other than to acquire Mexico, a fallen people, and to give them the penance of a monarchy paternally firm, even if this should require the spilling of a little French blood, in a little war: 'My Mexican war,' said the Empress, as Chateaubriand, forty years before, had said: 'My Spanish war.' Never had the plot of a courtly comedy been woven so tightly into the warp of a historical tragedy!"

But if it was Hidalgo who was chiefly effective with Eugénie, "Almonte," says Sierra, "achieved the personal predilection of the Emperor Napoleon, whose attention was attracted by his culture and judgment; because he was an intelligent man who knew much about his country, but who, in the manner of a cunning *mestizo*, knew how, with extraordinary seriousness, to present matters in a perspective that suited his interests."

Obviously these personal influences would have achieved nothing if Napoleon himself had not thought that he saw, rising above and beyond the fogs of conspiracy, the mountainous wealth of Mexico. It may have been Almonte who gave him the implausible idea that the Mexican customs receipts—already gripped for the most part by more realistic entrepreneurs in the City of London—might pay the costs of the intervention. Beyond, there gleamed the phantasms of millions for the Jecker bonds, the mineral wealth of Sonora, on which the Emperor had long had an eye, and above all, a satellite empire, Latin and Catholic, in the new world, that might at last make the mere nephew of the man who had been the master of western Europe, excepting England, into the master of an empire in America. As this strange man had dreamed while imprisoned at Ham, the sun on the snows of Orizaba might yet equal the sun of Austerlitz. This was in 1841, not long after Juárez, jailed much more briefly and uncomfortably at Loxicha, had been dreaming in his very different manner of a free and just Mexican society. William Bolitho summed up this Napoleon, speaking of the moment of his ruin at Sedan: "Poor devil, he never had much style." There were others at the time who could not be as tolerant as this essayist sixty years later. To feed or destroy this man's vision of himself while he laced in his belly and waxed his long moustaches, many thousands of good men of many nations spilled out their blood and entrails in the Crimea, in Italy, and on the rocks and dust of Mexico.

The most conspicuous of these victims, Maximilian, had been born in the vast imperial palace of Schönbrunn, Vienna, in 1832, when Juárez was twenty-six and struggling for every peso as a neophyte lawyer and teacher in Oaxaca. After the usual royal tutoring and travels—during which he had felt very superior to this mere Bonaparte, this self-made Emperor, on first meeting him in 1856—Maxi-

milian had married, in 1857, the Princess Charlotte of Belgium, born
in 1840. In the portraits of Maximilian there are evident his in-
born vanity and feeble benevolence, and in those of Charlotte a
wounded and sulky ambition throbbing within the fine china fig-
urine. As Governor of Lombardo–Venetia, for a brief period before
the French intervention in Italy, Maximilian was portentously too
liberal for the taste of his brother, the Emperor Francis Joseph; and
later as Commander-in-Chief of the four ships of the Austrian navy
stationed at Trieste, he was happy as a sailor of sorts but, he must
have felt, that was hardly a position worthy of a scion of what
was then still one of the most august of the royal families of Europe.
The palace of Maximilian and Charlotte, called Miramar, on a rock
just above and beside the Adriatic Sea, near Trieste, was a gem of
its flamboyant type, but to these two it must have seemed a gilded
cage. Perhaps their romantic hungers had been sharpened by reading the *True History* of the conquest of Mexico by Bernal Díaz,
who himself had entered the halls of Moctezuma. Might not Maximilian be received with his bride as the holy savior, and might they
not then become the loving and beloved parents of all those millions
of poor, devout, and flower-loving Indians? With its people thus
lifted up and regenerated, and with its vast wealth at last made
available, might not Mexico finally stand up, led by its Emperor, as
an equal even of France and Austria?

Gutiérrez de Estrada, Hidalgo, Almonte and other Mexicans in
Europe dreamed and schemed without rest, tried to flatter and deceive all the royal persons and the politicians of power, in any capital, with whom they could make any contact, and watched each
other with green eyes and with knives sharpened and ready for each
other's backs. Slowly the plot was matured, and more slowly revealed, while the activity became more complex and intense. For
example, Miramón, when in Paris, tried to warn Napoleon that there
was no strong monarchical party in Mexico, but for obvious reasons
was kept from seeing him by other Mexicans; while old Santa Anna,
then on the island of St. Thomas, inevitably tried to intrude by writing to Napoleon with his familiar hypocrisy that "the overwhelming
majority of the nation is longing for the restoration of the empire of
Moctezuma." Probably he was having designed for himself a new

family tree, Hapsburg grafted upon Aztec.

Hidalgo claimed that he first thought of Maximilian as a candidate for the throne, but the credit, if that is the word, should probably go to Gutiérrez de Estrada, who had long admired the Austrian Archduke. Napoleon selected Maximilian in order to appease the Hapsburgs, whose armies he had defeated in the Italian war, and whose help he might well need against Bismarck. This calculation was to be proved totally in error: the Emperor Francis Joseph had no high opinion of the project from the beginning. Its end was not one to endear its manager to him and his family, and his army was soon to be shown to be feeble enough.

In October, 1861, Maximilian, who had heard of the idea and surely begun daydreaming about it long before, was at last formally approached by Gutiérrez de Estrada, with the backing of Napoleon. Maximilian replied that he would accept the throne of Mexico if he had the permission of his brother, if he had the military support of France and England, and if the Mexican people voted to offer him the crown. In March, 1862, Almonte sailed for Veracruz to prepare the way by proclaiming himself President, while the French still issued disclaimers. Miranda had already returned, and Miramón, returning, had, as we have seen, been temporarily deported to Havana by the British, who considered him a thief. It was unfortunate for Juárez and Mexico that this soldier had not been handled more decisively.

In this interval, Maximilian received plenty of warnings. Archbishop Labastida was still sceptical. The Pope insisted on the restoration of all the privileges and properties of the Mexican Church, a measure now impossible to achieve and dangerous to attempt, yet the support of the Pope and of the Mexican clergy would clearly be essential for the secure establishment of an empire. Charlotte's father, King Leopold I of the Belgians, uncle to both Queen Victoria and Prince Albert of England, and royal confidant and meddler *par excellence*, kept warning that his daughter and son-in-law would have to have the support of the English as well as the French. However, the English had withdrawn from the whole enterprise, and Lord John Russell opposed it. Early in 1863, with the support of Leopold, the English went so far as to offer to Maximilian the vacant throne of Greece, then at their disposal, but he declined it, because the Greek crown had been "hawked around," and because he neither liked nor trusted the Greeks. The Emperor Francis Joseph remained unenthusiastic.

Intrinsically as important as any of these, but totally disregarded, were the warnings implicit in all of Seward's communications on the intervention, which Maximilian ignored, if he ever saw them. Mr. Sandburg records: "In the American language, and in plainer words than the covert phrasings of diplomacy, Lincoln had answered General John M. Thayer's query, 'Mr. President, how about the French army in Mexico?' He shrugged his shoulders and wrinkled his eyebrows. 'I'm not exactly "skeered," but I don't like the looks of the thing. Napoleon has taken advantage of our weakness in our time of trouble, and has attempted to found a monarchy on the soil of Mexico, in utter disregard of the Monroe Doctrine. My policy is, attend to only one trouble at a time. If we get well out of our present difficulties and restore the Union, I propose to notify Louis Napoleon that it is about time to take his army out of Mexico. When that army is gone, the Mexicans will take care of Maximilian.' " Napoleon and Maximilian did not hear these remarks, and if they had, would probably not have been impressed. At this time, the Union cause looked dim enough, and operators more astute than Napoleon III were to underestimate the democratic will and the military power of the United States.

The French defeat at Puebla on May 5, 1862, clearly meant a long postponement, but a year later the situation was reversed, and meanwhile the dreaming doves of Miramar had by no means lost interest. Maximilian was incorrigibly a wishful thinker, he was a hopeless amateur in the most dangerous of arts, politics, and his imagination fed on the Hapsburg past and on his own future rather than on the true nature and possible future of the Mexican people. Like all confidence men, Napoleon III found his strongest support in the greed of his dupes. He himself had advanced, incredibly, and survived, only because of his bold and cunning use of the Napoleonic myth, and the nourishment of that myth now demanded not only Forey's victory at Puebla but also the successful establishment of the empire in Mexico and solid gains in cash.

Accordingly, on June 16, 1863, Forey decreed that Saligny should name a *Junta Superior de Gobierno*, consisting of 35 Mexican citizens who were to elect an executive triumvirate of three and an Assembly of 215 Notables. This was done, and the triumvirate consisted of Almonte, Archbishop Labastida, still in Europe but replaced by a temporary substitute, and Mariano Salas, a minor politician and general who had served briefly as President before Santa Anna's return in 1846. On July 8 the Notables, duly coached in advance, proclaimed a monarchy and offered the throne to Maximilian of Austria, or if he should decline, to some other prince to be chosen by Napoleon III; meanwhile the triumvirate was to act as a Regency. In the long history of the reactionaries in Mexico, this was perhaps their basest hour.

Gutiérrez de Estrada, who never returned to Mexico, was appointed head of a commission to communicate these decisions to Maximilian at Miramar and to offer him the crown. This was done on October 3, 1863, and in reply, Maximilian accepted, on a condition now insisted upon by his brother, that the offer be confirmed by a vote of the Mexican people. The withdrawal of England and Spain was ignored.

The Regency was having its troubles about Church property and other matters. On October 1, partly as a result of intrigues by Hidalgo and Almonte, General Bazaine replaced General Forey, who was made a Marshal of France and summoned home, and Saligny also was at last withdrawn. Napoleon and Bazaine tried to pacify the Mexican people by being more liberal than the Church desired, and this effort, pursued later more vigorously and foolishly by Maximilian, was to prove disastrous. Napoleon and his Ministers also tried to calm the fears and resentments that they had aroused in the United States. Corwin was recalled without any recognition of the Regency, but the Confederacy sent an envoy to Mexico City. In Washington and New York, Romero continued to argue for his cause, and in the United States Congress, various resolutions were passed, opposing France's imperial intentions in Mexico more strongly and clearly than Seward had thought he could do. Meanwhile, the French forces and the smaller Mexican ones allied with them spread out from Mexico City and usually defeated the republicans. The French seized Tampico; and Yucatán, always a trouble spot, went over to the Regency.

Early in 1864, the Regency held as many elections as it could, or as it felt necessary before informing the commissioners in Europe that Maximilian had won overwhelmingly the plebiscite he had required. That these scattered and rigged "elections," held among a people mostly illiterate and indifferent, while the opposition was busy fighting a war, were a farce, was probably apparent to everyone, including Napoleon and excepting only Maximilian and Charlotte, who at this time would have accepted any assurance. The chosen pair proceeded as though to their second wedding. In Paris, they were gorgeously fêted, and in odd moments Maximilian and Napoleon made extensive agreements, in part secret, about the nature and gradual withdrawal of the French forces in Mexico—they were to be replaced by a new imperial Mexican army—and about the payment for the support of the French forces, which of course was to come out of the hides of the Mexican people. Napoleon promised firmly never to desert the new empire.

In England Maximilian borrowed money at exorbitant rates and there ignored the advice of Charlotte's French grandmother, Queen Marie-Amélie—which had been that of Maximilian's own parents—to have none of Mexico. Much the same good advice was given by Count Rechberg, the Austrian Minister of Foreign Affairs, and by Prince Richard Metternich, the Austrian Ambassador in Paris. Maximilian also brushed aside a warning given face to face by Jesús Terán, whom Juárez had sent to Europe to warn everyone concerned.

Especially interesting are two letters written to Juárez at this time by one J. W. Zerman, who, with a Mr. Howell, and with the support of Charles Francis Adams, the brilliant American Minister to Great Britain, was negotiating for the sale and shipment to the Mexican republican forces of 40,000 rejected Prussian muskets. The first letter was written in French in Amsterdam on March 19, 1864, reporting an interview with Maximilian in Brussels, and the second letter was written in English in London on May 9, 1864, reporting a second interview with Maximilian in that city. In these letters, Zerman reported to Juárez that he had warned Maximilian that he would find very little support among the Mexicans. Maximilian replied that he wished he had heard of this earlier, before giving his word to Napoleon! Maximilian also said, according to Zerman, that in any case he had reserved for six years his rights of succession to the throne of Austria (just in case), that he intended to support all of Juárez' Reform measures, and that he would not establish his government with foreign force and against the will of the Mexican people. Zerman also enclosed a letter from Baron du Pont, Ambassador of Austria in England, urging an interview between Maximilian and Juárez.

Reports by Mexican republican agents abroad are always open to suspicion, but considering Maximilian's rather flighty mind, these two seem plausible. Maximilian sounds rather like a bridegroom who is having serious doubts at the last minute, but is appalled by the prospect of the uproar that would surely be caused by his withdrawal. It was Vidaurri, somehow involved in this mysterious affair, who sent to Juárez a copy of Adams' "certificate" in support of Zerman and Howell, and in thanking Vidaurri on June 22, Juárez says that he has received no news of what chiefly interested him, the arrival of the guns, and considering the risks being run, "we must preserve the greatest possible discretion." On the margin of one of Zerman's letters he noted simply: "Letter from Zerman containing some curious news." In these seven dry words there are foretold the history of the next three years and revealed the character of the man who wrote them. They almost make one pity the flustered young man about to leave forever the fêtes of Europe, and of this world.

When Maximilian and Charlotte returned to Miramar to do their final packing, another difficulty arose: the Emperor Francis Joseph demanded that Maximilian renounce all rights of himself and his descendants to the Austrian throne. The Emperor's son Rudolph—he of Mayerling—was already six years old, but in these matters some legalistic care seems to be quite appropriate. This bridge-burning was a revealingly painful emotional event for Maximilian and Charlotte, but finally it was accomplished, and on April 10 Maximilian formally and fully accepted the throne of Mexico—which of course did not exist, except as a piece of furniture. Four days later, he and his wife left Miramar in the Austrian frigate *Novara*. First they went to Rome to get a blessing from the Pope, which they received, but they did not get something that would have been more useful: a relaxation of His Holiness's stand on Mexican Church property. The *Novara* then proceeded westward, and the royal pair were delighted when ships of the British Royal Navy off the Canary Islands gave them the salute of twenty-one guns that they considered due them in their new rank. On the voyage westward, Maximilian spent much of his time writing a manual of court organization and protocol: that was one thing *he* knew how to do. They arrived at Veracruz on May 28, 1864.

19

TOIL AND TROUBLE

MEANWHILE, the President of the Republic whose destruction was being plotted in the palaces of Europe went about his usual complex and arduous business. For him there were few fêtes and no apparent blessings, papal or otherwise. His only supports and comforts were his absolute faith in the independent and democratic future of Mexico, his devotion to his own task, the outrageous difficulties of which never daunted him, and the unfailing love that he gave to and received from his remarkable wife and their children.

Family life, which is of the greatest importance to most Mexicans, even when the men have erotic interests elsewhere—and this Mexican apparently did not once wander, after his marriage—was soon to be taken away from Juárez for a long time, but during this year of 1863–64 he was near his beloved family. In the grim month of May, 1863, just before their departure from Mexico City, Juárez and his wife and children were all greatly strengthened by the marriage of the oldest daughter, Manuela, to Pedro Santacilia, the Cuban liberal who had become Juárez' devoted friend when they were both in exile in New Orleans, and who had later arrived in Mexico. Whenever the family had to be sent onward, for safety, Santacilia guarded and cared for them and kept up a regular correspondence with Juárez, who in his letters discussed with this younger man not only family affairs but also those of state. This important correspondence does not give an impression that these two men were equals and very intimate friends—Juárez remains almost always the self-sufficient father-in-law—but it does prove without question that Pedro Santacilia did indirectly an enormous service to the Republic.

The French army and the traitors, as Juárez almost always called

the Mexican imperialists, could not at once move out of Mexico
City and defeat all of the republican forces, so that he had a respite
of sorts for several months (June 9–December 22, 1863) in the dignified and beautiful small city of San Luis Potosí, on the high plateau to the north, ringed by mountains, by a few dry but fertile
fields, and to the north by the very long and utterly savage desert
that extends up through Matehuala to Saltillo and Monterrey. It
was only a "respite of sorts" because there continued the usual
steady drumfire of "one damned thing after another."

For example, Doblado complained that an aide of Juárez' purloined a letter of his, when Juárez, on his trip north, had had no
aides. In Matamoros, Tamaulipas, a rebellion broke out against
Vidaurri and Manuel Ruiz, whom Juárez had appointed Governor
there, and whose considerable talents do not seem to have included
that of handling such situations. In traveling north from Guanajuato, Ortega and Llave—he of the escapade at Antón Lizardo—were
both attacked by their own escort, intent on robbery, and although
Ortega escaped because he had a good horse, and because some of
the robbers had served under his command previously, Llave was
mortally wounded.

In April, discouraged by Union reverses, by what he considered
the softening of American policy towards France, and by his continued bad health, Romero sought again and finally received permission to return to Mexico. He left Washington on April 29 and
reached San Luis Potosí on June 28. He requested permission of
Juárez to join the army of Porfirio Díaz, and he also suggested to
the President and his wife that they send their younger children to
the United States, to be educated there, "an idea that was well received." While renewing his friendship and exchanging news, opinions, and schemes with Juárez and other major and minor figures
then in San Luis, he played cards and managed, as he always did
when he could, to go to the theatre, and saw Bretón's *Everything
in This World Is a Farce.* Juárez at first wanted Romero to go back
to his job in Washington, but it soon became apparent that he could
be very useful as a liaison officer between the government in San
Luis and Díaz, training troops near Acámbaro.

Meanwhile, in August, another cabinet crisis boiled up in San Luis.

In response to criticisms that his cabinet was inert and lacked prestige, Juárez finally reorganized it, with Doblado in Foreign Affairs, Lerdo in Justice and Development, Nuñez in the Treasury, and Comonfort in War. During the few days in which he held the Foreign Ministry, Doblado insisted that Romero should replace Fuente in Washington, although Juárez had already sent Fuente on his way. Juárez complied, and Romero, who happened to be in San Luis on military business at the time, accepted the appointment with keen regret, because he wanted to visit his family—to whom he sent money whenever he could—in Oaxaca. Romero overtook Fuente in Matamoros, and Fuente accepted this sudden change with excellent grace. With Ignacio Mariscal, another cultivated and English-speaking lawyer from Oaxaca as his able secretary, Romero arrived in Washington and went back to work on October 26.

In another affair, however, even Doblado went too far. Francisco Zarco, the eminent journalist who had served as Foreign Minister and was now President of the Permanent Deputation serving as a sort of temporary, advisory Congress with the traveling government, and Manuel Zamacona, who had also been Foreign Minister and was then serving in the Deputation, had long opposed Doblado as being too conservative. Doblado now took the extreme liberty of ordering Zarco and Zamacona to leave San Luis for Monterrey within a fortnight, and to leave the Republic within a month. Ten Deputies led by Ponciano Arriaga protested, but Juárez had already had Doblado's order canceled, on the legal ground that Zarco and Zamacona, as a result of the extraordinary powers granted the government, were immune to such an order. Doblado resigned on September 7, and Juárez accepted his resignation, so that this prima donna returned to Guanajuato, promising, however, to continue to support the government with the forces of that state.

Lerdo, who had been in the Deputation, now replaced Doblado in Foreign Relations and was also given the Interior; while José María Iglesias took Justice and presently replaced Nuñez in the Treasury. Lerdo and Iglesias stoutly and efficiently remained in these offices during the rest of the war, and Iglesias also served as what we should now call director of information or propaganda by writing monthly a series of articles defending the republican cause, chiefly for the consumption of foreigners.

Doblado was by no means the only prima donna. When a unified command of the army seemed advisable, Juárez, Lerdo, and Comonfort all tried to persuade General José López Uraga to accept this command, but he refused to do so, on the shocking grounds that he would not get enough men and munitions to be successful, and that therefore his reputation would suffer. After his escape from the French, Ortega returned to the governorship of Zacatecas, and there refused to hand over the federal government's share of the taxes, or to supply other assistance. He promised to explain this to Juárez in San Luis, but never did so. One bright figure was Díaz, who left Acámbaro in the autumn to begin a brilliant campaign in the south.

Although the government of the United States could do nothing, arms kept coming across the border for the Mexican republican forces. Because of the dangers in delivery, Juárez insisted that they be paid for only on receipt in Mexico, and he kept hoping for a Union seizure of Texas, which would of course facilitate this traffic. Juárez also objected strongly and quite naturally to the delivery of used rifles that had been rebuilt but that broke down on the first firing. In discussing arms shipments, Juárez instructed Romero to refer in his letters to Texas as Tabasco, and to the Rio Bravo (Grande) as the Coatzacoalcos.

Although Uraga declined the supreme command, he did accept the post of second in command, under Comonfort, who at Querétaro assumed the chief command himself. "Soon after," Juárez wrote to Romero on November 22, "he [Comonfort] came here to discuss with the government some questions about the campaign. On the 11th he returned, and on the 13th of this month he left San Miguel de Allende on the road to Chamacuero [later Chamacuero de Comonfort and now simply Comonfort] with an escort of a hundred men; in the afternoon he left this village, but within a few leagues a party of bandits surprised the escort, dispersed it, and assassinated Sr. Comonfort and eight of his company, including soldiers and civilians. I cannot express to you all the pain that has been caused me by this misfortune: the loss of a man who, whatever one thinks may have been his political errors, was at the present time dedicated to the defense of his country. The command of the army has fallen definitely to Sr. Uraga." Juárez adds that for the present, action will have to be limited to guerrilla warfare, in the hope that later the enemy, now in Querétaro, can be put on the defensive.

Nearly thirty years later, Prieto remembered: "The dawn of the day of his death, I saw him [Comonfort] in San Luis in the house of Sr. Lerdo, where he had passed the night: he had a thousand glorious plans for the salvation of Mexico, and he spoke to me of Sr. Juárez with veneration and tenderness; availing myself of the intimacy between us, I put my hand on his neck and said: 'Take care of it,' and he replied, alluding to Juárez: 'The little Indian takes care of that.' At six they had assassinated him, although he was defended to the last by General Nuñez, who survived. Comonfort was goodness itself; that was his character!"

A firsthand account of this event, written to Juárez a week later, shows that Prieto, not Juárez, was off on the dates, and explains that Comonfort's death was at least partly caused by his rash treatment of his escort and of republican troops they met on the way. At Chamacuero a priest complained to Comonfort about the theft, by republican guerrillas, of his horse, which was worth $150; Comonfort ordered that he be given another horse, just as good, and this was done. The ambush was effected at the Rancho de Soria, six miles towards Celaya from Comonfort, near the River Laja. Some of Comonfort's escort deserted, and Comonfort's body was left stripped. Some important republican military plans were captured and sent to Bazaine. Comonfort's body lay for three days in a chapel in San Miguel, and was later buried in Mexico City. The word "assassination," used in connection with his death by Juárez, Prieto, and other republicans, seems extreme and unjust, considering that the killers were reactionary soldiers whom Comonfort and his escort would certainly have attacked, if they had seen them first. In any case, this able and surely unhappy man died in action, for his country, thus redeeming his weak and destructive folly of six years before.

Some time about the middle of November, because of the advance of the enemy, Juárez thought it wise to send his whole family north to Saltillo in the care of Santacilia. The desert between San Luis

Potosí and Saltillo in an upland valley, some two hundred miles long, walled by mountains, is very wild. The mining village of Matehuala is the only one on the way. Elsewhere there was no water except from rare and severe thunderstorms, and at that time the valley was probably infested by enemies of the government, as well as by jaguars.

On November 26 Juárez wrote to Santacilia in Saltillo: "I am desperate because I know nothing about you all, and the only thing that consoles me is the fact that up to now I have heard nothing bad, and that is something." He reports gratefully that don Eugenio Aguirre of Saltillo has offered to go out to meet the party and has already secured a house for them; and he reports the advance of the French to Querétaro and Maravatío. "A thousand things to Nela, to Pepe, and to all of 'the battalion.' You know that I love you all. Your most affectionate friend, Benito Juárez." Two days later he is rejoicing in response to the news, in Santacilia's letter of November 24, of the safe arrival of his family in Saltillo, and on December 3 he wrote the following letter to Santacilia in Saltillo, that is worth giving in full because we have so few of these homely details:

My dear Santa: Your welcome letters of November 25 and 26 have filled me with joy, because I see that you are all as usual and established in the best possible way. Now I have some tranquillity, and always I have the consolation that you, who care for our family, are another self.

I am so glad that those good people have received you well. I have already written to Sr. Aguirre to thank him for his kindnesses.

I am informed that the menservants were paid, and that as soon as he sends me the bill, I should pay to Sr. Larrache the other expenses and the value of the dead mule. I shall try to ask him for it first.

If the mules of the cart can be kept conveniently, their sale could be postponed, because it is always advantageous to have ready that means of transportation. You will ponder whatever is best, and whatever you decide will be right.

The thought of placing Beno in Monterrey, should there be an opportunity to do so, seems to me a good one. I am happy that Nela is already well, and that you will take her to Monterrey so that she may amuse herself and become acquainted with that city.

I fear that there you will not find the same good disposition that there is in Saltillo with regard to us, because don Santiago Vidaurri does not look favorably on the general government or its personnel. That does not matter, because—as I suggest to you for your guidance—most of the people think otherwise.

The French continue as far as Celaya and Acámbaro, but although when Bazaine left Mexico he said he would be in Guanajuato by November 25, it seems that this is not as easy as he had figured it to be, because although our army is not yet ready to meet him on the field of battle, Uraga has distributed and placed it in such a way that it does not allow the enemy to move with the liberty and impunity he might desire. Negrete is in San Felipe with the division. The newspapers that I am sending will give you other details of the situation. Say many sweet things to Nelita, give many kisses to Negrito, and remember me to all.

In a letter to Santacilia dated December 10, and in a letter to Vidaurri of the same date, Juárez expresses his gratitude to Vidaurri for his numerous kindnesses to the Juárez family. In the former letter, Juárez asks Santacilia to call on Vidaurri with his thanks, to ask Vidaurri to extend sympathy to the Comonfort family, and to explain to Vidaurri that he, Juárez, has not been sheltering Vidaurri's personal foes, because such personal relations do not interest him. He cites the fact that he has given important posts to the men who accused him of treason in Congress, simply because he considered them useful to the country. He also explains that he takes care to remain personally independent of Zarco and all other journalists. During all of this period Juárez was in steady correspondence with Vidaurri—who as usual did not agree with him or fully support him —about the rebellion against Juárez' friend and appointee, Governor Manuel Ruiz, in Matamoros. In a letter to Santacilia dated December 12 Juárez explains this complex small rebellion in detail, but more interesting are two short paragraphs towards the end of the letter:

May God enlighten the representatives of the North [in the United States] so that they may find a speedy solution to the Civil War, and thus put themselves in a position to call Louis Napoleon to order. I believe that the end of the war in the neighboring republic would be enough to make Napoleon change the tone of his mad policy with regard to ourselves. . . .

I am happy to hear that my dear Pepe does well in that climate. Thus he will grow strong and also develop his intellectual powers: *mens sana in corpore sano.* I charge you to take much care that neither he nor his sisters become impregnated with the biased notions produced by the superstitious practices of those poor people. I am glad that the girls are dancing, because that will do them more good than praying and beating their breasts.

He also mentions the continued advance of the enemy, and until the last minute he did not decide where, in the event of being forced to leave San Luis, he would establish the government. In an attempt to recover the city of Morelia, which had been taken from Berriozábal on November 30, an army of 9,000 men under General Uraga was badly defeated by General Márquez on December 18. Doblado had evacuated Guanajuato on December 9, and Tomás Mejía proceeded towards San Luis. On December 22 Juárez finally had to leave San Luis with the other members of the government, and they arrived at Saltillo on January 9, 1864. After yielding San Luis to General Mejía on December 23, General Negrete tried four days later to recover that city, only to be disastrously defeated. Juárez reported to Romero that this was because General Alcalde, by not obeying exactly General Negrete's orders, threw the attack out of order, but Sierra blames the defeat on Negrete himself, "to whom the death or absence of other commanders had given an importance that was unfortunate." In his letter to Romero, Juárez urges him to rush the delivery of arms, in particular at least two or three thousand rifles that could be obtained in Philadelphia.

It seems possible, if not certain, that the fall of San Luis and the retreat of the government to the north was the occasion of a more intimate blow to Juárez than has hitherto been mentioned anywhere. More than four years later, in Mexico City, among the numerous letters of the kind, Juárez received one from a certain Refugio Álvarez, who at the time of the fall of San Luis had been a lieutenant of cavalry in the republican army there, and had been captured. In this letter he asks Juárez for the restoration of his commission in the army. What alone makes this letter notable is the fact that twice within it, but with no special emphasis, Álvarez mentions that this was the same action in which Juárez' own son was taken prisoner by Mejía. Now, Juárez' two sons by doña Margarita living at that time, Benito Jr. (Beno or Negrito) and José (Pepe), were both children, and the third son, Antonio, was not yet born. If this Álvarez was not grotesquely in error, or his letter, although marked a "copy," is not a fabrication—and there is no apparent reason for believing that either is true—Álvarez could only have been referring to Juárez' illegitimate son before his marriage, Tereso, who presumably would have been old enough to be in the republican army at San Luis in December, 1863. This writer has found no other mention of this son, or of this event, in any other letter, document, or book, and risks mentioning him here only because such an event seems quite possible, and because, if it did happen, it must have caused Juárez, within his steely reserve, deep pain, and at a time when he was in any case under extreme pressure.

What is certain is that the strains on Juárez continued and increased. Five days after he arrived in Saltillo he faced a major challenge thrown in his face by leaders of his cause. In a memorandum he carefully recorded the following:

On the night of January 14, 1864, there presented themselves to me the Sres. D. Juan Ortiz Careaga and General D. Nicolás Medina, representing Sr. General D. Manuel Doblado; D. Martín W. Chávez, representing Sr. D. José María Chávez, former Governor of Aguascalientes [replaced by Ponciano Arriaga and resentful]; and D. Trinidad García de la Cadena and D. Manuel Cabezut, sent by Sr. General D. Jesús Gonzále Ortega, and they stated to me that they came in the name of the Sres. Doblado, Chávez, and Ortega [all then in Zacatecas] to ask me to resign the Presidency of the Republic, in order to deprive the enemy of a pretext he put forward in saying that while I remained in power there could be no entering into treaties: that the said Señores had decided to take this step because Sr. Cabezut, on returning from San Luis Potosí, had reported to them that I had decided to leave the post, and they considered this a very natural thing, because they judged me to be overwhelmed and weakened by the difficulty of the situation; that they did not make this request officially, but confidentially, and for this reason they did not bring with them a communication expressing this objective; and whether the answer I gave them was affirmative or negative, it would be respected and obeyed, for they did not wish in any manner to put pressure on me while I made my decision—a fact that they stated under the explicit direction of the Sres. Doblado, Ortega, and Chávez. Sr. García de la Cadena, in support of his position, stated frankly that he could conscientiously guarantee that in the state of Zacatecas, from the first to the last of its citizens, the opinion was uniform and explicit that it would be better if I abandoned the office.

In view of all this I answered that before arriving in this city on the 9th, I had received on the road a letter from Sr. Ortega in which he announced to me that a commission was coming to discuss with me matters of the greatest importance; that on that very day [the 14th] communications and letters had been received from Sres. Ortega and Doblado that were dated the 8th, and in the letters of Sr. Doblado to the Sres. Prieto and Nuñez he told them that he had been assured that I was resolved to leave the post, and that he was writing to me about the matter.

Since I did not receive the letter to which Sr. Doblado referred, I thought it well to write to him, saying that "I had not received his letter and it was not true that I wished to resign, because in the present circumstances, in which power had no attraction, neither my honor nor my duty permitted me to abandon the power with which the nation had entrusted me. Only when it withdrew its trust from me by legitimate means should I resign, for it was not appropriate for me to dispute over this office with the will of my country . . ."; that this answer that I had already given to Sr. Doblado was the same that I was giving now to the Señores of the commission, adding that if, as they had explained to me, it was believed that I, perhaps, was weakened and tired by the difficulty of the situation, and for this reason wished to retire, this was not true, and they could assure those who had sent them, on my behalf, that far from being wearied and debilitated by the events, I was as encouraged and determined as I had been six years before, when this struggle began; that at the time when I assumed command I foresaw all the consequences, and for this reason the reverses and disasters did not terrify me, that they were the natural consequences of a war such as our nation was enduring; that my conscience and my honor counseled me that it was my imperative duty to keep the power that the vote of the nation had confided in me, and that in these moments of common peril, cowardly to abandon the office would be to put a stain upon my conduct, to envelop my name with the curses of my fellow citizens, and to foul the memory that I wished to leave untouched to my children.

With this the conference came to an end, and the Señores of the commission repeated to me that they would transmit my decision to the Sres. Doblado, Chávez, and Ortega, and that it would be obeyed. *Benito Juárez.*

In letters to Chávez and Ortega, Juárez stated the same position more briefly, and in a letter to Doblado he elaborated it, explaining that his resignation would be both dangerous and ridiculous, plunging the country into anarchy; that the French might well not treat with Ortega or with any other Mexican who did not accept the intervention; that their purpose was to establish a government useful to France; and that some of the states might well refuse to accept Ortega, an outcome that would strengthen only the French. "Meanwhile, I shall continue to do everything in my power to help my country in the defense of its independence, its institutions, and its dignity." Then once more he pays his respects to Doblado's intentions, and appeals for his co-operation. In a letter to Romero, Juárez repeats all this, while asking him to keep the event from the press, in order to avoid increasing the scandal. He also reports that Doblado has written his acceptance of the President's decision, and shelves the whole matter in his characteristic style: "Thus ends this disturbance."

Doblado was now hardly in a position to do anything but co-operate with Juárez, within his own strictly limited resources and military talents. He had been driven out of Guanajuato, and in his independent and unauthorized negotiations with Bazaine he had discovered that the French were as little inclined to compromise as Juárez had predicted. Ortega was in no stronger position, because he was about to be driven out of Zacatecas on February 7. Soon after that, Chávez was captured and shot. Three leading governors, General Luis Terrazas in Chihuahua, General José María Patoni in Durango, and General Pesqueira, fighting off savage Indians in Sonora, vigorously repudiated this attempt to persuade Juárez to resign.

"Thus ends this disturbance"; but the testing of this man was far from ended.

20

TREASONS, DEFEATS, AND
A HARD FAREWELL

JUÁREZ' forbearance towards Doblado now paid off, after a fashion, because Doblado was able to join Juárez with a force of 1,500 men and four pieces of artillery, while General Florencio Antillón was near by with 2,000 men. This support was most fortunate, because Vidaurri's independence and arrogance had at last become intolerable. The federal government was now as usual hard pressed for money to keep its armies in the field. Nuñez, as Minister of the Treasury, had lost his nerve and shown some vague signs of going over to the enemy; relieved of his office, he had been briefly confined to his quarters and replaced in the Treasury by Iglesias. Vidaurri had been profiting by heavy trading with the Confederacy, and when Juárez and Iglesias demanded from him the funds due the federal government from the customs and other taxes, he refused to hand them over, claiming that he needed them for the protection of his own state of Coahuila—Nuevo León.

Juárez decided to move in on Vidaurri in Monterrey for a showdown, and on February 10 Doblado and his forces led the way down the winding, narrow road, between precipitous mountains, that drops about 3,500 feet in some sixty miles. At Santa Caterina, Doblado was joined by Antillón and his forces, but received a message from Vidaurri telling him to stay where he was, although the President would be received in the city with due honors. Doblado then committed the amazing folly of sending his four pieces of artillery into the city to provide the salute for the President. Vidaurri promptly seized the artillerymen and the four guns, took them to the Citadel, and prepared to fight. When Juárez arrived, he and his

Ministers spent the night of February 11 at a ranchhouse called El Mirador, near the foot of the hill of the Bishop's Palace, which had been the scene of important actions in all the wars. The next morning, Juárez wrote the following note to his wife in Saltillo:

> My dear Margarita: At ten to-day I shall make my entrance into the city. I did not do so yesterday because this Sr. Governor, who is extremely fond of swallowing gossip, has been believing that we came to attack him, and as a result has taken steps to defend himself, going to the Citadel to seize the artillery and spreading the word that he does not have to help the government. As all this was nothing more than talk and boasting, I ignored it and continued my march. I could have entered last night, but against my custom and my character I want to make a solemn entrance. Since in general there is good feeling among the people, they are already preparing decorations for the reception. To-day we shall see what other trick this gentleman will come up with.
>
> Do not prepare your journey until I send you word.
>
> Tell Santa 'this is for him also and he need not worry.
>
> Pick up for me some clothesbrushes that I left on the table where I was shaving.
>
> Remember me to our friends and many embraces for our children.
>
> I am your husband, who loves you. *Juárez.*

As usual, Juárez was optimistic, and at some peril to himself, because "this gentleman" Vidaurri still had a trick or two up his sleeve. Juárez entered Monterrey about noon, with a notable lack of public welcome, and he may or may not have been met by Vidaurri. There is a story that Vidaurri met him and said: "How are you, don Benito?" Juárez crossed his arms and said: "Are you unable to call me Señor Presidente?" and when Vidaurri did not answer, Juárez turned away and got back into his coach. Vidaurri's men followed him into the city, but did not dare to attack him. "At full speed," suggested a frightened aide, but Juárez contradicted him: "At a trot. The President of the Republic cannot run." In any case, Juárez occupied the statehouse and sent for Vidaurri, who remained in the Citadel and stipulated, along with effusive protestations of loyalty to Juárez, that Doblado's troops should first be withdrawn from the city—a move already suggested by Doblado himself, without Juárez' authorization. Juárez did not care to go to the Citadel, nor Vidaurri to the statehouse.

"There was a solution proposed by Doblado," says Sierra, "and he had to confess himself less adroit—he, not deceived until then by a living soul! [Actually, he had been deceived by Vidaurri himself the day before.] The idea was that Doblado should go as a hostage to the Citadel, occupied by Vidaurri, while Vidaurri went out to confer with Juárez. 'But Señor Doblado,' said Vidaurri, 'are you ingenuous enough to suggest to me the ruin of us both? My mother, who is no diplomat like yourself, but who has natural shrewdness, tells me that this is absurd, because if the President shoots me, and my men shoot you, Juárez will come out of it the winner, having got rid of both of us.' "

When Vidaurri was reinforced by his friend General Pedro Hinojosa, he threatened to attack, and Juárez thought it well to accede by ordering Doblado and his force, which had no artillery, out of the city. When this was done, on February 14, Vidaurri emerged and went to see Juárez in the statehouse, taking with him swarms of supporters who cheered him on the way. According to Prieto, vivid and unreliable as ever, Vidaurri now made extreme demands, and after a few minutes his son drew a pistol. With as much dignity as possible, Juárez, Lerdo, and Suarez Navarro withdrew to the street and joined Prieto in escaping in a coach prudently stationed there in advance by Lerdo. Defended by a few soldiers against a mob, the party made its escape.

Back in Saltillo, even Juárez must have been depressed by this whole fiasco, in which both he and Doblado had made dangerous errors in judgment, and from which he had escaped with little dignity and with lowered prestige. Although his health was usually invulnerable, this time he fell seriously ill with a fever.

Vidaurri's rebellion was now at least open, and in reply, Juárez separated the states of Nuevo León and Coahuila, which Vidaurri had joined some years before, declared both under siege, and as a technical gesture, ordered Vidaurri to come to Saltillo for trial. He added weight to these measures by concentrating his generals and troops at Saltillo, to prevent Mejía and the French, in San Luis and even in Matehuala, from coming to the assistance of Vidaurri. Meanwhile, Vidaurri revealed that he had been negotiating with Bazaine, who had tried both bribery and threats to make him come over. (Bazaine had also made totally vain approaches to both Lerdo and Díaz.) Unwilling to take any major step without the support of the people in his huge barony, Vidaurri now foolishly held a plebiscite of sorts, asking the people to choose between peace, meaning surrender to the French, and war, meaning support of Juárez. Juárez declared Vidaurri, and anyone who voted, a traitor, and the few votes cast were for war. Juárez now had 7,000 men and Vidaurri tried to "retire to private life," but Juárez naturally would have none of that, and Vidaurri had to flee to Texas. Only his friend General Julián Quiroga, with some cavalry, returned as a threat. So Vidaurri, the perpetual nuisance and would-be menace, was finally exposed and eliminated, but the concentration of forces required for this purpose had weakened the defenses elsewhere against the French. Juárez attributed this victory to the moral force of a legal position supported by the people of Coahuila and Nuevo León, which was undoubtedly an element in it, but so was the force of 7,000 armed men.

On February 27 a curious interlude occurred at Veracruz. Santa Anna himself arrived there from St. Thomas and Havana, hoping to seize political control of the parts of Mexico then held by the French, before the arrival of Maximilian, so that he might become the second figure, and perhaps the most powerful one, in imperial Mexico. Gutiérrez de Estrada had long supported the old schemer's pretensions to be still the most powerful Mexican, but Hidalgo and Almonte, jealous for their own positions, had succeeded in arousing Napoleon's suspicions of him. Furthermore, Bazaine, who had given Santa Anna permission to return to Mexico "as a simple citizen," and who had, through the authorities in Veracruz, forced him to swear to abstain from all political activity, was naturally enraged when Santa Anna issued one of his magniloquent and mendacious proclamations to the Mexican people, flattering the French but making it quite clear that this old professional conspirator could never have the slightest intention of staying out of politics. He was promptly deported.

On April 2 and 3, as a result of Vidaurri's flight, Monterrey was firmly occupied and the government established there, but Juárez left his family in Saltillo. There on June 13, "at nine fifteen was born Antonio Juárez y Maza," Juárez' last child. Within the next month the family was moved to Monterrey, where on July 12 Manuela Juárez y Maza de Santacilia gave birth to a daughter, Juárez' first grandchild, recorded by him as follows: "At 3:35 A.M. took place the birth of Nelita."

While Juárez' family increased, his associates fell away: discouragements, misunderstandings, disaffections, desertions, and treasons continued. Zamacona could never be a traitor of any degree, but at this time he certainly lost heart. On June 16, 1864, from Saltillo, he wrote a long, pessimistic letter to Juárez in Monterrey, saying that the Empire was in fact establishing peace and order, and that the morale of the people was deteriorating. Zamacona's frequent letters of criticism continued, and when Juárez evidently became irritated by them, and said so, Zamacona replied that he wished he could retire and farm in Puebla or Tlaxcala.

With Luis Terrazas, a rich and largely self-made rancher and a strong character, who was at that time, when only thirty-four years old, Governor of Chihuahua, Juárez had a serious misunderstanding. The difficulties between this state and the federal government were the usual ones over the disposition of Church property, over the division of customs receipts and taxes, and over the drafting and arming of men for the army. In the case of Chihuahua, these difficulties had been exacerbated by additional ones with Americans and with the savage Indians. In this case we can accept Sr. Fuentes Mares' interpretation that Juárez had been made irritable and oversuspicious by his troubles with Vidaurri, was legalistic in his response to Terrazas' decisions, and was influenced by enemies of Terrazas; but we must remember that if Juárez had been fully considerate of the difficulties of every governor, the Republic would not have survived. In any case, Juárez sent General Patoni into the state to take it over and to install a new governor, Jesús José Casavantes. While Patoni executed this task, as Sr. Fuentes Mares admits, "with the greatest tact," the probably maligned Terrazas, protesting his loyalty and offering the governorship to Patoni himself, to keep it out of the hands of Casavantes, withdrew with a cavalry escort to El Paso del

Norte, now Ciudad Juárez. Casavantes, a belligerent bungler, was soon replaced by Ángel Trías, who tried to undo his mistakes, while Patoni enlisted a battalion and, violating Juárez' orders to return to Saltillo (for which he was sharply rebuked), moved on to his own state of Durango. By July 13 Juárez himself apparently had some doubts about his action in this case.

In several army units there occurred mutinies and desertions, but probably the worst event of this kind was the treason of General José López Uraga, commander of the Army of the Center, whose correspondence with the enemy was exposed by Generals Corona and Arteaga. When proof of General Uraga's treachery arrived, on July 1, the government turned the command over to General Arteaga and recalled Uraga. Naturally he did not appear, and instead went openly over to the enemy. Then he tried without success to suborn other generals, including Díaz. Meanwhile, the French and the Mexican imperialists slowly continued their advance into the north.

Juárez naturally had difficulty in getting accurate reports about what was going on elsewhere in Mexico and in the outer world. Usually the news was bad, but he was optimistic whenever he possibly could be, as in the following reports to Romero. April 20: "Things go well. From Mexico they write on April 10 that the Emperor Napoleon has approved all of the acts of General Bazaine against the clergy. What will Señor Labastida do? We shall see." May 15: "To-day we have seen newspapers from New Orleans that come down to May 5. They report that the Archduke finally accepted the throne of Mexico on April 10, saying (an obvious lie) that he accepted it because a great majority of the Mexicans had confirmed by their vote the decision of the notables. Either all of this is false or the brother of Francis Joseph must be mad." June 8: "To-day we have letters from Mexico up to May 28. They report the arrival of Maximilian in Veracruz. I sincerely rejoice in the arrival of the Archduke, because I am convinced that the actual creation of the throne will facilitate the triumph of our republican institutions." July 6: "To-day I saw a letter from Mexico dated June 23. Referring to a person who had just arrived from Oaxaca, the writer says that Porfirio already has 14,000 men, much ammunition, and thirty pieces of artillery, and is waiting to take the field in a campaign only until his soldiers are skillful and disciplined." Of course in all his letters to Romero in Washington Juárez was chiefly concerned with securing Northern support. Members of both House and Senate kept offering and sometimes secured the passage of resolutions condemning the French intervention and the Mexican Empire, and similar resolutions were passed in both the political conventions of 1864. Romero supported all such actions in any ways he could, but Lincoln and Seward could not at that time risk any serious offense to France. On April 13 Juárez wrote to Romero that Corwin was returning to the United States—an event not important in itself, since he had never recognized the Regency, but perhaps fortunate, since he could not read Spanish and was discouraged, and his reports might have a bad effect. Juárez continued, as he did in many letters, to urge Romero to make every effort to counteract the effects of articles that had been copied into American newspapers from French publications in Mexico. He also instructed Romero to send him, via Matamoros, the weekly edition of the New York *Herald*. On March 29, 1864, a banquet was given to Romero in New York by thirty-one sympathizers with the Mexican Republic, including William Cullen Bryant, Hamilton Fish, John Jacob Astor, Jr., and George Bancroft, and when Juárez received Romero's report of this affair, he replied, April 20, that he was happy to hear about it, but added: "Up to now we have had only toasts and speeches and sterile sympathies," whereas he would appreciate more solid aid. On May 15, Juárez expressed his pleasure in the efforts of the American Congress, his belief that Seward was intimidated by the French, and his hope that the mutual sympathies of Vidaurri, the French, and the American Southerners would draw the North closer to the Mexican Republic. Actually, Confederate sympathies were divided and vacillating. What was wanted there above all was French recognition of the Confederacy, which never came. On June 29, noting European interventions in Santo Domingo and Peru, Juárez expressed his hopes that the United States would not remain indifferent to these violations of the Monroe Doctrine, and to this end that Grant would defeat Lee in the battles near Richmond.

Juárez' optimism buoyed up the spirits of the republicans, but on a short view it cannot be called well founded. During this period, the most important of the defeats of the republican forces was that sustained by Doblado at Matehuala on May 17. On April 22 Juárez had written to him warning him to avoid a major battle and ordering him to defend a line between the states of San Luis Potosí and Nuevo León and Coahuila; and on May 13 Patoni in Durango, on a basis of reports from Ortega, wrote to Juárez in alarm that Mejía might cut Doblado off. But Doblado attacked Matehuala and its mine, Catorce, only after Mejía had got wind of the attack and detained French reinforcements from San Luis. Doblado lost 1,200 men and all of his artillery. At first Juárez received encouraging reports of this action, but he soon heard the truth and sent for General Ortega and his forces. Fortunately for Juárez and his government, the French and imperial forces did not immediately attack Saltillo and Monterrey.

After handing in a report on his defeat at Matehuala, Doblado was exonerated and given the passport he had requested for entry into the United States. From Matamoros there came a report that when Doblado passed through that town, he and his friends had a riotous party in a brothel and gave to each of the "Russian-Austrian princesses" therein ten pesos and one of the medals that had been captured from the French: a report possibly slanderous, but too vivid to be overlooked. During Doblado's next and last year in the United States, he caused Juárez great concern by trying, without any authority whatever, to negotiate with American officials, assuring them that the Mexican government would cede territory in exchange for additional aid. On June 19, 1865, he died at 39 East 15th Street, New York, N.Y.

When Juarez' critics try to picture him as a dictator, they might be reminded that on July 16 and 17, 1864, with the enemy almost upon them, he and the cabinet were planning to hold elections somehow for a Congress to be convened in September.

On July 14 Juárez wrote to Romero: "Recently the bandit Quiroga has appeared with 200 men recruited in Texas, on the Sabinas road, and this circumstance has completely paralyzed the commerce of Piedras Negras," whose customs were one of the few sources of federal income. Amidst all the usual concerns about finances, personnel, and strategy, this Colonel Quiroga and his cavalry, formerly and perhaps still allied with Vidaurri, became an intrusive and dangerous problem. He indicated that he wanted to come over to Juárez' side *and* be paid for it, and although Ortega and his cavalry had arrived in Saltillo and Monterrey, it was evidently felt that the government was not strong enough to brush Quiroga aside. Negotiations were entrusted to General Hinojosa, who on July 25 "returned, saying that Quiroga demands the military and political command and all the forces and materials of war, besides money." This fantastic demand was of course rejected.

On July 28 Ortega presented himself to Juárez in a very low state of morale, with the familiar request that the cabinet be changed. Ortega said "it was believed that the government was going to disappear, I [Juárez] going to Matamoros and thence outside the Republic. . . . I answered that it was not true that I was going outside the country, and that I had resolved to die in my country, even if in the mountains."

Ortega and others now undertook the negotiations with Quiroga, but it was only after Juárez had received reinforcements that Quiroga submitted without conditions, promising to obey and to fight the foreign invader. Recognizing Ortega's demoralized condition, Juárez nevertheless had to make plans for him and the other republican generals at hand to defend Saltillo against the French and imperial forces. General Hinojosa was to remain in Monterrey as Governor and Military Commander of Nuevo León, with Colonel Quiroga as his second. In this area, the government was clearly now scraping the bottom of the barrel.

The rumor that had reached Ortega about Juárez' leaving the country may have been started by servants actually preparing for the departure of Juárez' family for the United States, by way of Matamoros. Quiroga offered the President an escort of cavalry for his family, but this offer Juárez, who still knew a hawk from a handsaw, declined with polite thanks. Just before the family left Monterrey in the care of Santacilia and for a while also in the care of a cavalry detachment provided by Ortega, Juárez bought his Margarita a dress, and then he went with them as far as the village of Cadereyta. There he saw every living being that he loved disappear in a cloud of dust. What their fate would be in the huge and mighty country that he respected but had no reason to love, where they knew little or nothing of the language, and might have to go for long periods without mail or money, and how long it would be before he could see them again, if ever, he could not know. On August 12 he noted simply in his diary: "The family left for Matamoros."

On August 14, he noted, a servant named Luz left Monterrey to catch up with the family. She must have been a brave woman. There exist letters written months later by a loyal servant named Manuel Ochoa, to doña Margarita, explaining his difficulties in taking care of her furniture left in Monterrey, because somebody had claimed to own pieces of it, and because the rest had been confiscated by imperial decree. But Ochoa reports proudly that he had got a receipt, and also: "You have a new *criado!*," or servant, meaning that he himself had a new son. Two years later Santacilia wrote to Juárez from New Rochelle, New York, opposing a suggested return of the family by way of Chihuahua: "I remember with horror the dangers of all kinds that we ran with Quiroga, when we had no other guarantee of security than the vigilance of the Quesadas. That [to travel thus] would not be to live, and I prefer anything to the frightful anxiety I felt at that time." Much later, Juárez and Ochoa learned that when the family was in New Orleans, on the way north, Benito Jr. had been temporarily but frighteningly lost in the streets of that city.

Two days before their departure, with the approval of the cabinet, Juárez had felt obliged to issue a decree that is a measure of his closeness to despair. To foreign volunteers who came armed to fight for the republican government in defense of Mexican independence, this decree offered, besides the regular army pay, lands worth a thousand, fifteen hundred, and two thousand pesos, depending on the rank of the volunteer, but not to exceed 1,084½ acres. Hitherto Juárez had always rejected any foreign volunteers unless they would become Mexican citizens, and he had expressed doubts that American volunteers would endure the hardships and low pay of Mexican soldiers, or remain well disciplined. As it turned out, during the next three years, a number of small units of American volunteers did go down into Mexico to fight for the Republic, and on several occasions proved themselves very useful.

The French were driving north. As early as August 4 the republican forces began to leave Monterrey for Saltillo and points south and west, and this withdrawal was gradually continued. On August 14 the government announced that it would leave Monterrey the next day for Saltillo, preceded by the remaining infantry and escorted by cavalry, "and that when opportune, it would announce the place in which it had decided to continue sustaining the laws of the nation." It was a brave statement, considering that on the way out of Monterrey the government party was treacherously attacked by Quiroga and his son. While the escort fought them off, one soldier was killed and another wounded, and Juárez' carriage was riddled with bullets. They spent the first night, after this attack, in Santa Catarina. They could not even reach Saltillo, which meanwhile had been taken by the enemy, and within a few weeks the entire northeast of Mexico, including Matamoros, had been occupied by the French and imperial forces. The dark little Indian in the worn black clothes, riding in old carriages with a few friends, followed by a wagon with the nation's archives, and escorted by a few horsemen, disappeared into the deserts of the north.

PART FIVE

The Tinsel Empire
and One Mexican

21

THE STEEL NET

JUÁREZ' difficulties were obvious enough. Presumptuous and alien as the Empire was, it was supported by French money and prestige, and by some thirty-five thousand French soldiers who were brave and tough, relatively well trained and equipped, and commanded with enough skill to enable them to defeat most republican forces in the field and to extend the imperial jurisdiction over most of inhabited Mexico. Disheartened or ambitious and unscrupulous, many of the republican leaders, military and political, and even a good many of the common soldiers, were deserting or going over openly to the enemy. Although Juárez was usually warmly received by the people wherever he went, and although republican guerrillas remained numerous and active, there were still several thousand Mexicans fighting savagely for the Empire, and the extent of solid popular support of the Republic remained an open question. Income, arms, and supplies from the unoccupied customs houses, states, and American sources remained a trickle. The American Civil War dragged on, and Napoleon's difficulties in France and elsewhere in Europe were not yet sufficiently clear to embolden Lincoln and Seward or Juárez himself. While the President and his little group of Ministers and stout supporters had repeatedly to flee for their lives from place to place in the deserts of the north, Maximilian maintained a court and something that looked much more like a government, in the capital of Mexico. Democracy might be "the future destiny of mankind," but in Mexico at that time it was only a few men writing letters that were often ignored, a vague dream or hope in the minds of a few thousand fighting men and scattered civilians, and the clear vision and indomitable will of one Mexican.

Every desertion, every lost battle, every flight of the government to another town farther north, every passing day, suggested more strongly that after fifty years of struggle the Mexican people were not yet capable of democracy and independence, and that Juárez, like all the heroic Mexican liberals before him, was doomed. Juárez himself must have known that it is quite as possible to become the victim of idealism as of greed. The princeling from Austria might be "mad," as Juárez had suggested, but he had the army, if not the votes; and on those long journeys, when Juárez looked out of his old coach at the scattered Indians, laboring, suffering, and ignorant as always, he may possibly have had moments of wondering whether he was not himself a victim of a madness more subtle but equally destructive.

Yet there is no evidence that he ever had any such moments, which are characteristic of minds more complex and introspective than Juárez'. He had been a shepherd boy living in an ancient Indian community that may have had a wise and strong old leader, he was notably paternal himself, and everything that he said and did as a politician suggests that he envisioned Mexico as a larger family ranch or community that could and must be pacified, ordered, enriched, and liberated, but under democratic law, and under elected leadership that was firm but gentle and wise. There were and are such communities and leaders in Mexico, and he must have seen them—in his mind's eye, at least—as well as the ignorant, isolated, and exploited peons. In any case, like any good rancher or father, he was going to realize his dream, he was going to save the Republic, if it killed him.

Besides, there is solid evidence that Juárez was strengthened not only by his dream, but also by his informed and shrewd appreciation of the dissensions and weaknesses within the Empire, and even of some of the problems of the confidence man who had promoted it and was supporting it but would not do so if it meant his own ruin. Despite the difficulties and delays of communication, he received, from Romero in Washington, Terán in Europe, and republicans watching and working secretly in Mexico City, a stream of letters and periodicals in which he could see more than shadows of the steel net of facts that was closing in on the doves of Miramar and Chapultepec and on the enemies of the Republic.

The pathetic drama of Maximilian and Charlotte in Mexico, enclosed within the tragedy of Mexico itself, began when they landed at Veracruz. Almonte did not meet them on time, and the people of the city ignored them completely. On the arduous climb to Mexico City, their coach broke down, yet the receptions in Puebla and the City, carefully arranged by the reactionaries and the French, were warm and colorful. Even so early, the poverty, ignorance, and disorganization apparent beneath the *fiestas* seemed to them "appalling." The National Palace turned out to be the vast barracks and office building that it remains today, rather than a residence, and like other tourists, these two quickly encountered vermin and dysentery. However, they began to acquire and make residences, with gardens, in Chapultepec Castle, Orizaba, and Cuernavaca. The views from the castle out across the old city and the valley to the two great snow-capped mountains were superb, and we can imagine how, living there in that heady altitude, and having been assured since birth that they were born to rule, these two young people who had found no country and people of their own to rule in Europe, could for a while imagine themselves strangely at home at last, and the destined saviors of the Mexican people and nation. They were genial, superficial, and supremely privileged yet insulated tourists, trying to go native. Given their powers of self-delusion, their youth, the extreme beauty of the country, the feudal devotion of their servants, and the gay fatalism of the Indians, whom they began to see as the true Mexicans, they must have had some happy hours. Now totally committed, they naturally wrote home that they were active, happy, and confident that they would solve all problems—in fact, that if they had left Miramar with their present knowledge of Mexico, they would have done so with no conditions whatever.

They were inept in personal and public relations, and from the moment they arrived they became snarled in a fish-line tangle of intrigues and plots even worse than the ones of which they had been the center in Europe. Leopold advised them to use Mexicans as much as possible, while Napoleon advised them to cleave to the French soldiers and diplomats. Except for Maximilian's elaborate court ceremonial, which nobody understood, they tried to dress and live like Mexicans, while the Mexicans who did not reject them were disappointed that they did not live like an Emperor and Empress. Maximilian courted such mild liberals as were not his open enemies, and eventually gave the Ministries of Foreign Affairs and War to two so-called "liberals," which of course did not please the conservatives. In between himself and the actual Ministers he allowed to intrude itself a private cabinet led by a Belgian mining engineer named Eloin, and he also depended entirely too much on a private secretary named Schertzenlechner, who had been a valet. The Emperors of the French and of Mexico corresponded steadily, as did their Empresses, in a style originally effusive but presently strained, while Napoleon received confidential reports on the side. King Leopold, Hidalgo in Paris, Gutiérrez de Estrada in Rome, and of course Almonte in Mexico, all remained as active in the drama as they safely could. Also, of course, Maximilian had to try to deal steadily, in an increasingly difficult division of authority and responsibility, with General Bazaine and with the Marquis of Montholon, the French Minister who had succeeded Saligny. There were even discords between Generals Bazaine and Douay. Importantly involved were Archbishop Labastida and the Papal Nuncio, named Monsignore Meglia, who finally arrived. Also, increasingly, and only partly kept in privacy, there developed strains between Maximilian and Charlotte themselves: Charlotte had a stronger will and a sharper tongue, and her neurotic tendencies were intensified by her failure to produce an heir to the fragile throne. When he had the time, Juárez could only guess about all of the intrigue and dissensions within the enemy camp, but when he did so, from hints in his correspondence, his surmises may have eased for him his dealings with Vidaurri, Ortega, Uraga, and the unauthorized operators in Washington and New York.

Maximilian wrote volumes of letters, memoranda, and plans for the reorganization and "implementation" of this and that, and he also traveled whenever he could, but none of this eager activity had much relation to reality. Soon after arriving in Mexico, and almost before he had even begun to try to solve the dangerous problems of taxation and finance, a Mexican imperial army to replace the French army, the Church property, and so on, he was actually scheming to

obtain control of all of Latin America between Mexico and Brazil!
On the night of September 15–16, 1864, he was in Dolores Hidalgo, the cradle of Mexican independence, and at the sacred hour of eleven he made a speech in his new Spanish from the balcony of Father Hidalgo's house. "You can imagine," he wrote to his brother, "how embarrassed I was before a tightly packed, silent mass of people. It went off well, thank God, and the enthusiasm was indescribable." That mass of silent Indians is wholly credible, and so, in a way, is the enthusiasm—but of course it was for the coppers that had been spread about or promised, with instructions for applause, for the pulque those coppers would soon buy, for the fireworks, for the uniforms, and for the independent Mexico that had somehow acquired this tall, blond, foreign *jefe* of some sort, and that would survive him, as it had all the others.

For more than two years after Maximilian's arrival, the French army and the Mexican imperial forces, under Bazaine, Douay, and Mejía, won all of the pitched battles and spread over most of Mexico, but they could not remain everywhere, and as soon as they withdrew, the republican guerrillas returned. Even at Chapultepec Castle there had to be sentries and a system of alarms and of defense, so that the imperial couple could almost never have felt truly triumphant and secure in their new semi-private, semi-detached empire. During 1864, Porfirio Díaz, with headquarters at Oaxaca, managed to keep a republican army active in the field. After the French army had seized most of the important cities and large areas in the north, and after Bazaine, using the traitor Uraga as an intermediary, had failed to seduce Díaz to the empire, it became clear that Bazaine had to defeat and if possible capture Díaz and occupy Oaxaca.

With great care and at great expense, Bazaine organized an expeditionary force of some 9,000 French and Austrian troops and 1,000 "traitors," well supplied with artillery. To defend Oaxaca, Díaz could muster only 2,800 men, with few guns, and his men were demoralized by the size of the force opposing them and by the influence of civilians in the city, including some former republicans. He wanted to fight outside the city, but did not have the transport to evacuate his necessary supplies for a campaign in the mountains, and was also dissuaded by the low morale of many of his officers and men. French artillery on Monte Albán and other near-by heights was able to bombard the city steadily, while Díaz' artillery did not have sufficient range to reply effectively. On the night of February 8, 1865, having exhausted his ammunition and food, Díaz went personally to Bazaine's headquarters and surrendered. With a group of officers and Lic. Justo Benítez he was imprisoned in Fort Loreto and then in the convent of Santa Catarina, both in Puebla, and once more he refused to swear that he would not again take up arms against the Empire. Four months later, after uselessly digging an escape tunnel under a wall, he found himself transferred to the Colegio Carolino. From this place, thanks to his daring, ingenuity, and physical strength, he made a remarkable escape (September, 1865) into the state of Guerrero, and there, starting from scratch, renewed his guerrilla warfare against the Empire. His later career can never obscure the fact that until 1867 "our Porfirio" was the most brilliant and reliable soldier of the Republic.

After his victory at Oaxaca, Bazaine became overoptimistic and sent home a French brigade, which was ill replaced by 6,000 Austrian and 1,200 Belgian volunteers. Of equal importance, Bazaine did not effectively co-operate in the organization and training of a Mexican imperial army, a task for which the Austrian "former naval person" was ill equipped, and the relations between the Emperor and the French commander, who held the real power, became increasingly strained. Also after his victory at Oaxaca, while his greatest prize, Díaz, was planning escape, Bazaine allowed his armies to take care of themselves while he, at fifty-four, courted and married a well-bred Mexican girl of seventeen. Both the Emperor and the Empress called the bride "charming" and gave the honeymooners a large house, while the Emperor remarked ironically of the General: "May this hazardous conjugal happiness agree with him." He himself was suffering from a liver complaint, and hopeless that the Empress could bear him a child, he took into the palace and prepared to adopt small Augustín Iturbide, the grandson of the first man to reign briefly as Emperor of Mexico.

When the Papal Nuncio demanded the full restoration of the properties and privileges of the Church, Maximilian, on December

27, 1864, issued what was probably one of the most disastrous of his numerous decrees: that which confirmed all the laws of the Reform on this subject. "The clergy," this startled idealist had observed, "are lacking in Christian charity and morality." With one stroke he had deprived himself of the support of the clergy, of the reactionaries, and of the Empress Eugénie; yet this extraordinary measure gained him the support of no liberals, because it included a hedging clause about the restoration of properties "irregularly" purchased, and more importantly, because no true liberals conceded Maximilian the right to decree anything whatever.

Juárez commented on this measure:

> The clergy are now disgusted with Maximilian, who has betrayed them by adopting in effect the Laws of the Reform, because he believed that the true liberals were so naïve that we should become his partisans only because he adopted some of our laws of the Reform, without recognizing that even if he adopted them in full he would never gain our submission, because above all we are defending the independence and dignity of our country, and when a foreigner intervenes in our affairs with his bayonets, and seeks, as Maximilian does, to impose his despotic will on us, we shall make war on him to the death, and we shall reject all of his offers, even if he accomplishes miracles. We do not need to have a foreigner come and establish reforms in our country: we have effected all of them without needing anyone.

Partly because the military expenses—for the capture of Oaxaca and for all the other expeditions—had been great, and partly because a thriving economy and sound taxation were still remote, Mexican finances under Maximilian were not even as solid as they had been under Juárez, with the result that most of a new French loan was assigned to the payment of old debts, and French officials took over not only those old foreign beachheads, the customs houses in the ports they controlled, but also the Ministry of Finance itself. The tricks of imperialism, even against subject "empires," are inevitably banal, and all that Napoleon and Maximilian had to learn was to call Mexico a "people's democracy."

On April 9, 1865, Lee surrendered to Grant at Appomattox. As the war drew to a close, Chambrun, the French Ambassador in

Washington, alarmed by widespread talk about the Union army going south to attack the French, had approached Lincoln to ask him about his government's present attitude towards France, and Lincoln had replied: "There has been war enough. I know what the American people want, but thank God, I count for something, and during my second term there will be no more fighting." Without intending to, Lincoln had comforted Maximilian, who by this time had taken note of the Monroe Doctrine and American military power. On April 14 Lincoln was shot, and he died the next morning. When Maximilian sent a letter by personal emissary to the new President, Andrew Johnson, neither the letter nor the emissary was received. The wind from the north was now cold indeed, and when Maximilian asked Napoleon for a guarantee of defense against the United States, his request was ignored.

The hostility of the victorious North had other causes than resentment over the violation of the Monroe Doctrine, democratic sympathies with Juárez, and the prolonged threat, now at last removed, of an alliance of France, the Mexican Empire, and the Confederacy, against the United States. Even before Maximilian had accepted the throne, Napoleon had supported a scheme by Dr. W. M. Gwin, a former United States Senator from California, to colonize Sonora with American Southerners and eventually to turn it over to France. Maximilian, as a new "Mexican," opposed this scheme, but later was forced to make some concessions to it. As late as the summer of 1865, Matthew Fontaine Maury, already the world's greatest oceanographer, promoted a plan to colonize parts of Mexico, including an area near Orizaba, with former Confederates, and Maximilian made him Imperial Commissioner of Immigration and Councilor of State. Maury wrote some gloomy and realistic reports on the condition of the Empire, which Maximilian ignored. The former Confederate General John B. Magruder was made surveyor of the lands destined for colonization, and he also fought for the Mexican imperialists. On September 5, 1865, Maximilian, the "liberal," issued a characteristically unrealistic decree to induce Southern planters to migrate to Mexico with their former slaves, who would become peons.

In response to events in the United States, Napoleon ordered

Bazaine to concentrate his troops into better defensive positions, and when this was done, republican forces took over the cities thus evacuated. The rats now began to leave the sinking ship, and it must have been very painful to Maximilian to discover, for example, that both Hidalgo and Gutiérrez de Estrada were chiefly interested, not in his glorious imperial regeneration of Mexico, but in the restoration of their family estates. Hidalgo appeared briefly in Mexico, was terrified by what he saw and fled back to Europe. Gutiérrez de Estrada never left Rome. Such were the men who had been heard when they presumed to speak for Mexico.

The defections to the republican side irritated the French officers into complaining to Maximilian that he had been too lenient in pardoning persons convicted of desertion by courts-martial. At this time a report was received from the French Baron de Aynard, in Mazatlán, that Juárez had abandoned his cause and country and fled to Santa Fé. Using this report as an excuse, on October 3, 1865, Maximilian issued a decree that began as follows: "The cause sustained by don Benito Juárez with such valor has already succumbed, not only to the will of the nation, but also to the very law invoked by that leader in support of his legal claims. To-day, except for the little band into which it has degenerated, that cause has been left abandoned by the departure of its leader from the fatherland." The decree then went on to order the summary execution of all persons caught bearing arms against the Empire. This decree was even more severe than that of Juárez dated January 25, 1862 declaring traitors all who supported the intervention; and it was more ruthlessly put into effect. In its chivalrous opening, expressing his temperament, and in its brutal purpose, dictated by others but accepted by Maximilian, this document is sadly characteristic of its author.

A few days later, a Mexican imperialist, Colonel Méndez, in Michoacán, defeated and captured two leading republican generals, José María Arteaga, commanding the Army of the Center, and Carlos Salazar, Governor of Michoacán; whereupon, in accordance with Maximilian's decree, he promptly executed these prisoners, along with two colonels and a priest. There was now much less chance of a spirit of compromise, or even of mercy, being shown by either side, and Maximilian had in effect condemned himself to death.

22

THE LAST DITCH

For about two years after his flight from Monterrey on August 15, 1864, Juárez' unfailing confidence that the Empire was doomed found little support in the hard, immediate facts, and if he had ever lost his nerve, the liberation of Mexico would have been long delayed and incidentally—he would have thought it incidental—he himself would have been destroyed.

All the travels of Juárez, his Ministers, and their small party of supporters, over vast distances in northern Mexico, were extremely arduous, in calabashes and carts drawn by horses and oxen over almost nonexistent roads, in country that was usually rocky, arid, and mountainous, in weather that could be freezing cold at night or as hot as an oven by day. Often the party was short of food and water and had good reason to bless the republican ranchers who gave them food, water, and shelter. The national archives, however sacred, were a heavy burden, and Juárez finally entrusted them, at a place called Gatuño, now Congregación Hidalgo, west of Saltillo, to eight devoted followers, "who deposited them near the stream El Jabalí, and later in a cave with a small entrance situated on the slope of the Sierra del Tabaco, near Matamoros, Coahuila. These men [to whom historians should raise a monument] zealously guarded the archives, suffering cruel persecutions by the imperialists, until 1867, when they could restore them to the federal government."

On August 29, from San Lorenzo near Parras, Juárez sent out an urgent summons to eight generals in the north, who met him at the *hacienda* of Santa Rosa, near Torreón, on September 2. There he grouped the available forces into the First Corps of the Army of the West, and unfortunately placed it under the command of Ortega, who was still saying what he would or would not do, with Patoni as his second in command. Under the impression, perhaps correct, that the French forces had been thinned out in that region, he ordered Ortega to move on Durango and Zacatecas. As the army marched south, Juárez and his party went by way of Mapimí, northwest of Torreón, to Nazas, on the River Nazas, in the state of Durango, there to await the outcome of the military operations, and there, on September 15–16, at a friendly *hacienda*, with a small body of troops, they celebrated, with who knows what rueful thoughts, the Mexican Independence Day.

On September 22, from Nazas, Juárez wrote cheerfully to Santacilia and Romero about the troop movements and his own, saying to the former: "In short, the struggle begins again, and I shall soon send you good news, because the nation still has life, and its government and defenders, far from being disheartened, feel every day more spirited and determined." Yet beneath his military and political optimism, he was painfully anxious about his family: "In my earlier letters I told you that since my departure from Monterrey and up to my arrival in this state I had not received any news, nor have I up to this date, but I have been in a continual torment from knowing nothing of your fate, for since you left Cadereyta I have learned nothing of your trip. You can well imagine my anxiety, from which I hope to escape at the moment I receive a letter from you or Margarita. . . . This letter and all those that I have written or shall write are for you and for Margarita. Poor Margarita! How much she will have suffered!" And he closes, as usual, sending many kisses and embraces to the children.

The day before he wrote these letters, the republican army under Ortega had been badly defeated at Cerro de Majoma, or La Estanzuela, near Durango. In this action the republicans had perhaps 2,500 men to perhaps 600 on the French side, and the following explanation of this disaster, written by Juárez to Santacilia, is supported by other reports:

We lost that action, when we had every chance to win, and all the odds on our side, simply because Sr. González Ortega did not send into combat all of his forces, but only a small part of them, which fought heroically; and the other part, which was larger, he left in formation and ordered to retire in order, without firing a shot; and the worst of it was that when this force, at least 1,500 infantrymen, was ten leagues from the enemy and was not being pursued, their commander-in-chief, either carelessly or from spite, allowed them to disband. These facts have not been published, and should not be, because the enemy is at hand, and I report them to you only so that you may be informed of one of the causes of our misfortunes.

From Nazas Juárez had therefore to move northwards, by way of San Pedro del Gallo, La Zarca, Cerro Gordo, Río Florida, and possibly Allende, to the city of Chihuahua, where he arrived on October 12. On the way or in Chihuahua Juárez received from Patoni a report on the defeat, with a footnote that throws a harsh light on republican morale in high places at that time: in a quarrel over lodgings one general struck another in the face, whereupon the one who had been attacked shot his assailant dead.

When Juárez and his party arrived in Chihuahua they were warmly greeted and the President and the former Governor, Luis Terrazas, whom he had removed, were somehow reconciled, to remain friends thenceforth. On October 15 Juárez wrote to his wife about his anxiety over having gotten no news from her and the family, and almost cheerfully about the defeat at Majoma. "I have fixed the seat of the government here because it is distant from the enemy and because the good will of the inhabitants will make our stay here tranquil and secure . . . and you receive the heart of your husband, who loves you dearly."

Juárez and his Ministers found quarters in the statehouse, "which adjoined that of Sra. Pía Rubio de Morón, whose husband, Dr. Roque Jacinto Morón, was a deputy and had accompanied them on their travels since San Luis Potosí. Sra. Rubio de Morón relates that they arrived in the afternoon, and from that time she attended and served them, becoming one of the family. The statehouse communicated with hers by a false door that provided a passage for the service. In order to equip the statehouse, furniture was borrowed here and there from families devoted to the republican cause. Don Benito would read and write until very late, slept very little, would rise at dawn, and would at once go out to enjoy the fresh air in the public garden. Most of the time he remained indoors," and he never locked his door. Years later, Sra. Rubio de Morón said to Ángel Pola of Juárez: "Ah, in his manners he was so sweet, I cannot tell you!" Iglesias and Prieto often went out together in the evening, but Lerdo, the urbane bachelor Rector of San Ildefonso, usually went out alone. Lerdo's influence on Juárez steadily increased, and while Juárez, Lerdo, and Iglesias drew closer together, Prieto became jealous. Tempers had grown frayed in Veracruz, years before, and Chihuahua was more isolated and provincial, but Lerdo at least had some of Juárez' stoicism. From one hard journey he wrote: "However bad our situation may be, we have all been able to foresee it and we have all known for some time that what is needed is more time and more constancy."

It was not until December 22 that Juárez was able to write, rejoicing, to Santacilia, that he had at last, more than four months after the parting, received his letters about the family, which had been settled safely in New York, at 210 East 13th Street, the address of the Mexican Consulate. At this time the mail usually went via Franklin, Texas (now El Paso), Santa Fé, and Kansas City, and took five or six weeks. Often the correspondents sent letters in duplicate by different routes. "This Chihuahua," wrote Juárez in the same letter, "is a jail in which one is held rigorously incommunicado, but not distant is the day on which we shall open our way into the interior with bayonets."

It is in this letter that Juárez also reports the first thunder of a storm that was on its way. Immediately after the passage already quoted on the battle of Majoma, he says: "Ortega is now living here in retirement in his house. However, he has been sufficiently active to ask me to turn over my office to him, claiming that my term had expired. He did not read the Constitution, and found himself in a ridiculous position." Under the Constitution, the President was to take office on December 1 and hold it for four years. In the critical period of 1861, Juárez had necessarily called an election, and when elected, had taken office early, on June 15. Ortega's claim at this time was based on the assumption that Juárez' term had actually begun on December 1, 1860, and would come to an end, or had come to an end, on December 1, 1864. When the defeated and ambitious General who also happened to be President of the Supreme Court, and next in line for the Presidency, asked the senior Minister for an opinion on this point, Lerdo told him that in his view, "under the Constitution the President could serve until the last day of November of the fourth year following his election, which meant that Juárez' term did not expire until 1865, an interpretation which Ortega accepted."

In a letter to Juárez on December 28, Ortega requested a leave of absence and a passport to go elsewhere to fight the enemy, a passport that would permit him to leave the country if necessary. He explained that he did not expect to leave the country, but thought that it would be an act of an imbecile to be captured by the enemy, and that it would be even worse if both he and Juárez were captured. Clearly misled by this request, the government granted the passport in this form, whereupon Ortega went to New York and stayed there a year—a distant refuge and a long time for a brief evasion of the enemy.

On December 22 Juárez also wrote to Romero in Washington, elaborating instructions already sent to him by Lerdo about his conduct in relation to the government of the United States:

"The instructions you seek have already been sent to you. Except for mortgaging or alienating national territory, steps for which the government has no power, you can do everything that may be advantageous to the defense of our cause. Forgive my recommending to you what you know better than I: that in the manner, form, and substance of any agreement, there must always be preserved the integrity and dignity of our nation, for this is precisely the objective of our present struggle. Bear in mind the *fortiter in re y* [*sic*] *suaviter in modo* of Lord Chesterfield.

"I await the report you offer me on the result of your visit to the army of General Grant." On October 24–27 Romero had visited the front in Virginia and had been cordially received by Generals Grant, Meade, Butler, and other officers, all of whom expressed the greatest sympathy for the Mexican Republic. The Union army was at this time wearing down the army of Lee and Early, but the results were still very uncertain. "If he [Grant]," continues Juárez, has succeeded in taking Richmond, our cause will advance somewhat in moral force, but if the question of arms remains undecided, we shall gain little or nothing, because we have to convince ourselves that the governors of that country, no matter what may have been the desires of their party, must work above all to re-establish and to consolidate peace within the country, and cannot dissipate their resources and attention in order to help other peoples, no matter how good their intentions towards us may be. This is the truth of the situation that we must always bear in mind in order not to deceive ourselves. However, in every case we must be grateful for the signs of esteem and sympathy shown us by generous hearts that wish to help us, although it is not possible for them to realize those desires. Thus I believe that in that Republic we should try to get what we can properly, without compromising our dignity, while not resting exclusively on that aid the hope of our victory. We shall manage to win that with our own limited resources. Thus the triumph of our cause will be more glorious, and if we should succumb, an event that I consider most unlikely, we shall have saved the honor of free men, to leave to our children so that they may bless us. There will not be lacking men who with creditable enthusiasm but insufficient patience, because they do not know how to suffer and wait, or possibly because they are ambitious, will suggest to you as a clever measure of high politics that you accept any offer, even when it involves some degree of sacrifice of our national honor.

Listen to these with caution; reject their hints with energy, and do what you think proper for the dignity and interests of the country.

If I had not proceeded in this manner when I was in Veracruz, and when similar suggestions were made to me repeatedly, I should have been condemned by Congress when the deputy don José M. Aguirre accused me of treason in the year 1861.

I am grateful to Mr. Seward and to his family, and also to the Secretary of the Interior for the wishes they have expressed to be presented to my wife. I do not know whether she will have been able to go to . . . [incomplete].

These instructions are further proof that the charges of treason that have been made against Juárez for a hundred years are absurd and incorrigibly biased. The warnings and instructions given to Romero by Juárez and Lerdo were necessary because towards the end of 1864 the Mexicans in the United States were alarmed by a rumor that after the American elections, in exchange for a promise by Napoleon not to recognize the South, the United States would recognize the Mexican Empire; and because this rumor, which had no basis in fact, had caused Doblado to suggest to Romero the cession of Lower California and part of Sonora to the United States, if the United States would reject any such agreement with Napoleon and would send an armed expedition into Mexico to aid the republican forces. Romero was no fool, but as Juárez knew, his health was always very poor, and the influence of Doblado was always to be feared. Meanwhile, Northern American sympathizers managed to keep sending a fairly steady if inadequate flow of supplies across the border.

At this time the French were advancing on the west coast and there was some threat to the state of Chihuahua, but for the time being the threat did not materialize. In reporting these operations to Santacilia, Juárez expresses concern about his family and also commends to Santacilia an old friend returning by way of New York from imprisonment in France: "My *compadre* D. Ignacio Mejía, who is in that [city], is a friend whom I love, and he was the support of my family in my days of misfortune. I recommend him to you highly."

On January 12, 1865, Juárez wrote to Santacilia: "I suppose that Pepe and Beno are going to school. I beg you not to put them under the direction of any Jesuit, or of any sectarian of any religion; they should learn to philosophize, that is, to learn to investigate the cause or reason of things, so that on their passage through this world they may have as a guide the truth, and not the errors and prejudices that make men and peoples unhappy and degraded." In this connection, we may quote another remark by Juárez that was heard and remembered by Sierra: "I should like to see Protestantism become naturalized in Mexico, conquering the Indians; these need a religion that would oblige them to read, and not oblige them to waste their savings on candles for the saints."

In his concern and love for his children, Juárez was about to receive a blow more crushing than would have been any other except the death of his wife or the decisive extinction of the Republic. On November 8, the American election day, the orderliness of which impressed him, Romero was in New York on Mexican business, and

"I went to see Sra. Juárez. I was with Santacilia for some time and he informed me of the grave condition of the son of the Señora." On January 26, only a fortnight after writing to Santacilia about the boys' education, Juárez was writing to him as follows:

My dear Santa: I write to you under the effect of the most profound sorrow, which crushes my heart, because in his letter of November 14, which I received last night, Romero tells me that my beloved son Pepe was gravely ill, and since he adds that even the physician was fearful for his life, I have understood that he wrote to me thus, merely of the seriousness of the case, only to spare me the blow of the sad news of the death of the little one; but really my Pepito did not then exist and does not now exist—isn't this true? You will appreciate all that I suffer from this irreparable loss of a son who was my delight, my pride, and my hope.

Poor Margarita! she will be inconsolable. Strengthen her with your counsels so that she may resist this severe blow with which evil fortune has struck us, and care for our family. Only you are their refuge and my consolation, in this impossibility in which I find myself, of reuniting myself with you all.

Farewell, my son; accept the heart of your inconsolable father and friend. *Benito Juárez.*

Excuse the blots, because my head is lost. *Juárez.*

A letter written by Juárez to Romero on the same day, January 26, 1865, is in part transcribed, cast in bronze, and mounted in a place of honor in the Juárez Museum in the National Palace; and this is appropriate, because it shows that although this man's will was made of bronze, he had a living, human heart that suffered greatly for his country and his family, and a brain, penetrating and civilized, that was equal to his great task. It follows in full:

My dear friend: By your letter of November 14 and by the official communications that you send to the Ministry, I am informed that in that [country] matters have changed in a manner that is favorable to our cause, and in this I rejoice, because I was much disturbed by the current reports that that government was disposed to recognize the empire of Maximilian. Thus we shall have at least the negative co-operation of that Republic, although as for any positive aid that it could give us, I consider that remote and superlatively difficult, because it is improbable that the South will abandon one iota of its pretensions, and therefore that government will have to settle the question by force of arms, and this will require much time and many sacrifices.

The idea that some persons have, as you tell me, that we should offer part of the national territory in order to obtain help is not only anti-national but also prejudicial to our cause. The nation, through the legitimate organ of its representatives, has shown in an explicit and decisive manner that it is not its will that its territory should be mortgaged or alienated, as you can see in the decree in which I was granted extraordinary powers to defend its independence, and if we should violate that directive, we should arouse the country against us and give the enemy a powerful support for the consummation of its conquest. The enemy may come and rob us, if that is our destiny, but we do not have to legalize that crime, handing over voluntarily that which they demand of us by force. If France, the United States, or any other nation whatever should take possession of any part of our territory, and if because of our weakness we should be unable to eject it therefrom, we should nevertheless leave alive the right of succeeding generations to recover it. It would be a serious evil for us to be disarmed by a superior force, but it would be superlatively worse if we should disarm our sons by depriving them of an unquestionable right that some day men more brave, patriotic, and enduring than ourselves would know how to value properly and to regain.

The idea of alienating territory under these circumstances is even more destructive in that the states of Sonora and Sinaloa, which are those most coveted, are to-day making heroic efforts in the national defense, are the most jealous of the integrity of their territory, and are giving the government firm and devoted support. Whether it may be for this consideration, or because of the prohibition that the law imposes on the government against mortgaging or alienating national territory, or in short because this prohibition conforms entirely with the opinion on this matter that I have always held and sustained, I repeat to you what I have already said in my letters of December 22 and earlier, namely: that you must not only hold fast to the patriotic attitude that you have held of not supporting any such idea, but also oppose it by working to dissuade its originators by making them become aware of the disastrous consequences that would result from its realization.

I am happy that you are satisfied with the opinion of our cause that you have found in the army of General Grant. That opinion and the one expressed by Mr. Seward are a sure guarantee that the empire of

Maximilian will not be recognized by that government. It is the only positive good that we can hope for at the present time from that Republic.

I cannot say more, because the death of the son that I loved so much presses with such a dreadful weight on my heart that I have hardly been able to write these lines. I say the death of the son that I loved so much because between the lines of your letter that I received last night I read that you do not wish to give me such dreadful news with one blow; but actually my beloved son was not then and is not now alive. Isn't this true? With all my soul I hope I am deceiving myself, and I should be very happy if by the next mail, which I am awaiting with painful anxiety, you should tell me that my son was recovering. But that is a dim hope that a grim presentiment wipes out, telling me that there is no remedy!

Juárez had to wait almost a month for the confirmation of his horrible premonition, and from the interval there remain at least six letters to Romero and Santacilia in which expressions of his agonizing suspense and grief are mixed with discussions, with which he seems to be trying to distract and calm himself, of events in the United States, policy towards that government, Maximilian's relations with the clergy, and the financial problems of the republican government, which for revenue could now count only on the customs receipts from Guaymas. In a later letter he reports the seizure of Oaxaca by Bazaine but characteristically—in this case with some accuracy—ventures the opinion that Maximilian will have to keep a large garrison in Oaxaca while he already lacks sufficient forces to pacify the people in areas he has already conquered. On February 23 he wrote to Santacilia that Romero had confirmed the dreaded fact of his son's death, and in this letter he grieves especially for his suffering Margarita; in a postscript he adds that he has just heard of the death in Cuba of Santacilia's father, and he tries to comfort his son-in-law in this new sorrow.

On March 21, Juárez' birthday, although he himself, because of his mourning, had planned nothing, and had objected to any celebration, the principal citizens of Chihuahua, including don Luis Terrazas—who was presently re-elected Governor—gave him a "sumptuous dinner," complete with toasts. When don Francisco

Urquidi offered a toast to Juárez' wife and children, Juárez is reported to have wept, and to have replied, in effect, that his country had to be placed before even them. "Friend Guillermo [Prieto]," he reported, "was admirable with his lyric poem, and has taken a very active part in everything that was done to celebrate my day." Juárez was evidently touched by the whole affair.

So must he have been later, in June, on receiving a letter dated May 28, in Acapulco, from Ignacio M. Altamirano, who had bitterly opposed Juárez in 1861, offering condolences and reassurances and reporting that to persons who think Juárez will flee the country, he has said: " 'It would be easier for the earth to move from its axis than that man from the Republic; that man is not a man, he is duty incarnate.' 'But where is he?' they have replied. 'I do not know the name of the bit of earth where he is just now, but he is in the Republic, he works for the Republic, and he will die in the Republic, and if only a corner of the country remains, in that corner will certainly be found the President.' " More important reassurance came in August, when Juárez learned by way of the Colombian Minister in Washington that in May the Congress of Colombia had passed a resolution in his honor, declaring him well deserving of America, or as it is usually expressed—and with heavy-handed irony by some of his hostile critics—*El Benemérito de las Américas.* On this honor, Juárez wrote simply to Santacilia that he did not deserve it and had only done his duty.

To go back, by March 27 Juárez was able to write to General Mariano Escobedo in Monterrey to congratulate him on having retaken that city and Laredo and begun to stamp out imperialism in the north. Escobedo, who had begun life as a farm laborer in Nuevo León, had learned soldiering in a hard school by fighting in the American war, in the war of the Reform, and against the French under Porfirio Díaz at Puebla and in the south. It is in this letter that Juárez makes his acidulous comment, already quoted, on Maximilian as a liberal reformer. As for the imperialists who now wish to come over to the Republic, they can do so only by proving their new loyalty with their blood, in action against the invaders. The lands of rich ranchers who have accepted commands under the enemy shall be seized and sold, and outright rebels and traitors like

Vidaurri and Quiroga shall "suffer all the rigor of the law" of January 25, 1862, namely, execution. Juárez appoints Escobedo Governor and Military Commander of Nuevo León, and gives him orders as such.

On April 6, to Santacilia, Juárez rejoices that Nela and her brothers are learning English, and that she will soon be able to go to the market and to shops without an interpreter. (Once in sending greetings to his children, he wrote: "For children are, as says the author of *Uncle Tom's Cabin* [*La Choza de T. Tomás*], roses of Eden that God casts upon the road of the unhappy." From Lord Chesterfield to Mrs. Stowe!) He then goes on to discuss the current state of our Civil War. He approves of "the inflexibility of Mr. Lincoln," and says: "If the North destroys slavery and does not recognize the empire of Maximilian, that will satisfy us." (In a letter written to Romero on the same day he says much the same thing, and shows that by "inflexibility" he means Lincoln's unwillingness to compromise with the Confederacy.) In view of recent Northern triumphs, he says, and the continued refusal to recognize the empire of Maximilian, Napoleon and the invaders and traitors may have to reconsider. Yet Juárez is still extremely careful to state that any aid from the North, even after a quick end of the Civil War, will have to come from "a friend, not a master," and with no loss of Mexican soil or dignity. As for private American volunteers to aid the Mexican Republic, Juárez is very sceptical: he says that he knows from experience that Americans are not accustomed to the misery of Mexican soldiers, and have to be well paid and equipped, or will become insubordinate. To what experience Juárez refers, and with what justice, is not apparent.

In a letter from New York dated May 9, Ortega himself brings up the same subject of volunteers, claiming with some truth that he has been warmly received by all kinds of persons, including generals, bankers, and businessmen, that there are heavy enlistments to serve in Mexico under the terms of Juárez' decree of August 11, 1864, and that these are being held up for approval by the American government and by Juárez. On the margin of this letter Juárez notes that it is not well to relieve the person already commissioned to buy arms and munitions, and that Ortega should be denied authority, with thanks. The authorized commissioner for this purpose, an unfortunate choice, as it turned out, was General José María de Jesús Carvajal. By April 27, the authorities (if any) of Doblado, Berriozábal, and Ortega had all been withdrawn.

On May 11, Juárez was able to write to Santacilia much more cheerfully about some family photographs and jokes he had received from New York. "In short, the mail that came recently from El Paso has made us all happy, and our pleasure would have been complete had it not been for the fatal news of the infamous assassination of President Lincoln, who labored with such constancy for the complete liberty of his fellow men, and who deserved a better fate than the dagger [*sic*] of a cowardly assassin. I await the next mail with the greatest anxiety, in order to learn what course will be taken by affairs in that Republic after the decisive victory of the government's army and the unfortunate death of Lincoln. I do not know the antecedents of Mr. Johnson, or his opinion on the Mexican question, although I assume that he will be favorable to our cause, because belonging, as he has said, to the people, he should share their opinion in not wanting a European monarchy in Mexico. We shall see, and meanwhile we shall keep up our fighting, undismayed." He then reports military operations and says that he does not think the enemy will come to Chihuahua, for fear of being attacked on their right flank and having their retreat cut off. In a letter to Romero on the same date, Juárez says of the death of Lincoln, "I have felt this disaster deeply," and he expresses a hope that Secretary Seward's wounds are not serious, while asking Romero to give Mr. Seward his best wishes. A week later he was relieved: "I have read the speech of Mr. Seward, and also that of Mr. Johnson, and there could not have been any declaration more explicit in our favor and against the tyrant of France."

On May 18: "It is not strange that now many of the turncoats and the admirers of the invader are already turning their eyes towards Chihuahua, and that Miramón and other reactionary leaders are cheering the liberal party. This is the world and the Mexican world, which is capable of astounding Louis Napoleon himself, if he came to live for a few days in Mexico. These Mexican people are singular; anyone who does not know them, and who is stupid, is intoxicated by their ovations and their fawning, and when they toss him aside and ruin him, if he is weak, their insults and curses will ruin him also." He then reports the return to the fold of two other liberals who had opposed him, and concludes: "The truth is that my enemies have no reason for being such. If I do any evil to the traitors, it is from misunderstanding, and not from conscious will. Vengeance is not my forte."

On June 29 he had to report to Santacilia that General Negrete, acting in accordance with Juárez' orders not to engage in battle unless he had a good prospect of winning, had been forced by the French General Brincourt, who had been successful under Bazaine at Oaxaca, to withdraw from Saltillo, but Negrete had then disobeyed orders by retreating to Chihuahua instead of aiding republican guerrillas to the east and south. On the reports of large groups of volunteers coming from San Francisco and New York, Juárez says:

I take these bits of news with some salt, but false rumors that they are, and much as the imperialists would wish to deny it, they give them a scare. What Ortega has said about parties coming from New Mexico into this state is not true. It would be easy to recruit men on the other side of the Bravo, but the lack of money for maintaining them will not permit us to do so. The miserable life of the poor does not agree with the sons of the rich.

Your idea that Beno should study civil engineering seems to me excellent, unless the boy shows a decided inclination for some other field.

Going as far back as Juárez' decree about volunteers on August 11, 1864, and continuing down through 1866, there was much activity in the United States in various projects to get arms and men into Mexico to aid the republican government. Some of this activity was legitimate, and a considerable amount of arms and a few volunteers did reach their destination, but many of the Mexicans and Americans involved in these activities were unauthorized by either government, many on both sides were either trying to inflate their own reputation or to line their own pockets, and some few were simply naïve. Insofar as they were able to keep themselves informed about these affairs, the legitimate authorities on both sides, Juárez and Lincoln (followed by Johnson), and Seward, Lerdo, and Romero, were more harassed than helped by them. Clearly the American people and their government wanted to help the Mexican Republic, and clearly that Republic and its soldiers and people needed any reasonable help they could get, but the "snafu" in this example of unauthorized "foreign aid" was extreme. Perhaps a few episodes taken from it will suffice.

Doblado died in his bed, but General Carvajal was there to take his place. He had been educated in Virginia, spoke English, and had had a good record in all the Mexican wars until the French cleaned him out of eastern Mexico in 1864, when he bustled off to Washington and New York. He was authorized to act under the decree on volunteers, but did not accomplish much in that direction and became the victim or accomplice of a crooked American named Daniel Woodhouse, who promoted the "United States, European, and West Virginia Land and Mining Company," demanding huge tracts of land, mines, and railroad rights in Tamaulipas and San Luis Potosí, in exchange for selling $30,000,000 in Mexican bonds at 40 per cent of their face value. Romero exposed the fraud, but not until after it had touched Juárez and his family in a way that was very painful to his scrupulous nature: Carvajal discovered that doña Margarita sorely needed money, so he sent to her warrants for $20,000, against Juárez' salary (of which he was getting only driblets at the time), secured by an illegal contract with the Woodhouse company. As soon as he heard of it, Juárez vehemently insisted to Santacilia that all the papers be returned to Carvajal at once, withdrew his commission, and took steps to raise funds for his family on his properties in Oaxaca. Involved with Carvajal's numerous schemes was General Lew Wallace, an honest man but a glory-hunter who had been relieved of his military command after his mistakes at Shiloh. He then became a rabid and troublesome Mexicophile who worked on a mad scheme to take Texas, Arkansas, and Louisiana out of the Confederacy and into support of Juárez. Some Confederates showed an interest in this scheme, seeing it as a means of absorbing northern Mexico into the Confederacy. Involved with Carvajal and Wallace in the Woodhouse fraud, until it was exposed, were two honest Americans, General Herman Sturm of Indiana and Robert

Dale Owen, also of Indiana, the son of the great Robert Owen and himself a distinguished man. (It should be noted that the bonds were ultimately redeemed by Porfirio Díaz.) Owen withdrew but Sturm went ahead and by 1866 managed actually to secure the delivery of substantial shipments of arms to Carvajal, then in Matamoros, and to Díaz, in Minatitlán, southeast of Veracruz, and these shipments had a part in the final victory. Matamoros became a hornets' nest of fighting, intriguing, and rebelling Mexican republicans, Frenchmen, Mexican imperialists, Union soldiers fighting on their own, and ex-Confederates—in other words, an Algeria of the time, worthy of a study of its own. A cheering gesture with intangible results, if any, was a meeting held at Cooper Institute in New York, on July 19, 1865, organized by American citizens "to express sympathy and respect for the Mexican republican exiles," who formed an impressive but most heterogeneous group. Always actively pro-Juárez, and at last very effectively so, if not always with proper authority from the government, were Generals Grant, Sheridan, and Schofield. On June 20, 1865, Romero reported to Juárez: "Grant could not do more if he were a Mexican."

Altogether, it is a very complex and human story, and Juárez watched it as carefully as he could under the circumstances, sceptically, and warily; his semi-detachment, while he kept his mind firmly on the larger issues, reminds one of the attitude of Lincoln. Those two were more like each other than they were like the hotheads and schemers among their own countrymen. Lincoln was dead now, but the new President, like the durable Seward, was rarely a fool, and times were changing.

Juárez' happy recognition of the fact, and such things as the salute from the Republic of Colombia, which came at this time, did not dispose of the French army, which in July, 1865, began to advance into the state of Chihuahua. On August 5 Juárez and his party had to leave the city of Chihuahua for El Paso del Norte, on the border itself. Luis Terrazas had not yet been inaugurated as Governor, and Manuel Ojinaga was appointed Governor *pro tempore*. Ojinaga had to withdraw into the mountains, where he was killed by imperialist sympathizers. The French entered the state capital on August 13. The country between Chihuahua and the border is a sandy desert, and in the blazing heat of summer, the retreat of Juárez and his party to the Rio Bravo, the last ditch of the Republic, must have been one of the most severe of their many hard journeys. They arrived on August 14.

On July 27, Reuben W. Creel, the American Consul in Chihuahua, who probably accompanied Juárez to the border, had written to Brigadier General James H. Carleton in Santa Fé, commanding the Department of New Mexico, about the advance of the French and the preparations of the Mexican government to go to El Paso del Norte; and on August 14 Carleton telegraphed this letter to the Adjutant General in Washington, adding that Juárez would probably have to seek refuge in the United States and eloquently suggesting that he be offered hospitality. While awaiting permission, he ordered the commanding officer at Franklin, Texas, "to have the dwellings at Hast Mills at your [Juárez'] disposal." Reporting these measures to Juárez on August 25, he concludes: "I hope your Excellency will not hesitate to call upon me for any favor or assistance which I can properly give. That in your reverses you have our heartfelt sympathy you must believe, and I am one of those who have faith that not many months will elapse before you will be at the Capital of the Mexican Republic, amidst a loyal, free people as their chief Executive, with neither foreign influence nor foreign bayonets to bias or threaten you in the free discharge of your duty." With equal courtesy and his "profound gratitude," Juárez declined the invitation, explaining simply that he had established the government in El Paso del Norte. In several letters to others he expresses his usual confidence, in this case that the French are not in a position to advance farther north, because of guerrilla operations. In this estimate he was probably correct, but it might also be noted that without Carleton's or Juárez' being aware of the fact, Napoleon had ordered Bazaine not to risk complications by getting too close to the United States Army.

Having just dug into the last ditch precisely at the time when he was being exasperated by Carvajal's unauthorized operations, and worried by the very serious problem of Ortega, Juárez was struck down, in September, by another blow: the news of the death of his youngest child, Antonio, who had been born in Saltillo fifteen months before. The father's grief could not have been as great as that which he felt over the death of his second son, José or Pepe, whom he had known and especially loved, but this time he was even more worried about his wife. "I imagine all that my poor wife is suffering, I greatly fear that she will not be able to endure this blow, and this almost deprives me of any judgment. . . . My mind is overwhelmed, and I can hardly write these lines."

23

THE LAW AND THE FACTS

NEXT to his permitting the negotiation of the McLane–Ocampo Treaty, the act of Juárez that has been most severely criticized is his decision about the Presidency in the autumn of 1865. During that autumn and winter in El Paso del Norte he had many other problems on his mind, but this was probably the most serious and oppressive one, and it is mentioned in one way or another in almost every one of his letters for months on end.

When Ortega had first raised the question, the year before, it had been fairly easy for Lerdo to answer it, for the time being, but then Ortega had tricked Juárez into giving him a passport, and had then proceeded to make an endless nuisance of himself in the United States, interviewing President Johnson and everyone else he could buttonhole, and trying to raise and arm a corps of volunteers—all without any authority from his government, and to the acute embarrassment of Romero, Lerdo, and Juárez. The Constitution clearly stated that when the Presidency fell vacant at the end of a term, and elections could not be held, the President of the Supreme Court, in this case Ortega, would become interim President.

All during this year, nobody could have doubted that on or before December 1, 1865, Ortega would claim the Presidency, and might well persuade a body of politicians, generals, and soldiers to back up his claim, in which case, if Juárez and his supporters resisted him, this new civil strife within the Republic itself, such as it then was, would almost surely result in its extinction. Juárez had always been the embodiment and the paladin of the law as "the sword and shield" of freedom and order, and he himself had educated an uncertain but increasing number of Mexicans in this view of it. If he denied Ortega the Presidency, that act would perhaps in some degree betray both them and himself. Like all other strong Presidents, in Mexico and elsewhere, Juárez had been called a would-be dictator, but at least until 1871—and as to that date it can be refuted—this accusation has no evidence to support it. Without vanity, of which Juárez had abnormally little, any man who had fought so tremendous a fight for so long would have wanted to finish it himself, but even this man must have had moments of great weariness, and he clearly had more than moments of tremendous longing for an honorable reunion with his wife and children. If someone other than Ortega, possibly Lerdo, had been the claimant, it seems quite reasonable to imagine that Juárez would have yielded up the Presidency on December 1, 1865.

But Ortega was Ortega: a man undeniably vain and personally ambitious, avid for money and glory. As a soldier, he had been phenomenally lucky once, at Calpulálpam, and gallant, at the siege of Puebla, but elsewhere mediocre or worse. As a governor, he was obviously ignorant of the law and indifferent to it, tricky, and subject to flattery. Above all, he was a man easily discouraged and in discouragement wide open to deals that seemed advantageous to himself. Juárez apparently did not know, but he may well have suspected, that already the French were at least considering an attempt to make a deal with Ortega to supplant Juárez on terms favorable to themselves, and that Ortega himself had taken steps in this direction. Once declared President, Ortega, returning, might sell the Republic down the Rio Bravo. After the sacrifices of Ocampo, Degollado, and Valle, not to mention Hidalgo, Allende, Morelos, and thousands of other Mexicans, was the Mexican Republic to be turned over to this flamboyant and slippery character who might even, as Vidaurri had done, sell everything in his power for high office in the tinsel Empire? There was one thing that Benito Juárez loved more than the law and the Constitution, more than his reputation as their defender, more than peace and order, more even than his family, and vastly more than his own life, and that was the Mexican people and their future; and these Mexican people had entrusted him with these vague but very great powers to defend them against all of their many enemies. During those months, Juárez may well have thought of the return of Ortega to the National Palace, perhaps amidst the plaudits of the "singular" Mexican people who gave them so easily, and thought of that possible return in terms of what Ortega might do to the people of Guelatao and ten thousand other hamlets all over Mexico. "I am a son of the people, and I shall not forget it," he had told them eighteen years before; he had not forgotten it, and when confronted with that passionate loyalty, what was the worth of his own happiness, his reputation, and even the explicit law?

It will be recalled that in May, 1865, Ortega, in New York, requested and was denied authority to enlist American volunteers. On May 18, Juárez wrote to Santacilia:

I have already told you in one of my earlier letters that González Ortega did not take to that Republic any commission from the government. After he had been answered that the day had not yet arrived on which he would assume the Presidency, he requested permission to go to one of the points in the interior, where there was action against the intervention, in order to offer his services, and since it was possible that it would not be easy to go by way of areas occupied by the enemy, he also requested permission, in case of necessity, to travel through foreign territory or by sea. His request was granted, with the warning that with any forces he should raise he should put himself under the orders of the commander named by the government in the state in which he arrived. I believed he was going to Sonora, Sinaloa, or Coahuila, where they were fighting in the nation's defense, and where the road was free of the enemy; but he chose the road to Santa Fé and New York; as he told me once, he is tired and discouraged, and needs to be far from the enemy in order to restore his lowered spirits.

I shall tell you a contretemps that occurred to this good man when he was at Parral and I was here in Chihuahua last October. He went to a ball given him by the inhabitants of that place, and at the time of toasts, Ortega took his glass and gave a toast to the withdrawal from command of Benito Juárez, who had brought so many evils upon the Republic; but he had not even finished speaking his last words when Dr. Don Manuel Robles, a resident of that place, stood up, indignant and energetic but with poise, and offered a toast demanding that Ortega withdraw those words injurious to the First Magistrate of the Republic, of whom the nation thought otherwise than did Ortega, for if Sr. Juárez had not been able to do all the good that he desired, it was because those who coveted the supreme command had served him only as obstacles, confronting him with systematic opposition. Ortega did not expect this volley, which disconcerted him, and he had the humiliation of withdrawing his toast, giving thousands of apologies to Sr. Robles. What worse pain could be given so high a personage as Ortega? Although this story is notorious in this state, it would be well for us to keep it to ourselves.

It is in this same letter that Juárez claims with justice that vengeance is not his forte, but this little anecdote may be relished not only for the courage and poise of Dr. Robles, who is otherwise apparently unknown, but also for this rare and humanizing little display of personal pique on the part of Juárez himself, a display that he did not want to have go further than his son-in-law.

On June 13, Ignacio Mariscal, Romero's second in Washington, wrote to Santacilia in New York about his approach to General Schofield, in Raleigh, North Carolina, in an effort, which General Grant advised be kept secret, to get General Schofield to command fifteen or twenty thousand American volunteers in Mexico. In connection with this effort, Romero told Mariscal, Ortega proposed to Romero that they buy guns from the Americans for $5 and then sell them to the Mexican government for $15! When Juárez received this letter from Santacilia, he wrote on its back: "Important letter from I. Mariscal about General González Ortega."

In a letter to Santacilia on June 15 Juárez repeats that only Carvajal has a commission to act in the United States, "so that if the Yankees put any trust in the promises and arrangements of Ortega, they will make fools of themselves. I will tell you also that Ortega has said that I should do well to recommend him [to the Americans?] as the future President of Mexico; this I do not believe, for although Ortega, with his characteristic indiscretion, may have said so, it is not certain." The Spanish is a bit vague, but momentous as the issue was, at this date, from this remark, we may assume that Ortega's chances of succeeding were somewhat slight.

On August 18 to Santacilia from El Paso: "I have been advised of the speculations of G. Ortega, which do not surprise me, because I have long known about his love of money and his lack of scruple in selecting methods of obtaining it. This love is one of the motives that make him ravenous for the Presidency of the Republic, which he considers a means of enriching himself and satisfying all of his vicious tastes. In this respect Ortega is of the school of D. Antonio López de Santa Anna." He then repeats that Ortega has no commission.

But whatever his proven character, Ortega could not be brushed aside. On September 27, in a confidential postscript to Santacilia:

On the matter of the extension of my tenure as President of the Republic, a step that many persons [including notably, without doubt, Lerdo] advise me to take for the good of the country, I have decided nothing, because the point is too grave. Although I believe that the extremely broad powers given me by Congress empower me to make such a declaration, there are not lacking those who cast doubt on the legality of the measure, and it would suffice for Ortega, any governor, or any commander to dispute the authority extended by myself, to light off a civil war, and in that case the dissolution of this unhappy society would be complete. The time has not yet come for such a declaration, and already, mark you, Guillermo Prieto and Manuel Ruiz are talking and are preparing to protest against the declaration: the former to get himself in well with Ortega, and the latter because he believes that if Ortega does not take the office upon himself on December 1, it will devolve upon himself, for no other reason than that he is a member of the Court of Justice. However, by the end of November, circumstances, the law, and public opinion will indicate the course that should be taken. Let us hope so, and wait.

The reader will remember that Juárez' close association and friendship with Prieto and Ruiz had continued throughout the whole tumultuous decade; and with Ruiz even longer, for he, sixteen years younger than Juárez, had also attended the seminary in Oaxaca, and then the Institute to study law, and Juárez had led him, as a protégé, into civil service and politics in the state government of Oaxaca. He had been Minister of Justice under both Comonfort and Juárez, and in Veracruz had been one of the authors of the Laws of the Reform. During the Intervention he had followed Juárez into the north and been named Governor of Tamaulipas, an office he held whenever Cortina or Vidaurri did not take it away from him, until he became a Justice of the Supreme Court and in this mad moment had fallen victim to the presidential disease and come to consider himself in the line of succession. The attitudes of Prieto and Ruiz at this time may not have been a total surprise to Juárez, who knew them well, but they must have given him some pause and more pain.

On the first two days of October, in El Paso del Norte, Juárez and Prieto exchanged six letters that record the alienation of these old friends. Within Mexican towns, important letters were and are delivered by servants, and in this crisis, both men may have found letter-writing more precise and less painful than personal interviews. Both used the familar second person. Prieto writes first to the "old and much loved friend of his heart" that on the last two times he has seen him, Juárez has made him feel his displeasure, apparently because he, Prieto, heated by wine, and at an almost public gathering, had perhaps indiscreetly expressed his opinion, which was in accordance with the law and with honor as he understood it, on a matter that had begun to be discussed in the town—meaning, of course, the presidential succession. Somewhat reproachfully asserting his loyalty and services over eight years, he asked Juárez to close down the postal service, of which he was director, and which was already in fact inoperative, in order to relieve everyone concerned of embarrassment. He also asks to be excused giving any verbal explanation. In reply, Juárez says that only the enemy will close any part of the administration, if he can help it; on the incident in question, Juárez refers Prieto to his conscience; and finally, Juárez urges Prieto to remember that he had never told or authorized him to write to Ortega in Juárez' name, to the effect that Ortega had permission to remain abroad indefinitely. This painful and repetitive correspondence continues until Juárez finally says he will pass Prieto's resignation on to the appropriate Minister.

On October 6, in a postscript to Santacilia, Juárez comments sarcastically on Ortega's pleasure trip to Niagara Falls: "Perhaps when he hears that Chihuahua is occupied by the enemy, he will hesitate about coming to these deserts, where there are no amusements of any sort." On October 13 he repeats this jibe and then says: "I remain unperturbed, watching the arrival of events without worrying about anything but the national defense, which is my first duty while I occupy the post with which the nation has entrusted me. Prieto and Ruiz remain much worried and agitated, out of pure love of . . . our country. The question of the Presidency does not permit them to sleep. It is pitiful to see what these little angels suffer." On the same date, Prieto himself ventured to write to Santacilia, ridiculing the government and telling of many disagreements with Juárez and the Ministers. "I do not think that on balance, I owe more to Juárez than he does to me." Prieto and Ruiz are pitiful, and Juárez' own response to his old friends is slightly chilling.

At this same time Luis Terrazas rejected an appointment as Prefect of the Department of Chihuahua, under the Empire, and ironically enough, Maximilian was proposing to his Imperial Council the idea of his appointing Juárez President of the Imperial Supreme Court! On October 26 Juárez wrote to reassure his family that the French would not dare—and did not have the money necessary—to cross the desert between Chihuahua and El Paso. He reports the defection of Generals Miguel Negrete and Rafael Quesada in support of Ortega and of his claim to the Presidency, but says he doesn't regret their action, because there are plenty of good patriots left, and because "it is better to be alone than to have bad company."

In due time, Juárez made his decision. On November 3, evidently as a legal gesture, he ordered the arrest of all officers outside the country without permission, and of all officers outside the country with permission but absent longer than necessary for safe return to the scene of action. On November 8 Juárez, with the assistance of Lerdo, issued two decrees that were more specific and decisive. In the first, acting under the extraordinary powers granted him by the last Congress, Juárez extended the terms of both the President and the President of the Supreme Court until the end of the war and the elections that victory would make possible. The extension of both terms was a legal necessity, but it was obvious that Juárez could not leave Ortega in office as an heir apparent who had been denied the Presidency, so in a second decree of the same date Juárez declared that Ortega had abandoned his office as President of the Supreme Court when he accepted the governship of Zacatecas—something of a legal quibble considering the frequent and unconstitutional tenure of several offices by the same man—and also, much more plausibly, that Ortega had abandoned both his judicial post and his commission in the army when he had remained outside of Mexico for a long period without permission. For "abandoning the army, its flags, and the cause of the Republic" in time of war, Ortega was ordered to return to Mexico for trial by the appropriate courts. We may assume that he was not expected to do anything of the kind, and that this measure was merely intended to supply a basis for legal action if and when Ortega should return furtively or with an armed force and be defeated and captured. In sending the decrees to Santacilia, Juárez said that he expected criticism, but felt confident that he had reached the right decision, and that the nation would support him.

At this time Juárez was again almost trapped by his optimism. On October 29 the French withdrew from Chihuahua, and evidently acting on military information that was insufficient or incorrect, Juárez prepared to return to that city. On November 12, the day before his departure, he calmly reported his plans to Santacilia, while also reporting an exchange of parties between his government and friendly Americans across the border, the Mexicans having been hosts on September 16 and the Americans having reciprocated with a farewell party to Juárez in *El Paso del Norte* on November 11. "They were very agreeable to me and to all those who accompanied me. Of course there were dancing, drinking, and toasts to the victory of the Republic and to my return to Chihuahua." The Americans had brought along a military band. We may hope that he enjoyed himself, but there is an undated photograph of him playing cards with some merry Americans in El Paso del Norte in which he is shown scowling, perhaps at his thoughts about Ortega but probably at the hand he had drawn. His pleasure, if any, was brief. He arrived at Chihuahua on November 20, and the French promptly drove northward again from Durango. On November 24 and December 1 he wrote cheerfully that if the French approached Chihuahua he would go elsewhere, and that the French were in any case demoralized and doomed, both by increasing Mexican opposition and by the recent warning of Mr. Seward. He also chats cheerfully about the futile reunion of Ortega's supporters, Prieto, Ruiz, Negrete, Quesada, and Aranda in Piedras Negras. He discusses Carvajal's antics and the disposition of his houses and furniture in Oaxaca and Mexico City, and he warns the family against becoming too dependent on the fireplaces of New York, which can bring on other ills, since an alternation of heat and cold is natural and salubrious. There is always a short view as well as a long view, and on December 9, with General and Governor Terrazas in command of the escort, Juárez and the Ministers and others had once more to start for El Paso del Norte, which they reached on December 18. "Probably Maximilian will now say, with his usual precision, that I have gone to the United States, and I don't know what other things, but pay no attention: you know how credulous he is." And after citing instances in which the French might have caught him but did not: "Now we can say to them what the *gachupin* said to the chicken that he had caught alive and that was squawking not to have his head cut off: 'Too late, friend chicken.'"

In the most vital respect, Juárez' optimism was promptly proved well founded: all the governors and all the generals except Patoni and one Huerta supported his extension of his tenure of office and his condemnation of Ortega. This support was more important than any other, and Juárez' relief must have been great, but then he must also have been cheered by a letter from Giuseppe Mazzini in London, recommending an Italian artillery officer who wanted to serve under Juárez and going on to applaud Juárez' struggle against the French, comparing it to Garibaldi's fight in Rome in 1847. Mazzini also broached the idea of a Republican Legion made up of elements from Europe, the United States, and South America. From New York on January 5, 1866, Zarco wrote to Juárez in full approval of the legality and necessity of the first decree of November 8, but deploring the second as being illegal and unnecessary. He said that he had kept this second opinion to himself and was glad that only the first decree had been published in New York. In a careful reply, Juárez argued, among other points, that if Ortega had not been deprived of his office as President of the Supreme Court, any rebellion by him would have had much more encouragement and force. Six months later, Zarco conceded the wisdom of Juárez' second decree: in his view, Ortega's behavior in New York had justified it. So this great problem had been solved successfully, but despite other problems that followed hard upon it, for months and even years it remained on Juárez' mind and found mention in his letters. Stuck on the outermost edge of the Republic, he had both to make sure of support in the interior and to follow as well as he could the movements and activities of Ortega and his supporters.

Poor Ruiz went to El Parral and there issued a protest against Juárez' decrees, ending with an announcement that he was then returning to private life. This was the common ambition of republicans and imperialists who got into serious trouble, but it was rarely achieved. When the French took Ruiz prisoner, he appealed to General Patoni, who had not yet gone over to Ortega, to release some French prisoners he had captured, in order to induce the French to release him, but General Patoni merely passed this "impertinent request," as Juárez styled it, on to the government, which was then being forced out of Chihuahua. Juárez heard no more of him and assumed that his protest had been accepted by the French and that he was in Mexico City. "Thus has ended the political career," wrote Juárez, "of a man whom I wanted to make a good citizen, [and it ended] because he insisted on being the opposite. *Con su pan se lo coma.*" Or as we should say: he has made his bed and now he must lie in it. Three years later, in Mexico City, Ruiz published a defense of his own bizarre claim to the Presidency. He died on October 26, 1871, and because of his record, Congress appropriated money to pay part of his debts.

"As for Guillermo Prieto," continued Juárez to Santacilia on December 21, "shortly before I left Chihuahua he came to see me with the pretext of appealing for my compliance with the request of Ruiz. He told me that he loved me very much, that he was my minstrel and biographer, and that if I wished him to continue writing whatever I wanted him to, how would that do? I thanked him, pitying his weakness and paying no attention to his lies" about his disputes with Lerdo and Doblado concerning the administration of the postal service. "It seems that he has gone to Presidio, [Texas] or some other place in that state. I have read the letter that he wrote to you. He does not say a word of truth. . . . In short, this poor devil, like Ruiz and Negrete, is out of action. They had value because the government made use of them. Now we shall see what they can do on their own. As for G. Ortega, I suppose that he has already seen my decision on tenure and on his trial. If he has any judgment and good sense left, the best he can do is give himself up or be quiet." Even the report of this scene is slightly embarrassing. Prieto was in Brownsville and San Antonio until December, 1867, when he returned to Mexico City and there occurred a reconciliation. He returned to Congress, wrote voluminously, became a poet laureate and grand old man, of sorts, under the Porfiriato, and died in 1897.

Of course Ortega did not keep quiet. On December 26 he issued a statement disputing the legal validity of the decrees, while also claiming that his labors in the United States for the Mexican Republic could not be called desertion. But after this, Ortega's decline, caused at least as much by his own character as by Juárez' decrees, was rapid. In New York in the summer of 1865 he had been associated with a Colonel William H. Allen, formerly of the 1st and the 145th Ohio Volunteer Infantry Regiments, in an abortive effort to raise a force of American volunteers. This effort had an enthusiastic response, but mostly from ex-officers who wanted to be paid. On October 14 Allen sued Ortega in the Superior Court of New York in an effort to recover certain funds. Romero reported several conversations with Ortega in which the General was obscure on his plans in relation to the Presidency. In November, with $1,300 oddly supplied by Romero, he left New York and also left his lawyer, who had been procured by Romero, unpaid. For the honor of Mexico, Romero and Navarro, the Consul in New York, paid this bill.

Ortega next appeared in Texas; and at Matamoros, in the autumn of 1866, at the time when Maximilian was considering abdication and the French were considering replacing him with Ortega as a republican figurehead favorable to themselves, some Mexicans rebelled in favor of Ortega. This event was not really dangerous, but the American General Sedgwick took it upon himself to invade Matamoros, arrest Ortega, and send him to New Orleans. General Sedgwick's superior, General Philip H. Sheridan, rebuked him for this intervention, but it had disposed, if briefly, of Ortega. He soon returned to Mexico and was joined by Patoni, but both were imprisoned in Monterrey. When they were liberated, in 1868, Patoni was murdered and Ortega issued a manifesto trying to justify his behavior in 1864 and 1865 but also accepting Juárez' title and authority and offering to go into exile. Juárez assured him that this was not necessary, and ordered the Treasury to pay him some money due him. Jesús González Ortega, the not quite perpetual storm center, died in 1881.

At the end of 1865, almost alone except for Lerdo and Iglesias, in the shabby town at the northern edge of the Republic, Juárez still stood like a tower. If he had become a little more frosty, who can wonder?

24

TWO MEN, TWO WOMEN, AND DESTINY

In watching and comparing Juárez and Maximilian, doña Margarita and Charlotte, and others, as they were caught up in the tides of history, we need not commit the common error of assuming that these great forces were above and beyond the decisions and control, and hence the responsibility, of individual human beings. Millions of unknown persons in North America and Europe were deciding what they wanted most, and it was their decisions and actions, and not any inhuman laws or powers, that determined the results that constituted destiny.

One tide of history came from the north. Even before the Union victory and the death of Lincoln, enough Americans in the North were sufficiently irritated and humiliated by the presence on the continent of an empire supported by the French army to arouse their congressmen, and so indirectly to make it possible for Generals Grant, Sheridan, and John M. Schofield, acting just within the limits of their authority, to take steps towards the Mexican border. In May, 1865, after various schemes of an American auxiliary force to go to the aid of the Mexican Republic had come to nothing because of the prudent reserve of Lincoln and Juárez, General Sheridan was sent by President Johnson to the border, and in time his well-armed force grew to the formidable number of 100,000 men. While Gwin, Maury, Magruder, and other ex-Confederates were busying themselves within the Empire, this force just beyond the Rio Bravo undoubtedly had more influence on Bazaine and Maximilian. Whenever there were rumors of imperial advances to the north, more American soldiers appeared at El Paso, and although he rebuked General Sedgwick for meddling in the cauldron at Matamoros, Sheridan relieved himself by staging demonstrations all along the border, and by "condemning" large supplies of arms and ammunition, leaving them conveniently beside the river, and then making sure that the Mexican republicans knew that he had done so.

Seward had a broader view than the eager generals, whose pressure on the civil government was becoming troublesome, and he pulled a trick from his sleeve by sending General Schofield on a futile mission to France. Then in a long series of communications of various kinds, notable among which were those of September 6, 1865, December 16, 1865, and February 12, 1866, he slowly drew the velvet glove from the steel fist. On the last date he declared, in reply to French fictions and evasions, "that the proceedings in Mexico were regarded in the United States as having been taken without the authority, and prosecuted against the will and opinions of the Mexican people; that the United States had not seen any satisfactory evidence that the people of Mexico had spoken and called into being or accepted the so-called empire, and that the withdrawal of the French troops was deemed necessary to allow such a proceeding to be taken. He concluded with a virtual ultimatum: 'We shall be gratified when the Emperor shall give to us . . . definite information of the time when French military operations may be expected to cease in Mexico.' "

President Johnson had made a similar statement on December 4, 1865, and Juárez' comment on it deserves study:

I said in my last that we were entirely in agreement in judging the message of Mr. Johnson in relation to the cause of Mexico. He said what he had to say, and that harms us in no respect. On the contrary, what he said surprised me agreeably, because I was hoping for very little or nothing. I have never had illusions with regard to the open aid that that nation could give us. I know that the rich and the powerful do not feel or try to alleviate the miseries of the poor. The former fear and respect each other and are not able to break lances in the quarrels of the weak or against the injustices with which they are oppressed. This is and has been the way of the world. Only those who do not recognize it deceive themselves. Instead of complaining, Mexicans must redouble their efforts to free themselves from their tyrants. Thus they will be worthy to be free and respected, for thus they will owe their glory to their own efforts and will not, like miserable slaves, need others to think, work, and speak for them. It may happen occasionally that the powerful will find it advantageous to defend a poor, oppressed people, but they will do that for their own interest and gain. The weak can never have any sure hope in that outcome. This could happen in our present situation; only for that reason may Napoleon withdraw his forces, no matter how many troops he has sent and kept on sending, only to withdraw them, if his fear of the United States, or his other interests, or more probably both, counsel him to do so. His plan may be to reinforce his troops in order to make as advantageous a bargain as he can with the power that he fears and respects because it is strong. We shall see. We shall continue our defense as though we were self-sufficient.

Discouraged by the continued guerrilla warfare in Mexico and by the refusal of Juárez and his government simply to disappear, menaced by Seward's threats and by the ominous rise of Prussia, and failing in health and will power, Napoleon in April, 1866, finally decided to cut his losses by abandoning the great intercontinental confidence game . . . and his victim. He decided that his army should leave Mexico in three detachments, in November, 1866, March, 1867, and November, 1867. In his threat of February 12, Seward had astutely allowed Napoleon to save some face by assuring him that the United States would stay out of Mexico after the French withdrawal. Had not Seward heard Lincoln predict that after the French withdrew, the Mexicans would take care of Maximilian? Meanwhile there was coming to a head, within the Germanic Confederacy, a struggle for domination between Austria and Prussia. Just before the war with Prussia, and under Seward's added pressure, Austria abandoned a plan to send further volunteers to the aid of Maximilian. At Sadowa, on July 3, 1866, after a war of only seven weeks, Bismarck inflicted a crushing defeat on the Austrians. In the peace negotiations, and in the settlement of the future of Luxembourg, it became clear that the French Empire was sooner or later to face a serious challenge from Prussia, with the result that the French withdrew even ahead of their timetable. "Bismarck," wrote Juárez, "has alarmed and stirred up the other wolves of Europe."

During these great events a Mexican side show, small and shabby, but enough to cause some worry to Juárez and others, was going on in the United States. In January, 1866, Seward was cruising in the Virgin Islands, to take a look at them with a view to purchase, and to restore his own health. At St. Thomas, in an accidental meeting, he talked with the old clown Santa Anna, who thereupon conceived the characteristic idea of going to the United States and offering himself as a replacement, satisfactory to both the United States and France, for both Juárez and Maximilian. He tried to float a loan, secured by his own properties, to equip an American force, nominally in behalf of Ortega or Juárez, but actually, of course, in behalf of himself. Seward refused to see him, and Juárez ordered Romero, to whom he had made advances, to reject him as a traitor despised by the Mexican people. Even this little farce had one astonishing and one may say deplorable result. While old Santa Anna was living in Elizabethport, New Jersey (far from the Alamo and thirty years later), trying to see Seward and being victimized by his own followers, a young American named James Adams saw him chewing chicle, asked him about it, and proceeded to invent and manufacture chewing gum.

Slowly but steadily, while Juárez waited it out in El Paso del Norte, and later again in Chihuahua, hearing only scraps of all this increasingly good news, the steel net closed in on Maximilian and Charlotte.

Jesús Terán, Juárez' emissary in Europe, worked intelligently and indefatigably for the Republic, and in the autumn of 1865, he called on Baron De Pont, an old friend and diplomatic agent of Maximilian's, in order to give a warning of Maximilian's plight, and to suggest his withdrawal. Impressed, De Pont reported this warning to Maximilian himself, who replied, on December 8, 1865, speaking of Juárez: "If, as I believe, he really desires the good of Mexico, he must soon see that no Mexican has such warm feelings for his country and its progress as I, and that I am working with the utmost good will and honesty; so let him come and help me faithfully and sincerely, and I will receive him with open arms, as I would any good Mexican." What a cloud of naïve illusions, and what vast if unconscious impertinence! While Maximilian was indulging in such fantasies, others were more realistic. The Jecker bond claimants, for example, were still squeezing millions from the hard-pressed Mexican treasury, which had never been able to repay the more legitimate English debt while paying for the war and the Empire.

Maximilian now lost two important friends and supporters: Lord Palmerston died in October, 1865, and Charlotte's father, King Leopold I of the Belgians, in December. While Bazaine drew the French units towards the center of Mexico, the republicans swarmed in after them, eager for vengeance on the Mexican imperialists, and Maximilian protested vehemently and in vain to Bazaine, Napoleon, and everyone else. Napoleon's decision to withdraw entirely was of course a bitter wound to Maximilian, who until that moment had trusted him greatly. Charlotte suffered also, of course, and the falling out of the imperial couple was clearly painful to Napoleon and Eugénie as well. These two were not utterly unscrupulous, and felt their responsibility for what they had done, and for what might happen in Mexico; but in 1866, and especially after Sadowa, it was clear to them that they had to abandon Maximilian and Charlotte or imperil their own throne, and possibly France itself. As imperial dreamers and operators they were the more guilty because they had been the more intelligent and powerful originators and executors of the whole scheme, but we cannot wholly agree with Juárez' judgment that since Napoleon "has a greater interest to insure, the permanence of his dynasty, it little matters to him if Maximilian goes to the devil."

Trying to do what he could to avoid disaster to Maximilian and dishonor to himself, Napoleon gave Bazaine the impossible task of wiping out the republican forces entirely, before leaving Mexico. Under such direction and control as could be provided from the north by Juárez and by Ignacio Mejía, now back in action as Minister of War, General Mariano Escobedo in the northeast, Generals Vicente Riva Palacio and Nicolás Regules in the center, General Ramón Cortona in the west, and Generals Juan and Diego Álvarez and Porfirio Díaz in the south were now reinvigorated and more experienced, and were all closing in on the tottering empire. A turning point was the defeat of the imperial General Tomás Mejía by General Escobedo at Matamoros on June 22. After this event, there were frequent mutinies among the Mexican imperial troops and also among the remaining Belgian and Austrian volunteers, whose pay was in arrears. If our feelings for the Mexican people leave us any sympathy to spare, it might go to the French soldiers who survived this long and nasty campaign to go back to Sedan.

Maximilian was about to abdicate, that July, when Charlotte, always more ambitious and decisive than her husband, kept him from doing so by appealing to his sense of honor as a sovereign. They then agreed that she should depart for Europe, to act as his ambassador in demanding further support from Napoleon. She left Mexico City on July 9, and her husband accompanied her part of the way to the coast. Their parting may have been as painful, in its own way, as that of Juárez from his wife and children at Cadereyta two years before. The republicans were singing a satirical love song by General Riva Palacio, with the refrain: *"Adiós, mamá Carlota, adiós, mi tierno amor!"*

Monterrey and Tampico were now given up to the republicans, while Maximilian frantically conceded almost everything demanded by the reactionaries and the French officers without getting in return a more vigorous fight against the republicans. Guaymas and Mazatlán fell next, and then Maximilian heard of the humiliation of his brother and of his native land at Sadowa, but also of a victory by his own Austrian navy.

Charlotte's embassy in Europe was a total and pathetic failure. When she arrived in Paris, Napoleon was ill and was also being humiliated by a triumphant Bismarck. Charlotte's eloquence and tenacity were great, but Napoleon, Eugénie, and the French Ministers, with whom she pleaded and argued, were all tightly bound by the European situation, and by their own fears and ambitions, so that they would or could do nothing for the young Empress and her husband in their plight. In writing to Maximilian the worst possible news, Charlotte was able to add: "I am inheriting money from all sides, and the jewels too were very fine. I have a magnificent Golden Fleece for you."

But these were toys for doomed children. When in August Napoleon firmly refused to send any further help to the Mexican Empire, Charlotte's anger, disappointment and fear were so great that her mind began to give way to paranoia: Napoleon was the Devil, and at St. Cloud he had tried to poison her in some orange juice. After a rest in northern Italy, she went on to Miramar, where further bad news from Mexico—defeats, withdrawals, and concessions to the French—again upset her, without for a moment making her reconsider Maximilian's abdication. She next went to Rome to plead with Pope Pius IX, who of course could not tolerate Maximilian's attitude towards the Mexican Church, and who was at that time dependent, like Maximilian, on French arms. When the Pope, while receiving her with splendor, refused to try to intercede with Napoleon, Charlotte lost her mind completely, insisted that she was served by murderers, and declined to leave the Vatican, where she was the first and last woman, it is said, to spend the night. Her brother came from Belgium and took her to Miramar, but her illness became more severe, and she was eventually taken to Belgium, where she lived, totally insane, until 1927.

In October Maximilian, himself usually ill, received Napoleon's refusal of further aid and his advice to abdicate, and also the brutal news of Charlotte's fate. With the help of his loyal friends Stefan Herzfeld and Count Ollivier Rességuier, Maximilian left Mexico City for Orizaba and prepared to abdicate and return to Europe. The military disasters, and the confusions and tensions within the French command and between the French and Maximilian, continued, but the semitropical beauty of Orizaba, where he passed the time studying flowers and butterflies, permitted him to delay taking the decisive step. While he pondered and avoided it, he listened to the blandishments, reproaches, and arguments of all the persons whose only hope, however slim, lay in his refusing to abdicate. These included Gutiérrez de Estrada, taunting him from safety in Rome; the Mexican reactionaries led by Theodosio Lares, then Chief Minister in the Empire; Generals Marquéz and Miramón, who had just returned from Europe; and for some reason the British Minister, Peter Campbell-Scarlett. There was another influence; after Sadowa and the Austrian naval victory, Maximilian's popularity in Austria had revived, and there now came to Orizaba a report that Francis Joseph, perhaps fearful of being replaced by Maximilian, had said that the latter could not return to Austria if he persisted in any claim to the succession.

After hesitating for six weeks, on November 28 Maximilian decided to remain—if a National Assembly wished him to do so! He returned to Mexico City, rejected Bazaine's plea to him to abdicate, and tried to organize his forces under Generals Tomás Mejía, Marquéz, and Miramón, while a majority of one in a sham assembly of thirty-three persons requested him to remain. Thanks to reactionary intrigues, the relations between Maximilian and Bazaine became ever more bitter. When the last of the French garrison left Mexico City on February 5, 1867, with Bazaine at its head, Maximilian, who had refused Bazaine a final audience, watched the French troops from behind a curtain and said: "At last I am free."

The fate of Juárez' wife was not so disastrous as that of the young Empress, but her sufferings were also great. Most of her letters to Juárez have not appeared in the archives, but we have a score of harrowing ones written to him from the United States between November, 1865, and July, 1866. These letters are incoherent and incorrect, but they are more intimately expressive than Juárez' letters, and they show that the gallant woman who had crossed the mountains from Oaxaca to Veracruz with her children, seven years before, was now driven almost to insanity by the death of her two sons while she was in a strange land without the support of her husband. They show that Juárez' worries about her were more than justified, and that they must have been a much more severe strain upon him, when he was fighting off both his enemies and his "friends," in the last ditch of the Republic, than one might imagine from his poignant but few expressions on the subject in those of his own letters that we have.

On November 10, 1865, she wrote to Juárez from New York: "I write this to tell you that we are all well, and that we have learned with delight from your last letter of the 29th that you also are quite well. But my grief is so great that it makes me suffer keenly. The loss of my sons is killing me. From the moment I awaken I think of them, remembering their sufferings, blaming myself, and believing that it was my fault that they died. This remorse makes me suffer much, and I believe it is killing me. I find no remedy, and the only thing that calms me for a few minutes is the thought that I shall die, and I prefer death a thousand times more than life. My present life without you and without my sons is insupportable. You will remember the fear that I used to have of death: well now it is the only thing that consoles me. I do not much blame persons who kill themselves when they have lost all hope of regaining any tranquillity. If I had been braver, I should have done it a year ago. At that time I wept night and day, having lost the hope of regaining I do not say pleasure but peace of mind—even to the point that if God does not relieve me of this, he might not, because the only thing that would give me life would be the return of my sons. One hope remains to me: that you should come to us, and that would be a great consolation." And five days later: "When the children see me crying, they can only do the same. . . . It is hard to be resigned, above all in this separation." The poor woman's desperate sorrow and self-reproach are expressed in every letter, but simply, directly, without self-pity. "I do not wish to afflict you," she says, "but it consoles me greatly to tell you of my sufferings. They would anger a stranger, but you will not be angry, you will be kind." The cause of the children's death is not known, but they may well have been the victims of one of the cholera epidemics of the time, which later drove the family out of the city, and doña Margarita's self-reproaches must have been purely neurotic.

Obsessive as her grief was, she was always able to write also about other matters that concerned her and him. She was naturally worried about Juárez' premature return to Chihuahua and flight back to El , Paso del Norte, although Juárez' optimism and consideration concealed from her the extent of that danger. She was worried about his housekeeper and about his crude way of living; she feared that he lacked decent clothing, and told him that if he would send her his neck size, she would send him shirts by some friend returning to Mexico. She sent him pictures of herself and the children, and finally induced him to send her a picture of himself; when it arrived, she said she would try to have it made darker. She feared that she was aging rapidly, and losing her looks and disposition, but she could joke about that: ". . . and you, old man, receive the heart of the young woman who will be forty in March." Often she sends her greetings to "Lerdo, Iglesias, Goytía, Sanchez, Contreras, and the other good friends." She also was concerned about the Ortega problem, but in her womanly and not wholly incorrect manner, she saw it more simply as a matter of personalities. "Everyone knows what a mule Ortega is," "Tío Ruizito" is a fool, Prieto only wants to be a Minister and it is not the first time he has been up to tricks, and all of them are only making themselves ridiculous.

Very often a much more cheerful postscript is added to these letters by the oldest daughter, Manuela, who wants to add a few lines to her "beloved *papacito*," to tell him how mischievous and charming his little granddaughter is, and that the little one now speaks more English than Spanish. Sometimes Felicitas and the younger Margarita add postscripts or write letters of their own, to tell Juárez of their progress in school, and especially in English and in piano-playing. These seem to have interested him most, and he had warned them to pay special attention to the English verbs. Also, Felicitas and Margarita are proud to report that they are helping Beno and the other younger children with their lessons. The happy prattle of the children and the cheerful good sense of Santa and Manuela must have done much to distract Juárez from his harrowing anxiety about his wife. When Juárez was about to return to Chihuahua more safely and permanently, his daughter Soledad wrote to him gaily: "They [friends in El Paso del Norte] have written to Santa that they are thinking of giving you a ball [in Chihuahua]. I hope that you will enjoy yourself and dance with a Señorita Chihuaheña." We can only hope that in his courtly and reserved manner, he did just that.

Romero repeatedly invited doña Margarita to visit him in Washington, but her low spirits forced her to decline until March 13, 1866, when she went because she thought she could be helpful, since Romero had with him at the time his sister and his aging mother, who was ill, who could not speak English, and who had to be informed of the death of her own sister. The first week was very good, she reported to Juárez, because nobody knew that she was in Washington, but when her presence there became known, the invitations poured in, and then she had to go out steadily, while mentally upset and while knowing no English. Fortunately she could take along her daughter Margarita, whose English was now sufficient. However, she much preferred to be alone, and every night she dreamed of her sons and would awaken while calling out their names. In the midst of this public strain and private anguish she be-

came briefly the center of wide attention. On March 28 she wrote
her husband:

> My dear Juárez: To-morrow is the terrible day on which I complete
> forty years, and I should greatly enjoy passing it at your side, but that
> is not possible, and one can only resign oneself to death, because there
> is no other remedy. We are all well. I am still here, but next week I am
> going to New York. The night before last, Romero took me to the
> President's reception, and as you will see in the *Herald*, they say that
> I was elegantly dressed, with many diamonds. That is not true. All of
> my elegance consisted of a dress that you bought me in Monterrey
> shortly before I left, and having so many cares and sorrows, I had not
> worn the special dress that I keep in order and save for the times when
> I have to make formal visits, and for nothing else; and as for the dia-
> monds, I had no more than some earrings that you gave me once on my
> saint's day, because my other little things I left in New York. I tell you
> all this because they shall not say that when you were in El Paso in such
> poverty I was here enjoying luxury. All this was caused by the novelty
> [of my being here?] and by the affection and sympathy felt for you.
> Many people have called on me here, and on the night of the reception
> many persons were presented to me, including Sr. Hamersly, who has
> called on us ever since our arrival in New York, and has done so here.
> Every day during the illness of my son Pepillo, he left his card; he and
> his wife escorted me to the salons; in short, what is certain is that the
> people I have met and who know me are very kind to me. I am only
> mortified by not being able to speak, but fortunately Margarita, who
> was here with me, already speaks fairly well.
>
> I am glad that the French will have retreated, so that you can go to
> Chihuahua, where there will be more resources. God grant that you
> have a happy journey. I am fearful of your having to pass some nights
> in the desert during the winter: take care of yourselves as well as you
> can.
>
> Greetings to [ten persons] . . . and tell Salomé that I am very grateful
> to her for accompanying you and caring for you; she is not like Secun,
> who behaved so badly that I had to discharge her.

Doña Margarita then criticizes severely and specifically various
Mexican emissaries, official and self-appointed, in the United States.
"With this roost full of useless specimens, what hope do you expect
me to have that we can do anything? Only God can drag us out of

this quagmire, and I have already wasted enough of your time with my foolish remarks that will go into one of your ears and come out of the other." This criticism is fully supported by all the other accounts.

Besides the President's reception, there was a dinner at the house of the Secretary of State—which Lerdo heard was "the most sumptuous party of the winter"—and a ball given by General Grant. Reporting these briefly to Juárez, Santa calls Seward an old fox, and says he would have preferred guns and bullets. "When Margarita had dinner in the house of Mr. Seward, he said to her: 'I hope that within a year I shall see in Mexico my two friends, Juárez and Santa Anna.' Margarita said to the interpreter, the Minister of Colombia: 'Tell Mr. Seward he will see one or the other, but not both.' " It seems that even great Secretaries of State can put their feet right into it, and also that doña Margarita's depression did not deprive her of her wit or her dignity, although Juárez may have prepared her for this. Romero reported that her visit to Washington had made Seward more cordial, and every liberal newspaper left in Mexico reported her reception at the White House. Imperial papers did also, with envy and rage. A couple of months later, Felicitas and Soledad visited Romero in Washington and were taken by him to another presidential reception, and by sons of General Grant to an English opera.

Although doña Margarita's visit to Washington was in every other respect a distinct success, and although her letters from Washington are more animated than her others, it gave her no real pleasure. "Last night we went to the ball of General Grant, and he was very kind. If at any time you had told me that the day would arrive on which all diversions, and even a ball, would torment me, I should not have believed it. . . . I shall have peace only when at last I am with you." At this time she would have had even less peace if she had known what Santacilia wrote to Juárez from Washington on March 23: he had received reports from Mexico City that the French and the traitors were planning to send a group of men to Juárez in El Paso, to pose as republicans, offer their services, and then assassinate him. Naturally Santacilia urged him to take the greatest care. When Juárez was about to return at last to Chihuahua, his wife also warned him: "I know that you are very trustful, but you do not lack enemies that you do not recognize, because with your good heart you never believe anyone capable of doing evil." Another cause of her unhappiness in Washington was the religious fanaticism of Romero's wife and sister, who, she wrote to Juárez, were always confessing and fasting, and who believed that only religiously fanatic Roman Catholics like themselves would go to heaven. All this evidently irritated doña Margarita, but she went on to say that because of her sons she envied them their religious faith in immortality.

Cholera had arrived from Europe and there was a distinct change for the better for the family when in June, they moved from Manhattan to New Rochelle, New York, to avoid the epidemic. Santacilia reported on June 28: "We arrived in this delicious place four days ago, and all of us, thank God, are well. We live in a house perfectly situated, on a picturesque hill surrounded by magnificent trees, and we are three miles from the village that gives its name to this place. . . . We hear only the songs of the birds and the sound of the wind." On July 26 Juárez' wife also wrote to him much more cheerfully than usual, worrying because she had not yet heard of Juárez' safe arrival in Chihuahua, but rejoicing in all the good news from Mexico, including that of Charlotte's departure. "This suggests that they are thinking of leaving, which appears to me impossible. I shall have to see it, and I still shan't believe it. . . . As I have told you in my last letter, I have decided to go to you wherever you want, in Chihuahua or at whatever other place you may move to. Don't worry about the roads: there can't be any worse than those of Cualimulco, over which I went in a month with all my small children, while having to take along all there was to eat. Here they say that to go by way of Chihuahua is the same. I shall take care to take along food. Unhappily I have no little ones to whom I could do such harm. Nelita [Manuela] and Santa, because of the baby, could not go with me." On August 28 Santacilia wrote, in connection with a projected publication in Spanish, in New York: "It would be truly mad to spend a thousand pesos on paper when we have to take care of the needs of so large a family, mostly of women, who always need to be in good society, and who must, therefore, spend what is necessary to appear as they should among gentlefolk.

Luckily, I don't think we need to publish anything now, because Santa Anna and Ortega are not only dead but in a veritable state of putrefaction." Some day, someone may set up in Mexico City a statue of Pedro Santacilia, above a bas-relief of all the women and children for whom he cared so well, so long. Unlike some of his compatriots then in the United States, he might well have found life easier in the army.

In April and May there occurred some slight strain between Juárez and Romero, who perhaps had been overactive and overeager. Juárez told him to communicate with the government of the United States only under instructions from Lerdo. Romero replied that he was trying to keep a complete historical record, in order to justify the Republic, and that he wanted fuller instructions. For a reply, Juárez noted on the back of this letter: ". . . the American government should not concern itself in what is strictly our business, and although the powerful must be treated with tact, we must do nothing to suggest in the slightest degree any humiliation on our part." If Romero was perhaps overzealous, there are times when Juárez himself seems oversensitive about the honor of Mexico. Romero replied rather testily that the United States never made inquiries, that his reports to the American officials had been effective, and that he thought he had done nothing to affect adversely the "decorum and dignity of our country, of which I am as jealous as yourself." He then went on to add that he had not been paid for fourteen months, that he had not been able to give a dinner for a year, that he had to spend a thousand pesos a month, including four thousand a year for rent, and that his forced economies might well have an adverse effect on the American opinion of Mexico. Apparently most governments, including the American, and their representatives abroad, are always quite familiar with such difficulties, though Juárez' were extreme. The Republic's emissaries abroad seemed to have fared better than the President and cabinet.

With daring maneuvers, General Luis Terrazas and Colonel Joaquín Terrazas recaptured the city of Chihuahua on March 25, 1866, and one of them, probably the former, was wounded, an event for which doña Margarita wrote regret to Juárez, to be passed on, with her congratulations, to the General. Unfortunately this victory was preceded and followed by the brutalities and reprisals that had become altogether too familiar on both sides. French cavalry remained in the neighborhood, so Juárez, not wishing to subject the government and himself to another quick exit, remained in El Paso del Norte until June 10, and arrived in Chihuahua on the 17th. The reception was elaborate, including an escort, a parade, speeches—with, as often the custom in Mexico to this day, an emotional oration by a school child—a champagne supper with numerous toasts, and a ball—this last to celebrate General Luis Terrazas' birthday. Juárez' reports to Santacilia and Romero show that he was touched and gratified.

During this whole period in the north, Juárez personally, as well as the government, suffered a good deal from sheer poverty, and he was often worried about what his family was using for money in New York, although Santacilia was sometimes able to support them himself. On June 8 Juárez noted that he had not received any of his own salary (nominally $30,000 a year) since being paid $1,250 in January, 1865, but that recently Romero had been authorized to advance $4,000 to the family, against the President's salary. In July, a patriot named Jesús Carranza, who had a seven-year-old son named Venustiano, later President of the Republic, loaned Juárez $1,000 without interest, to cover his small personal expenses. This was repaid in September. In August, the soldiers of the Army of the North, under General Escobedo, sent Juárez $5,000 as a gift, with their thanks and homage, and he returned the money with deep thanks, saying that under the circumstances, they needed it more than he did. Juárez knew, however, that the Empire too was having financial troubles, and he was able to rejoice in the idea that Napoleon would get no more booty without fighting the Mexicans for it, and that he could not do that without dangerously violating his promise to the United States to withdraw his forces.

In late August Carvajal, who had returned to action of a sort, capitulated to Tomás Mejía in that perpetual trouble spot, Matamoros, but Generals Hinojosa and Canales rebelled against Carvajal, and under Juárez' orders, Generals Escobedo and Tapía handled the situation, and Juárez even gave General Sheridan some of the credit for the restoration of peace and order, under the Republic, along the entire northern frontier. However, Juárez was sceptical when he heard that Placido Vega, with 600 men that he had enlisted without authority in California, and with arms and ammunition, had arrived in Sinaloa. Insofar as communications would permit, Juárez and Ignacio Mejía directed all the operations in the north and center, which continued with success, but the greatest victory at this time was perhaps that of the brothers Porfirio and Felix Díaz in the battles near Miahuatlán, south of Oaxaca, on October 3, and at La Corbonera on October 18, victories that resulted in the reoccupation of the city of Oaxaca by the republican forces on October 31. In this campaign, Díaz captured large quantities of arms and supplies that made possible his later victories. "That's excellent. Díaz is a good boy," said Juárez. By this time only Mexico City, Veracruz, the constantly threatened road between them, and a few other scattered areas remained in the control of the Empire.

Now again, as in 1861, the difficult question arose of what to do with the imperialists found in the areas recovered by the armies. These prisoners included some men who had been republicans and deserted, and who now wanted to return to the fold. In a letter to General Escobedo in Monterrey, November 3, 1866, Juárez orders him to jail the deserters and send them to the government for trial. "The triumph of the national cause is certain, imminent, and inevitable, and for its realization we need neither foreign forces nor bargains with traitors." Towards the end of a long and savage war involving treacheries, outrages, and reprisals, with the commanding officers of necessity possessing wide powers, horrible injustices inevitably were perpetrated by both sides. In writing to Governor Domingo Rubí of Sinaloa, an able man who had begun life as a miner, to congratulate him and Governor Ramón Corona of Jalisco on their victories in the west, and on Rubí's careful selection of honorable persons for public office, Juárez said: "We are entering upon an era of recovery and morality, and for this we need men who are honest, loyal, and patriotic."

As early as May Seward had designated Mr. L. D. Campbell and General William T. Sherman as representatives of the United States to the Juárez government, the victorious General to add prestige and to give military advice. In reporting the appointment of this mission to Colonel Ascención Gómez in Tampico, where they might appear, Romero stated that the United States would recognize only the Republic, that it desired no territory, that it would not recognize the alleged debt of Mexico to France, and that if invited it would send forces to help restore order, but would not meddle in the internal affairs of Mexico. Campbell and Sherman did not get under way until November, and they could not disembark in Veracruz because that port was still controlled by the fading Empire. They proceeded to Tampico, where they conferred with Gómez and with General Escobedo and tried unsuccessfully to get in touch with Juárez. Then they returned to New Orleans, after a curiously delayed and ineffective mission. A meeting between Juárez and Sherman would have been very interesting.

Between December 3 and 9 Juárez wrote to Santacilia a string of hurried notes about his plans. He would leave for Durango on the 10th, with the expectation of arriving in Mexico City by March. He approved of Santacilia's plan of bringing the family by ship to Veracruz—although they might be delayed by the hold of the French on that city, as Campbell and Sherman had been. He had just heard of the liberation of Oaxaca. From as early as June 8, nearly every letter from Juárez to Santacilia had included a discussion of the possible routes for the return of the family, and Juárez always said that he trusted Santacilia's judgment in this matter completely.

Governor Terrazas escorted Juárez and his party, which included Lerdo, Iglesias, Ignacio Mejía, Manuel E. Goytía, and an American engineer named George E. Church, as far as the *hacienda* and Arroyo de la Parida, on the boundary between the states of Chihuahua and Durango, which they reached on December 17. Although Juárez and Terrazas, whose relation had begun so badly, remained friends for life, they never saw each other again. When Juárez and his party arrived in the city of Durango, on December 26, they were, he wrote Santacilia, given a magnificent reception, "naturally, because," quoting an old saying with his familiar irony, " 'it isn't the same Viceroy who is coming as the one who is going.' " Meanwhile, Guadalajara and San Luis Potosí had been liberated. All of this was all very well, but the war was not yet over, by a good deal, and fifteen days later Juárez himself had one more very narrow escape.

Towards the end of December Miramón had set out from Mexico City for the north with four or five hundred men and two pieces of artillery. Juárez noted this movement, but counted on Escobedo and other forces for defense. On his way north, Miramón absorbed other imperial forces, and with a characteristically rapid maneuver he distracted Escobedo and on January 27 fell upon Zacatecas. We turn now to Juárez' own report, on February 2, to Santacilia, of what happened:

On December [he meant January] 22 I arrived at this city [Zacatecas], where the government was given a splendid reception: fireworks, balls, and a cane worth two thousand pesos were the gifts they made me. After three days there was reported the march of Miramón towards this city with 2,500 men and fourteen pieces of artillery. Defensive preparations were made at once. On the 25th General Aranda arrived with 500 infantrymen, 200 cavalry, and ten pieces of artillery, that he brought from Durango. On the 26th the enemy appeared and made a reconnaissance.

Although many thought that the government should withdraw from the city, and supported this view with weighty arguments of a political nature, nevertheless, I did not think it wise to accept this view, and decided to share the fortune of our troops. The almost frantic enthusiasm with which these people received me, and the decisive idea that my proposed withdrawal from this city would discourage the troops and the people, confirmed me in my resolution. In short, my view was that if the city was to be lost, this disaster should not be the result of the retreat of the government, but its cause. On the 26th, accompanied by Sr. Auza, who was the commanding general, I passed twice along the line of defense. The enthusiasm of the troops and the people was great, and so was their faith in victory; but in war, one can hardly be sure of the results, and whatever circumstances, even the most insignificant, can upset the best arrangements. The report to the commanding general from the commander at the Bufa bridge, to the effect that the enemy attacked that bridge before dawn, did not arrive, and this fact prevented the sending of reinforcements; and between six and seven in the morning of the 27th, the bridge was taken and the enemy at once penetrated the city. Sr. Auza sent me word to save myself. Then I mounted a horse, and Sres. Lerdo, Iglesias, and Goytía accompanied me. Mejía had been sick for a week, and the night before, I had sent him out of the city.

As we left the Palace, my escort was already firing on the French, face to face. My idea was to set out for Fresnillo, but already the enemy was directing his movements and fire towards the road going thence, so I set out for Jerez, or Ciudad García, fourteen leagues from Zacatecas. Our force took the same road. Miramón with most of his force took it for about three leagues, but as often as he tried to destroy our force, he was repulsed, until he was obliged to give up the attempt and return to Zacatecas. On the same day I arrived at Jerez, and the next day there arrived a force of 2,500 men.

On the 30th our force marched to reunite itself with that of Escobedo, who was coming to the relief of Zacatecas, and I set out for Fresnillo, where I arrived on the 31st. On that day General Auza informed me that at noon Miramón had evacuated the city of Zacatecas, taking the road to Aguascalientes. Sr. Auza, under orders from General Escobedo, advanced to take the city and to harass the rear guard of the enemy. On February 1 I returned to this capital, and at dawn to-day I received the report of the complete defeat of Miramón. Now I have given you a brief, running account of everything that has happened here in the past week. There is no personal news. In the moments of my departure on the 27th Salomé took my baggage to a house adjoining the Palace which was later searched by Joaquín Miramón and other myrmidons. All that was left was my cigar case and the cane that had just been given me. A houseboy that we had brought from Chihuahua was murdered by the French as he left the Palace. The rabble and the traitors busied themselves in sacking and destroying the public offices. In the Palace they destroyed everything, and I have had to find lodging in a private house.

With the defeat of Miramón our victory draws near, for now the enemy has only the half-organized forces of Castillo and Méndez, which will soon be destroyed. Perhaps within a week or ten days I shall proceed to Guanajuato or to San Luis.

Later Juárez added this comment: "If we had delayed a quarter of an hour more in leaving the Palace, we should have given a happy moment to Miramón, but we escaped because the hour had not arrived." It is also said that General Diódoro Corella performed prodigies of valor at Jerez to protect the President and his cabinet. One would like to know what happened during this affair to Juárez' loyal housekeeper, Salomé (whom one may imagine as a middle-aged

Indian woman, sexless and hard as nails), and to the American named
Church. There was also a small American force involved, called
"The Legion of Honor," and one of these Americans, George W.
Blasdell, later testified: "Many of Juárez' officers gave us the credit
of saving his life at the battle of Zacatecas. Whilst the Mexican soldiers were retreating, we dashed into the town and attacked the
French-Austrian troops under the command of the brother of General Miramón and kept them at bay, so that Juárez was able to get
away in safety, when otherwise he would have been taken." Blasdell
himself fell a prisoner during the siege of Querétaro, and he claimed
that he was saved from death at that time by the personal intervention of Maximilian. Blasdell's story about the fight at Zacatecas was
supported by other Americans who were present, and we can only
hope that it was not the inevitable embroidery of veterans. There is
another story that an empty carriage was sent off in the wrong
direction, and that this trick deceived and delayed Miramón until
reinforcements came. There is still another story that when Maximilian heard of this near triumph, he wrote to Miramón, ordering
him, should he capture Juárez, to try him by court-martial but not
to execute him without the Emperor's sanction, and that this letter
was captured by the republicans. Any episode so vivid, in the life
of a great man, is bound to become encrusted with legends.

The imperial forces could not get together rapidly enough to
withstand Escobedo, who, as noted in Juárez' letter, on February 1
crushed Miramón's army at San Jacinto, but Miramón himself escaped to make a later rendezvous. This victory was badly stained by
Escobedo's shooting 109 French prisoners. Escobedo offered as a
defense the claim that these men were freebooters, because Bazaine
had ordered all French soldiers to withdraw with him and had
explicitly denied protection to any who remained. Escobedo also
claimed that these Frenchmen had committed many "excesses" at
Zacatecas, this being a euphemism of the time, used by Juárez also,
for who knows what atrocities. However, this mass execution has
been generally condemned. This war, like all wars, grew more foul
every day, and both sides were becoming more deeply and permanently scarred by guilt.

Luckily, the end was near.

25

QUERÉTARO AND VICTORY

AT ABOUT THE TIME when he heard of Miramón's brief and meaningless victory at Zacatecas, Maximilian received letters from his mother and younger brother, urging him as a matter of regal and family honor to remain in Mexico and keep the imperial crown; yet these fatal promptings were not so much quixotic as ignorant, because Maximilian had never been quite candid towards his family in reporting his situation in Mexico. He at last began to see clearly how desperate his situation had become. Miramón, with what soldiers he had left, retreated to Querétaro, while Márquez was defeated on the Monte de las Cruces.

On February 9, 1867, Maximilian wrote a letter to his chief Minister, Theodosio Lares, in which he revealed that he knew that the Empire was collapsing, both materially and morally, while the republicans gained daily in power, and in which he sought Lares' advice—because of course Maximilian had never been capable of making any major decision alone. Lares and the other reactionaries now saw that the Empire was doomed, and they also saw that their own futures depended considerably on how strong Maximilian was or seemed to be at the end. If Maximilian remained in Mexico City, under the influence of the ambassadors to the Empire, he might very well abdicate and leave the country, and in that case their own ruin would be assured. At the head of the whole imperial army in the field, Maximilian might get a tolerable settlement of some sort from Díaz, or even from Juárez himself. Through a M. Carlos Bournouf, Maximilian made some kind of an approach, in Acatlán, to Díaz, who firmly rejected it but took care, before sending this emissary back to Mexico, to march his small force several times beneath the curtained window of the room in which the emissary was received, in order to have delivered in Mexico an exaggerated report of his strength. On February 13, Bazaine, who had not yet embarked, sent word to Maximilian that the way home to Europe was still open but would soon be closed. Maximilian never got the message: he and Márquez had joined none other than Vidaurri, who was now Minister of Finance and War, and with the 1,500 men they had been able to muster, they were on the way to Querétaro.

This beautiful old city of domes and towers, and of 40,000 people, on a high, fertile plain surrounded by low hills, was chosen partly because the imperial forces were already gathering there, under Generals Miramón, Tomás Mejía, Márquez, and Méndez—who with Maximilian himself made "the five M's"—and partly because the citizens had always been religious, reactionary, and imperial in their sentiments. Unfortunately these sentiments were not an adequate substitute for a strategic position, or for a soldier-emperor. If Maximilian had been even a fraction of one, the situation might not have been hopeless. He had 9,000 men at the beginning, and although outnumbered by the republicans—Escobedo was approaching with 12,000 men, Corona with 8,000, and Riva Palacio with 7,000—they came slowly, as usual, and with vigorous action the imperialists might have struck them down unit by unit, as Miramón urged them to do. However, Márquez was made Chief of Staff and insisted upon delay, while the Emperor himself, as usual, had no opinion: all he could do was to inspire the troops by wandering about in dangerous places, exposing himself to enemy fire.

Near the end he heard, and believed until the report was corrected, that Charlotte had died, but long before that he knew that he had no future in Europe. Instead of dominating his generals and directing the campaign, which could not thus have ended more disastrously, he fell ill with dysentery and fever, and had to be cared for by his physician, Dr. Samuel Basch. His close associates were a picturesque adventurer named Prince Felix zu Salm-Salm, and a polished villain named Colonel Miguel López, to whose child he had stood godfather. And in the midst of this final campaign Maximilian actually sent an agent, Antonio García, to open negotiations with

Juárez, who refused to see him. In short, the Empire had no vital core.

Juárez arrived in San Luis Potosí on February 21 and from there kept in touch with the armies as well as he could, while still speculating in his letters to Santacilia on the date when his family might be able to return, and on the best route that they might be able to take. Of his birthday there is no mention except by Maximilian, who said, while writing to a friend in Mexico City about the care or burning of the archives there: "While I am dictating this letter to you, our adversaries are celebrating the birthday of their leader by sending us grenades that are swarming like flies in this vicinity." Juárez could not have wished any better fireworks. Perhaps thinking also of certain prisoners in the future, he wrote to Díaz: "I forgot to say to you in my letter of yesterday . . . that it seems to me well for you to follow your accustomed rule of not shooting the enlisted men who fall prisoner, whether they are Mexicans or foreigners, except when you find among them some whose known acts make them worthy of the penalty of death, in which case they should not go unpunished. As for the prominent leaders, commanders, and officers involved in aggravating circumstances, they should be dealt with with the full rigor of the law. The soldiers, commanders, and officers who are not executed should be put at the disposal of the government, as was done with those at Puebla." Evidently Santacilia or his wife or both lectured him about his behavior at Zacatecas, because he replied: "I have received the sermon on what seems to have been my tomfoolery on January 27 at Zacatecas. There are circumstances in life in which it is necessary to risk everything, if one wishes to go on living physically and morally, and it is thus that I see those of that date. I got away with it, and I am happy and satisfied with what I did." He notes: "All the people of Querétaro are hostile to us. Not one man or woman has come out to report to our commanders what the enemy is doing." More ominously, in view of what was to come, he expresses or implies some impatience with the scarcity of reports from Díaz. Yet again he seems to rebuke his own impatience: "From Porfirio I have had no news for some days. Surely he is following his plan, as when he took Oaxaca and Puebla, of not writing to me until he can date his letter in the conquered capital. Impatient people are limbs of Satan, for they want everything to end instantly, even if great criminals go unpunished, without guarantees of the future peace of the nation; but the government pays them no heed and continues to do firmly what is best for the country, without being influenced in its decisions by personal vengeance, by compassion ill understood, or by any foreign threats, no matter how disguised: we have fought for the independence and autonomy of Mexico, and that must become a reality." This was written on May 15, and the great news of that date came only in time to be mentioned in a postscript, with a *"Viva México!"*

By March 6 the republicans had surrounded Querétaro and begun to cut off the supplies of food and water. The siege was not at first a tight one, and both sorties by the imperialists and attacks by the republicans were indecisive. The only large escape occurred when Márquez got out of the city by night with Vidaurri and 1,200 cavalrymen. He had orders from Maximilian to take over the government in Mexico City, return to Querétaro with reinforcements, and attack the republicans from their rear. He was also to bring in some books and burgundy. When he reached Mexico City, Márquez increased his force to about 4,000 men, and then, instead of returning to Querétaro, which in his acute vision may have begun to resemble a rat trap, he started for Puebla, in an attempt to relieve that city, which was being vigorously besieged by Díaz. When Díaz learned of this move, he attacked Puebla on April 2, taking the city on the 4th. On April 10 his force attacked and defeated Márquez, who managed to flee to Mexico City with 400 Austrian and Belgian cavalrymen.

On April 22, when he heard this bad news, Maximilian also received an offer from the republicans of his personal freedom in exchange for the surrender of the city and his whole army, but with his invariable chivalrous loyalty to his own partisans, he declined this offer; and when Miramón began to suggest a settlement at Juárez' cost, the republican envoy withdrew.

On the night of May 14-15, just before the imperialists were going to attempt a breakthrough, Colonel López treacherously allowed the republican forces to enter the city as far as the imperial headquarters. General Méndez, who had executed Generals Arteaga and Salazar, was trapped in hiding and shot. General Miramón was wounded. At one point, Maximilian was clearly given a chance to escape, a fact suggesting either that General Escobedo felt that the imperial prisoner would be an embarrassment to Juárez or that he had made this chance to escape part of his agreement with Colonel López that led to the collapse. General Mejía and the Emperor made their way to the low Hill of the Bell, just outside the city to the west, and were there surrounded and forced to surrender. There is a story that Maximilian first approached the American Colonel George M. Green, who sent him to General Corona. There were at this time a considerable number of Americans, Canadians and Europeans in the republican forces.

A few days later, Maximilian asked General Escobedo for permission to return to Europe with all his European troops, after abdicating and swearing "never to interfere in Mexican politics again." Escobedo properly replied that he would refer this request to President Juárez, which he did; and Juárez then ordered that Maximilian, Miramón, and Mejía be tried by court-martial in accordance with the law of January 25, 1862, which provided the death penalty for foreigners conspiring against Mexican independence and for Mexicans assisting them. (As for López, who had betrayed the Emperor, his wife left him, all Mexicans scorned him, and a few years later he was bitten by a mad dog and died of hydrophobia.) Maximilian appealed to Juárez for an interview, and was told through Escobedo that he could say whatever he had to say at his trial. When the trial began, on June 12, in a theatre, other charges against Maximilian were that his decree of October 3, 1865, had caused the death of many Mexicans, as had his prolonging the war after the departure of the French. Maximilian, who had been given good attorneys, refused to attend the trial. Three of the officers of the court voted for his banishment, and four for his death. Miramón and Tomás Mejía were also condemned to death.

From the moment of Maximilian's surrender, schemes were hatched by his friends for his escape, but he always hesitated, for fear of deserting Mejía and Miramón, or of sullying his honor and dignity. He did, however, tolerate an attempt by Prince and Princess Salm-Salm to bribe his guards. One night the Princess, an Amer-

ican and a former circus rider, asked one of these guards, a Colonel
Palacio, to escort her home, and in her bedroom she promised him
$100,000. When he hesitated, she started to undress, offering him,
so to speak, a more tangible down payment, whereupon the upright
Colonel, in consternation, declared that his honor was doubly compromised, and that "if she did not open the door at once, he would
jump out of the window into the street." Meanwhile, the Austrian,
Italian, and Belgian Ministers, who had been summoned from Mexico
City by Maximilian, were about to sign bills to guarantee the bribes
—although the request for this was probably a republican trick to
establish their complicity—when Colonel Palacio told General Escobedo of the Princess's overtures. All the Ministers and the Princess
were then ordered to leave Querétaro at once. The Emperor kept his
dignity to the end, but the pathos of his story was not spared these
intrusions of melodramatic farce.

Nor were the alarums and excursions limited to Querétaro. As
early as March 5 Prince Metternich, the Austrian Ambassador in
Paris, had been ordered to speak to Napoleon about Maximilian's
safety, and Napoleon had told him that since Maximilian had chosen
not to leave with the French troops, nothing more could be done.
In April the Austrian Minister in Washington, Baron Wydenbruck,
had become alarmed for Maximilian's safety, and at his request,
Seward ordered Mr. L. D. Campbell, who was still in New Orleans,
to ask Juárez to treat the Emperor, if captured, as a prisoner of war.
When a messenger from Campbell finally reached Lerdo at San
Luis Potosí, the request, which contained a somewhat insolent reference to Escobedo's shooting of prisoners at San Jacinto (perhaps
the cause of Juárez' remark about "foreign threats, however disguised"), was politely denied. On June 1, Seward telegraphed Campbell to go at once to Mexico, see Juárez, and urge clemency.
Campbell still delayed, until Seward telegraphed him for his resignation and then "requested Romero to notify his government promptly
that the United States, seeking no undue advantage in Mexico and
apprehending no future European intervention there, strongly recommended clemency towards Maximilian, who had developed into
a Mexican partisan chieftain." This last, incidentally, had been one
of the arguments put forward by the defense during the trial. This

recommendation arrived too late, but it is doubtful indeed that it would have altered Juárez' final decision.

At San Luis Potosí the appellants for mercy for the Emperor, and the others who sometimes succeeded in getting past the Ministers to Juárez himself, were numerous and must have been either irritating or harrowing. Baron Magnus, speaking not only for his master, the King of Prussia, but also, he claimed, for the other royal houses of Europe and even for the United States, was denied. The passionate, telegraphed appeals of Giuseppe Garibaldi and Victor Hugo, unquestionable liberals and friends of the Mexican Republic, surely moved and interested Juárez much more. To appeals from Manuel Lozada of Nayarit and Plácido Vega, to Generals Escobedo and Corona, who forwarded them to Juárez, he replied that he had considered all their arguments deeply and conscientiously, in terms of justice and the nation's good.

According to Princess Salm-Salm, she kneeled before Juárez and gripped his knees during her appeal, and he said: "I am grieved, Madam, to see you on your knees before me; but if all the kings and queens of Europe were at your side, I could not spare his life. It is not I who take it away; it is my people and the law, and if I did not do their will, the people would take his life as well as my own." This famous story has been embodied in a painting in San Luis Potosí, but remains wide open to doubt.

Juárez postponed the execution from June 16 to June 19, which proved to be an act of doubtful mercy. On June 18, Maximilian telegraphed Juárez to ask for the pardon of Miramón and Mejía, in the hope that he himself might be the only one executed. Once when captured, Escobedo's own life had been saved by Mejía, and when Escobedo offered to do what he could to have Mejía pardoned, Mejía said that he would not accept a pardon unless the Emperor and Miramón were pardoned also.

The execution of the three men took place on a sunny morning, June 19, 1867, on the Hill of the Bell, where Maximilian had surrendered. The three men were stood with their backs to a wall that formed one side of a square, the other three sides being formed by 4,000 armed men. Maximilian gave Miramón the honor of standing in the center, forgave the members of the firing squad and presented gold to them, and said finally that he hoped the shedding of his blood would be for the good of Mexico. When he fell into the dust, he murmured, "*Hombre*," and had to be given a final shot through the heart.

The news reached Paris on June 30, at the moment when Napoleon and Eugénie, the Prince Imperial, the Sultan of Turkey, and the Prince of Wales were attending a prize-awarding ceremony at the "Universal Exposition." "Hardly had the twelve-hundred-piece orchestra struck up an anthem by Rossini," records M. Guérard, "when an aide handed the Emperor a telegram. The sovereign remained impassive, went on with the show, gave a speech on peace, progress, good will. But the Austrian Ambassador and his staff quietly withdrew." Napoleon and Eugénie seem to have grieved honestly for this victim of their dream and their bad faith, but they probably felt more keenly the peril to themselves, their dynasty, and France caused by the whole misbegotten enterprise. For political reasons, the Emperor Francis Joseph became reconciled with Napoleon, and in November he sent an admiral in the *Novara* to return Maximilian's body to Vienna; later the Hapsburg family built on the Hill of the Bell a small and ugly chapel that cannot be called an extravagant expression of familial devotion. (Next to it there has since been built something that would interest Juárez much more: a state fairgrounds in which Mexicans can amuse themselves without homicide and learn how to farm better.) Long after Maximilian's death, in Belgium, poor Charlotte was speaking of him as "the Lord of the Earth, the Sovereign of the Universe."

During the siege of Querétaro and the critical period after it, Juárez' letters are brief and impersonal, recording the great events almost as though he were no more than an observer. In his address to the Congress on its opening on December 8, 1867, Juárez said: "The execution at Querétaro was necessitated by the gravest motives of justice, combined with the imperious necessity of securing peace in the future and putting an end to the internal convulsions and all the calamities inflicted by the war on our society. The application of the law to those in the first rank among those most guilty has permitted the use of great clemency towards all the others." For the execution of these three men, and especially of course for that of Maximilian, Juárez has been condemned to this day by a large and heterogeneous collection of persons. In our view, these executions at Querétaro were just and necessary for the reasons stated clearly by Juárez himself, and Maximilian was "a wretched, rash, intruding fool" who was honored by being shot in the company of two gallant Mexicans who died for considering their Church and the old ways more important than the chosen government of their growing country.

After defeating Márquez, Díaz penned him, the remaining imperial garrison, Vidaurri, and other imperial officials, within Mexico City. The defense was maintained only because false and cheerful reports came from Querétaro, and although some people escaped to Díaz' headquarters at Tacubaya, the sufferings of the civilians left within the city were great. Even after the surrender at Querétaro, Márquez refused for a while to believe it, but republican armies were transferred from Querétaro and the siege of the city was tightened. After a sortie by Márquez was thrown back by forces led by Díaz in person, as was his wont, the Austrians and even a few French soldiers who had remained in the imperial army sought and were granted by Díaz separate terms, so that they could withdraw from the fighting into the National Palace and a convent until the capitulation, and then return to Veracruz and Europe. On June 19 Márquez, Vidaurri, and others, having heard of the execution on the Hill of the Bell, went into hiding. Various proposals of betrayal and compromise were made to Díaz, but he rejected them all, and General Ramón Tavera, remaining in command, had to surrender unconditionally on June 21. Demanding the surrender of all the leading imperialists, Díaz received little response until he caught and executed Vidaurri, after which the imperialists flocked into three prisons. A few were shot, but most of them were banished, or heavily fined, or pardoned. After six months of painful hiding, Márquez disguised himself as an Indian burro man selling charcoal and successfully made his way to Veracruz and thence to Havana, where he lived out his wretched days as a pawnbroker and as an apologist for his life.

Juárez left San Luis Potosí for Mexico City about July 3, and on July 13 he wrote to Santacilia from Chapultepec:

Although I had intended to arrive in Mexico on the 9th, this was not possible because with the rains the roads have become impassable, and it was necessary to make short journeys and to wait in some places to allow for the repair of the carriages of the party, one or two of which broke down nearly every day. Iglesias' carriage was left in Tepeji in pieces. Finally, yesterday afternoon, we arrived here safely. I did not go directly to Mexico because the Council and friends insisted that the entry take place on Monday, since it is not possible to complete the preparations sooner for the reception, which they wish to be the best possible.

Excuse my saying that my journey has been, up to my arrival here, a constant ovation that the people have offered to the government. That on Monday will be an extraordinary affair, according to the preparations they are making.

I suppose you will be on your way to Veracruz, whither I direct this letter, to be delivered to you on your arrival. Inform me by telegraph as soon as you arrive. [Veracruz had fallen to the republicans on June 27.]

Díaz had gone out north of the city, farther than Tlalnepantla, to meet the President and his party, and when they met over breakfast, Juárez told him that the presidential escort, composed of one regiment, two battalions, and half a battery, had gone for some days without pay, and he asked Díaz whether he had funds for this urgent necessity. Díaz replied that he had indeed, and also for their pay due the next fortnight. Encouraged, Juárez then revealed that the Ministers also lacked their salaries, and Díaz was able to advance $10,000 from the funds of his army. His army funds were more substantial than those of the government because he had taken the taxes of the various states from time to time under his control, had confiscated the properties of imperialists, and had borrowed from various foreign businessmen, including $200,000 from Americans, with the help of Mr. Marcus Otterbourg, the American Consul General in Mexico City. He had also seized large quantities of military supplies abandoned by Bazaine. After paying all his debts, loaning the government money as noted, paying his own army, and paying for the reception and lodging of the government in the City, he was still able to turn over to the government the sum of $87,232.91. This was obviously a matter of considerable pride to him. The government then owed him $21,000 in back pay, assuming, at his suggestion, that he had received a third of his pay, whereas he guessed he had only received about a quarter of it. He wanted to go into business, but Juárez urged him to remain in the army. He used $18,000 to finance a newspaper for Justo Benítez, and then lost half of the remainder in the robbery of the house of a Sr. José de Teresa. It is necessary to mention these facts because even this early there seems to have developed some coolness between Juárez and Díaz, the latter feeling, although he does not say so explicitly in his *Memoirs*, that he had done more for the government and for Juárez than they had done for him.

There were other causes for irritation on both sides. Díaz says that beginning on the day of the fall of Mexico City he tried to resign from the army, but Juárez did not designate an officer to relieve him, nor even answer his letters. Díaz also admits that he did not obey Juárez' order to imprison M. Danó, the Minister of the French Empire, and to seize the French Legation archives; but he adds that when he saw Lerdo that morning of the arrival of the government, Lerdo expressed the opinion that he had done right in disobeying this order, "which could have compromised the government." Also, when Juárez ordered Díaz not to name anyone Governor of the Federal District, because Díaz was about to name Juan José Baz, the memorable eccentric involved in Comonfort's *golpe de estado*, Díaz obeyed the order but made Baz political boss of the capital and neighboring villages.

We are confronted here again with the subtle relation, discussed in Chapter 14, between Juárez, as a man and as a power, and his military and civil colleagues. The relation between Juárez and Díaz was especially dramatic and important. Both men had been poor boys in Oaxaca. Juárez, twenty-four years older, had briefly been Díaz' teacher, and in his paternal way, he made the familiar mistake of forgetting that students grow up and can equal or surpass their teachers. Díaz, as a civil and military chieftain, had performed innumerable personal exploits, had carried on the war almost alone in the south, and had emerged, even more than Escobedo, as the final military victor. Furthermore, he had always been obedient to Juárez' will, when he knew it, and had not, like Doblado, Ortega, and so many other republicans in high places, openly aspired to the Presidency or in any way conspired for it. Yet at the end of the war Ignacio Mejía, also a Oaxacan, and in Díaz' view a minor soldier who had once betrayed him in a small but dangerous military action within the city of Oaxaca, was now, as Minister of War, his superior, and one who had increasing influence on the President. In Díaz *at this time*, personal ambition, vanity, envy, and all the other forms of egotism do not seem to have been marked characteristics—they were perhaps only normally and humanly present, while in Juárez they were almost abnormally and inhumanly absent. Yet no two men, placed thus facing each other from peaks of very different kinds of political power and personal character, each enormously indebted to the other, could have avoided being somewhat wary and critical of each other.

To Díaz, in time, Juárez must have seemed a legalistic, paternal but authoritarian, chilly, shabby, and above all, intolerably durable old politician—if, alas, a hero; and to Juárez, even this early, Díaz may have seemed brave and talented soldier, but otherwise unreliable, effusive but cold at heart, basically a killer without culture or democratic love and vision—if, alas, a hero. At Tlalnepantla, at this time, Díaz was to remember, for example: "Sr. Juárez made to me some very obvious observations about how difficult it would be for me to devote myself to some other career," and Juárez—if quite unreliably—is reported to have said soon after of Díaz: "He is a man who kills while weeping."

However, for the moment—the glorious, incredible moment—even to each other, Juárez was the great President of the Republic and Díaz was his loyal and victorious general. "The President remained at Chapultepec," Díaz remembered, "while there were prepared his appropriate reception and lodging in the capital. This gave me time to order the making of a large flag to be flown on the National Palace on the day of the solemn entrance of the President; because he had said to me in one of his letters during the war, when the recovery of the capital seemed difficult, that we should return to raise the Mexican flag about the National Palace, and remembering his enthusiastic expression, I prohibited anyone from raising the flag on that building until Sr. Juárez should do so personally; and this is what he did on July 15, 1867, the day of his entrance."

The streets of the old city, then so much smaller than now, were packed with Mexicans, some of whom, at least, knew not only the cost, but what had been won for them, and by whom, and if Juárez distrusted their cheers, he also enjoyed them. While the cannon thundered, all the bells rang, the rockets shot into the clear air, the bands played, and the confetti fell on the dark, stolid little Indian, the procession moved into the huge plaza in front of the National Palace, where the President himself raised the flag again, and the dark day of the withdrawal, May 31, 1863, was wiped out. Seventy years later, an old lady remembered that day: "She had been one of three little girls chosen to offer a wreath to President Juárez when he drove into Mexico City . . . and being the tallest, had been told to put it over his head. But either her nervousness, or the President's ugliness, had made her get it wrong way round, so that the strings hung down in front of his face, and he looked uglier than ever, and extremely comic." Juárez himself, with his ironic humor, could have enjoyed that moment and found in it some relief from the overwhelming celebration, and from his memories of the dead, and of their families, who had paid for it. Eight days later he wrote to a war widow: "For me it is a sad and grievous pleasure to receive the congratulations with which I am honored by persons to whom the price of the triumph of the Republic has been the life of the most beloved of their kindred. Each Mexican who died for his country is to me a brother. . . . You may be sure that I shall always remember your good husband and other kinsmen who died for the independence and liberty of my country."

On the day of the triumph, Juárez published a manifesto to the nation in which he paid tribute to "the good sons of Mexico" who alone had saved the Republic and its liberties, promised to temper justice towards former enemies with all possible mercy, and promised to uphold the Constitution and the laws. "The people and the government," he said, "shall respect the rights of all. Between individuals as between nations, respect for the rights of others is peace: *el respeto al derecho ajeno es la paz.*"

Thanks to Secretary Seward and to Hugh McCulloch, Secretary

of the Treasury, acting through Mr. W. P. Kellogg, Collector of the Port of New Orleans, and Captain Freeman of the U. S. Revenue Cutter *Wilderness*, that vessel, with despatches for Mexico, was held at New Orleans from July 6, her sailing date, until "Madame Juárez and party, fourteen persons in all," came aboard on the morning of July 10. The *Wilderness* cast off at once, and after a partly rough passage, anchored in the harbor of Veracruz on the night of July 14. Doña Margarita and party went ashore the next morning. Her party consisted of her five unmarried daughters, her only remaining son, Benito, Jr., Simon Pedro Santacilia and his wife Manuela, three gentlemen, and two servants. Benito Jr. had written to his father that he wanted to stay in the United States, but Father thought he had better return with his mother. Sr. Tamayo says that doña Margarita took with her on this voyage the bodies of her two sons, José and Antonio, for burial in Mexico, but there is no mention of this in the ship's log or related correspondence. When the family arrived in Mexico on July 25, Juárez installed them, during August and September, not in the huge and grim old National Palace, where he had rooms, but in the Hotel Iturbide. There is no direct evidence about doña Margarita's state of mind after her return to Mexico, but from all the indirect evidence or lack of it we may assume that she recovered her mental if not physical health, and was her husband's strong support and candid critic, as before.

For Juárez, as for Mexico, despite all the sad memories, life was beginning again.

PART SIX

A Democratic Tragedy

26

MEXICO ALONE

AFTER FIFTY-SEVEN YEARS of internal chaos and two major invasions, including the last ten years of the War of the Reform and the War of the Intervention, Mexico had reason to rejoice. Thanks chiefly to Juárez, who had continued the work of his liberal predecessors and succeeded where they had failed, and who had drawn out the force of the Mexican people, Mexico was now for the first time an independent and democratic nation. It was neither occupied nor threatened by foreign powers. The Church, the army, and the privileged classes had been separated from and subordinated to the power of a secular, civil, and constitutional state. Mexico was governed—not yet by, but on the whole for, the people—by a group of politicians who in their different ways were struggling to create, under the law, a peaceful, just, and free society. For nearly ten years they struggled, and at the end of that decade they had failed, and were followed by a dictatorship.

Because these people and their cause were great, and because their fatal weakness, egotistical individualism, was closely related to their strength, a passion for liberty, this was a true tragedy, and not the least of the many in the history of democracy. Juárez died in the middle of this decade of transition from victory to surrender, but he was the greatest figure in it, as he had been in the decade before. He embodied in his own character the Mexican people at their best, and his one tragic error was not wholly different in kind from those of the Mexicans under Díaz who finally sacrificed liberty for material progress. He had worn himself out, alone, and so had Mexico. Especially in our time, this tragedy of a young republic bears watching.

What it comes down to is that even with national independence, and with a Constitution much respected, a democracy cannot survive without a thriving citizenry, more or less educated and more or less equal in opportunity; nor can there be such a citizenry without a thriving economy, more or less free, taxable, and regulated in the public interest—and such an economy in itself depends on that kind of citizenry; nor, without outside help, can that kind of economy, that kind of citizenry, and a strong democracy be created from the raw material of a people recently released from a very long period of oppressive colonialism.

After only fifty-seven years of struggle, compared with centuries for the older democracies, and after "the great decade" of civil and defensive war, Mexico was exhausted, its economy was still primitive, its citizens were still mostly illiterate and without opportunity, and its government was democratic almost only insofar as it was at last secular and violently argumentative. (The United States, in contrast, had been born fully armed with English liberal experience and French liberal thought, had been given a rich continent with only a few savage inhabitants, and had been protected for decades by the British Navy. Our only vast misfortune had been Negro slavery, and now that we are comparing, our own tragic weakness may be compounded of our good luck and our collective self-satisfaction.)

From this date, looking back on "the restored Republic" in Mexico between 1867 and 1876, we may imagine that the surrender to dictatorship—in this case, fortunately, a Mexican one—might have been averted by foreign aid of the best kinds: international loans, foreign capital and enterprise under Mexican law, international trade, technical and educational assistance, personnel exchanges, a Peace Corps, an Alliance for Progress, and all the rest. It is obvious, however, that at that time British and American capitalists had their hands full with their own concerns and were naturally disinclined to risk their money and their lives in a very unstable Mexico; that except in colonies foreign trade and enterprise were relatively undeveloped, with tariffs high and growing higher; and that the strengthening and union of all democracies had not been made imperative by the threats of Fascism and Communism. In 1867 the Mexican Republic had to make its own way alone, had very good reasons for wanting to do exactly that, and eventually paid a terrible price, in the dictatorship (1876–1910) and subsequent Revolution (1910–20), for doing so. Mexican isolationism is no longer prudent, and could cost much more in liberty and blood. This forward glance is necessary in order to understand what happened to Mexico and to Juárez at the time.

"If at that time," says Sr. Cosío Villegas, "there had existed agree-able economic prospects, a rich foreign and internal trade, for example, the most ambitious and competent among the disinherited would have tried to acquire riches in private rather than public activities; but as things were, the easiest and one might even say the only way seemed to be in politics: to acquire political power, and with it, the property of others." Such persons, including unemployed and restless generals and governors who still amounted to feudal chieftains, besides more disinterested but equally violent, articulate, and egotistical lawyers and journalists, soon brought the new political pot to a rolling boil. Juárez and his colleagues, politicians themselves, if for the most part poor men and content to remain so, had to keep their minds mostly on politics in the narrow and superficial sense of keeping the government functioning and solvent, and suppressing rebellions. They also wished, naturally, to keep themselves in office—that is to say, to do their own chosen work, in a cause for which they had already sacrificed much. Nevertheless, Juárez continued his lifelong effort to promote and finance road-building, and the government continued to make real sacrifices in other fields in order to complete the railroad between Mexico City and Veracruz.

But Juárez had never been either a businessman or an economist; he had been a teacher and the director of an institute. He knew what a hard-won education had done for himself, and he knew as well as anyone at the time that Mexico's social and economic and political problems could be solved in the long run only by a great advance in the education of the people. He also knew very well that hungry people cannot be interested in education, even for their own children; but he had never been one to do nothing simply because he could not do everything. In the autumn of 1867, he and his Minister of Justice and Public Instruction, Antonio Martínez de

Castro, appointed a committee, with Gabino Barreda as Chairman, to reorganize public education. It so happened that Barreda had received a degree in medicine in France, and had been converted to the positivist philosophy of Auguste Comte; also, many of his collaborators were positivists. This meant a concerted effort to separate education from religion and to base it on science and humanitarianism. To-day, even those who would applaud such an effort in itself would have to admit that it was both scientifically superficial and singularly un-Mexican. More important, its authoritarian and almost Hegelian tone was partly responsible for the so-called "scientific" and undemocratic aspects of the imminent dictatorship. Comte's works are not included in the books that Juárez collected in these later years, and it is unfortunate that he was kept too busy at this time by political turmoil and open rebellion, and was perhaps too modest intellectually, to call the attention of these eager pedagogues to the more liberal, spiritual, and truly humane if airy philosophy of Pierre Joseph Proudhon, to which he had been introduced by Melchor Ocampo. Yet it would be absurd to deny that for all its philosophical defects and unhappy results, this was a noble effort to make Mexican minds both more enlightened and more realistic, and that these men and Juárez, as well as such early religious teachers as Bartolomé de Las Casas and Vasco de Quiroga, were the progenitors of the valiant and underpaid teachers of Mexico to-day. Unfortunately Mexico's isolation and turmoil did not permit the government to develop and tax an economy that would have permitted a more vigorous educational program at this time. However, a national literature began to appear.

A more immediate and pressing problem was the old and nasty one of what to do with all the traitors, collaborators, and imperialists of widely varying degrees of guilt and danger to the Republic, and then with those taken in open rebellion against the government after July, 1867. Juárez and his cabinet at first attempted to follow his old policy of severe punishment for leaders and of lesser punishment or total amnesty for most of the followers, but these decrees and the decisions based on them were severely criticized by the journalist Zarco and others for lack of uniformity and justice, and as the rebellions continued and the government felt it needed a stronger hand, it was accused of identifying mere political opponents with rebels.

A more pressing and important problem was the reorganization of the army, and under Ignacio Mejía as Minister of War, this was accomplished on the whole very effectively. During the preceding four years, according to a work on which Juárez congratulated the author, about 40,000 Mexicans on both sides had been killed and about 10,000 wounded. At the time of the victory, the republican army included more than 60,000 men. An army of this size was not necessary and could not be supported, so in decrees of July 20–23 it was reduced to four divisions, of the Center, East, North, and West, of 4,000 men each, under the commands, respectively, of Generals Régules, Díaz, Escobedo, and Corona, with a fifth division under General Juan Álvarez at Acapulco. Although he had wished to retire to go into business, Díaz retained his command, first in patriotic compliance with Juárez' request, and later for his own political purposes. The army was reduced slowly enough to 18,853 men by December, 1867. Even then it cost more than half the national budget and caused a deficit; Iglesias, in the Treasury, naturally considered it still too large. The veterans received compensation from the confiscated properties of imperialists, and many were settled in colonies. Furthermore, in the new army, new officers, such as Generals Sóstenes Rocha and Ignacio R. Alatorre, and a new, more professional spirit replaced the older one of improvisation and independence of the civil government. If all of this had not been accomplished, the restored Republic would not have lasted as long as it did.

In any event, there were now many more than 40,000 veterans in Mexico, and of these, many had never lived and worked as civilians, many that had did not now want to return to the hopeless drudgery of their civilian lives, and many of those who did were sure to find their families scattered, their homes and villages ruined, and their former occupations gone. When the officers sought government appointments, many felt that they were being discriminated against in favor of party regulars. As a result of all this, many veterans became bandits, such as the former General Miguel Negrete, and others found themselves ready and eager to support the disgruntled generals and politicians who arose in a long series of minor rebellions against the government. Furthermore, the victory had not eliminated the Mexican theory of federalism or altered the views, habits, and assumptions of the governors and politicians who still ruled large areas of Mexico as neo-feudal lords; these were uneducated and irrational men who had found it easier and more natural to fight for the vague Republic than they now found it to help rebuild that Republic into a more solid institution that might well threaten their own interests and privileges. The politicans and journalists in Mexico City were better educated, but in too legalistic and theoretical a manner, so that now again, as in 1861, they thought that the Constitution in combination with more liberty, purely political, would solve everything. Mexico City became a vast beehive of angry, shouting, stinging men who consciously or unconsciously encouraged rebellion all over the country and made it very difficult for the government to get on with all the work at hand. For ten years the Republic had been nothing but a hope, a flag, an inappropriate and inadequate but sacred Constitution, and Juárez; and now, when Juárez wanted above all to create a peaceful and thriving nation beneath these symbols, most of the articulate and able Mexicans were heartily sick of Juárez and wanted some power and glory for themselves.

It was in this developing situation that Juárez, then only sixty-one years old and as full of quiet energy and stamina as ever, made the greatest mistake of his career. On August 14, 1867 he issued the *convocatoria* or summons to elections to the Presidency, the Supreme Court, and Congress. No one has ever blamed Juárez for running for President this time: after all, he had only been elected to that office once, during the bitter year 1861, and if re-elected, this would be his first chance to govern in peace, of a kind. With the people, the army, and a few loyal civil servants, he had saved the Republic, and if most of the politicians and generals were tired of him, his prestige among less prominent people was still enormous.

However, the *convocatoria* went much further than a summons to elections. The citizens were asked to vote at the same time either to give or to refrain from giving to the next Congress *alone* the power to adopt five amendments to the Constitution. This method was unconstitutional because the Constitution provided that it could be amended only by a two-thirds vote of Congress, approved by a majority of the state legislatures, as in the United States Constitution. The amendments proposed were: to establish a bicameral Congress to give the President a veto that could be overruled by a two-thirds vote in Congress, instead of by a majority; to permit executive reports to Congress to be made in writing, instead of orally; to restrict the right of the permanent deputation of Congress to call special sessions of the whole body; and to determine the presidential succession in case both the President and the President of the Supreme Court were eliminated. Furthermore, the *convocatoria* decreed outright that the clergy could vote, that Ministers and priests could be elected to Congress, that a member of Congress did not have to reside in the district from which he was elected, and that the decrees against "traitors" be relaxed to permit the less guilty among them to vote.

This document was probably written by Lerdo, but when it was attacked, and later before Congress, Juárez assumed full responsibility for it. He defended the attempt to bypass the authorized method of amendment on two grounds: that greater speed of decision was necessary, and that in any case the people were sovereign. The problem of the presidential succession had been pointed up by the claims of Ortega and Ruiz in 1866. All the other proposed amendments were designed to strengthen the executive branch in a paralyzing struggle against a Jacobin Congress such as had occurred in 1861, and the arguments in their defense need not be summarized. Several of the proposed amendments were adopted much later, but their adoption was certainly delayed by this *convocatoria*. The changes in the electoral law were intended to help in the pacification of the country and also in the election of the ablest men possible to the Congress. In a number of letters Juárez expressed a surprise that seems somewhat ingenuous over the opposition aroused by these measures and proposals. Repeatedly he insisted that the government was not attempting to impose anything on the people, whose will was sovereign. In an especially interesting passage Juárez explains his attitude on votes for the clergy: "We desire complete liberty of cults, we want no religion of the State, and we ought therefore to consider the clergy (be what may their religious creeds) to be simple citizens, with the rights that all others have." There can be little doubt that Juárez was legally if not morally entitled to issue this *convocatoria*, under the extraordinary powers granted him in June, 1861, powers which he could have held until thirty days after the meeting of Congress on December 8, 1867, but which he voluntarily gave up on that date.

We cannot turn from the defense of this document without calling attention to a possibility that has received little notice, except by Sr. Valadés, and that is that consciously or not, Juárez was groping towards a method of government that can be called *presidencialismo*, or presidentialism, in which the President would assume wide, paternalistic powers, within the Constitution when possible, and always based on the will of the people. We may note this tendency in his two terms as Governor of Oaxaca; and after long use of executive powers that were almost unlimited, it may have been strong enough in his mind, by August, 1867, to blind him to the fact that thanks chiefly to himself, the Constitution had become sufficiently sacrosanct to make this *convocatoria* something that his opponents could seize upon and magnify as a betrayal and an outrage. (An American may venture to suggest again that this *presidencialismo*, or something like it, which may well seem to us vague and dangerous, has been the peaceful and effective mode of government in Mexico since about 1934. An important difference is that recent Mexican Presidents have risen from within an oligarchy by which they have been selected, supported, and in some degree controlled.) In short, Juárez' great error in 1867, like Ocampo's in 1859, and Woodrow Wilson's in 1919, was that of moving too far ahead of his time and of his support.

The opposition to the *convocatoria* was immediate, violent, and prolonged. It was led by Manuel María de Zamacona, an able and honest but irritable egotist who, feeling neglected, had been allowed to drift away from Juárez and his supporters in 1864. He now became "the most penetrating pickaxe that undermined the reputation, the fame, and even the glory of Juárez." Each of the proposed amendments, the decreed changes in the electoral law, which was held almost as sacred as the Constitution, and above all, the irregular method of amendment and its doubtful basis in Juárez' extraordinary powers, granted only to fight the war, were all effectively criticized. Governors Leon Guzmán of Guanajuato and Juan N. Méndez of Puebla both refused to publish the *convocatoria* and were, somewhat rashly, replaced. Generals Corona and Escobedo declared correctly that their duty was to support the civil government and stay out of politics. Díaz refused to make a public statement, but in private letters he attacked the *convocatoria*, and especially the granting of votes to the clergy. A public banquet that was organized to effect a union of some kind between Juárez and Díaz fell short of its purpose, and the widespread criticism of Juárez stimulated Díaz' supporters, and Díaz' own ambition. By this time he was supported for the Presidency by a considerable number of former generals and politicians, including even José María Mata and Ignacio Ramírez.

In the more or less popular voting on September 22, many abstained on the constitutional questions and some wrote in their own ideas: for example, the reform of the postal service and of the pavements, and "that don Benito reform himself." In these elections and in their confirmation much later in the electoral body and in Congress (December 19), the Mexican people, insofar as they expressed themselves at all, showed not only their humor but finally their good sense: Juárez was overwhelmingly elected to the Presidency and Lerdo somewhat less enthusiastically to the Presidency of the Supreme Court. The administration decided not even to count the votes on the constitutional amendments. Yet for Juárez, for Lerdo, and for the Mexican people, these events were to be proved anything but a happy ending of a minor episode. Juárez had lost many of his most able, articulate and influential supporters, at a time when he had a tremendous job to do and hardly a party, much less an organization, behind him; Lerdo, although vilified and slandered as a scheming "Jesuit," had emerged, in his defense of the *convocatoria*, as a brilliant centralist when centralism was obviously needed; and Díaz had become an open schemer for the Presidency, with vast prestige, a formidable group of supporters, and no principles.

In connection with Juárez' passionate and lifelong support of secular education, and with his remark just quoted on the freedom of the religious sects, it should be noted that at this time or soon after, Juárez' support of Protestantism, not by any means as a Protestant, but for the good of the Mexican people as he saw it, seems to have become more open. An Episcopal clergyman has said that his church was stronger in Mexico at that time than it is today. On January 15, 1868, Juárez wisely recalled Romero from Washington to make him Minister of the Treasury. Thirty years later Romero remembered that although he himself was a Catholic, he thought Protestantism might be good for Mexico, and when a Protestant clergyman, Mr. Henry C. Riley, wanted to buy "the Franciscan convent, which had been built by the Spaniards, located in the best section of the City of Mexico, and which could not now be duplicated but for a very large amount of money; and with the hearty support of President Juárez, who shared my views and who was perhaps a great deal more radical than I was myself on such subjects, I sold the building, which had become national property after the confiscation of the Church property, for a mere trifle, if I remember rightly about $4,000, most of that amount being paid in government bonds, which were then at a nominal price. The magnificent building sold to Dr. Riley's community was bought recently by the Catholic Church to restore it as a Catholic temple, for the sum of $100,000, as I understand." But, one may ask, does religious freedom extend to profiteering, and cannot Protesant missionary activity in Mexico, by foreigners, be considered presumptuous?

But of course such transactions were trivial in comparison with Romero's valiant efforts to restore the economy and establish fiscal order. The railroad from Mexico City to Veracruz was continued and two others begun. Romero also tried to revive mining and agriculture by blasting off the barnacles of numerous internal and export taxes, hoping that trade thus revived would augment revenues, and by affording interim substitutes in the form of stamp and other new taxes. He also advocated the issuance of treasury notes for the regular payment of government bills while the customs receipts were irregular. These were but a few of Romero's intelligent efforts, backed by Juárez, but the government did not on the whole make much progress in this direction because Congress was argumentative, critical, and recalcitrant. All but liberals had disappeared from political life, yet a disciplined liberal party did not exist, so that Congress was made up of warring factions and of individuals, often talented, who loved their country less than their own ideas and voices. If the method of the *convocatoria* had been proved disastrously in error, its purpose, the strengthening of the executive branch, was now vindicated. Even if Juárez and his cabinets had been able to dominate Congress, it is doubtful if more than a beginning of economic reconstruction could have been made without foreign capital and technicians, to be replaced as soon as possible by the profits and talents of a new Mexican middle class, then nonexistent.

A chief reason why foreigners were not attracted and why even Mexicans were not tempted to go into production and commerce was that minor rebellions and major banditry, all over the country, caused by ten years of warfare, made such efforts almost impossible. In December, 1857, a reactionary rebellion broke out in Yucatán, and in the following years there were others of different kinds all over the country. All these the government and the new army managed to put down, but at such cost that public works and education had almost no chance. Equally serious was the crime wave: murders, armed robberies, kidnapings, and all other crimes were so common that everyone not in rags had to travel armed and preferably with an escort. The articulate members of the public cried aloud for peace and order, and the government was at least as eager to establish them, but every time it asked for appropriate legislation and money it ran into weeks and months of violent discussion and rarely received any effective authority. This was not entirely the fault of a Congress composed mostly of legalists and egotists, because Juárez and the Ministers were inclined to ask rather hastily for extraconstitutional powers, such as they had enjoyed so long during the war, and for the revival of harsh laws of that time and even earlier, instead of showing greater ingenuity in devising measures that would have been effective in the new situations and within the Constitution. Thus the deputies and journalists were able to ask why the government never seemed to be able to function under the Constitution, and to accuse the government of asking for laws so vague that they could be used against political opponents as well as against bandits. Yet more precise laws within the Constitution were also opposed. The age of Santa Anna had not been forgotten, and having fought so long for their Constitution and their liberty, Mexicans now demanded both, apparently without quite understanding either.

The general uncertainty about just how the government could and should function under the Constitution also found expression, of course, in the activities of the Supreme Court. After the defeat of the *convocatoria* it refused Lerdo leave of absence as its President to serve as Foreign Minister, but later granted him this leave. (He was also serving at this time in Congress.) In 1869 the Court exercised its rights under Article 101 of the Constitution to act on *amparo* (civil rights) cases directly, asserted successfully its independence of Congress, and succeeded in establishing, for the time being, at least, its right to declare acts of Congress unconstitutional. This was a gain, although in its decision of April 12, 1869, declaring unconstitutional an act of Congress "suspending individual guarantees for one year with regard to kidnapers and bandits," probably hampered the efforts of the government to restore order. (In this connection, Americans might be reminded that our Supreme Court did not establish this right until John Marshall's opinion in *Marbury vs. Madison,* 1803, fourteen years after our Constitution was ratified, and that this right is still disputed in the South.)

The isolation of Mexico at this time was the inevitable result not only of its internal disorders, but even more of the painful relations that Mexico had had with most of the great powers of the world for nearly fifty years. The attitude of Juárez and Lerdo in foreign affairs now was that since most of the European powers had recognized an empire illegally and aggressively imposed on Mexico, relations could be resumed with those powers only at their request, and on a basis of settlements wholly acceptable to Mexico of any remaining financial claims. Relations with the United States had not been discontinued, and were now cordial on both sides, while a Mixed Claims Commission, meeting in Washington, managed to settle all claims of both Americans and Mexicans since the Treaty of Guadalupe Hidalgo. With the help of the United States, Mexican relations were resumed with the German Confederation and Italy. In the summer of 1869, Juárez was very happy to hear from General

Prim, who had recently overthrown Queen Isabel II of Spain, in favor of a liberal constitutional monarchy, with a sovereign yet to be found, that Prim, that ancient and important friend of Mexico, wanted to renew relations.

In the autumn of that year Seward, having retired from public office, visited Mexico with his wife, son, and several friends, and he was warmly received by Juárez and especially by Lerdo, although of course many Mexicans were quick to express their fears that Seward, to them a sinister American expansionist, and Juárez, the perpetrator of the McLane–Ocampo Treaty, would get together in some dark corner and arrange the robbery of another large part of the soil of Mexico. Seward hastened to declare that Americans were now much more interested in dollars than in dominion: a remark that during the American economic penetration of Mexico under the Porfiriato and later has been taken up in bitterness by the always considerable number of Mexicans, chiefly intellectuals, who fear and hate the United States. In a speech at Puebla, Seward, who had not only known and served Abraham Lincoln but had also known many of the other most distinguished men of his age, declared that Juárez was the greatest man that he had ever met in his life. Romero records that Mr. Thomas H. Nelson, then United States Minister to Mexico, present on this occasion, was startled by this declaration, later asked Seward whether he would stand on it, and was told: "What I said about Juárez was after mature consideration, and I am willing to stand by my opinion."

More interesting to Juárez than such tributes must have been the news that came the next year from France. On July 19, 1870, having used Prim's hunt for a new Spanish king as part of his plot, Bismarck tricked Napoleon III, a gravely ill man, into a war for which, partly as a result of his Mexican adventure, Napoleon was not prepared. On September 1, he and 100,000 of his soldiers were captured at Sedan, and he was eventually released to join his wife and son in exile in England. Marshal Bazaine, who had thought at one time that he had conquered and pacified Mexico, was forced into surrendering with another French army at Metz, and was later convicted of treason. Conflicting French governments, including the Commune of

Paris, were set up, and Paris was not forced to surrender until January 28, 1871.

On June 17, 1870, Juárez had warned his eager old colleague Armando Montluc in Paris that the Mexican government had no intention whatever of opening any kind of relations with the French Empire. On October 10 he wrote again to Montluc to thank him for sending a tribute to Juárez clipped from a French journal, and to rejoice in the formation of a new French Republic: "I have hopes, not unfounded, that the French, under the form of government that they have just adopted, will be able to undo the evils of all kinds brought upon them by the madnesses of the empire; and I ardently hope that the result of the war between the kings may be the conquest of liberty for the peoples."

Juárez had long known that democracy was one fabric, damaged or strengthened throughout by its defeats or victories anywhere in the world. Although vengeance, as he had truly said, was not his forte, he was a human being, and he could not but have felt some slight and more personal pleasure in the news of the collapse of an empire and of two men who had nearly destroyed the Republic to which he had given his whole life, and who had, in a sense, taken the lives of his two sons and the health of his strong and beloved wife, when they were in exile in New York. Yet his wife was now very ill, and so was the Republic.

27

SR. JUÁREZ ALONE

LIKE most Indians who survive infancy and childhood, Juárez was physically very tough, and his only recorded illnesses up to this time are a fever in New Orleans during his exile there in 1854 and another in Saltillo ten years later. However, his long travels under difficult conditions, his worry about his family, his narrow escapes from death, and above all, the severe strain of his work and his responsibility for so many years would have worn down any man. In October, 1870, he suffered some kind of stroke, after which, for a few days, there was fear for his life. He recovered, only to face, a couple of months later, the worst blow he could have imagined. His wife had suffered a long and painful illness whose nature is not known, and on the afternoon of January 2, 1871, in their small house next to the church of San Cosme (No. 4, Calle de San Cosme, now Calle Serapio Rendón), she died.

Doña Margarita was only forty-four years old, but in her twenty-seven years of married life she had given birth to twelve children and lost five of them; she had had to improvise homes in many places in Mexico and also, without speaking English, in New York City and New Rochelle; she had often been hard pressed for money; frequently, for months on end, she and the children had been separated from her Juárez with very little surety that they would ever see him again; and there is no evidence whatever that at any moment in this very hard life—whether she was keeping a village shop in Etla, Oaxaca, while her husband was in exile, or was leading her family across mountains and jungles to join him in Veracruz, or was the guest of honor at gala affairs in the White House and of other great men in Washington, or was the first lady of Mexico in the

National Palace—she ever behaved with anything but total unselfishness, dignity, courage, and grace. Her character, which as we have seen included shrewdness, and her devotion, must have given Juárez no small part of his great courage and stamina, and it is clear that he appreciated her fully. The Mexican tributes to her naturally emphasize her abnegation and modesty, as well as the fact that she did not openly have anything to do with politics, which is the way Mexican women are supposed to behave; but Juárez' wife, surely like those of other Mexican politicians, had a mind of her own that was not without influence on her husband and on public affairs. During their anguish over the death of their two sons, Doña Margarita's near mental collapse in the United States, her long final illness, and after her death, Juárez must have asked himself more than once whether his tremendous work, however successful, however good for so many people, had justified him in asking her to suffer so much and die so young. This question, hovering over him in his loneliness like one of the vultures of Veracruz, must have given him more pain than the defections and the attacks on him of his old friends and colleagues in the long fight, and far more pain than the sight of the corpses of the men—his brothers, he had truly said—who had died for a Republic that was now showing no great vitality, no clear promise of being a great and blessed heritage for their children.

Shunning any display, Juárez invited no one to the secular funeral the next day, but when the procession moved through the streets to the cemetery, vast crowds appeared in silence. One of the newspapers remarked: "We have never seen a similar unanimity of feelings or an equal expression of sorrow among all classes of the population, without regard to party, opinion, or nationality." As to this nonreligious funeral, we may recall that Sierra, speaking of Ocampo's similar funeral, wrote that there were many such in those days. The practice deeply disturbed Mexican Catholics, but it planted in their minds the seeds of religious liberty. If this was true, Juárez probably knew or cared nothing about it: for most of a month he was almost unable to work.

It was after these shocks of illness and death, including whatever effects his stroke of the previous October may have had on his brain, that Juárez had to make one of the most difficult and important decisions of his career, namely, whether or not to run again for the Presidency in 1871 against Lerdo and Díaz, who remained the only other possible candidates. Because of its results, his decision to run has been called a tragic error, more serious than that of the *convocatoria*, but to make that judgment is to assume that if Juárez had stepped down, the results would have been better for Mexico, a hypothesis that the later behavior of Lerdo and Díaz does nothing to support. Juárez knew both Lerdo and Díaz very well indeed, and he may have feared that if he backed Lerdo, his obvious preference, and if Lerdo were elected, Díaz would not accept the decision of the electorate, and for all his intellectual brilliance, the former Rector of San Ildefonso would be unable to rally enough support behind the government to suppress the glamorous and now clearly ambitious General from Oaxaca. If, on the other hand, he backed Díaz, whose lack of democratic faith and principles he had almost surely detected, he would have made himself considerably responsible for a tragic relapse into the crudest authoritarianism. In other words, early in 1871 or before, Juárez, who left no record of his thoughts on this matter, may well have foreseen Díaz' eventual and disastrous triumph and decided to delay it as long as possible.

It has been well said that "Juárez believed he was indispensable; while Lerdo regarded himself as infallible and Díaz as inevitable." We might be allowed to qualify this dictum by observing, first, that Díaz' inevitability may not have been perceived by anyone; second, that Lerdo's infallibility, if it must be called that, was apt to be expressed with arrogance and legal trickery, and to be finally ineffective; and third, that if Juárez thought he was indispensable, his thinking so was by no means the same thing as a greedy attempt to hang on to the Presidency.

We must return briefly to this common charge that Juárez, whatever his previous merits, had by this time become a power addict. Once more we are somewhat frustrated by Juárez' extraordinary self-sufficiency and reticence. Since he never once used his office to make money for himself, always dressed and lived with great simplicity, usually viewed public acclaim with some cynicism, repeatedly made use of colleagues who he thought would be useful to the Republic, although they had tried to humiliate and replace him, and had even betrayed him, and was now undoubtedly, at last, very tired, we find that this common charge has very little substance. The most that can be said is that like any master, Juárez was addicted to his job, a very different thing from greedy addiction to power. No man who for many years has taken great risks, borne very heavy responsibilities, and done his job reasonably well, can be expected to turn it over lightly and easily to other men who, in his view, may well ruin everything he has done. In 1871 Juárez may have understood Mexican history, including what was to come, better than his professorial critics, and have decided to go down fighting.

Mexico had no organized parties to hold national conventions and nominate candidates. Neither, of course, did they have radio, TV, aircraft for the candidates and their parties and journalists, or even the railroad rear-platform speeches and the torchlight processions of our post-Civil War presidential campaigns. Obvious candidates were nominated by petitions published in the newspapers, and the candidates and their friends and political protégés then went to the "grass roots," namely, local clubs, cafés, barracks, and government offices, for support. The popular vote, when and where allowed, was small. The decision was probably made by the number of local politicians, also serving as electors, who saw in this candidate or that the best chance for themselves. The votes of the electors had to be counted and confirmed by Congress. Juárez gave the press complete freedom, which it used in a virulent manner. The two opposition parties accused Juárez and his supporters of all kinds of illegal pressures and maneuvers, and they were especially critical of (and curious about) the influence of the army, which was well under the control of the Minister of War, Ignacio Mejía, a candid partisan of Juárez.

During the preceding four years, Lerdo had quietly been building up a party of his own. "The Lerdist party assumed the character of its chief, being composed of men of property, a few capitalists, the intelligentsia, the socially prominent, and a minority of the bureaucratic element which Lerdo had erected in governmental posts during his long tenure as chief of cabinet." In December, 1870, a struggle for power had arisen between the *lerdistas* and the *juaristas* over the city council of Mexico and the Federal District deputies in Congress, and when Lerdo saw that Juárez was not going to withdraw in his favor, he felt obliged to resign as Foreign Minister, although for his purposes in the presidential election, he would have preferred to remain in that high office. His letter of resignation, dated January 14, 1871, which was not the first, cites the attacks on him in the press, and Juárez' acceptance sounds truly regretful, grateful, and affectionate. Lerdo returned then to his post as President of the Supreme Court.

The *porfiristas* included a wide variety of men who had grown critical of Juárez over the years, old radicals of the opposition of 1861, discontented veterans, strict constitutionalists who had been shocked by the *convocatoria* of 1867, and such able intellectuals as Zamacona, Ramírez, and Mata. The chief operator of this party was Justo Benítez, and the military "hatchet man" was Porfirio's younger brother and long-time comrade in arms, Félix Díaz, then Governor of Oaxaca. Juárez must have been suspicious of Porfirio Díaz, but he never showed any hostility towards him. In fact, when the General retired in 1868, Juárez insisted that he receive his legal two-thirds of active pay. For his part, until the elections of 1871, Díaz was careful not to criticize the President in public, although he did so in private correspondence. His claim that his military victories were not sufficiently recognized by the government when they took place is disproved by numerous letters of congratulation from Mejía and Juárez. Although the minor rebellions of these years were not openly supported by Díaz, many of the rebels were *porfiristas* whom he did not repudiate. Meanwhile, the *porfiristas* criticized the government for not putting down the rebellions more effectively.

The *juaristas* were led by more office-holders than Lerdo had in his camp, and by the current leaders of the army. These men, with access to federal funds and pressures, were in a strong position, but even they might not have been successful without the support of a good many unknown politicians, all over the Republic, who persisted in "liking" don Benito. They had no buttons saying "*Me gusta don Benito,*" but as it turned out, they had the votes.

The informal platforms of the three parties were, like all such statements, vague and almost indistinguishable, with the *lerdistas* emphasizing economic soundness, the *juaristas* the President's record, and the *porfiristas* strict constitutionalism, in which don Porfirio himself had never shown any interest or knowledge whatever. The *lerdistas* and the *porfiristas* often united in Congress, and soon the former proposed a change in the voting in Congress for President—should it go there for lack of an electoral majority for any one candidate—from block votes by states to votes by individual deputies, while the latter insisted that the army should be kept away from the polls. Congress was convened early by the opposition parties, and its sessions soon developed into a struggle that extended into several state legislatures.

The American reader may well see nothing alarming in all of this, which sounds enough like our own political campaigns, until he is reminded of the important differences. In Mexico, at that time, the actual meaning of the Constitution, the balance of powers, and the operations of the government remained very uncertain, while armed rebellion remained at least as likely as acquiescence in the election returns.

Of the electors voting in July and counted in August, 5,837 voted for Juárez, 3,555 for Díaz, and 2,847 for Lerdo: a majority for none, and sufficient proof that Juárez was no dictator, as we now understand the term "dictator." It was now "all over but the shooting." While the counting was going on, followed by the decisive struggle in Congress, there were armed outbreaks all over the country—a fact not to be inferred from Juárez' characteristically cheerful report to Armando Montluc in Paris, dated Mexico, August 9, 1871, or from his address to Congress on its opening on September 16, in which he asserted that with a few exceptions here and there, "peace reigns from one extreme of the Republic to the other." More somber is his letter of October 3 to Governor Ignacio Pesqueira of Sonora: "The day before yesterday we had in this very capital one of those shameful scandals that fortunately have become infrequent among us. The rebels managed to seduce the garrison of the Citadel, which pronounced there and liberated more than eight hundred prisoners from the [Belén] jail in this city. The rebels in the Citadel had at their disposal many elements of war and means of resistance; however, the scandal did not last long, because at eight o'clock the worthy troops of the federal government vigorously seized that place and left everything in peace, but not without having lost some good and loyal servants of the nation. There is no doubt that there are conspiracies in different parts of the Republic to ignite another civil war, but it is a fact that nowhere can the rebels count on the support of the people, and that is the best guarantee we can have that in the future we can preserve order and tranquillity." This uprising, led by General Negrete, was put down by General Rocha, and after the rebel leaders had escaped, Rocha had all of the remaining rebels, then prisoners, shot on the spot. It is said that the spectacle of the dead being carried through the streets created a deep and painful impression on the people of the city, and we may believe that it did the same on Juárez himself. Had the new army, including such hard characters as General Rocha, become the indispensable institution?

On October 12, after giving Juárez 108 votes, Lerdo 5, and Díaz 3, Congress declared Juárez legally elected President, to begin his new term on December 1. However, Governor Félix Díaz of Oaxaca had for some time secretly been gathering war materials, including rifles imported from New York by way of Puerto Ángel. On November 8 Porfirio Díaz published his rebellious Plan of La Noria, named after a *hacienda* given him near the city of Oaxaca. This Plan, probably devised by Justo Benítez, who, as Sr. Iturribarría says, played Witch to Díaz' Macbeth, accused Juárez' government of dictatorship and of rigging the election, demanded less government and more liberty, and proposed several specific measures to curb the power of the executive branch. It called for a return to the Constitution of 1857, yet at the same time shoved even Lerdo, Juárez' legitimate successor, aside in favor of a "provisional President," obviously none other than our Porfirio, and proposed an entirely new constitutional convention, to consist of three delegates from each state, to be chosen by direct election by the people. This Plan was supported by the Legislature of Oaxaca, 3,500 well-armed men, and twelve pieces of artillery. Porfirio Díaz' excuse for this outrage was: "I can only compensate for the immense disservice that I do to my country in plunging it into a civil war by putting it at some time in conditions that will make civil war definitely impossible." In short, one final rebellion, please, this time with the proper leader, who was hypocritical and cynical enough to assert also: "If triumph crowns our efforts, I shall return to the peace of my home, preferring in any event the frugal and tranquil life of the obscure laborer to the ostentations of power."

On November 18, Edward Lee Plumb, former American chargé d'affaires in Mexico, reported from Mexico City:

It appears it has been the deliberate intention of the Porfirio Díaz party, in any case, if not successful in the election, to appeal to arms, and notwithstanding the high opinion we had formed of that person, he has proven to be utterly without political capacity, character, or patriotism. For several months there have been constant rumors that there would be a revolution of which he would be the head, but so high has been the estimation entertained of him personally that there has been great reluctance to believe that this could prove to be true. . . .

On November 13 there reached here a proclamation issued (on November 8) at La Noria. It has caused a profound sensation, and I may also say, almost universal disgust, so great even that very many at first refused to credit its authenticity. Only one paper has come out in its defense. In the manifesto, Díaz, while pretending to sustain the Constitution, sets it aside entirely. And going even back of the times of Santa Anna, he proposes nothing less than a pure military dictatorship.

The result of La Noria has been to force a union between the Lerdo and Juárez parties and unite all who are opposed to anarchy and a return to the era of military pronouncements. These people are now supporting the government, and this has rendered impossible the permanent triumph of the revolution.

On December 1, when he took the oath of office, Juárez received from Congress extraordinary powers to suppress the rebellion, and in his inaugural address he expressed his revulsion at this attack on the principle of liberty under law for which the nation had fought successfully for fourteen years, and his confidence that the people would support the government. In Oaxaca in December and January General Ignacio R. Alatorre defeated the rebels and seized the state capital, and soon thereafter General Félix Díaz was captured by forces from Juchitán, and because he had in 1871 burned a church containing the image of their patron, San Vicente, they shot him forthwith. He was replaced as Governor of Oaxaca by Juárez' old friend, Miguel Castro. Juárez naturally took special interest in all of these events in his native state, and on January 16, 1872, he took time to write a letter urging upon the local citizenry the prompt completion of the bridge across the Rio Grande on the road between the city of Oaxaca and the towns of Guelatao and Ixtlán. He also had to suppress one more effort of the inhabitants of the Isthmus of Tehuantepec to secede from the state of Oaxaca. In the North, General Rocha defeated the *porfirista* General Jacinto Treviño in March, there were other victories by the federal forces, and Porfirio Díaz himself was forced to flee into the mountain wilderness of Tepic. Then a rebellion with local causes broke out in that perpetual hotbed, Yucatán, and the country was not actually pacified until well into the summer.

When Juárez asked for an extension of his extraordinary powers, in order to complete the pacification, he got it, but only after extended debates in which the opposition was led with great bitterness by Zamacona, who directed his fire chiefly at Juárez, Mejía, and Romero, and who made a scathing indictment of, among other things, Rocha's butchery at the Citadel. The opposition was also kept up, effectively, against Juárez' repeated proposals to create a Senate and to clarify the law on the presidential succession. On June 8, three cabinet members, including Romero, resigned, and the cabinet had to be reconstructed, amidst severe criticism as usual. Romero had worked fourteen hours a day for five years, as Minister of the Treasury. He had met nothing but opposition in Congress, and his health, never robust, seemed to be ruined. He retired to Chiapas, where he introduced scientific methods of coffee-raising and processing that were later used very advantageously in Oaxaca as well. He must have recovered his health considerably, but he may have lost some of his liberalism, because he was to serve later as Minister of the Treasury under Díaz, and again as Minister in Washington, where he died in 1898.

In that last year, after his wife's death, and especially in the early summer days of 1872, after the departure from his official family of his trusted Romero, Juárez may sometimes have looked back across the tumultuous years and felt very much alone, and at sixty-six, very old. Four years before, he had sold all but one of his small properties in Oaxaca, and it must have seemed doubtful to him that he would ever be able to return there and live in peace. His daughters undoubtedly took the best of care of him physically, but much as they loved him, they could not have understood him as his wife had done, through so much hardship and separation, for so many years. There is a plausible story that when Sr. Delfín Sanchez, the new husband of Felícitas Juárez, resisted the execution of a legal judgment against him, and was ordered arrested, Juárez had to explain to his daughter that he could not intervene; and it must have depressed him to recognize that even his own daughter did not understand something that he had been trying to explain and demonstrate to the Mexican people for forty years.

Juárez had never had, because he had never needed, a very close friend who was also his equal in character and intellect, although perhaps Melchor Ocampo had come as close to being such as anyone could have done, and Ocampo's body had been cut down from the tree eleven years before. Perhaps Juárez thought of him more often now. Yet if Juárez had gone his way almost alone, he had certainly known well and worked with and against an extraordinary group of men. Álvarez . . . Comonfort . . . Ocampo . . . Doblado . . . Degollado . . . Valle . . . Miguel Lerdo . . . Zaragoza . . . that strange Spaniard, Prim, and many more . . . all had died, and very few of them in bed. Other old colleagues, Prieto . . . Zarco . . . Zamacona . . . Ramírez . . . Mata of those days in New Orleans . . . had gone other ways, and some of them in open opposition to Juárez as a man, as well as to his principles. Manuel Ruiz had collapsed, and so, at last, had even that dangerous actor, González Ortega. Maximilian, Miramón, and Tomás Mejía had gone down on the Hill of the Bell, and Vidaurri soon after, while Napoleon III, self-made Emperor of the French, and his Eugénie, and the poor mamá Carlota, and everything they had hoped and stood for, were in ruins. Even that intolerable jack-in-the-box, Antonio López de Santa Anna, was at last a permanently discredited old wreck, in exile now in Nassau. In the quarter of a century since he had first become Governor of Oaxaca, in the fifty-three incredible years since the shepherd boy had walked down out of the mountains, how there had come and

gone all of these builders and wreckers, these schemers, talkers, and
fighting men! Along the endless galleries of the National Palace the
dark little Indian President with the somber eyes walked alone, a
stranger out of a heroic past, who had come now into smaller times.
When he walked in the streets of the old city, alone or with some
gesticulating politician or general, and perhaps with an armed guard
walking a pace behind, it may have been different and better, for
there he was among the people of all sorts and conditions for whose
freedom and dignity he had given his life. There, some little old
woman crouched on the stones behind her pathetic little display of
herbs for sale, or some boys playing the bull and the bullfighters, or
a tinsmith peering out of his dark little shop, may suddenly have
recognized don Benito, and smiled with true gratitude. But, he may
have wondered, were all of these people, including the solitary men
scratching the rocky soil behind their oxen in the mountains, the
women beating clean their clothes, nursing their babies, and chat-
tering to one another beside the muddy streams, and the little boys
watching their fathers' sheep and goats on the hillsides, alone with
their thoughts beneath the vast sky—were all of these people any
better off than they had been twenty, fifty, a hundred years before?
Would they ever feel themselves to be part of their government and
responsible for it, as one great family, trusting neither the plaster
saints, nor the rich and powerful, nor even wholly their President,
whoever he might be, but themselves, under God, to make their
own destiny? *Quien sabe? . . . Quien sabe?*

Meanwhile, the urbane and learned don Sebastián Lerdo de
Tejada, the next in line for the Presidency, thought he knew everything—but did he? and could he *do* everything necessary? For somewhere in the mountains there still waited and schemed Porfirio Díaz,
who had escaped from jail after jail to win battle after battle, once
for the Republic but now for himself, as the inevitable master, at
any price in their blood and suffering, of these people of Mexico.
The future of the Mexican people was always what mattered to
Juárez, but that spring he was at least twice reminded of his own,
by brief but unquestionable heart attacks. The second of these occurred in the National Palace, whither their guardian had taken, to
offer their thanks, twenty of the orphans in his care. Juárez had

personally supported them all, after the pursestrings of the Treasury had been drawn tight by the rebellion of La Noria. After half an hour of happy chatter, each child went to the President to say good-bye, and to each child he gave a peso to buy fruit. When the last, a boy of six, gripped his knees, he went pale, clutched his heart, and leaned on a table, but then quickly made light of it. He was completely a Zapotec Indian from the mountains, and if he did not talk about death and "the moment of truth," he had seen plenty of it, and it had come very close to himself, more than once. Almost certainly, because of his modesty and his rationalism, he had no hope of living after his death except in the lives of his children, who included, insofar as his love and his work might touch and help them, every child in Mexico. When death finally moved in upon him, implacably, he knew it and met it calmly, standing, getting on with his work.

Among his last acts were these: to order the return to the American Consul at La Paz, Lower California, of a boat lost by an American vessel in a storm, and then found by sailors and sold; to order the Treasury to pay "dowries" to nuns without them; to order amnesty for the enlisted men among the rebels who put down their arms and went home; to decree that a certain young man was old enough to administer his own property; and to free, under the vigilance of the police, a man who had been sentenced to death for assault and robbery on insufficient evidence. The book that he was reading in his last days was *Cours de histoire des legislations comparées*, by M. Lerminier.

On July 18, 1872, severe and intermittent pain drove him home early from his office, and he hoped that he could find relief the next morning, as he had before, by walking rapidly up the hill of Chapultepec, bringing on perspiration, and then going home to a bath. However, the pains became more severe, he had to lie down, and Dr. Ignacio Alvarado was summoned. At one point, when Juárez seemed very near death, this doctor poured boiling water on the region of the heart, this first time to good effect. The *angina pectoris* was almost surely a symptom of coronary occlusion, and although the treatments for this in our time are less brutal, they have the same purpose: to stimulate the heart into going on. When the family had withdrawn into the dining room, don Benito told the doctor tales of his boyhood in Oaxaca, in the household of his protector, don Antonio Salanueva. Suddenly he interrupted himself to ask:

"Is my illness mortal?"

When the doctor answered as gently as possible, but honestly to this patient, that it probably was, Juárez calmly continued his reminiscences of his boyhood. During another attack that was given the same painful treatment, Juárez remained quite impassive, without even a normal reflex action. The fact that the President was ill became known in the city, but the serious nature of the illness was kept secret, with the result that Sr. José María Lafragua, then Foreign Minister, and later a general, both of whom thought that he was having an attack of rheumatism in the knee, insisted on being admitted to receive the President's advice about their problems in hand. Juárez arranged his clothing, sat up in a chair, and gave the advice they sought, with no hint of the true situation. Just before eleven o'clock that night, Juárez asked his houseboy, from Ixtlán, named Camilo, to press his hand upon the place in his chest where he felt the most severe pain, and the boy obeyed, weeping. At half past eleven, Juárez quietly died.

NOTES

A formal bibliography seems unnecessary, because good bibliographies, not too far out of date, can be found in several of the works cited, and can be supplemented from these notes, which indicate my debt to books and manuscripts. The following symbols indicate the works most frequently cited and most important. In referring to other sources, after the first reference, I use the name of the author only. The numbers appearing in bold-face type at the left-hand margin refer to pages in *Viva Juárez!* Dates of books in parentheses are those of the first editions; dates without parentheses, those of the editions used.

AJ—Archivo Juárez, in the Biblioteca Nacional de Mexico.

AP—Juárez, Benito, and Santacilia, Pedro: *Archivos privados* . . . , Mexico, 1928.

AR—Archivo Romero, in the Banco de Mexico.

B—Bancroft, H. H.: *History of Mexico*, San Francisco, 1883–1888.

CV—Cosío Villegas, Daniel: *Historia moderna de Mexico: La república restaurada: La vida política*, Mexico, (1955) 1959.

D—Doblado, Manuel: *La Guerra de Reforma* . . . , San Antonio, 1930.

FM—Fuentes Mares, José: *Juárez y los Estados Unidos*, Mexico, 1960.

IG—Iturribarría, Jorge Fernando: *La generación oaxaqueña del 57*, Oaxaca, n.d.

IO—Iturribarría, Jorge Fernando: *Oaxaca en la historia*, Mexico, 1955.

INAH—Archivo histórico del Instituto Nacional de Antropología e Historia.

JD—Juárez, Benito: *Discursos y manifiestos*, Mexico, 1905.

JEp—Juárez, Benito: *Epistolario*, ed. Jorge L. Tamayo, Mexico, 1957.

JE—Juárez, Benito: *Exposiciones*, Mexico, 1902.

JM—Juárez, Benito: *Miscelánea*, Mexico, 1906.

NA—National Archives, Washington, D.C.

PRO—Public Record Office, London, England.

PS—Prida Santacilia, Pablo: *Siguiendo la vida de Juárez,* Mexico, 1945.

PV—Prieto, Guillermo: *Viaje* . . . , Mexico, 1877–1878.

RD—Romero, Matías: *Diario personal, 1855–1865,* ed. Emma Cosío Villegas, Mexico, 1960.

RJ—Roeder, Ralph: *Juárez and His Mexico,* New York, 1947.

SE—Sierra, Justo: *Evolución política del pueblo mexicano,* Mexico, (1900–1902) 1950.

SJ—Sierra, Justo: *Juárez, su obra y su tiempo,* Mexico, (1905–1906) 1956.

SMM—Simpson, Lesley Byrd: *Many Mexicos,* Berkeley and Los Angeles, (1941) 1960.

VO—Valadés, José C.: *Don Melchor Ocampo, reformador de Mexico,* Mexico, 1954.

VP—Valadés, José C.: *El pensamiento político de Benito Juárez,* Mexico, n.d.

CHAPTER 1

The passages from Juárez' *Notes:* AP, pp. 227–231.

30   Humboldt, Alexander, *Ensayo político* . . . , Mexico, (1807) 1953, p. 59 **/** "short biography": JE, pp. 5–119.

31   "strength of body" etc.: VP, pp. 23, 29 **/** "his character": JE, p. 12.

33   Salanueva's house: Calle Manuel García Vigil **/** photograph: Juárez Museum.

35   private library: in the State Library, Oaxaca.

36   populations: Humboldt, pp. 58, 64, 80, 85 **/** SJ, pp. 35 and 37.

40   "a natural faculty": VP, p. 44.

41   "incomprehensible": VP, p. 40 **/** Puritan: SMM, p. 248.

CHAPTER 2

This historical summary is based on the works of Sierra, Riva Palacio, Simpson, Parkes, Bancroft, Priestley, etc.

47   SJ, p. 38.

48–50 and **53–54**   *Notes:* AP, pp. 231–234.

50   On Santa Anna: Fuentes Mares, José, *Santa Anna* . . . , Mexico, 1956; and Hanighen, Frank C., *Santa Anna* . . . , New York, 1934.

51 Juárez as a Mason: IO, p. 143; and Velasco Pérez, Carlos, *El Coloso de Guelatao*, Mexico, 1957, p. 43.

52 federalism: SMM, p. 206; and Molina Enriquez, Andrés, *Juárez y la Reforma*, Mexico, (1905) 1958, pp. 69-78.

54 disturbances: IO, pp. 143-146 / course in civics: IG, p. 44 / young men: CV, p. 55.

CHAPTER 3

56 Aparicio: SJ, p. 49, and IO, p. 142 / teachers: SJ, p. 48, and Velasco Pérez, pp. 33-35.

56-57, 62-67 *Notes:* AP, pp. 234-239.

57 "this situation": VP, p. 37, and SJ, p. 47 / "this hope": JM, pp. 1-11.

58 "defended publicly": SJ, pp. 49 and 52, and Velasco Pérez, pp. 33 and 34 / "classmates": PS, p. 57.

59 patriotic address: JM, pp. 1-11.

60 colonial history: IG, pp. 13-14.

61 confrontation: Santa Anna, *Mi historia* . . . , Mexico, (1905) 1952, p. 94 / accepted by Fuentes Mares: *Santa Anna*, p. 295 / doubted in IO, p. 156.

62 "At a meeting": PS, pp. 371-372; and Sanchez, C. Juan, *Vida literaria de Benito Juárez*, Oaxaca, 1902.

64 test and certificate: Sanchez, *op. cit.*, and PS, p. 75.

65 Loxicha is the form now in use; Juárez spells it Loricha.

67 Fifty leagues is about one hundred and fifty miles, whereas Loxicha is about seventy miles south of Oaxaca.

68 two children: JEp, pp. 426 and 572.

69 in the parish record the name is spelled Masa / "very homely": RJ, p. 67.

70 twelve children: JEp, p. 19.

CHAPTER 4

71-73 Madame Calderón, Everyman edition, pp. 32-34, 124-125, 226-254, 410-432; but there will soon appear a better edition edited by H. T. and M. H. Fisher.

73 cultural flowering: SE, p. 163.

75 "resentment and resistance": letter from Zamacona to Juárez, June 16, 1864: AJ, 11/30.

76 colored stripes: Lempriere, Charles, *Notes on Mexico in 1861*, London, 1862, p. 48 / medical care: JE, p. 162; and Díaz, Porfirio, *Memorias, 1830–1867*, Mexico, (1892) 1922, Vol. I, p. 103.

77 an American scheme: FM, p. 19.

80 Vasconcelos, José, *Breve historia de Mexico*, Mexico, (1936) 1944, pp. 379–380.

81–84 *Notes:* AP, pp. 239–242.

81 "such criticism": SJ, pp. 63–65; but see VP, p. 99 / "as secretary": Iturribarría, *History of Oaxaca, 1821–1854*, Oaxaca, 1935, pp. 304–305 / "resigned in protest": JD, p. x, and IG, p. 159.

82 coalition: IO, p. 154.

83 Pola: JE, p. 31, and VP, p. 104.

84 "the man of law": SMM, p. 240.

CHAPTER 5

85 *Notes:* AP, p. 242.

86 Prieto: PV, Vol. II, p. 197 / "paternalistic": VP, and even Bulnes agrees.

87 "human fly": JEp, p. 449.

88–90 inaugural address: JM, pp. 11–15.

90 Pola: JM, p. ix / the peso: see RJ, p. 76; but to me it seems gently ironic.

91 short biography: by Anastasio Zerecero, JE, pp. 119–137; the original is in AR, with a transcription in AJ, 15/56, which I have translated. See also JE, pp. 151–154.

92 personal hatred: Fuentes Mares, *Santa Anna*, p. 295 / large house: corner of Hidalgo and 20 Noviembre, now Hotel Alameda / "When the bells": JEp, p. 24 / "an administration": JEp, 23–26, based on Iturribarría, *Historia*, pp. 359 ff. / on education, there is much disagreement, and I have relied on Viramontes, Leonardo S., *Biografía popular*, Mexico, 1906, p. 61 / "children do not go to school": JE, p. xxv.

93 reduction of debt: IO, p. 159.

94 cane: JE, p. 115 / Marcucci: JEp, pp. 30–34, and JE, pp. 153–154 / daughter: AP, p. 242.

95 cortège: IO, p. 157 / Isthmus: JD, pp. 9-11, FM, pp. 22-26, B Vol. V, p. 589 / "Meanwhile . . .": SE, pp. 185-195.

CHAPTER 6

99-102 *Notes:* AP, pp. 242-244.

99 directorship: JEp, p. 35, and Sanchez, C. Juan, *op. cit.*

100 Ortíz affair: IO, pp. 161-164.

101 different version: IO, p. 166.

103-108 Ocampo's early life, based chiefly on VO, but see also the works by Salvador Pinada, Jesús Romero Flores, and Tomás Contreras Estrada (for the Constitutions of 1857 and 1917), and Ocampo's own *Obras,* Mexico, 1900.

107 Dueñas: RJ, p. 83.

108 Josefa on Mata: VO, p. 311 / Arriaga: Ramírez Arriaga, Manuel, *Ponciano Arriaga,* Mexico, 1937.

109 filibuster: INAH, 50/03/16-19, and VO, pp. 272-273 / Comonfort's trip: INAH, 50/J/ Jan. 17, 1855, and VO, pp. 287-288.

110 Cabañas: PS, pp. 107-109.

111 Iturribarría: IO, p. 168.

112 slaves: PV, Vol. II, p. 40 / newspapers: *El Rayo Federal* in New Orleans and *Noticioso del Bravo* in Brownsville.

113 Order of Guadalupe: Parkes, Henry Bamford, *A History of Mexico,* Boston, (1938) 1950, p. 227.

114 packet of letters: INAH, 50/J/1-20.

116 Mata and Ocampo to Juárez: PS, p. 104; / *Notes:* AP, p. 244.

CHAPTER 7

117 arrival at Acapulco: Velasco Pérez, p. 59, PS, p. 109, and IO, p. 169.

118-133 *Notes:* AP, pp. 244-250.

120 Juárez to Ocampo: INAH, 50/J/19, 20 / arrival of Ocampo: VO, p. 294 / the various Plans: Molina Enriquez, pp. 95-114, and SE, p. 199.

121 Ocampo: VO, pp. 296-299, and Ocampo's "Mis Quince Días" in the *Obras.*

122 McLean, Malcolm D.: *Vida y obra de Guillermo Prieto*, Mexico, 1960; but the judgments are mine.

124 Sierra on Comonfort: SJ, p. 99.

125 Degollado's reply: INAH, 50/D/14, 15; and Muñoz y Pérez, Daniel, *Ensayos biográficos* (Ocampo, Degollado, and Valle), Mexico, 1961.

128 "Juárez later wrote": AJ 15/56 and AR.

130 Mariscal: IG, pp. 211–215 / Pola: JE, p. 46 / Sierra: SJ, p. 103.

131 Doblado: D, Castañeda's introduction / Sierra on Doblado: SJ, p. 370.

132 Romero and Juárez: RD, pp. x, 6, 7, 12.

133 situation in Oaxaca: IO, pp. 173–180, and IG, pp. 141–156.

CHAPTER 8

135 Te Deum: IO, p. 180, and JEp, p. 42.

135–149 *Notes:* AP, pp. 250–254.

136 the military: IO, p. 181, JEp, p. 42, and SJ, p. 108 / Díaz: IG, pp. 67–123, etc. / Werfel, Franz, *Juárez and Maximilian*, New York, 1926, p. 71.

137 "our Porfirio": JEp, p. 266, and elsewhere.

138 newspaper: IO, p. 182 / protest: JEp, pp. 44 and 48, and IO, p. 182.

139 Sierra: SE, p. 201, and SJ, p. 107 / Institute, IG, p. 132, and JD, p. 15.

140 Juárez as governor: JEp, p. 44, and IO, pp. 182–183 / Ley Lerdo: Molina Enriquez, pp. 115–136, SMM, pp. 242–243, and Paz, Octavio, *El laberinto de la soledad*, Mexico, (1950) 1959, pp. 127–130.

141 the Lerdo brothers: Knapp, Frank Averill, Jr., *The Life of Sebastián Lerdo de Tejada*, Austin, 1951; and Sierra, Carlos J., *Miguel Lerdo de Tejada*, Mexico, 1961.

142 description of Sebastián: Knapp, pp. 31–32.

143 the Constitution of 1857: SE, pp. 209–211.

145 Mejía and Miramón: B, Vol. V, pp. 754–755, and Vol. VI, p. 275.

146 Juárez on the Constitution: JD, pp. 300–302 / election: JE, p. 49.

147 Carvajal: IO, p. 190 / Juárez and the Bishop: IO, p. 189, and JM, pp. 144–145.

149 Ixcapa: Díaz, Vol. I, pp. 97–105.

150 correspondence with Romero: JEp, pp. 64–69.

151 "overthrow Comonfort": B, Vol. V, p. 719 / Comonfort to Juárez: JEp, p. 70.

CHAPTER 9

This chapter is based chiefly on Juárez *Diary*, AP, pp. 254–263; RD, pp. 126–144; D, pp. xii and 1–64; Baz, Juan José: *Manifiesto* . . . , Morelia, 1858; Payno, Manuel: *Memoria* . . . , Mexico, 1860, and *Defensa* . . . , Mexico, 1861; and Portilla, Anselmo de la, *Mexico en 1856 y 1857*, Nueva York, 1858, which includes Comonfort's own *Política del General Comonfort*, previously published in New York, July, 1858. See also the somewhat harsher interpretation in RJ, p. 154.

160 the election: B, Vol. V, p. 721, Vol. VI, p. 225.

161 the incriminating letters: Riva Palacio, Vicente: *Mexico a través de los siglos*, Mexico, 1887–1889, Vol. V, pp. 265 ff., by Vigil, José María.

165 Bulnes, Francisco: *Juárez y las revoluciones de Ayutla y de Reforma*, Mexico, 1905, pp. 269–275 (until Fuentes Mares, Bulnes was the most formidable critic of Juárez) / Sierra: SJ, p. 118.

166 Oaxaca: IO, pp. 192–193 / Parrodi: D, p. 63, and JEp, p. 74.

168 escape of the liberals: PV, Vol. II, p. 201; VO, p. 327; Ramírez, Ignacio, *Obras*, Mexico, (1889) 1960, p. xlv; Sierra, C. J., pp. 28–29; Knapp, pp. 45, 50; Viramontes, pp. 118–119; FM, pp. 89, 106–107.

CHAPTER 10

This chapter is based chiefly on RD, pp. 144–173; PV, Vol. II, pp. 202–210; and VO, pp. 334–338.

170 manifesto: JD, p. 206.

172 Prieto: PS, pp. 94–97, for Prieto's poem on this adventure.

175 Juárez' *Diary*: AP, p. 263 / manifesto: JD, p. 208 / Valle and Collin: Teja Zabre, Alfonso, *Leandro Valle* . . . , Mexico, 1956, pp. 62–67.

176 Juárez' narrative: JE, pp. 119–137; AJ, 15/56.

177 Prieto's report: quoted by Prida Santacilia in *Excelsior*, Mexico, March 18, 1962.

178 Prieto on Manzanillo: PV, Vol. I, p. 2.

179 Juárez' *Diary:* AP, pp. 264–265.

CHAPTER 11

180 the servant: PV, Vol. II, pp. 198–199 **/** Benítez: JEp, p. 78 **/** doña Margarita's journey: JEp, p. 76, and AJ, 15/199.

183 Oaxaca: IO, pp. 195–200, and JEp, pp. 94–95.

184 Márquez' sash: B, Vol. V, p. 764.

185–187 Laws of the Reform: JD, pp. 217–245; VP, pp. 165–167; JEp, pp. 97–99; IG, p. 23, 165–179; FM, p. 5.

187 "La Epistola": Ocampo's *Obras,* Vol. II, pp. 229–239, for instructions going back to the Council of Trent **/** Juárez' letter: JEp, p. 99 **/** poor men: McLean, p. 131; but the figures seem large.

CHAPTER 12

This chapter is based chiefly on FM, a well-documented book with the judgments of which, however, I cannot possibly agree. For further discussion of the treaty, see the works cited in FM's bibliography and Bulnes, *Ayutla,* pp. 413–485; Iglesias Calderón, Fernando, *Las supuestas traiciones de Juárez,* Mexico, 1907, pp. 580–604; Salmerón, Celerino, *Las Grandes traiciones de Juárez,* Mexico, 1960; Junco, Alfonso, *Juárez, intervencionista,* Mexico, 1961.

195 Lerdo's appointment: AP, p. 265.

196 Ocampo's proposal: FM, p. 146, and photostats 10 and 11; also, VO, p. 372.

197 Degollado and Miramón: B, Vol. V, p. 771 **/** the text of the treaty: FM, Anexos A and B, photostats 12 and 13.

198 Romero: RD, pp. 271, 313, 345 **/** Juárez' *Diary:* AP, p. 273.

199 McLane, Robert Milligan: *Reminiscences,* 1827–1897, privately printed, 1903 (Rare Book Room, Library of Congress), pp. 141–145.

201 defenders of Juárez: RJ, p. 214.

202 Sierra: SJ, pp. 193–203, and SE, pp. 222–223.

203 Valadés: VO, pp. 372–373.

CHAPTER 13

205 Turner and Juárez: JEp, pp. 93–94, and NA, 45/12 **/** customs receipts: SJ, p. 151 **/** Aldham to Russell: PRO, F.O., 50/347.

206 Black: FM, pp. 209-211 / Mathew to Russell: PRO, F.O., 50/343.

207 Jarvis must have been over sixty and Turner nearly fifty years of age: Hamersley, L. R., *Records of Living Officers* . . . , Philadelphia, 1870 and 1890 / "last order": NA, 45/letter from SecNav to President, March 29, 1860 / conspiracy: PRO, F.O. 50/343 and 347 / Elgee: FM, p. 212.

208 Alvarado: AP, p. 266 / conference: FM, p. 213 / Turner and Miramón: NA, 45/March 4 and 11, 1860; four sailors' report: NA, 45/with Jarvis' report of March 11.

209 action report: NA, 45/Captains' Letters, Vol. I, March 8, 1860 / protests: Iglesias Calderón, pp. 299-311 ff.

212 Jarvis to Toucey: NA, 45/March 11, 1860 / protests and judgment: Iglesias Calderón, pp. 340-346, 367-368.

213 legend: SJ, p. 210 / Fuentes Mares: FM, p. 217.

CHAPTER 14

217 Mathew on reactionaries: PRO, F.O. 50/343.

218 Degollado to Aldham: PRO, F.O. 50/347 / "bad moments": for all these negotiations, Juárez' *Diary*, AP, pp. 266-273, and *Continuación del expediente instruido en el Ministerio de Relaciones Exterior* . . . , Veracruz, June 14, 1860, in AJ, twenty-five documents on the negotiations between March 22 and June 10, 1860.

219 the cargo: B, Vol. V, p. 799.

221 Lerdo's resignation: JEp, pp. 111-112 / Juárez and Pacheco: JEp, pp. 109-111.

222 Mata and Romero: RD, p. 345 / fiat money—this is deduced from the steady value of the peso in relation to the dollar.

223 Sierra: SJ, pp. 225-232 / Degollado to Ocampo: INAH, 50/D/5/65.

224 Degollado to Juárez: JEp, p. 115 / settlement: AJ 18/unnumbered and B, Vol. v, p. 788.

224-226 Degollado, Juárez, and Ocampo: JEp, pp. 112, 113, 116; INAH 50/D/5/65-67: AJ 2/36-37.

226 Lerdo and Juárez: JEp, pp. 118-120.

228 Degollado to Ocampo: INAH 50/D/5/68.

229 surrender of Mexico: B, Vol. V, p. 794; but see McLean, pp. 29-30: Prieto claimed to have conducted the negotiations on behalf of

Ortega **/** *I Puritani:* PS, pp. 343–345, quoting from Zayas—others claim the opera was Meyerbeer's *Les Huguenots* **/** Ortega in triumph: SJ, p. 292.

CHAPTER 15

Opening difficulties: Juárez' *Diary:* AP, pp. 275–277; and Scholes, Walter V., *Mexican Politics during the Juárez Regime,* Columbia, Mo., 1957, pp. 58–60.

232   Ocampo: VO, pp. 396–400, and INAH 50/O/3/31.

234   finances: Romero, Matías: *Mexico and the United States,* New York and London, 1898, p. 139; B, Vol. VI, p. 9; and Scholes, p. 63 **/** Prieto: McLean, pp. 30–31 **/** Aldham: Lempriere, p. 55, and AP, p. 291 **/** Wyke: B, Vol. VI, p. 12, and AP, p. 285.

235   Montluc: *Correspondence de Juárez et Montluc,* Paris, 1885, and Mexico, 1905.

236   Sisters of Charity: SJ, pp. 249–250 **/** Lincoln: RD, p. 378.

238   greeting to Corwin: JD, pp. 38–39 **/** Vidaurri: B, Vol. VI, p. 12 **/** Juárez' address: JD, pp. 25–38.

240   Ocampo to Juárez: JEp, pp. 136–138.

241   death of Ocampo: VO, pp. 404–410; Márquez, Leonardo, *Manifiestos . . . ,* Mexico, 1904, pp. 281–297; VO, Plates XV and XVI; INAH 50/o/3/33.

243   Sierra on Valle: SJ, pp. 281–282.

245   Ocampo's funeral: SJ, pp. 283–284 **/** inaugural address: JD, pp. 40–45.

246   death of Degollado: Teja Zabre, pp. 117–126 **/** death of Valle: Teja Zabre, pp. 127–143.

CHAPTER 16

Juárez' *Diary:* AP, pp. 298–323.

251   Comonfort restored: JEp, p. 175.

252   Juárez to Fuente: JEp, pp. 140–142.

253   Thouvenel and Spain: B, Vol. VI, pp. 18, 21, and Scholes, p. 78 **/** Pickett: Callahan, James Morton, *American Foreign Policy in Mexican Relations,* New York, 1932, pp. 283–284 **/** the treaty: SJ, p. 253, and Callahan, pp. 282–285.

254   promotion of Díaz: IG, p. 80.

255 impeachment: Scholes, p. 82; Knapp, p. 69; JD, pp. 48–55.

256 the Convention of London: JEp, pp. 147–149, and Latané, John Holladay, *A History of American Foreign Policy*, Garden City, 1927, pp. 402–403; but there remains confusion about the date.

258 decrees: Fuentes Mares, José, *Y Mexico se refugió* . . . , Mexico, 1954, p. 53; B, Vol. VI, p. 30; SJ, p. 232; Scholes, p. 87 / Wyke–Zamacona: Scholes, p. 80, and Knapp, pp. 71–73.

259 last meeting: Lempriere, pp. 91–93 and 120, and JD, pp. 55–58 and 257–262.

260 Juárez to Vidaurri: JEp, pp. 151–153.

262 Juárez to Vidaurri: JEp, p. 160 / manifesto and address: JD, pp. 58–64 and 262–266.

263 the abortive treaty: Callahan, p. 287; Latané, pp. 404 and 406–407; and Lempriere, p. 305 / Juárez to Doblado: JEp, p. 159 (this letter and footnote are incorrectly dated).

264 French proclamation: B, Vol. VI, p. 44 / Acultzingo: JEp, p. 186 / Juárez' exhortations: JEp, pp. 164 and 166.

CHAPTER 17

266 Díaz, Vol. I, pp. 248–267, including Zaragoza's report, and B, Vol. VI, pp. 47–50, with map.

267 Zaragoza's report to Juárez: AJ 5/37.

268 Juárez' *Diary:* AP, pp. 323–324 / Bustamente and Romero: Brown, Robert B., *Guns over the Border* . . . , unpublished dissertation, Ann Arbor, 1951, pp. 11 ff.; RD, pp. 460–490; JEp, pp. 354–356.

269 Juárez to Montluc: JEp, p. 172 / Ortega and Saligny: JEp, pp. 168–172.

270 Vidaurri: JEp, pp. 172–173, 227–229 / Amada and Maza: AJ 4/10 / Doblado: AP, pp. 324–325; Scholes, pp. 89–90; B, Vol. VI, p. 52 / Montluc: JEp, pp. 174–176.

271 Romero: RD, pp. xvi and 490–515, and Romero, Matías: *Correspondencia de la Legación Mexicana* . . . , Mexico, 1870 / Álvarez: SJ, p. 406 / Forey: JEp, pp. 176–177 / address: JD, pp. 70–75.

272 T. Mejía: JEp, pp. 188–189.

273 seer: JEp, pp. 191–192.

274 siege of Puebla: Díaz, Vol. I, pp. 275–321; B, Vol. VI, pp. 62–69; Prida Santacilia in *Excelsior*, March 18, 1962.

275 Ignacio Mejía: IG, pp. 190–192 / withdrawal: Iglesias, J. M., *Revistas históricas* . . . , Mexico, 1867–1869, Vol. II, pp. 3 ff.; SJ, pp. 413–414.

276 address: JD, pp. 80–82; JEp, pp. 204–207; PS, p. 140.

277 French captain: RJ, pp. 512–513.

CHAPTER 18

This chapter is based considerably on Corti, Egon Cesar, Count, *Maximilian and Charlotte of Mexico*, New York and London, 1928.

279 Mexican monarchism: Hidalgo, J., *Apuntes para escribir la historia de los proyectos de monarquía en Mexico* . . . , Paris, 1868, a distorted record / Sierra on Gutiérrez: SJ, pp. 316–362.

280 Sierra on Hidalgo: SJ, p. 363.

281 Sierra on Miranda: SJ, pp. 364–365.

282 Napoleon: Guérard, Albert, *Napoleon III*, New York, 1955, may be taken as a convenient antidote to my view of Napoleon; Bolitho, William, *Twelve against the Gods*, New York, 1929, p. 303.

283 For a full account of Santa Anna's later antics, see Fuentes Mares, *Santa Anna.*

285 Sandburg, Carl: *Abraham Lincoln: The War Years*, New York, 1939, Vol. II, p. 395.

286 Congress and Seward: Callahan, pp. 291–298.

287 Terán's warning: JEp, p. 187 / the Zerman–Howell affair: AJ, 11/33 and 34, and JEp, p. 208.

CHAPTER 19

Except as noted, this chapter is based on JEp, pp. 207–247.

290 the Juárez–Santacilia correspondence: AP, and partly incorporated into JEp.

291 "respite of sorts": Knapp, pp. 80–81, includes a "Timetable of the Nomadic Republic," with map / Romero: RD, pp. 512–557, and Díaz, Vol. I, pp. 328–330.

292 Mariscal: IG, pp. 211–215 / Doblado–Zarco–Zamacona: Juárez' *Diary:* AP, pp. 325–329 (the only entries for the year 1863).

294 Prieto: *Lecciones de historia patria*, Mexico, 1891, p. 415 / "firsthand account": AJ 6/126.

297 Sierra: SJ, p. 419 / letter from Refugio Álvarez: AJ 16/90.

298 memorandum: JEp, pp. 240–241.

300 aftermath of "this disturbance": Scholes, p. 202; B, Vol. VI, pp. 124–125, and AJ 9/97, 10/2, and 10/78.

CHAPTER 20

301 Nuñez: AJ, 9/125 and 9/126, and JEp, pp. 247–249 / Vidaurri's trading: AJ, 10/84 / move on Monterrey: JEp, pp. 234–236 and 239.

302 "Señor Presidente": Reyes, Rodolfo, *Benito Juárez* . . . , Madrid, n.d., pp. 198–199.

303 Vidaurri's mother: SJ, p. 421 / Prieto, *Lecciones*, p. 503.

304 Bazaine: Knapp, pp. 83–85, and IG, p. 83 / "moral force": JEp, pp. 264–267 / Santa Anna: Corti, p. 314, and Fuentes Mares, *Santa Anna*, pp. 344–350 / April 2 and 3: these dates bring up the question of the famous letter (JEp, pp. 258–260, RJ, p. 565, etc.) supposedly written by Juárez in Monterrey on March 28, 1864, to Maximilian in reply to a letter supposedly written to Juárez by Maximilian aboard the *Novara* on February 22. The latter has never appeared, and from internal and external evidence too complex to discuss here, I regretfully consider Juárez' letter a forgery. Even less plausible is the letter of December 18, 1870 (JEp, pp. 492–497), on events in France.

305 child and grandchild: Juárez' *Diary*, AP, pp. 337 and 341; and JEp, pp. 274–275 / Zamacona: AJ 11/30 and 31; and JEp, p. 271 / Terrazas: Fuentes Mares, *Y Mexico* . . . , pp. 61–71 and 81–90; and AP, p. 341.

306 Uraga: AP, p. 339, and Scholes, pp. 105–106 / reports to Romero: JEp, pp. 255–271.

307 banquet in New York: Romero, *Mexico*, pp. 382–387, and JEp, pp. 262–263.

308 Doblado's defeat: AJ 8/69 and 10/12; B, Vol. VI, p. 125; AP, pp. 331–335 / Doblado's withdrawal: AJ 8/72; JEp, pp. 285, 294, and 300–301; D, p. xvi / elections: AP, p. 342 / Quiroga and Ortega: Juárez' *Diary*, AP, pp. 342–348 and JEp, pp. 274–275.

309 departure of family: JEp, pp. 276–277 and 350; AJ 9/13 and 15/190.

310 "loss" of Benito Jr.: JE, p. 117 / decree: AP, p. 348, and Brown, pp. 29, 44, 52.

311 withdrawal: Juárez' *Diary*, AP, pp. 346–349, and B, Vol. VI, p. 165.

CHAPTER 21

Again, this chapter is based largely on Corti.

319 Maximilian's brother: the Archduke Karl Ludwig, not the Emperor Francis Joseph **/** Bazaine, Uraga, and Díaz: Díaz, Vol. I, pp. 360–366 **/** siege of Oaxaca: Díaz, Vol. I, pp. 369–412, and B, Vol. VI, pp. 188–190.

321 Juárez' comment: JEp, pp. 304–308.

322 Lincoln: Sandburg, Vol. IV, p. 189 **/** Confederates in Mexico: Latané, pp. 409–410; in 1868 Maury returned to the U. S. and taught at the Virginia Military Institute.

323 Maximilian's decree: JEp, p. 289, and JD, p. 288 **/** Arteaga: JEp, p. 349.

CHAPTER 22

324 archives: JEp, pp. 237–238 **/** itinerary: AJ, 10/26–27, 10/33, and 10/35; JEp, pp. 276–278; Iglesias, Vol. III, pp. 25–26.

325 to Santacilia and Romero: JEp, pp. 276–279 **/** defeat at Cerro de Majoma: AJ, 10/47–48 and 10/88; B, Vol. VI, p. 167; JEp, pp. 283–285.

326 further itinerary: AJ, 10/128, 10/47; Fuentes Mares, *Y Mexico*, p. 94 **/** Juárez to his wife: JEp, pp. 279–280 **/** Sra. Morón: JE, p. 108.

327 Prieto: Knapp, p. 95 **/** Lerdo: Knapp, p. 90 **/** family: JEp, pp. 237, 283–285; Knapp, p. 97 **/** "first thunder": JEp, pp. 285–286, and Scholes, p. 111–116.

328 instructions to Romero: JEp, pp. 281–283; RD, pp. 635–637; SJ, pp. 432–436.

330 I. Mejía: AP, p. 32 **/** Jesuits and Protestantism: JEp, p. 293, and SE, p. 275 **/** death of José: RD, pp. 639–640; JEp, pp. 294–298.

333 birthday: JEp, pp. 302–304; Fuentes Mares, *Y Mexico*, p. 98; PS, pp. 204–210.

334 Altamirano: AJ, 12/1 **/** Colombia: JEp, pp. 317–320 **/** Escobedo: JEp, pp. 304–308.

335 Juárez' children, and Lincoln: JEp, pp. 298–302 and 308–310 **/** Ortega and others: JEp, pp. 310–311, and AP, p. 56.

336 death of Lincoln: JEp, pp. 311–313, and AR **/** turncoats and Mexicans: JEp, pp. 313–315, and AR.

337 Negrete: JEp, pp. 315–317.

338 the Carvajal scandal: JEp, pp. 322–326; Callahan, pp. 307–309; SJ, pp. 478–479; Brown, pp. 87, 131, 156.

339 Grant: AJ, 12/112.

340 Creel and Carleton: AJ, 12/14–16, and JEp, pp. 320–322 / Bazaine and U.S. Army: JEp, pp. 337–340; Corti, p. 442; Fuentes Mares, *Y Mexico,* p. 116; B, Vol. VI, p. 202 / death of Antonio: JEp, pp. 322–325.

CHAPTER 23

343 the French and Ortega: Corti, p. 743, and B, Vol. VI, pp. 233–235.

344 Juárez to Santacilia: JEp, pp. 313–315.

345 Mariscal on Ortega: AJ, 12/37 / Juárez to Santacilia: AP, p. 68, and JEp, pp. 317–320 and 325–327.

346 Ruiz: IG, pp. 159–163.

347 Juárez and Prieto: JEp, pp. 327–330 / Juárez to Santacilia: AP, pp. 93 and 95–96.

348 Prieto to Santacilia: AJ, 12/99 / Terrazas: Fuentes Mares, *Y Mexico,* pp. 104–106 / defections: AP, pp. 98–99 / decrees: AP, p. 100; JEp, pp. 333–334; Knapp, p. 101.

349 to Chihuahua and back: AP, 103–104, 112–113; JEp, pp. 335–337; Fuentes Mares, *Y Mexico,* p. 100.

350 Mazzini: AJ, 12/74; Zarco: JEp, pp. 345–347, and AJ, 15/267, 15/272.

351 Ruiz and Prieto: JEp, pp. 337–340; IG, pp. 159–163; Scholes, p. 114; McLean, pp. 32–45.

352 Ortega and Patoni: JEp, pp. 347–349, 377–379, 385–386, 473–475, 582; AJ, 12/160–162 and 12/166; Scholes, p. 114; Brown, pp. 65–69; SJ, pp. 451–455.

CHAPTER 24

354 Sheridan at border: Brown, pp. 220–222 and 231.

355 Seward: Latané, pp. 412–413 / Juárez on Johnson: JEp, pp. 347–349.

356 Napoleon's withdrawal: Latané, p. 415 / wolves of Europe: JEp, pp. 366–367 / side show: JEp, pp. 363–364; Fuentes Mares, *Santa Anna,* pp. 354–368; Callahan, pp. 326–327; Hanighen, pp. 295–299.

357 Terán: JEp, pp. 331–333; Corti, pp. 548 and 562; SJ, pp. 484–487 and 490.

358 Juárez on Napoleon: JEp, pp. 356–357.

359 Charlotte: Corti, p. 687.

360 Maximilian: Corti, p. 747.

361–367 doña Margarita and family in New York, Washington, and New Rochelle: AJ, 12/35, 39, 42, 44, 48, 49, 52, 56, 57; AJ, 15/30, 36, 37, 39, 40, 50, 115–210, 215; JEp, pp. 337–340, 342; AP, p. 157; AR, July 30, 1866; Brown, pp. 247–254.

367 Juárez and Romero: AJ, 15/30, 31.

368 return to Chihuahua: AJ, 12/51; Fuentes Mares, *Y Mexico*, pp. 117–124; AR, June 10, 1866; JEp, pp. 362–363 / poverty: JEp, pp. 342, 354–356, 358–362, 364–365, 368–369; AP, pp. 180, 188.

369 military operations: AP, pp. 177 and 193; JEp, p. 379; IO, pp. 212–213; B, Vol. VI, pp. 260–261; Díaz, Vol. II, pp. 31–44 / prisoners: JEp, pp. 373–379 / Campbell and Sherman: AJ, 15/81, 89, 258; JEp, pp. 358–360, 379; Callahan, pp. 325–329.

370 Juárez to Santacilia: AP, pp. 194–196 / Church: AR; on March 29, 1867, Juárez wrote for "Mr Church" a letter of introduction to Romero, praising Church highly and saying the latter had accompanied him since San Luis Potosí. This is probably George E. Church, author of *Mexico, Its Revolutions*, New York, 1866, revised from the New York *Herald* of May 25, 1866. It is to be hoped that Church left a more personal record. / moving south: JEp, pp. 344, 380, 384–386; AP, p. 199.

371–373 escape at Zacatecas: AP, 200–203, 208; SJ, 519–521; IG, p. 192; Brown, p. 75; B, Vol. VI, p. 246; and there are undocumented additions in Velasco Pérez, p. 132, and Pérez Martínez, H.: *Juárez el impasible*, Buenos Aires, 1956, p. 141.

CHAPTER 25

374 Maximilian to Lares: Corti, p. 773; SJ, p. 521 / Díaz and Bournouf: Díaz, Vol. II, pp. 95–97.

376 Maximilian on Juárez' birthday: Prida Santacilia in *Excelsior*, March 18, 1962 / Juárez to Díaz: JEp, p. 391 / Juárez to Santacilia: AP, pp. 210, 213, 216.

377 Díaz at Puebla: Díaz, Vol. II, pp. 103–152 / death of Méndez: JEp, pp. 395–396.

378 Green: Brown, p. 80 / "good attorneys"—Mariano Riva Palacio and Rafael Martínez de la Torre—Díaz, Vol. II, p. 159.

379 Princess Salm-Salm and Colonel Palacio: Corti, p. 812 / Campbell: Callahan, pp. 329–330.

380 Lozada and Vega: AJ, 17/256–259 / Princess Salm-Salm: Corti, p. 815.

381 Guérard, pp. 170–171 / address to Congress: JD, p. 87. The *Manifiesto Justicativo* reprinted in JD, pp. 307–366, is a forgery by a medium who claimed he had taken dictation from Juárez' spirit.

382 Juárez to Santacilia: JEp, p, 400.

383 Juárez and Díaz at Tlalnepantla: Díaz, Vol. II, pp. 193–201; see also CV.

385 Juárez on Díaz: Lerdo de Tejada, Sebastián, *Memorias* . . . , Mexico, 1911, p. 8; but CV, p. 931, reasonably considers this book apocryphal.

386 "seventy years later": Trend, J. B., *Mexico* . . . , New York and Cambridge, England, 1940, p. 170 / Juárez to the widow: JEp, p. 402 / manifesto: JD, pp. 286–290 / Seward, McCulloch, et al.: NA, Record Group No. 26, and JEp, pp. 406–407.

387 Benito Jr.: AR, October 22, 1866 / the bodies: JEp, p. 383.

CHAPTER 26

393 Cosío Villegas: CV, p. 55.

394 public education: Scholes, pp. 138–141, and Parkes, pp. 279–280 / national literature: SE, p. 275 / traitors: Scholes, pp. 129–131.

395 army: CV, pp. 74, 79–81, 84, 132–135; JEp, p. 403, to Basilio Gallardo, author of *Martirologio* . . . , Mexico, 1875; B, Vol. VI, p. 348; Scholes, p. 137; Knapp, p. 119; Negrete: JEp, p. 480.

396 "sick of Juárez": hard to pinpoint, but manifest in the letters, speeches, and articles of the time / *convocatoria:* CV, pp. 141–172; Knapp, pp. 122–128; JEp, pp. 407–410; AJ, 17/27, 112–113; JD, p. 92; VP, p. 175.

398 the opposition: JEp, p. 271; CV, pp. 75–76, 166–172, 175–176.

399 the election: CV, pp. 183, 187.

400 Romero on the sale: Romero, *Mexico*, p. 96; the economy and finances: Scholes, pp. 143–146; but see also JD, p. 110.

401 rebellions: JEp, pp. 453–454; CV, pp. 230–282.

402 the Supreme Court: Scholes, pp. 127–129, and Knapp, pp. 129–135.

403 Prim: JEp, pp. 482–483 / Seward in Mexico: Knapp, p. 135; JEp, p. 438; Romero, *Mexico*, p. 361.

404 Montluc: JEp, pp. 489 and 491–492; but, as noted above, I consider JEp Letter No. 355, pp. 492–497, a forgery.

CHAPTER 27

405 "their house": JEp, p. 498; but much of this part of the city has been torn down and rebuilt, and I have been unable to find this house.

406 doña Margarita's funeral: see *La señora Margarita Maza de Juárez* . . . , Mexico, January, 1871, a collection of articles, including the emotional funeral address of Prieto, who had been forgiven. On the reconciliation, see Reyes, p. 198 / Sierra: SJ, pp. 283–284.

407 "well said": by Knapp, p. 120 / Juárez' money: his will may be found in PS, pp. 378–379: total value of the estate: $151,233.81.

408 "The Lerdist party": Knapp, p. 153.

409 Lerdo's resignation: JEp, p. 501 / Juárez and Díaz: JEp, p. 465, and CV, pp. 212–216.

410 the opposition: for satirical attacks on Juárez, and on Mejía and other *juaristas,* see Ramírez, Ignacio, *Obras,* Mexico, 1960, Vol. II, pp. 391–550 / the election: B, Vol. VI, p. 378; Montluc: JEp, p. 512 / address to Congress: JD, pp. 150–156 / letter to Pesqueira: JEp, pp. 512–513.

411 the spectacle of the dead: Pérez Martínez, pp. 160–161 / the rebellion: IG, pp. 95, 203; SE, p. 279; Knapp, p. 157.

412 Plumb: quoted by Scholes, pp. 164–165 / inaugural address: JD, pp. 156–162 / death of Félix Díaz: IO, pp. 224–225.

413 letter on bridge: JEp, p. 540 / Zamacona: CV, pp. 276–278 / Romero: IG, pp. 221–227.

414 small properties: JEp, p. 440 / Delfín Sanchez: Pérez Martínez, pp. 156–157; Santa Anna was allowed to return to Mexico in 1874, was ignored or ridiculed, and died in 1876.

415 orphans: PS, pp. 348–353.

416 last acts: PS, pp. 354–356 / Dr. Alvarado's narrative is in PS, pp. 357–365.

INDEX OF PERSONS